Joseph Barbiere

Scraps from the Prison Table

At Camp Chase and Johnson's Island

Joseph Barbiere

Scraps from the Prison Table
At Camp Chase and Johnson's Island

ISBN/EAN: 9783744732307

Printed in Europe, USA, Canada, Australia, Japan

Cover: Foto ©Andreas Hilbeck / pixelio.de

More available books at **www.hansebooks.com**

FROM THE

PRISON TABLE,

AT

Camp Chase and Johnson's Island.

———

BY

JOE BARBIERE,

LIEUT. COL. LATE C. S. A.

———

DOYLESTOWN, PA.:
W. W. H. DAVIS, PRINTER.
1868.

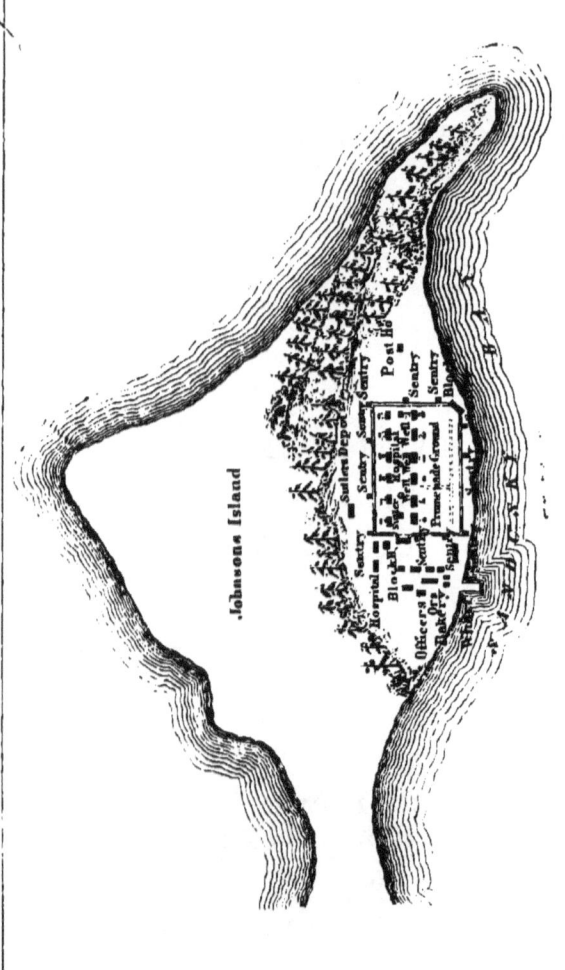

Johnsons Island

Post H[..]

Sentry Sentry

Sutlers Sto[..]

Sutlers Dep[..]

Sentry

Hospital
B[...]

Office[..]
Quar[..]

Plan of the Military Prison
Situated on the South side of
Johnsons Island
in the Bay of Sandusky Ohio.

Dedication.

To

MRS. F. M. PARKER, OF NEWPORT, KY.,

THIS VOLUME IS RESPECTFULLY INSCRIBED,

AS A TRIBUTE OF RESPECT TO A LADY,

WHOSE KINDNESS TO THE AUTHOR WHILE A PRISONER

OF WAR

IS YET FRESH IN HIS MEMORY,

THUS ADDING ANOTHER LINK TO THE CHAIN OF CHARITIES

THAT UNITES THIS NOBLE WOMAN'S HEART

TO THE ESSENCE OF ALL GOOD.

ILLUSTRATIONS.

CONTENTS.

ERRATA.

Preface, read Servres for "Serres."
Chapter 3d, page 71, read Marital for "Martial."
Chapter 10, read *Idiosyncrasies* for "*Idiosyn join crusen.*"
Page 238, read Miscreant for "Mother."
Appendix, page 322, read Editor for "Tditor."

PREFACE.

THIS literary loaf will be composed of scraps, whether they will be crumbs of comfort to the reader, is beyond the ken of the writer to determine, it is simply a question of preference, for the dainties of freedom from Serres' China in defiance of duty, or the more humble offerings from tin plates in a faithful performance of the same. It is not the intention of the author to write a history of the war, that laborious undertaking will be left to abler hands; yet I deem it due the public, who may honor these "scraps" by a perusal, to present them with a synopsis, which will be found in my first chapter, the creation of that distinguished Tennessean, A. O. P. Nicholson, esquire, of the causes which led the South to appeal to the arbitrament of arms, and in which I found justification in drawing my sword, in opposition to the encroachments of fanaticism, and to aid in staying the flood of ills let loose upon the land on the accession to power of the corrupt leaders of the abolition party of the country—confident that the programme of that party, if successful, foreshadowed the destruction of the Southern aristocracy, one of the most humane, social organizations with power known to History, and the annihilation of the Democratic party South by the political elevation of the Black, and disfranchisement of the White Man—thus obtaining and holding the reins of Government, by which

2

their diabolical purpose to inaugurate a war of races would be accomplished.

I have no regrets for my action in the matter—what I did was executed with an honest purpose—and, although not a *first-class warrior*, I endavored to *perform all* duties devolving upon me, during my four years' service in the armies of the Confederate States.

In publishing the "scraps" I am not prompted by any spirit of revenge or vindictiveness, but am performing an act of justice to the people of the South, in showing how prisoners were treated at camp Chase and Johnson's island at an early period of the war, before that spirit of demonism led to the atrocities at Fort Delaware—and at other prison pens at the North—and if we were badly treated, as I will clearly show we were in these "scraps," Heaven alone could have helped the suffering Confederate prisoner at a later period, to support the brutal treatment to which he was subjected.

The following letter from the provisional Governor of Alabama, Hon. Lewis E. Parsons, is attached as evidence of my treatment of Union men during the war:

"EXECUTIVE DEPARTMENT, STATE OF ALABAMA,
MONTGOMERY, Sept. 27th, 1865.

"To all whom it may concern. I, Lewis E. Parsons, Provisional Governor of the State of Alabama, do hereby certify that Joseph Barbiere, of Memphis, Tenn., late an officer in the so-called Confederate army, is personally known to me, having been stationed at Talladega, the town of my residence, as chief enrolling officer of the district. He was marked for his kind and considerate course towards those of our inhabitants who were so unfortunate as to be within the limits of the conscript law of the so-called Confederate States. His treatment of the poor of his district was so kind and humane that it was objected to by the more ultra portion of our people. In testimony whereof, I have hereunto set my hand and caused the great seal of the State to be affixed, this the 27th day of September, A. D. 1865.

"LEWIS E. PARSONS,

"Pro. Gov. of Ala.

"By the Gov. ALBERT ELLMORE, Sec. of State."

The following paragraph in a letter dated June 17th, 1864, from the then Governor of Alabama, Hon. T. H. Watts, is added to show that while considerate in my treatment of Union men, I was not derelict in my duty to the cause *I warmly espoused*:

"I cannot withhold the expression of my gratification on being informed of the kind and considerate manner in which you have discharged your unpleasant and onerous duties.

"Very res. your obt. sert.,

"T. H. WATTS."

In addition to the above, it is the intention of the writer to give a simple chronicle of a soldier's life from camp to field, thence to camp Chase and Johnson's island, with notes while in confinement. If I give offence to any officer whose name is in the book, I will exceedingly regret it, as I have used their names with a purpose single to their interest and amusement—and it is to be hoped that a little family history of those with whom I have associated may be laid upon the family altar an offering to courage and gallantry. Yes! let their children know that even if the voluminous pages of this Revolution's History neglect to record the name of many a brave man—it will be found in one little volume that may live—say a generation—that is some consolation, for I am sure I would give the price of a small library, to see my grandfather's name, who fought at Yorktown, complimented for gallantry, even in an almanac ; and I hope the grand-children of the officers mentioned in this work will appreciate the sentiment.   B.

SCRAPS

PRISON TABLE.

—

CHAPTER I.

—

COMPLETE SYNOPSIS OF THE ENCROACHMENTS OF THE RADICAL PARTY.—THEIR WAR UPON THE CONSTITUTION.

NEW England was settled by the Puritans who effected the Revolution of 1620, and decapitated Charles I. The Southern Colonies were occupied by a more loyal class. To the noble family of Baltimore was granted, by Royal Charter, the province of Maryland. To other staunch adherents of the crown were accorded grants and privileges in Virginia, North and South Carolina, and Georgia.

George Washington was the first Federal magistrate, chosen from a list of twelve candidates.

During his term, the people divided into two hostile parties, each striving for office through the profession of opposite principles. The New England States, led by John Adams, advocated the power of the Federal Government, even to straining the Constitution. This was the Federal party. The Southern States, led by Thomas Jefferson, maintained State rights against Federal encroachment. This was the Democratic party.

In 1797, John Adams, of Massachusetts, was elected President of the Confederacy. During his term, the Alien and Sedition laws were passed by the Federal Congress. These enactments were opposed by the statesmen of the South, since, in their opinion, they invested the Executive with powers not conferred by the Constitution and inimical to popular rights. The Creation of a National Bank was also a subject of keen controversy. The public men of the North sustained it with energy, while those of the South opposed it as unconstitutional and of doubtful expediency.

In 1801, Thomas Jefferson, of Virginia, was elected President. During this term, the New England States displayed a bitter animosity to the South, which arose, chiefly, from the South having put a limit to the slave-trade, in which these States were profitably engaged. When, therefore, President Jefferson proposed the purchase of Louisiana from France, the Eastern States violently resisted, because it increased the territory and power of the South. Congress empowered the purchase, April, 1803.

In 1805, Thomas Jefferson was re-elected to the Presidency. His second term was troubled by the war between England and France. The Berlin and Milan decrees of Napoleon, and the Orders in Council of the British Government, equally assailed American interests. Our vessels, bound either to English or French ports, incurred capture and confiscation. This left but one alternative, either to abandon our trade with Europe, or go to war to protect it. To escape the latter, President Jefferson recommended an Embargo Act, to put a temporary stop to all our foreign trade. This was vehemently opposed by the New England States, because their interests, being chiefly commercial, were seriously damaged. The Embargo Act was passed by Congress in December, 1807; whereupon the Eastern States threatened to secede from the Union, and form a Northern Confederacy.

In 1809, James Madison, of Virginia, was elected President. Soon after his accession, March 1809, the Embargo Act was repealed, to appease the New England

States ; and a less stringent law, the Non-intercourse Act, was passed by Congress, May, 1809, which prohibited trade with England and France. New England, however, carried on an indirect trade with Europe, through Canada. In spite of all these precautions by the Government, our interests and dignity were incessantly outraged by England. Finally, the indignation of the country compelled Congress to declare war, May, 1812.

In 1813, James Madison was re-elected President. During the war, the Government was supported by direct taxes and requisitions upon the States; but the New England States refused, for the most part to contribute. The war closed, January, 1815. To resuscitate the Federal treasury, a new financial policy was inaugurated. A tariff of high duties was passed by Congress, April, 1816. New England advocated this law, because, during the war, she had transferred her capital from commerce to manufactures, for which she desired protection. The South was injured by the tariff, but she supported it from patriotic motives. John C. Calhoun, of South Carolina, went so far as to introduce a *minimum* rate for *ad valorem* duties, that is, a rate below which the duties should not fall. A new National Bank act was also passed, April, 1816 ; the old one having expired in 1811.

In 1817, James Monroe, of Virginia, was elected President. During this term, the interests of the country prospered. No struggle occurred between the politicians of New England and the South, till 1820, when Missouri applied for admission into the Union as a Slave State. The Eastern States opposed it violently, on the ground of extending slavery. The Union was in danger of dissolution, when, finally Missouri was admitted by Congress as a Slave State, on the compromise that thereafter no Slave States should be created north of 36° 30′ parallel of latitude.

In 1821, James Monroe was re-elected Prsident. During this term, a new conflict arose between the politicians of New England and those of the South, on the subject of the tariff policy inaugurated at the peace. New England demanded more protection for her manufactures. This the South opposed, on the ground that her manufactures had protection enough, and next, because an increase of the tariff was seriously detrimental to the interests of the South.

In 1825, John Quincy Adams, of Massachusetts, was elected President. During this term, a heated contest was carried on between New England and the South, on the tariff policy. In 1828, a new act was passed by Congress, which raised the duties to an almost prohibitory standard. The average was 40 per cent. on imports. The South designated this act as the "Black Tariff."

In 1829, Andrew Jackson, of Tennessee, became President. During this term, the extreme Tariff policy of New England led to violent remonstrance in South Carolina, whose interests were seriously injured. She alleged that a policy to enrich one section of the country at the expense of another was unjust and unconstitutional. She threatened to resist this policy by force. A compromise was effected, March, 1833, by which the obnoxious tariff was modified by Congress.

In 1833, Andrew Jackson was re-elected President. During this term, an acrimonious struggle was carried on between the politicians of the North and South, on the National Bank, created at the peace. The former maintained it was necessary to their trade and commerce; the latter, while denying its constitutionality and expediency, also avowed their fears of its becoming a political machine, that might in the hands of unscrupulous politicians, do much harm. The charter was allowed to expire in 1836. A policy known under the name of "Internal Improvements," was also discussed in this term. It had the support of the North, but the South opposed it, as favoring one section at the cost of the others.

In 1837, Martin Van Buren, of New York, was elected President. During this term, great financial disorder prevailed in the country. The Northern politicians proposed, as a panacea, a new National Bank, a higher Tariff, and a Bankrupt Law. The South opposed them all, as unnecessary and sectional in their tendency.

In 1841, William Henry Harrison, of Ohio, was elected President. He died soon after his accession to office. The Presidency was then administered by the Vice President, John Tyler, of Virginia, as provided by the Constitution. During this term, Northern policy mostly prevailed. The Tariff was augmented, September, 1841, and August, 1842. A Bankrupt Law was passed, August, 1841. A law was carried through Congress, July, 1841, dividing the public domain among the respective States, in proportion to their population. The effect of this was favorable to the manufacturing States of New England; for, by cutting off from the Federal treasury the receipts from the public lands, it made a higher Tariff imperative, to insure a sufficient revenue. The new bank charter failed. At the end of eighteen months, the Bankrupt Act was repealed, 1843. A new Slave State, Texas, was admitted to the Union, March 3, 1845. The act for dividing the public lands was repealed, January, 1842, as it was found necessary to retain them as security for Federal loans.

In 1845, James K. Polk, of Tennessee, was inaugurated President. During his term, the Tariff, which was pressing heavily on the interests of the South, was modified, July, 1846. The President, in a special message to Congress, May, 1846, announced that the Government of Mexico had committed an act of war against the Confederacy. On this occasion, all sections of the country, North and South and West, united in declaring war against Mexico. The war closed, February, 1848. The treaty of Gandalupe-Hidalgo, which followed, ceded California and New Mexico to the United States.

In 1849, Zachary Taylor, of Mississippi, became President. During this term, the old issues between the politicians of the North and South were abandoned, to wit: the Tariff policy, a National Bank, a system of Internal Improvements, a Division of the Public Lands. The recent acquisitions of territory, however, afforded the public men of both sections a fertile field of discussion. The North contended against admitting slavery into the new territory. The South declared that its right to join occupation was incontestible, both in law and equity, and proposed that the compromise of 1820 should be renewed, by extending the Missouri line of 36° 30' to the Pacific Ocean. This the politicians of the North refused. The controversy became so violent, that a separation of the North and South seemed imminent. A compromise, however, took place in 1850, which stopped the discussion, but did not settle the main point in dispute, namely: the right of the South to joint occupation of all new territory.

In 1853, Franklin Pierce, of New Hampshire, became President. During this term, the discussion on slavery was renewed. A portion of western territory, named Nebraska, was divided into two territories. One of these was called Kansas and the other Nebraska. The compromise line of 36° 30' ran to the south of these territories, which would have given Kansas as well as Nebraska, the largest, to the North. On the proposition of the Senator from Illinois, Stephen A. Douglas, the compromise line was repealed by Congress. Emigrant societies were established in Massachusetts and Connecticut, in 1854, to furnish pecuniary aid to settlers in Kansas. In consequence, a hostile population from the North poured into Kansas. Bands of armed men from the North paraded the territory. The Federal Government, whose jurisdiction extended over this distant country, was finally forced to interfere. The leaders of the anti-slavery propaganda, having violated the Federal prerogative by passing a constitution and electing a Governor, were indicted for treason, and obliged to take flight.

In 1857, James Buchanan, of Pennsylvania, was inaugurated President. The whole of this term was disturbed by a heated contest between the politicians of the North, on the subject of slavery in the territories. Towards the close of this Presidency, the prolonged strife between the politicians, on the topic of slavery, was taken up by the people of the two sections, in an election for a new President, November, 1860. The Northern States, being in the majority, pronounced in favor of Abraham Lincoln, of Illinois, the exponent of their sectional views.

Under these circumstances, the Southern States have dissolved their connection with the Union. The civil compact they made with the Northern States, in 1789, guaranteeing equal rights to both, and equal protection to all, had been violated. Being in a minority in the Confederacy, they could oppose no legal barrier to the anti-slavery sentiments of the North, which, carried into legislation, would confiscate their property, and even involve their lives.

The abolitionist is a practical atheist. In the language of one of their congregational ministers—Rev. Henry Wright, of Massachusetts:

"The God of humanity is not the God of slavery. If so, shame upon such a God. I scorn him. I will never bow to his shrine; my head shall go off with my hat when I take it off to such a God as that. If the Bible sanctions slavery, the Bible is a self-evident falsehood. And, if God should declare it to be right, I would fasten the chain upon the heel of such a God, and let the man go free. Such a God is a phantom."

The religion of the people of New England is a peculiar morality, around which the minor matters of society arrange themselves like ferruginous particles around a loadstone. All the elements obey this general law. Accustomed to doing as it pleases, New England "morality" has usually accomplished what it has undertaken. It has attacked the Sunday mails, assaulted Free Masonry. Its channels have been societies, meetings, papers, lectures, sermons, resolutions, memorials, protests, legislation, private discussion, public addresses; in a word, every conceivable method whereby appeal may be brought to mind. Its spirit has been agitation—and its language, fruits and measures, have partaken throughout of a character that is thoroughly warlike.

"In language no element ever flung out more defiance of authority, contempt of religion, or authority to man. As to agency, no element of earth has broken up more friendships and families, societies and parties, churches and denominations, or ruptured more organizations, political, social or domestic. And as to measures! What spirit of man ever stood upon earth with bolder front and wielded fiercer weapons? Stirring harangues! Stern resolutions! Fretful memorials! Angry protests! Incendiary pamphlets at the South! Hostile legislation at the North! Underground railroads at the West! Resistance to the Constitution! Division of the Union! Military contribution! Sharpe's rifles! Higher law! If this is not belligerence enough, Mohammed's work and the old Crusades were an appeal to argument and not to arms."

It is a very common error that the Puritans persecuted themselves for opinion's sake, sought liberty of conscience in the wilderness of America, *and there erected its altar.* To Sir George Calvert belongs the imperishable glory of first establishing a government of which universal toleration and religious freedom were the chief foundation stones. It is a remarkable fact that the same spot—the shores of Maryland—which was thus embalmed in the affections of freemen, should, after the lapse of a little more than two centuries and a quarter, be the first territory of the great republic desecrated by the foot of the tyrant, and the extinction of political and civil liberty.

It is true that the Puritans fled from England on account of violent opposition, amounting to persecution. In thus expatriating these schismatics, the English of that day, as subsequent developments have demonstrated, exhibited a thorough insight into the nature and tendencies of their principles and character. One of their first acts, after their colony had assumed some form and substance, was the establishment of a spiritual despotism and religious intolerance as cruel and relentless as the Roman Inquisition in Spain. Professing to be themselves religious refugees, they denounced a dreary banishment against all heretics and non-conformists. Every student of American history is familiar with the sad but ever-glorious story of Roger Williams. He was a fugitive from the persecutions of the old world, but, unlike his fellow-sufferers, comprehended the nature and wrong of intolerance, and proposed the true remedy. He taught that "the civil magistrate should restrain crime, but never control opinion;

should punish guilt, but never violate the freedom of the soul." He contended for the abolition of all laws punishing non-conformists, requiring the performance of religious duties, enforcing pecuniary contributions to the support of the church ; and that equal protection should be extended to every religious belief—the peace of the State, like the vital fluid we breathe, surrounding and gathering alike over mosque, synagogue, cathedral, and the humble "house of God" of the Protestant, securing to their respective worshippers unmolested sanctity of conscience. For holding and advocating these just and truly sublime doctrines, now fully recognized and enforced by the free Constitution of the Confederate States, this "young minister, godly and zealous, having precious gifts," and whose opinions and teachings we have given in almost the identical language of the historian, was most cruelly persecuted by the Puritans, and forced to hide himself in the recesses of the howling wilderness "in winter snow and inclement weather, of which he remembered the severity even in his late old age." "Often," says Bancroft, "in the stormy night he had neither fire, nor food, nor company ; often he wandered without a guide, and had no house but a hollow tree." The savage of the forest, more tolerant than these narrow bigots, and who knew not his God at all, kindly rescued him from from the dread doom to which he had been consigned, to find a new home, and found a new State, by the undisturbed waters of the Narragansett. Mrs. Hutchinson, a most pure and excellent woman, for the same *crime*, suffered the same miserable persecutions. There is no more infallible criterion of the *tone* of a people than the position occupied by the weaker sex. Gallantry was the guiding-star of returning light in the mediæval ages. Devotion to women makes gentlemen. And where gentlemen inhabit, there woman "rules the court, the camp, the grove ;" her refined presence elevates him above his more grovelling nature ; and in return he is in very truth her slave, and with life and limb and manly honor devoted to her service. The historical fact which we last mentioned, therefore, truly illustrates Yankee character. Heavens! what a spectacle!

a horde of mean-spirited, whining Yankees pelting a
shivering, defenceless woman into a rigorous exile, for
entertaining a peculiar opinion, or not conforming to some
rite of public worship. And with what unutterable indignation does the blood boil at the hanging of Mary Dyer,
simply because she was a Quaker. This was her only
offence. She died, and died upon the gallows, because
she held a faith different from those people *who had devoted themselves a sacrifice on the altar of religious liberty.*
The ferocious and bloody fanaticism of the witchcraft
persecutions is too revolting for statement. It is enough
to recur to it.

Glance for a moment at the Puritans in power in the
colony of Maryland, in the year 1676. We have already
alluded to the fact that the Roman Catholics had there
established perfect freedom of conscience, and opened an
asylum for the persecuted and proscribed of every faith.
Availing themselves of this liberality of religious jurispru-
dence, many Puritans from New England entered the
colony, and in the course of a revolution, in the year we
have named, mounted into political power. The earliest
exercise of sovereignty by this new and godly *regime* was
an edict prohibiting the freedom of public worship to all
papists and prelatists. Here we see manifested the same
despicable spirit that now animates the Abolition party
of the country. Indeed, the Yankee is the same animal
in all ages, and in all situations. He is "universal."

The great fathers of the State were convinced that the
heterogeneous peoples, whom they had bound together,
would not long dwell in peace. Washington sincerely
desired the perpetuation of the Union, but he died in the
belief that, in the course of time, his tomb would become
the exclusive property of the South. And John Adams,
perhaps the next man to Alexander Hamilton, among the
Northern patriots, had a clear and unclouded vision of
the great rupture, though he was somewhat deceived as
to its proximity to his own day. The following passage
from Mr. Jefferson's diary, presents the views of Mr.
Adams upon this subject, and is also interesting as another

illustration of the supreme meanness of Yankee sentiment, even its most exalted type :

"December the 30th, 1803. The Rev. Mr. Coffin, of New England, who is now here, soliciting donations for a college in Green county, in Tennessee, tells me that when he first determined to engage in this enterprise, he wrote a paper, recommendatory of the enterprise, which he meant to get signed by clergymen, and a similar one for persons in a civil character, at the head of which he wished Mr. Adams to put his name, he being then President, and the application going only for his name, and not for a donation. Mr. Adams, after reading the paper and considering, said ' he saw no possibility of continuing the union of the States ; that their dissolution must necessarily take place ; that he, therefore, saw no propriety in recommending to New England men to promote a literary institution in the South ; that it was, in fact, giving strength to those who were to be their enemies, and therefore he would have nothing to do with it.' "

What was philanthrophy in our forefathers has become misanthropy in their descendants, and compassion for the slave has given way to malignity against the master. Consequences are nothing. The one idea pre-eminent above all others is abolition !

It is worthy of notice in this connection that most abolitionists know little or nothing of slavery and slaveholders beyond what they have learned from excited, caressed, and tempted fugitives, or from a superficial, accidental, or prejudiced observation. From distorted facts, gross misrepresentations, and frequently malicious caricatures, they have come to regard Southern slaveholders as the most unprincipled men in the universe, with no incentive but avarice, no feeling but selfishness, and no sentiment but cruelty.

Their information is acquired from discharged seamen, runaway slaves, agents, factious politicians, and scurrilous tourists; and no matter how exaggerated may be the facts, they never fail to find willing believers among this class of people.

In the Church, the missionary spirit with which the

men of other times and nobler hearts intended to embrace all, both bond and free, has been crushed out. New methods of Scriptural interpretation have been discovered, under which the Bible brings to light things of which Jesus Christ and his disciples had no conception. Assemblings for divine worship have been converted into occasions for the secret dissemination of incendiary doctrines, and thus a common suspicion has been generated of all Northern agency in the diffussion of religious instruction among the slaves. Of the five broad, beautiful bands of Christianity thrown around the North and the South—Presbyterian, old school and new, Episcopalian, Methodist, and Baptist, to say nothing of the divisions of Bible, tract, and missionary societies—three are already ruptured—and whenever an anniversary brings together the various delegates of these organizations, the sad spectacle is presented of division, wrangling, vituperation, and reproach, that gives to religion and its professors any thing but that meekness of spirit with which it is wont to be invested.

Politically, the course of abolition has been one of constant aggression upon the South.

At the time of the old Confederation, the amount of territory owned by the Southern States was 647,202 square miles; and the amount owned by the Northern States, 164,081. In 1783, Virginia ceded to the United States, for the *common benefit*, all her immense territory northwest of the river Ohio. In 1787, the Northern States appropriated it to their own exclusive use, by passing the celebrated ordinance of that year, whereby Virginia and all her sister States were excluded from the benefits of the territory. This was the first in the series of aggressions.

Again, in April, 1803, the United States purchased from France, for fifteen millions of dollars, the territory of Louisiana, comprising an area of 1,189,112 square miles, the whole of which was slaveholding territory. In 1821, by the passage of the Missouri Compromise, 964,-667 square miles of this was converted into free territory.

Again, by the treaty with Spain, of February, 1819,

the United States gained the territory from which the present State of Florida was formed, with an area of 59,268 square miles, and also the Spanish title of Oregon, from which they acquired an area of 341,463 square miles. Of this cession, Flordia only has been allowed to the Southern States, while the balance—nearly six-sevenths of the whole—was appropriated by the North.

Again, by the Mexican cession, was acquired 526,078 square miles, which the North attempted to appropriate under the pretence of the Mexican laws, but which was prevented by the measures of the Compromise of 1850. Of slave territory cut off from Texas, there have been 44,662 square miles.

To sum this up, the total amount of territory acquired under the Constitution has been, by the

Northwestern cession	286,681	square miles.
Louisiana cession	1,189,112	" "
Florida and Oregon cession	400,731	" "
Mexican cession	526,078	" "
Total	2,402,602	" "

Of all this territory, the Southern States have been permitted to enjoy only 283,713 square miles, while the Northern States have been allowed 2,083,889 square miles, or between seven and eight times more than has been allowed to the South.

The following are some of the invasions that have been, from time to time, proposed upon the Constitution, in the halls of Congress, by these agitators:

1. That the clause allowing the representation of three-fifths of the slaves shall be obliterated from the Constitution; or, in other words, that the South, already in a vast and increasing minority, shall be still further reduced in the scale of insignificance, and thus, on every attempted usurpation of her rights, be far below the protection of even a Presidential veto.

Next has been demanded the abolition of slavery in the District of Columbia, in the forts, arsenals, navy yards and other public establishments of the United States. What object have the abolitionists had for raising all this clamor about a little patch of soil ten miles

3

square, and a few inconsiderable places, thinly scattered over the land—a mere grain of sand upon the beach—unless it be to establish the precedent of Congressional interference, which would enable them to make a whole-sale incursion upon the constitutional rights of the South, and to drain from the vast ocean of alleged national guilt its last drop ?   Does any one suppose that a mere micro-scopic concession like this would alone appease a con-science wounded and lacerated by the "sin of slavery ?"

Another of these aggressions is that which was propos-ed under the pretext of regulating commerce between the States—namely, that no slave, for any purpose and un-der any circumstances whatever, shall be carried by his lawful owner from one slaveholding State to another ; or, in other words, that where slavery now is there it shall remain forever, until, by its own increase, the slave popu-lation shall outnumber the white race, and thus by a united combination of causes—the fears of the master, the diminution in value of his property, and the exhausted condition of the soil—the final purposes of fanaticism may be accomplished.

We might also refer to the armed and bloody opposi-tion to the Fugitive Slave Law, to the passage of Per-sonal Liberty Bills, to political schemes in Congress and out, and to systematic agitation everywhere, with a view to stay the progress of the South, contract her political power, and eventually lead, at her expense, if not of the Union itself, to the utter expurgation of this "tremen-dous national sin."

In short, the abolitionists have contributed nothing to the welfare of the slave or of the South.   While over one hundred and fifty millions have been expended by slave-holders in emancipation, except in those sporadic cases where the amount was capital invested in self-glorification, the abolitionists have not expended one cent.

More than this : They have defeated the very objects at which they have aimed.   When Virginia, Maryland, Kentucky, or some other border State has come so near to the passage of gradual emancipation laws that the hopes of the real friends of the movement seemed about to be realized, abolitionism has stepped in, and, with frantic appeals to the passions of the negroes, through incendiary publications, dashed them to the ground, and producing a reaction throughout the entire community that has crushed out every incipient thought of future manumission.

We come now to the train of historical facts upon which we rely in proof of the foregoing assertions.

From what I have already stated, it may be seen that during the colonial existence of this country, African Slavery had been introduced and overspread its whole surface. The Southern Colonies had, from the fertility of the soil and the value of their productions, become the most profitable mart for Black labor; but the influx gradually outstripped their productive powers, and began, as elsewhere, to inspire the leading men of that section with serious alarm. They devised what means they could to check it, but commercial rapacity eluded or overpowered their remonstrances. While the Southern Colonies were thus suffering, at this early date, both inconvenience and detriment from the Blacks who were forced upon them, the Northern, or New England Colonies, were driving a brisk and profitable business upon the solitary basis of the African Slave Trade. The principal occupations of these Colonies consisted of Commerce and the Fisheries. The New England ships made the voyage to England with tobacco, rice, and other Southern products, and then took in British manufactures for the Gold Coast, which exchanging for Blacks, they returned with them to the Southern Colonies, sold them, and reloaded with tobacco, etc., for the North and Europe, as before, thus completing the round voyage. The fisheries employed a considerable number of persons, and the cured fish found sale chiefly in the Catholic countries of Europe, mostly in exchange for coin, which was always in demand for England. Large quantities of these fish were sold in the West Indies for sugar and molasses. The latter was distilled into rum, which, in the changing character of the Slave Trade on the Coast under the British Governors, rapidly became a favorite article of barter for Blacks, greatly to the dissatisfaction of the English manufacturers of coast-goods. Lord Sheffield, in his report to the Parliamentary Committee of 1777, states, that "out of the Slavers which periodically left Boston, thirteen of them were loaded with rum only, and that having exchanged this for 2,888 Negroes with the Governors of the Gold Coast, they carried them thence to the Southern Colonies." The same report mentions that during the three years ending with 1770, New England had sent 270,147 gallons of rum to the Gold Coast. Thus, from what I have stated, the startling fact will be elicited, that the Northern and Southern Colonies, long before the breaking out of the Revolutionary War, were engaged in a lively controversy on the subject of slavery; the South resisting the excessive flow of Blacks into their section, and New England persisting in the importation for the profits of the trade. The South was anxious to stop the Slave Trade and manumit their Blacks, but New England, like the mother country, was not disposed to listen to them, and abandon so lucrative a traffic.

Mr. Jefferson, of Virginia, seems to have been one of the most earnest advocates of the Southern sentiment. In 1777, being then a member of the Virginia Legislature, he brought in a bill which became a law, "to prevent the importation of slaves." He also proposed a system of general emancipation, as a preliminary to which he introduced a bill to authorize manumission, and this became a law. In these efforts he had the support and sympathy of the Slaveholding States, who were overrun with slaves, that returned no adequate remuneration. At this period their numbers reached some 600,000, a part of whom were employed in raising tobacco and rice. The majority of them, however, were occupied in domestic farm-labor, producing no exportable values. Hence there was no profit in slavery at the South, while at the North it was even a greater burden. Massachusetts found it so unproductive that, in 1780, she abolished it in her own borders, but she did not cease for that reason to force it, by her importations, on the South.

In the Congress of the Confederation, the views of the

North and South on the subject of slavery, founded on interests so antagonistic, frequently came into collision. It was at this epoch, too, that Virginia, Georgia, and other Southern States, ceded to the Federal Government, for the common benefit of all the States, their immense Western Territories. All the States were then Slave-holding, and the idea that a man could not hold his slaves in any part of the territory of the United States, had never yet been broached. On the contrary, the right to carry them everywhere was undoubted. The policy of Virginia, however, was manumission; and Mr. Jefferson, in 1784, prepared in the Congress of the Confederation a clause preventing slaves being carried into the said territories ceded to the United States, north of the Ohio River. This was a part of the Southern scheme of manumission, which was meant as a check to the trading in Negro slaves, carried on by Massachusetts with unabated activity. This clause did not pass at the time, but, in 1787, it was renewed by Nathan Dane, in the Federal Convention. The clause enjoining the restitution of fugitive slaves was then added, and it passed unanimously. By a unanimous vote it became a vital part of the Federal Constitution, and without it this compact could never have gone into effect. The Slave Trade carried on by the North became, also, the theme of much sharp discussion in the Convention. The North was not disposed, of course, to give it up, but with the South it had become an intolerable grievance. They had long and earnestly protested against it when carried on by the mother country, but their minds were now made up to break with the North rather than submit further to this traffic. The North then demanded compensation for the loss of this very thriving trade, and the South readily conceded it by granting them the monopoly of the coasting and carrying trade against all foreign tonnage. In this way it was settled that the Slave Trade should be abolished after 1808. Without this important clause, the South would never have consented to enter into a Confederacy with the North. The Federal Constitution, with these essential clauses, having passed into operation, it became,

henceforth, a certainty that the Slave Trade would finally
expire in the United States at the close of 1808.   This
left it still a duration of nineteen years, and the North
seemed determined to reap the utmost possible advantage
from the time remaining.   The Duke de Rochefoucault-
Liancourt, in his work on the United States, 1795, states,
that "twenty vessels from the harbors of the North are
engaged in the importation of slaves into Georgia; they
ship one Negro for every ton burden."   Thus we see,
that while New England was vigorously engaged in buy-
ing and selling Negro slaves, Virginia, on the other hand,
was steadfastly pursuing her theory of manumission.

In 1793, Congress, on the recommendation of President Washington, passed an act to put in force the clause
of the Constitution enjoining the restoration of fugitive
slaves.   It seems evident they were regarded by the
Constitution in the light of property only.   It likewise
provided for taxing them, and ordained that three-fifths
of their number should be a basis of representation.

This was, certainly, the view taken by the framers of
the Constitution, in their intercourse with foreign nations.
John Adams, afterwards President, and Doctor Franklin
signed, 1783, the Treaty of Peace with Great Britain,
which contained provision for payment of "Slaves and
other Property" carried away during the War.   These
Treaties were examined and approved by the Government, composed also of the very men who had taken the
leading part in drafting the Constitution.   In the Treaty
of Peace at Ghent, in 1814, the same clause recurred,
and the British Government paid a million and a half of
dollars for Slaves that had been carried off by the enemy.
The accounts of Hon. Richard Rush, when Secretary of
the Treasury, contain the various sums paid by the United
States Government to the "Owners of Slaves and other
Property."   Our Government has also made frequent
demands for the payment of Slave-property since the
Peace.   Some twenty years since, the American Minister,
Mr. Andrew Stevenson, conducted a negotiation with
England for the payment of sundry slaves that had been
cast ashore from wrecked American vessels, and set free

by the authorities of Bermuda. The demand was finally acknowledged, and the sum of £23,500 was paid as an indemnity. In a word, the action of the Federal Government has been uniform and consistent in asserting and protecting the rights of our Slave-owners against all Foreign Powers. The right to this property has been just as positively recognized in our domestic relations. In all the State Conventions held to discuss the Federal Constitution prior to adopting it, the right of property in slaves was never contested. The law at that time for recovering that property was of a summary nature. The owner might seize his property wherever he found it, and on making an affidavit before a Federal Judge, a warrant was issued for the removal of it. There was no provision for trial by jury, or for writ of *Habeas Corpus*, which would be indispensable if Black Slaves were considered as persons

In 1797, John Adams, who signed the Treaty of Peace, and was the leader of the New England or Federal Party, succeeded Washington in the Presidential chair. At this period, the Slavery question was frequently agitated by the Democratic Party of the South, with a view to its modification. In 1800, January 2, Mr. Waln, of Philadelphia, presented a petition to Congress, from the free Blacks of Philadelphia, praying for a revision of the Fugitive Slave Law. On this occasion, Mr. Harrison Gray Otis, a leader of the Federal party, thus expressed himself: "Although he possessed no slaves himself," he said, "yet he saw no reason why others might not; and that their owners, and not Congress, were the fittest persons to regulate that *species of property*." Mr. Brown, of Rhode Island, on the same occasion, declared "that the petition was not from negroes, but was the contrivance of a combination of *Jacobins*, (meaning the Democratic party,) who had troubled Congress for many years, and he feared would never cease to do so. He therefore moved that the petition be taken away by those who had brought it there." The motion being supported by Messrs. Gallatin, Dana, and other Northern members, the petition was withdrawn. In this debate the Northern

members who represented the Slave-trading interests,
naturally adhered to the Property in Blacks, although
the new doctrine of the British Abolitionists began to
make converts in this country, outside of the body of
Quakers, who had always opposed slavery.

It may be as well to remark here, that it does not appear any laws were ever enacted in Great Britain authorizing the trading in, or possession of, Black Slaves as
property. Nevertheless, that they were so regarded, is
evident from the opinion of the Eleven Crown Judges,
given in pursuance of an Order in Council, and in consequence of which the Navigation Act was extended to the
Slave Trade, to the exclusion of Aliens. The laws by
which England allowed the holding of slaves, extended,
of course, to the Colonies; and all those of North America
held slaves, without any special enactments for that purpose. The right was inherent, like that to any property;
and when the separation of the Colonies from the mother
country took place, that legal right, like the Common
Law of England, survived the Revolution, and remained
in force in all parts of the country.

It is claimed by the Anti-slavery party that slavery exists by local law only, and cannot exist out of the State
sanctioning it. Whereas, it is maintained by their opponents that it originally existed all over the land, whether
as Colonies or States, and that it required a special law
to exclude it. This fact is beyond cavil. It should be
also recollected that the Spanish and French Colonies,
that afterwards became a part of the United States, derived the right to hold slaves from the head of the Church,
as well as from the State.

To return to the record of events. During Mr. Jefferson's first term of office, the State of Virginia proposed
to the Federal Government that the proceeds of the public
lands that had been ceded to it should be appropriated to
the manumission and removal of slaves, with the sanction
of the respective States. This movement was not successful.

It is necessary to notice two very important events that
occurred during the administration of Mr. Jefferson, which

wholly changed the destiny of Black Slavery in the United States. The first was the invention of the cotton-gin, which gave great additional value to this staple, and hence opened a broader field to the employment of the Blacks. The next was the purchase of Louisiana, which added new and valuable territory to the South and its special products. These two events revolutionized completely the value of Slave labor at the South, and the Blacks, instead of continuing a burden, as hitherto, became henceforward a source of profit.

On the other hand, the approaching termination of the Slave Trade, which had profitably employed for so many years the commercial interests of New England, rendered that section not only indifferent to the prolongation of slavery, but even out of chagrin from having been forced by the opposition of the South to give it up, they began to nourish a species of spite against it, and which has since manifested itself with uninterrupted bitterness.

The cessation of the Slave Trade, and the purchase of Louisiana, both of which were so distasteful to the North, were followed, as already stated by the Embargo Act, in Mr. Jefferson's administration; and all this together, gave nearly a quietus to the commercial interests of New England. The exasperation which followed these measures, that seemed to threaten ruin to this section, led shortly to a desire to break up the Confederacy. In February, 1809, the Governor-General of Canada, Craig, deputed his agent, John Henry, to go to Boston and treat with the leading Federalists there; and by the arrangement, then made, Massachusetts was to declare itself independent, and invite a Congress to erect a separate Government. Mr, John Q. Adams, Ex-president, in a letter to Mr. Otis, 1828, states that the plan had been so far matured, that proposals had been made to a certain individual to put himself at the head of the military organization. These schemes went on until they resulted in the Hartford Convention, 1814, where the subject of a Northern Confederacy, in all its bearings, underwent discussion. The sentiment of the Abolitionists at that time may be seen in the party cry : " The Potomac for a boundary—the Negro

States to themselves." This was the favorite phrase of
the day all over the Eastern States. The peace with
Great Britain soon afterwards occurred, and the stimulus
this gave to business of all kinds, together with the con-
ciliatory conduct, as stated of Mr. Calhoun, of South
Carolina, diverted New England from her resolute menace
to break up the Union.

While this irritation was still lingering in the Abolition
mind, a bill was introduced into Congress, 1818, to
authorize the people of Missouri to form a Constitution,
preparatory to admission into the Union. This territory
was a portion of that same Louisiana whose purchase had
been so vehemently resisted by New England. During
its ownership by Spain, and afterwards by France, slavery
had existed in the whole of this territory, and it remained
undisturbed after its purchase by the United States;
nevertheless its admission into the Union as a Slave State,
was violently opposed by the Eastern States. An ardent
political struggle ensued, that threatened the safety of
the Confederacy, but which was, finally allayed by admitting Missouri as a Slave State, but on the condition
that no more Slave States should exist north of the 36°
30' parallel of latitude. This is the well-known Missouri
Compromise. It was at this time, also, that the Slave
Trade was declared to be Piracy, and punishable with
death.

Meanwhile, slavery had become so manifestly unprofitable at the North, that most of these States abolished it.
New York did so in 1826, and many other States, even
Delaware, Maryland and Virginia, were moving in the
same direction. New Jersey, Ohio and Delaware, passed
resolutions desiring Congress to appropriate the proceeds
of the Public Lands to the manumission of slaves, with
the consent of the Slave States. In 1825, Rufus King,
of New York, made the same proposition in Congress,
where it had been originally introduced by Virginia. At
this period, in the Southern States the utmost favor was
extended to Emancipation. Societies for this purpose
were formed to co-operate with the Colonization Society,
then in full vigor, and whose object was to free Blacks

and transport them to Liberia. In March, 1825, Virginia passed an act to furnish the Colonists in Liberia, under the direction of the "Richmond and Manchester (England) Colonization Society," with implements of husbandry, clothing, etc. The emancipation of Blacks to be sent to Liberia, were frequent all over the Southern States, and on a liberal scale. *Alabama, Louisiana and Missouri, passed laws prohibiting slaves to be brought within their borders for sale, and further enacting that those brought in* by settlers should not be sold under two years.

The sentiment of Emancipation was making steady progress ; but, at the same time, a decided repugnance to free Blacks began to manifest itself. Ohio, Illinois, and other Northwestern States, forbade by law free Blacks coming into the State, under any pretence ; and a white person who brought one in, was required to give bonds in $500. They were not regarded as citizens of the United States, and from their idle habits, were considered as a nuisance everywhere. The Southern States also enacted that free Blacks arriving there as seamen, should be under surveillance while in port. In consequence of this general antipathy to free Blacks, and in view of the difficulty of deporting them, Mr. Tucker, of Virginia, proposed in Congress, 1825, to set off the territory west of the Rocky Mountains as a Colony for free Blacks. This effort failed ; but all the leading statesmen of the South, Mr. Mangum, Mr. McDuffie, etc., urged the adoption of some scheme of emancipation.

About this time, a new movement was initiated in New England. The doctrine of Abolition was then at the zenith of its popularity in England, where it was already proposed to transplant it to our Southern States, which would then be converted into a great free Black cotton-growing country. This utterly impracticable idea was seized upon by various individuals of the New England States, who forthwith began to sow the seeds of agitation. It is impossible to attribute to them any very philanthropic motive ; for only twenty years had elapsed since Massachusetts had been forced to give up her slave-trading, and

and it is not at all credible that the tastes thus acquired should, in so short a time, have been supplanted by so ardent a love for the Negro of the South as to desire his manumission at the risk of breaking up the Confederacy. No; it really looked more like the renewed expression of that old grudge which the Eastern States have for so many years nourished against the South.

In 1828, a Mr. Arthur Tappan subscribed, with the aid of friends in Boston, sufficient funds to establish a newspaper in New York, called the "Journal of Commerce," whose object was to promote the borrowed English theory of Abolition. Its editor was a certain David Hale, an auctioneer of Boston, and a teacher in the Presbyterian sunday-school there. At the same juncture, the Baltimore "Genius of Emancipation" fell into the hands of another Abolitionist, named W. Lloyd Garrison. This individual was the grandson of what was known as a "Tory" during our Revolutionary War, and who, at the Peace, was compelled to fly the country to Nova Scotia, whence his widowed daughter and her only son returned, some years after, to Boston, to seek a livelihood. The young Garrison readily caught up the doctrine of Abolition, as most congenial to his English antecedents and education, and set to work with baleful energy to urge its propagation, fraught with so many dangers to the country of his adoption. On assuming the editorship of the Baltimore paper, he instantly assailed both Colonization and Emancipation as only obstructions to Abolition, and openly avowed that the Union of the States was equally an obstacle to Abolition. By some it was supposed that this treasonable denunciation of the Union was out of deference to the memory of his Tory grandfather, who had done all he could to prevent it.

In the year 1830, the same Garrison founded a new journal in Boston, called "The Liberator," whence he propounded his extreme views in the most extravagant language. In the following year, the "New England Anti-slavery Society" was formed. This was followed in due course by the "American Anti-slavery Society," under the leadership of Messrs. Garrison, Tappan, and

Birney. The sunday-schools of the Eastern States became active coadjutors in the same cause. These societies adopted precisely the same tactics as their British
prototypes. They circulated tracts and books, full of
inflammatory appeals. Highly-colored engravings too,
representing the Black undergoing every kind of torture,
were distributed for those who who could not read.
These were meant more especially to excite the Blacks
at the South, and were sent through the mails. These
proceedings were considered, at the time, so dangerous
to the peace of the community and to the integrity of the
Union, that popular indignation frequently broke out into
riot. In New York, in 1832, the dwelling of Arthur
Tappan and the church of Dr. Cox were both demolished
by a mob. Many influential citizens sanctioned these
violent demonstrations of public feeling, and the well-
known editor of the "Courier and Enquirer," Mr.
James Watson Webb, boasted of his share in this vindication of Southern rights.

The Abolitionists of Boston, meanwhile, continued
their operations with all the ardor of their puritanical
descent. Garrison was sent to England, to obtain funds,
by the Anti-slavery Societies; and in 1834 he returned
home with Mr. George Thompson, a Member of Parlia-
ment at that time, and an Abolition lecturer. This led
to so violent an outcry, that Thompson, alarmed for his
safety, went back to England. A new mode of excitement was then devised by the Abolitionists, who got up
a clamor against South Carolina for detaining free Blacks
who came into her ports. Massachusetts claimed that
free Blacks were her citizens, and that as such they had
a right to go to South Carolina; but as she made no
complaint against Ohio, Illinois, and other States who
also excluded free Blacks, it was evident that she sought
a quarrel with South Carolina, for the very purpose of
spreading the Abolition infection.

A Mr. Hoar was sent by Massachusetts as an agent to
Charleston to make a formal complaint of her alleged
grievance, and, as was anticipated, Mr. Hoar was sum-
marily dismissed. Upon this the Abolitionists professed

great indignation, and the Legislature was appealed to for a measure of retaliation, which was soon got up under the title of a "Personal Liberty Bill," which was designated, under a transparent plea, to obstruct the restoration of fugitive Blacks.

Up to this time, Abolition had been discussed merely as a moral question, but the agitation had gained such strength among its unsuspecting converts, that it was thought high time by its designing leaders to carry it into the political arena, where they anticipated making it a stepping-stone to power and emolument.

It will be seen in the sequel that these ingenious schemers were doomed to disappointment, and that the *spolia optima* of the agitation they began were destined to be gathered by the hand of the professional politician, leaving but a "barren sceptre in their gripe."

In 1838, the Abolition party was too weak and too ignorant of political strategy to dare to take the field in person, therefore, they began coquetting with the prominent politicians of the day. Mr. Marcy and Mr. Seward were, at that time, the candidates of the two rival parties for Governor of the State of New York, and perhaps the two most influential men of the North. The occasion was thought opportune by Messrs. Smith and Jay, the New York sponsors for the untoward bantling of Abolition, to put these gentlemen to the test. It happened that there existed a statute in New York, called the "Sojournment Law," which allowed a slaveholder to bring his Black servants with him, and remain there nine months, without prejudice to his rights; for it had been decided in the Federal Courts that a slave taken *voluntarily* into a Free State, could not be recovered. When Mr. Seward was interrogated in relation to this law, he sustained it as "a becoming act of hospitality to Southern visitors." Mr. Marcy made no reply. Mr. Seward, however, changed his views afterwards on this subject, and refused, in 1840, while Governor, to restore a fugitive slave, on the requisition of Virginia.

The evil results of this sectional issue were foreseen by many States; and among others Ohio, in 1840, passed resolutions in her Legislature to the effect that " Slavery was an institution recognized by the Constitution," and that " the unlawful, unwise, and unconstitutional interference of the fanatical Abolitionists of the North with the institutions of the South, were highly criminal." The violent proceedings of the Northern Abolitionists did not escape the attention of the South, where they created not only alarm, but aroused a deep and natural feeling of indignation. The change of sentiment that had occurred may be seen in an act of the State of Alabama, to the effect that " all free Blacks remaining in the State after August 1, 1840, should be enslaved.

At the very close of 1839, a handful of Abolitionists met in Warsaw, N. Y., and decided formerly to transform their doctrine from a moral into a political question; and they set to work at once, on a political organization. Determined to eschew any affiliation with the parties of the day, they selected one of their own band, Mr. Birney, as a candidate for the Presidency of the United States. It was now evident to all dispassionate observers, that the motives of the founders of Abolition were not so much the emancipation of the Blacks, as their own elevation to place and power. It is clear enough the North regarded them with just suspicion at that day, for in the Federal election of 1840, Birney received but 7,000 votes.

The agitation of the Slavery question received a new stimulus at this period, from the discussion awakened by the revolt of Texas. This fine country had once formed part of Louisiana, but was ceded by France to Spain, and then became a part of Mexico. In 1836, an insurrection, headed by Americans, broke out, and was soon followed by the independence of Texas. Speculations now ran high in the price of her lands, and the project was broached of re-annexing her to the United States. The celebrated Daniel Webster, among others, favored this scheme; but he was afterwards induced to change his views and oppose it. Just as in the case of Louisiana, in 1805, the New England States resisted the Annexation of Texas, during the Presidency of Mr. Tyler, on the same pretext of extending slavery, but on the real ground

of jealousy of the South. The leading politicians of the
day were sorely embarrassed whether to support Annexation or not;- and by opposing it, Mr. Clay lost his election
in 1844; and for the same reason, Mr. Van Buren failed
to obtain his renomination by the Democratic party.
The difficulty was terminated by the admission of Texas,
March 3, 1845, but on the agreement that four States
should be formed out of the territory, besides the one
existing, and that the States so formed south of the line
36° 30' should be admitted with or without slavery, as
their inhabitants should decide, but that slavery should
not exist north of that line.

A temporary lull followed; but the Slavery question
was soon again evoked, to gratify a political grudge.
The rejection of Mr. Van Buren as the Democratic candidate in 1844, by Southern influence, in consequence of
his opposition to Texas, led him, from motives of irritation, to raise up a new party in New York, on the cry of
"Free Soil, or no more Slave States." This act was a
violation of the agreement made with the South on the
admission of Texas, and was frowned upon by the Democratic party; but the issue started by Mr. Van Buren was
successful enough to divide the party in the State of New
York, and to give the election to the Northern party.
This incensed and alarmed the South, who were at last
pacified by the Compromise Measures of 1850, which,
however, were stoutly opposed by Mr. W. H. Seward,
who had become already the chosen and wily representative of the Anti-slavery sentiments of the North.

One of the prominent measures of the Compromise of
1850, was the new Fugitive Slave Law, which Daniel
Webster declared to be far more favorable to the Blacks
than that recommended by Washington, in 1787. Yet
it was seized upon by the cunning of the Anti-slavery
politicians to keep up the subsiding agitation, and several
of the Legislatures of the Northern States were induced
to pass "Personal Liberty Bills," in imitation of the example set by Massachusetts.

In 1852, the Abolitionists dropped Mr. Birney, and
selected for their Presidential candidate Mr. Hale, of New

Hampshire. He received 157,000 votes, against the 7,000 thrown for Birney, in 1840.

Among other ingenious modes of excitement, a discussion was regularly kept alive at the North as to the citizenship of free Blacks. Several States bestowed the suffrage upon them, as a practical proof of their right to rank as citizens. This controversy was rather inflamed than otherwise, by a decision of the Federal Supreme Court, in the Dred Scott case, 1853, which settled that no Blacks are citizens of the United States. In 1854, the Slavery question re-appeared in Congress, and the action of the North on this occasion was pregnant with serious consequences. Two new territories of the West were pronounced sufficiently occupied to render legislation necessary, and a bill to create a territorial government in Kansas and Nebraska, was reported by Mr. Douglas, of Illinois. His bill contained a clause to repeal the famous Missouri line of 36° 30', running south of the territories in question. This line was the basis of compromise in 1820, and was again a means of adjusting the dispute that arose on the admission of Texas, in 1845. The constitutionality of this line was, however, more than doubtful, for the reason that Congress never had any power conferred on it by the Constitution to legislate on slavery; nor was it at all necessary, since individual States could retain or exclude slavery, according to their pleasure. Besides, the line in question was really a nullity, because slavery was so unprofitable to the north of it that it would never be carried there. It was only to the south of this line that the cotton culture made slavery a profit and a necessity, Hence the South made no objection to its repeal, in 1854 ; but it is difficult to perceive what motive Mr. Douglas could have had in proposing this repeal, unless it was merely to fan the glowing embers of the Slavery question.

No sooner was this Missouri line revoked, than a prompt and significant movement was made in the New England States. Emigrant Aid Societies were formed, as already mentioned; and settlers for Kansas, one of the territories just organized, were lustily summoned as recruits

4

in the new crusade against slavery, and funds in the way
of bounty were liberally distributed. This unusual means
to stimulate emigration was designed to secure Kansas as
a Free State, by obtaining a majority for the Northern
people. Such an attempt, made with demonstrations of
vehement hostility to the South, was sure to provoke
anger and resistance. This, of course, was calculated
upon by the Anti-slavery propaganda, and they were not
disappointed. The Slave State of Missouri, directly ad-
joining Kansas, was not disposed to be forestalled, and,
as it were, forced out of their legal share to territory in
such close proximity; so they did their best to encourage
emigration too, but the slaveholders were naturally chary
to carry their Blacks with them, as they were sure to be
tempted away. As a matter of course, it was impossible
for the people of the two opposite sections, in their
intemperate state of mind, to live long in peace together.
Collisions occurred, and occasional loss of life ensued.
The Abolitionists were eagerly waiting for some such
news as this, for it was rightly anticipated that a conflict,
sooner or later, was inevitable.

When the looked-for intelligence at last arrived, a wild
and furious shriek for "bleeding Kansas" vibrated in a
thousand echoes through all the valleys of New England.
The organs of the Abolitionists teemed with the most
discordant appeals to the passions of the people, and
nothing but imprecations of the most startling description
were launched against the "Border Ruffians," as the
settlers from Missouri were forthwith christened. Public
meetings were called in the Eastern States, and the pulpit
soon became a rostrum for clerical agitators. Subscrip-
tions were rapidly set on foot to buy arms and ammunition
for the sacred defenders of anti-slavery in Kansas, whose
brows were encircled with the halo of martyrdom.
Speculators in "Sharp's rifles" joined in the well-sus-
tained chorus of the Abolitionists, and a considerable
profit was the result. At a public meeting in New Haven,
a well-known Abolitionist, Rev. H. Ward Beecher, of
Brooklyn, and brother of the authoress of "Uncle Tom's
Cabin," aided by his presence and language to swell the

clamor fast rising in the North.   He desired his name to
be subscribed for "twenty-five Sharpe's rifles," and announced he would collect the money to pay for them, in
his church, the following Sabbath, which was done.

Such ingenious modes as these, and so skilfully handled,
could not fail to excite the sympathies and stir the passions of any community.   Ever since 1828, the Abolition
party had been laboriously engaged in sapping the mind
of the North on the subject of Black Slavery; nor must
it be forgotten that they appealed to something more
than its philanthropy, when they raised the cry of "No
more Slave Territory," which simply meant that all that
vast extent of country stretching from the Mississippi to
the Rocky Mountains, should be given up to Northern
emigration.   It was natural, certainly, that so palatable
a doctrine should be acceptable at the North; but just as
natural that it should be unwelcome at the South, whose
equal claims were so unceremoniously ignored.

The now-called Republican party met in convention in
Philadelphia, June, 1856, and made, for the first time, a
sectional issue the basis of party action.   They selected
for their Presidential candidate Mr. John C. Fremont,
known in the country as an officer of the army, but without any political antecedents.   It was thought judicious
not to nominate a politician too closely identified with
the anti-slavery movement, lest the possible consequences
might alarm the "sober second thought" of the North.
Thus accoutred, the Republican party went to the polls,
November, 1856, and brought off a vote of 1,334,553.
They were defeated by the Democratic party, which was
now the only link between North and South; but the
Republican leaders felt quite sanguine that, with the tactics their experience would suggest, they would carry off
the Presidential prize in 1860.   It was thus that the
moral question as to the sin of slavery, borrowed from
England by our Abolitionists, and kept alive by their
address till the North was thoroughly infected by it, was,
at last, converted into a party question and made a party
issue.

In October, 1859, an event occurred which amazed the

whole country. We allude to the invasion of the State
of Virginia, by John Brown and his retinue of men.
This man Brown had figured in "bleeding Kansas" as a
daring ring-leader of the anti-slavery bands that had contended for the mastery there. When these bloody con-
tests subsided, he was reduced to inaction; and he chafed
at the loss of the stern excitement congenial to his fierce
nature. Whether it was fanaticism or ambition that
inspired him, no one can say; but he conceived the horrible project of setting on foot a servile insurrection.
Followed by a handful of desperate men, he suddenly
entered the State of Virginia, seized the arsenal of the
Federal Government, to obtain the arms he needed, and
raised the cry of "Freedom to Slaves." To his astonishment, no doubt, the affrighted blacks ran to their masters
for protection, and some were shot in seeking to escape.
This nefarious attempt was quelled by the arrest of
Brown and his confederates, and their subsequent trial and
execution.

One thing was proved by the utter failure of this daring
outrage, for it showed that the blacks were contented
with their homes, and desired not the emancipation of the
sword. Another thing, if not quite so clear, at least
looked ominous. This madman, Brown, had been known
as an efficient instrument in the hands of the anti-slavery
party of New England; and it was, therefore, a matter
of conjecture at the South how far he was incited to this
fearful attempt against their very existence. Had they
not some reason to think the act met the approval of the
Abolitionists of the North, when 300 bells tolled for the
fate of Brown, and when the organs of the party honored
his memory, while affecting to disapprove his conduct?

This event sank deep into the mind and heart of the
Southern States. They were led to believe, for the first
time, that the ultra wing of the Republican party contem-
plated the confiscation of their property and the destruction of their lives.

Another incident occurred in the summer of 1860,
which deepened their conviction that the Northern States
had entered into a dark conspiracy to desolate their land

with fire and sword. It was discovered that a book, called the "Impending Crisis," was being secretly circulated all over the North as a "campaign document." The purport of this volume was to show, by assertion, as well as by figures, that the free labor of the North was more profitable than the black labor of the South. The tone of the book was violent in the extreme. We will add a few extracts, which will enable the reader to form a correct opinion of the character and object of the work:

"Slavery is a great moral, social, civil, and political evil, to be got rid of at the earliest practical period."— (page 168.)

"Three-quarters of a century hence, if the South retains slavery, which God forbid! she will be to the North what Poland is to Russia, Cuba to Spain, and Ireland to England."—(p. 162.)

"On our banner is inscribed—No Co-operation with Slaveholders in Politics; no Fellowship with them in Religion; no Affiliation with them in Society. No Recognition of Pro-slavery men, except as Ruffians, Outlaws, and Criminals"—(p. 156.)

"We believe it is, as it ought to be, the desire, the determination, and the destiny of the Republican party to give the death-blow to slavery."—(p. 234.)

"In any event, come what will, transpire what may, the institution of slavery must be abolished."—(p. 180.)

"We are determined to abolish slavery at all hazards —in defiance of all the opposition, of whatever nature, it is possible for the Slavocrats to bring against us. Of this they may take due notice, and govern themselves accordingly."—(p. 149.)

"It is our honest conviction that all the Pro-slavery Slaveholders deserve to be at once reduced to a parallel with the basest criminals that lie fettered within the cells of our public prisons."—(p. 158.)

"Shall we pat the bloodhounds of slavery? Shall we fee the curs of slavery? Shall we pay the whelps of slavery? No, never."—(p. 329.)

"Our purpose is as firmly fixed as the eternal pillars of

heaven; we have determined to abolish slavery, and, so help us God! abolish it we will."—(p. 187.)

The volume containing the above quotations, not by any means the most bitter, was endorsed by 68 members of Congress of the Republican party, whose names were given for publication. The South, under manifestations like these, felt they had a right to infer that, if a party making such declarations of hostility were elected to power by the North, they must either consent to the early abolition of Black Slavery, or retain it by seceding from the Union.

When the British Government emancipated the Blacks in her colonies, she acted with the strictest commercial equity; but the book in question repudiates any compensation to the "curs and whelps of slavery." One more extract:

"The black god of slavery, which the South has worshipped for 237 years."—(p. 163.)

Now, the writer is ignorant that the South protested for years, first, against the mother country, and, next, against New England, importing slaves within her borders. However, the object of the book was to inflame the mind of the North against the South, and therefore falsehood was as good as truth.

In April. 1860, the Delegates of the Democratic party met in convention at Charleston, South Carolina, to make their nomination for the Presidency. The Northern wing of the party proposed Senator Douglas as the most eligible candidate at the North, from his doctrine of "Popular Sovereignty." The Southern wing objected, as they considered said doctrine only a concession to the Anti-slavery dogma. Mr. Douglas did not withdraw his name, and a rupture of the party ensued. The Northern delegates nominated Mr. Douglas, in Baltimore, June 18; and on the same occasion, the Southern delegates nominated Vice-President Breckinridge.

This schism doubled the chances of the Republican party, which met in convention to select their candidate at Chicago, Illinois. May, 1860. It was generally supposed that Mr. W. H. Seward, the acknowledged leader of the Anti-slavery party at the North, an able and wily statesman, would be its chosen companion in the electoral lists about to open; but, to the surprise of all, an almost unknown politician of the West, Mr. Abraham Lincoln, was selected as its standard-bearer.

On the 6th of November, 1860, the long agitation on the slavery question, that began in 1803, ended with the election to the Presidency of Abraham Lincoln, the representative of the Republican party, but which contained within its bowels, like the Trojan horse of old, the armed men of the Abolition party. Shortly after this event, Governor Andrew, of Massachusetts, declared at a public meeting, that "the election of Mr. Lincoln was only the first step towards forcible emancipation."

The whole territory of the States, North and South, was originally slaveholding—-English, Spanish, and French. Not for any local law, but from the laws of the mother country.

Slaves were regarded only as property in all the thirteen States that formed the Union; since it would have been a manifest absurdity for the Slaveholders who made the Declaration of Independence, to declare " all men were born free and equal," had they not conidered the slaves as property.

In forming the Union, the thirteen Slave States conferred upon the Federal Government the power to tax slave property; to protect it from foreigners, as well on the national territories as at sea, and also from domestic escape; and conferred no other power, either to prohibit or to extend it.

The Abolitionists North clung to the profits of the Slave Trade as long as possible, and attacked the slave system when they were deprived of those profits.

The territory that was once all slave, has become free; 1st, by the Ordinance of 1787, prohibiting slaves north of the Ohio; 2d, by eight Northern States abolishing slavery in their borders; 3d, by the Missouri Compromise of 1820, prohibiting slaves north of 36° 30'; 4th, the act admitting Texas re-enacting that line. Thus the North has driven slaves out of half the Territories of the United

States, showing a constant and large aggressions upon the South.

The duty of the Government is undoubtedly to protect the property upon the Territories, until people there settled form their own laws.

The agitation of the slave question grew originally out of the chagrin of New England, at being deprived of the Slave Trade and its profits. It was prolonged by the mutual irritation that the opposition of Massachusetts to the purchase of Louisiana occasioned.

Emancipation made steady progress in all the States, until Abolition forced the Slaveholders upon the defensive.

Abolition made little progress, until unscrupulous partisans coquetted with it for party issues.

The question of the power of the Government to exclude slavery from the Territories, has been blended with the moral question as to the "sin of slavery."

The cry of "Free Soil" was raised in 1848, by Mr. Van Buren, to avenge his non-nomination by the South, at Baltimore.

The compromise measures of 1850, were carried by the influence of Henry Clay.

Violation of these compromises, by the "Personal Liberty Bills" of the Northern States, soon followed.

Repeal of the Missouri Compromise, in 1854.

Attempt, by the Abolition party, to make Kansas a Free State by force, which was resisted by the South.

Rise of Republican party, under the lead of Mr. W. H. Seward, and its defeat in 1856.

Violent agitation of the slavery question at the North, followed by the invasion of Virginia by John Brown, in 1859, and the circulation of the Helper Book, in 1860.

The theory of a "Higher Law" at the North, to justify resistance to the Constitution and laws of Congress, has begotten the Higher Law of Self-preservation at the South, to justify resistance to a dominant party, which embraces the "sin of slavery" among its tenets.

The Southern States have been for nearly sixty years the object of political persecution by the North, which they have borne with patience and returned with kindness.

In 1820, the North entered into a compromise, which has been broken. In 1850 they made new agreements, which have since been violated. In 1860 a legal majority elected a President on the "Platform" that "Slavery must be restricted to its present limits." Outraged in our rights, and threatened in our interests, what course is left the South? To fold their arms and await more injury and endure more obloquy? Would this check the aggressions of the North till both North and South were swallowed up in the vortex of ruin? It is clear that the South have no alternative. Far better they should have no alternative. Far better they should have abandoned the Confederacy than remain only to engage in bitter feuds that compromise the dignity of the country, and sow the seeds of undying hatred.

In 1789, according to our view, the South entered into a civil compact with the North, on certain conditions and guarantees. These have been broken, and the South returns, in her opinion, to her original sovereignty. Even were it otherwise—were it true that the South owed allegiance to the Federal Government—still, she asserts our Declaration of Independence in 1776, and the present practice of Europe justify all people in repudiating a government which assails their rights and sacrifices their best interests. If the Northern States do not acknowledge these truths, then are they false to their origin, and seek to substitute for a government of opinion the tyranny of force.

A few general considerations, and we conclude our narrative. After tracing the course of events recorded in the foregoing pages, the questions naturally arise— What has been the result? What have the Abolitionists gained? The answers may be briefly summed up as follows:

"With the fairest portions of the earth in their possession, and with the advantage of a long discipline as the cultivators of the soil, their constitutional indolence has converted the most beautiful islands of the sea into howling wastes. It is not too much to say, that if the South should, at this moment, surrender every slave, the wisdom of the entire world, united in solemn council, could not solve the question of their disposal. Freedom would be their doom. Every Southern master knows this truth and feels its power."

1.   Touch the negro, and you touch cotton—the mainspring that keeps the machinery of the world in motion.   In teaching slaves to entertain wild and danger- ous notions of liberty, the Abolitionists have thus jeopardized the commerce of the country and the manu- facturing interests of the civilized world.   They have likewise destroyed confidence.   In short, all the kind relations that have ever existed between the North and the South have been interrupted, and a barrier erected, which, socially, commercially, and politically, has sepa- rated the heretofore united interests of the two sections.

2.   They have held out a Canadian Utopia, where they have taught the slaves in their ignorance to believe they could enjoy a life of ease and luxury, and having cut them off from a race of kind masters, and separated them from comfortable homes, left the deluded beings, incapable of self-support, upon an uncongenial soil, to live in a state of bestiality and misery, and die cursing the Abolitionists as the authors of their wretchedness.

3.   They have led a portion of the people of the North, as well as of the South, and to plant themselves upon the broad principle that that form of government which re- cognizes the institution of Slavery in the United States, is the best, the condition of the two races, white and black being considered, for the development, progress, and happiness of each.   In other words, to regard servi- tude as a blessing to the negro, and, under proper and philanthropic restrictions, necessary to their preservation and the prosperity of the country.

4.   Step by step they have built up a party upon an issue which has led to a dissolution of the Union.   They have scattered the seeds of Abolitionism until a majority of the voters of the Free States have become animated by a fixed purpose to prevent the further growth of the slave power.

The power of the North has been consolidated, and, for the first time in the history of the country, it is wielded as a sectional weapon against the interests of the South. The Government is now in the hands of men elected by Northern votes, who regard slavery as a curse and a crime, and they will have the means necessary to accomplish their purpose.

The utterances that have heretofore come from the rostrum, or from irresponsible associations of individuals, now come from the throne. "Clad with the sanctities of office, with the annointing oil poured upon the monarch's head, the decree has gone forth that the institution of Southern Slavery shall be constrained within assigned limits. Though Nature and Providence should send forth its branches like the banyan tree, to take root in congenial soil, here is a power superior to both, that says it shall wither and die within its own charmed circle."

Abraham Lincoln, President of the United States, says: "I believe this Government cannot endure permanently, half slave and half free. I do not expect the Union to be dissolved; I do not expect the house to fall, but I do expect that it will cease to be divided. It will become all one thing, or all the other. Either the opponents of Slavery will arrest the further spread of it, and place it where the public mind shall rest in the belief that it is in the course of ultimate extinction, or its advocates will push it forward until it shall become alike lawful in all the States, old as well as new, North as well as South."

"I have always hated slavery as much as any Abolitionist. I have always been an old line Whig. I have always hated it, and I always believed it in a course of ultimate extinction. If I were in Congress, and a vote should come up on a question whether Slavery should be prohibited in a new Territory, in spite of the Dred Scott decision, I would vote that it should."

"Abolitionism and fanaticism is a blood-hound that never bolts its track when it has once lapped blood. The elevation of their candidate is far from being the consu-

mation of their aims.   It is only the beginning of that
consummation ; and if all history be not a lie, there will
be coercion enough till the end of the beginning is reached
and the dreadful banquet of slaughter and ruin shall glut
the appetite."

CHAPTER II.

HOW I GOT INTO THE ARMY.—GENERALS POLK, CARROL AND PILLOW.
—SCENES AT FORT PILLOW.—NEW MADRID, AND ISLAND 10.—REL-
ATIVE FORCES.—COMPLETE LIST OF CONFEDERATE BATTERIES
AND THEIR OFFICERS.—INCIDENTS OF THE ENGAGEMEMT.

I WAS a pretty fair Union man until South Carolina seceded, then felt the time had arrived to define my position.

I was at a fair in Macon, Georgia, when the news came that the Palmetto had refused to shade the enemies of the South, thus casting an electric spark into the political magazine of the country.

Being called upon, as a representative of Tennessee, to make a speech, my response was a definition of my position as alluded to; satisfying myself, if not my hearers, that I was a *dyed in the wool* seceder. My peroration was, as follows: "There was not a Tennessean in that broad domain from Shelby, to Carter, but would shed the last drop of blood that coursed through his veins, in stay-ing the advance of an enemy, that would desecrate your household and political Gods, and make your hearths and firesides desolate." That's what I said, *my* boy. But I *lied* under a mistake, for very many, too many, *you see*, didn't do any thing of the kind. The above speech was made under the patronage of those two distinguished Maconites, Captain Conner and General Frank Bloom, who were my friends, and presented me to the large and enthusiastic crowd, who were yelling, "No more bounty on cod-fish;" "Hurrah for Tennessee;" "Bully for South Carolina;" and were *waking things up* generally, all of which excitement had its effect on the speaker, not mentioning the influence of that mysterious Georgia combination, "peach and honey."

On returning to Memphis, Tennessee, I joined an organization, called the Sixth Ward Company; found them alive on the " drill," and drilled with them. This continued until the gun fired at Sumpter, 13th day of April, 1861. Lincoln's proclamation followed, and the South rushed to arms. The excitement in my company became so intense, owing to the fact, that Memphis had appropriated $50,000 for defense, an act based on her close proximity to Cairo, 247 miles disant, and the fortifying at Fort Harris, with my old schoolmate, Captain Marsh Patrick, and his Crockett Rangers. Marsh being one of the most recklessly brave men I ever saw, and his Rangers just like him—that not deeming it safe to risk my military prestige with such imflamable material, I transferred my ardor to an organization called the Gayoso Guards, commanded by Captain Tank Wilson, a gentleman and a soldier, whose bad health prevented a display of that efficiency demanded by the service. We were drilled by Captain John Cameron, of the "Young Guard," who, although barely out of his teens, was unexceptionable in drill and military decorum. His lieutenants, Will. Bourne and Otis Smith, the former as gallant a boy as I ever knew, son of my old friend Captain Jim Bourne, one of Memphis's most useful citizens, the latter a good soldier and genial companion, were effective aids to their captain, in all matters pertaining to drill and discipline. Captain Bowdoin Locke gave us the finishing touch which his West Point education enabled him to do, and the company prepared for active service, by organizing on the 8th of June, 1861, with the author as captain, on the 22d of July following, was mustered into the service of the State of Tennessee, whose army was raised as a provisional.force under a legislative act of May 6th, 1861, by Major W. B. Campbell, A. D. C. to General J. Pillow, the former a scholar, soldier, and gentleman, the latter an impetuous, rash, brave, generous hearted soldier, with one of the best executive heads in the country.

The following order was my first introduction to military life :

" *Head-quarters Inspector General's Dep't, Provisional Army of Tennessee, Memphis, July 31st, 1861.*

" Captain Joe Barbiere is authorized by me to take command of the regiment to rendezvous at Colliersville, Tennessee, under the commission given me by General Leonidas Polk, to raise regiments for the Confederate service.

" WM. H. CARROL,

" Inspector General, Tennessee Army."

This kind offer of promotion by General Carrol was declined, owing to a promise I made my company not to leave them, which I fulfilled, and have no cause to regret it.   General Carrol was the son of Governor Carrol, of Tennessee, who with Jackson, at New Orleans, made Tennessee and her sons famous.   There are few better men than Bill Carrol ; and I am sure none braver.   His A. A. G., Colonel Cayce Young, was the coolest soldier under fire I ever saw, with an undying energy, that had it not been for an impaired constitution, would have placed him in the highest niche in the military temple of the South.   Colonel Young did much towards organizing and rendering effective the military arm of the State. Captain William Carrol, Jr., A. D. C., was a model soldier, devoted to his father—the soul of honor and a fitting shoot of that worthy stock that has shed so much lustre on the name of " Tennessean."

Captain John Wilkerson, I. G., on the staff, was a *reckless of consequences* officer, distinguished himself at Belmont, and was ever foremost when there was danger in the van.   John's motto was a stereotyped one, " be it on the scaffold high, or in the battle's van, the noblest death for man to die is where he dies for man ;" and if John has not died, it has been because a kind Providence has held him in reserve for years of future peace and plenty, which his big heart so eminently deserves.   Captain John Harris, ordinance officer, whom I have known from his infancy, is a promising soldier, and bids fair to **take** prominent position among the cavaliers of the Con-

federate army. The order from General Carrol attracted
the notice of General Leonidas Polk, who immediately
summoned me to his head-quarters.

"General Polk, I believe?"

"Walk in, captain."

"General, you have sent for me, and I am here. My
name is ——."

"Well, sir, I knew who you were before I sent for you.
General Carrol's order is irregular, sir; the General has
permission to raise regiments for the C. S. A., while you
are in the service of the State of Tennessee."

"Very true, General ; but you can muster me into the
Confederate service, thus harmonizing matters at your
convenience."

"Well, sir, that settles the question. I will attend to
your case at once," and with a bow and salute the interview terminated, leaving me impressed with the greatness
of the man.

Major Anderson was post-quartermaster during the
reign of Dixie in Memphis. Everybody abused him, and
not one gave him credit for half he did. The mass of the
troops from Arkansas, Mississippi, Louisiana, Texas, and
Tennessee passed through Memphis ; a host of officers
had to be paid, tents, canteens, haversacks, etc., had to
be supplied. He was banker, merchant, book-keeper,
appraiser, and stable-keeper—for one hundred and sixty
dollars per month. He had able assistants ; but the bulk
of the duties devolved upon him alone.

The post-commissary, Major Calvin Fackler, was one
of the best business men I ever knew; they say he had
faults; who has them not? He with Anderson were
attentive to my military wants, and I remember them
kindly for it. After being mustered into the general
service I was ordered to take charge of a battery at the
mouth of Wolf river, which I held one month *for bunkum,*
knowing that when an enemy came in range of my guns
his projectiles would reach the city, showing the military
follies committed, the first year of the war, although
the order placing me in charge emanated from a West
Pointer, Colonel Bonham, a stern and inflexible discip-

linarian. Colonel Marsh Walker, on relieving Colonel Bonham, with that good judgment for which he was always celebrated, ordered me to give up the battery and remove my command to Germantown, a village about fifteen miles from Memphis, on the M. & C. R. R.; at this point we attempted the organization of a regiment which was to assist in forming a brigade, to be commanded by General W. H. Carroll. The Thirty-seventh Tennessee, already formed, commanded by Colonel Moses White, one of the most perfect specimens of manliness and chivalry to be found throughout the world of humanity. The Thirty-eighth Tennessee, commanded by Colonel Robert Looney, a personal friend of years standing, and whose many genial qualities and splendid oratorical powers has earned him a host of friends in the social and political circles of his section. My own regiment not forming rapidly enough for the emergency, the brigade left for East Tennessee, and we were left out of it. In a few days I was ordered to move my battalion to Fort Pillow, 80 miles above Memphis, on the Mississippi river; we were two days in making the trip, and only had one day's rations; this soured the men, who had obtained whiskey and were very hard to manage. We reached the Fort, mud a foot deep, and the weather excessively cold; this was the initiative of genuine soldiering. I immediately reported to the colonel-commanding's head-quarters: had on blue coat, staff buttons, blue pants with gold stripe an inch wide, broad-brimmed hat with gold band, and a sweeping feather; in fact, Brummel never felt better dressed, nor Wellington more grand.

I had known the commandant from boyhood—yet approached him deferentially, he remarked :

" Captain, what is that feather in your hat for ?"

" 'Tis the style in Tennessee," colonel."

" I was not aware of it captain, I thought you wore it possibly to keep the rain off'

The next day the hat and feather *went up*—then the gold stripes—and in a few weeks I became a respectable looking soldier. We were ordered to consolidate our

5

battalion with two Mississippi and four Alabama companies, which we did. I was defeated for a field office, and resolved into my old position of senior captain, after the election. I dropped into surgeons' head-quarters—the two chiefs of this department being Messrs. Cobb and Benjamin, whose pleasant attentions to their friends made their mess the centre of attraction at the post. Colonel Walker, who was present, remarked to me:—

"Captain, you are looking dull to day!"

"I hope your defeat has not given you the hypo."

"Oh, no, colonel, not at all."

At this moment Lieutenant McCall, a bluff old U. S. A. officer, addressed me.

"Never mind, captain, a major is nothing but a d—d stick."

Colonel Walker, interrupting, "Let me introduce Major Minter, of the Fortieth."

"Oh, I beg pardon, major," exclaims the waggish McCall. "but you must admit he is nothing but a d——— file-closer."

Minter being an amiable man accepted the apology. I was appeased—consoled for my defeat, which is an event common to all men.

After charging around in the mud at Fort Pillow for three months, amused by drills and false alarms, stopping boats unnecessarily, very much to the annoyance and disgust of their officers, the only boat that attempted to run the batteries of the fort, was one with despatches from General Polk, and she was successful, as the officer at the gun rammed his ball in before his cartridge, greatly to his discomfiture and the amusement of his brother officers. I've tried stopping boats, and find it a very difficult matter, even if you load regular, having attempted it with Commodore Walke, at "Island Ten."

I had been promised a leave of absence for some time, and to kill two birds with one stone, the commanding officer gave me leave and an order at the same time, authorizing me to take charge of the steamboat "Winchester," said boat being employed to carry surplus war material and extra baggage of the fort, the command being ordered to New Madrid, Missouri, as well to convey the families of several of the officers to Memphis.

It was a trying period, and the first time the stern realities of war were realized by devoted wives and innocent children, the latter, of whom there were several, seeming as if their little hearts would break.

DEDICATED TO MY LITTLE FRIEND WINNY JAMES, SON OF A. R. JAMES, DOYLESTOWN, PA.

There is nothing so softening, so humanizing, as the influence of the innocent child upon the coarser nature of the man, next to woman's love, it has no equal in the physical world in paving the rough elements of our nature with the flowers of innocence. Who that dandles the little prattler upon his knee, but feels that he imbibes that spirit that tells us we must "become as a little child" before we "can enter the Kingdom of Heaven," and has the better feelings of his heart invoked to think of soothing sentences, and to devise artless tales to please the child he descends to, as the Great Federick ever did.

The man who will amuse the little ones with "cherries are ripe, O give the baby one," "sing a song of six-pence," and "little Jack Horner," even, if a bad man, will feel most beneficially the modifying influence of "baby talk" in his household. He who loves children may be unfortunately constituted as regards passion and impulse, but he cannot be a very bad man. God bless the little ones, and don't be cross to them, as for every word so spoken there will be many an after pang, should the little eyes cease to wink and blink, the little mouth to prattle, and the tiny shoe of the little toddler of the household be placed carefully away in the bureau drawer, when the little one's spirit has gone to the God who gave it. Yes, be kind to the children. The author will never forget the friends of his childhood, and can hardly forgive that man who insulted him, while a child.

We reached Memphis in safety, I delivered my precious charge of living freight, remained in the city for a few days, when it was rumored they were fighting at New Madrid. I immediately left to join my command; reached Tiptonville, found the river blocked by the enemy's batteries at Point Pleasant, walked through to Island Ten, thence by boat to New Madrid, in time to participate in the engagement.

As historians will speak of these engagements, I deem it due the officers, now my fellow prisoners, to give a synopsis of the two engagements, as I witnessed them. They were not bloody affairs, but were evidences of the powers of endurance of a soldiery, taken fresh from the plow, loom, and anvil, the office and bar, when engaged in a cause holy to them, and to which they had pledged their "lives, fortunes, and sacred honor." The force in front of us at New Madrid, was reported thirty-two regiments of infantry, seven of cavalry, two of engineers, twelve light batteries, and some heavy siege guns. Our force aggregated not exceeding thirty-five hundred effective men. For the first few days after our occupation, nothing of moment transpired excepting picket firing, and a skirmish of the Fortieth Tennessee, under Colonel Henderson, with some of the enemy's cavalry, driving them back, and the unfortunate killing of the gallant Captain West, (Billy West, as his comrades called him.) He had been provost marshal of New Madrid, and was acting as a scout, reconnoitering the enemy's picket lines, when killed by mistake by one of our own pickets. West was a noble fellow, and died as he had lived, cool and unflinching. His effects were taken charge of by Drake McDowell, his old friend and companion in arms.

Dr. Drake McDowell is the son of the famous doctor of the same name in St. Louis, Missouri, after whom the college is named, now used for imprisoning "Southern sympathizers." McDowell acted the scout for us at New Madrid, penetrated beyond the enemy's lines, discovered their strength and intentions, and predicted all that afterwards occurred.

The morning of the 13th of March, 1862, found us enveloped in a heavy fog, under cover of which the enemy advanced their columns, in three divisions, under Schuyler Hamilton, Stanley, and Payne, with Pope at his head-quarters "in his saddle," at the rear—with the reserve. We were in a miserable condition. Our camps in the upper fort were immediately on the bank of the river, ditches from one to three feet deep through our camp, as it was the rainy season, and they were usually full of water. The sinks were about ten steps from the writer's tent; no protection for our wounded or sick; one-third of our number ill—cause, fresh pork and Mississippi water; all of which the enemy were aware of, and deemed us easy prey. We were supported by five gun-boats, among the most prominent being the Ponchartrain, commanded by that polished officer, Captain John Dunington. It was the look-out on this boat that discovered the advancing columns of the enemy, who were preparing to form, for the purpose of storming our position. We immediately opened on them, with a fire so destructive, as to drive them back, and, as per their official report, a hasty council of division officers was called, at the suggestion of their superior, decided to withdraw their forces—an act of cowardice, only equalled by our disgraceful evacuation of the place. They could have driven us into the river at any time, had they stormed us, rather than amused themselves by desultory firing; one of their balls striking our medical director, Dr. Bell, a most accomplished surgeon and estimable gentleman. He was conversing with General McCown, when a solid shot, passing between the legs of the General, shattered the feet of Dr. Bell. They were amputated above the ankle, and he died the next day.

On the morning of the 13th of March, Charlie Logan lost his life. He was a member of Captain Frank A. Ragsdale's company, Company B, Fortieth Tennessee. He was a brave, courageous fellow, and died regretted by his command. His death was accidental and instantaneous. We could not bury him in the lines, and it was impossible do be done outside, so he was cleanly dressed and shaved, under the supervision of his captain, and left with evidence in writing who he was. The report of our leaving our dead unburied, originated in this single case.

On the night of the 13th, as mentioned, it was decided to evacuate New Madrid. The writer was in charge of the reserve picket that night, one of the most terrific ones ever passed. It was stormy, the reverberating claps of thunder, in their sublimity, drowning the recollection of the roar of artillery the day previous. The lightnings flashed, darting into the river in perpendicular streaks, with a hissing sound, like some angry spirit in the world of torment. I had quartered my picket in the court-house, and here was witnessed one of those scenes of vandalism ever attendant upon the movement of large bodies of men, be they either friends or enemies. The records of the county for half a century, titles and licenses, with other valuable documents, were lying on the floor, a foot deep covered with mud, and trampled upon by the soldiery, and those upon the shelves scattered and torn, to gratify an idle curiosity.

About midnight, a tall figure, shrouded in a large military cloak, with a lantern beneath, Major Jim Alexander, General Walker's adjutant, as true an officer as ever wore the Confederate uniform, notifying me to " bring in the reserves, we were evacuating." I immediately aroused my picket, and, after some trouble, reached the sally-port with them, only losing four or five, who were captured by the Federals the next day. On reaching our camp, I found the troops had all left, the gun-boat Ponchartrain alone remaining ; and had it not been for General Marsh Walker, I think it would have gone also, leaving the picket to their fate. The General remained on the bow of the gun-boat, in the drenching rain, posting the writer at the foot of the single plank that communicated with the shore, and where he remained one of the last to leave the shore.

Captain A. S. Levy, quarter-master of the First Alabama, Tennessee and Mississippi volunteers, deserves much credit for faithful performance of duties entrusted to him.

The troops were divided ; some going to Tiptonville, others to Island 10, the regiment to which the writer belonged four miles below the island, on the main shore, and seven miles above New Madrid; thence to the interior for picket duty; thence up to the main land facing the island, which they crossed to, and picketed alternately with the other regiments on the main shore.

The island and main land batteries have been over-rated by writers. The following is a correct statement of the location, and number of batteries:

Battery No. 1, two eight-inch Columbiads, four thirty-two-pound smooth-bore, commanded by Captain E. W. Rucker, of Memphis, Tennessee, whose gallantry on this occasion was heralded throughout the Confederacy, and received special notice, in general orders from the commanding General.

Senior First Lieutenant John E. Saunders is an educated gentleman, and a brave officer.

Second Lieutenant W. B. Clarke, of Alabama, was a courageous and promising soldier, and was killed at his post, while performing duty, in company with Lieutenant Chapman, during the terrific bombardment of the 17th of March. This battery was supported by the First Alabama regiment, under the command of Colonel Steadman, a thorough officer, who was ably seconded by Capt. J. F. Whitfield, of Montgomery, Alabama, formerly connected with the press of that city, who, like all printers, is brave and generous and warm in his attachments, and whose friendship the author is proud of.

Battery No. 2, four thirty-two pound rifle-guns, commanded by Captain R. S. Sterling, Senior First Lieutenant A. Munch, Second Lieutenant Thomas James Finnie, Junior First Lieutenant Roe, Second Lieutenant Hagan. This battery was skillfully managed and well served, the officers and men behaving like veterans. Lieutenant Finnie deserves especial mention, and performed the duties of his office in a manner that would have distinguished him on any field. The lieutenant is a Memphian, and is as enthusiastic to all that appertains to the moral improvement of his city, as he is at serving his battery. Messrs. Sterling, Munch, and Roe proved themselves skillful and effective.

Battery No. 3, three thirty-two pound rifle cannons,

commanded by T. W. Hoadley, Senior First Lieutenant Parks, Junior First Lieutenant Baggett. This was a small battery, but one that would have done much execution, had the enemy come within effective range.

Battery No. 4, one eight-inch Columbiad, three thirty-two pound rifle guns, commanded by Captain A. Jackson, junior, Senior First Lieutenant Brown, Second Lieutenant Chinn, Junior First Lieutenant Nowlan, and Second Lieu-'enant McClure. The commander is well known to Tennesseans, is a graduate of West Point, and an accomplished officer. Lieutenant McClure, although young, is of much experience, both in Australia and America. Messrs. Chinn and Nolan performed the duties to which they were assigned, creditable to their corps.

Battery No. 5, one thirty-two pound rifle-gun, three sixty-four pound smooth-bore, and three thirty-two pound smooth-bore, commanded at the passing of the gun-boats by Senior First Lieutenant S. R. Hayman, Second Lieutenant J. A. Forrey, Junior First Lieutenant W. B. Michie, Junior Second Lieutenant G. W. McCown. Hayman had one of the best handled batteries on the main shore, it was a perfect specimen of order and cleanliness, he himself acting with firmness and calmness. Lieutenant Forrey is a chip off the old block, and those who know his father, Major Jim Forrey, of Tennessee, will not question the fighting qualities of the son. Messrs. Michie and McCown performed creditably their allotted duties. The foregoing list is complete, of the guns and officers on the main shore, being a total of twenty-four guns. The batteries on the island proper, were near and on the head of the island, and so situated as to be defenseless to a rear attack. The principle battery was one of seven guns ; one one hundred and twenty-eight pound rifled gun, which burst after two or three discharges; two eight-inch Columbiads, one twenty-four pound rifled; three thirty-two pound smooth-bore, commanded by Captain W. Y. C. Humes, Senior First Lieutenant, George Martin, Second, George R. Hill, Junior First Lieutenant, W. C. Winston, Second, E. C. McDowell. The captain of this battery, must have had nerves of steel. Day after day did the air resound with shriek of shell, and the roar of the mortars, as they discharged them, the air being literally filled at times with fragments, yet Captain Humes remained at his post. He was ably seconded by Lieutenant George S. Martin, a nephew of General Pillow, and one of the most fearless young officers in the service. Their junior officers displayed nerve equal to veterans.

Washington Heavy Artillery, three thirty-two pound smooth-bore, commanded by Captain P. W. Bibb, Senior First Lieutenant Lipscomb, Second Lieutenant L. F. Burke, Junior First Lieutenant John J. Lane, Second Lieutenant W. H. Rupert. This battery was well officered. Bibb looks every inch the soldier: Lipscomb belongs to the press, and is one of the many game men the "Fourth Estate" has thrown into the field. Lieutenant Rupert has the reputation of writing the worst piece of poetry I ever read.

Nelson Artillery, one eight inch Columbiad, two twenty-four pound rifled guns, two thirty-two pound smooth-bore, commanded by Captain John A. Fisher, Senior First Lieutenant J. J. McDaniel, Second Lieutenant R. J. Polk, Junior First Lieutenant Thomas L. Bransford, Second Lieutenant Daniel D. Phillips, and Lieutenant Thomas B. Cook. This last completes the list of guns on the island proper. Captain Fisher had a good battery, and was assisted by good officers. Messrs. Polk and Phillips, I know personally to be gentlemen unexceptionable in bearing, of courtly manner, flushed with the hopes of youth, yet displaying the fortitude of veterans. Messrs. Bransford and Cook are unknown to the writer personally, yet have the reputation of being competent officers.

The total of effective guns on the island proper, was fourteen. The sum total of main shore and island (that kept Pope and his forty thousand men at bay, with Foote and his iron-clad fleet, for weeks,) was thirty-nine guns, only a few being of any important weight, and they sustaining the entire brunt of the attack. During the occupation of the main shore, Battery No. 5 was in charge of Captain Joseph B. Caruthers, Senior First Lieutenant

Thomas J. Caruthers, Senior Second Lieutenant Pleasant
B. Roe, Junior First Lieutenant James Moore, Second
Lieutenant Stephen J. Lett. There are few officers in
the service who stood higher than Captain and Lieutenant
Caruthers.

Our chief of ordnance on the main shore was Lieutenant Tidmarsh. There are but few who were at island 10,
who have forgotten Tidmarsh, with his genial face, sallies
of wit, jokes and and repartee. "Tid," as we call him,
is the only knight of the "sock and buskin" within the
prison limits, and if we are ever exchanged, then "after
the fitful fever (war) is over," and Tid should live to
"star" it, there is no hero, comic or dramatic, that can
touch the bumpers, we will ovate to old "Tiddy." Lieutenant Tidmarsh is of English extraction, a native of Hal-
ifax, of aristocratic connections, has a fund of information,
the result of travel over the four quarters of the globe,
He distinguished himself on the 17th of March, at Island
10, in supplying the famous Rucker's battery with ammunition. Being constantly exposed during the heaviest
firing of the day. The lieutenant relates a little incident
that occurred during the severest part of the firing, that
must have been affecting. When one considers the men
and the occation : "I was observing the gallantry with
which Captain Rucker was directing the fire of his guns,
under a perfect storm of shell, when I noticed Captain
Winters, of the engineer corps, a brave and able officer,
passing. He and Rucker, had been at "dagger's points"
for months, and I thought the opportunity a favorable one
to reconcile these two brave, yet sensitive spirits. Bringing them face to face, I said : Gentlemen, at such a time,
and under such circumstances, be friends. They grasped
each extended hand, and the tear drop glistened in the
now moist eye. "Tid" doesn't inform us, but the
lines upon his begrimed face, made by trickling tears—
after the fight was over, is proof of the "milk of human
kindness," dwelling in the heart of the whole-souled Tidmarsh. His constant occupation in prison is in making
soup and delicacies for the sick in our hospital. All being
a gratuity, and a labor of love.

The few lines below, written by him, to please a child, show the freshness of a heart, that had experienced the vicissitudes of life for half a century :

"LU LU.

"Sweet Lu Lu, your papa to-day
Tells me, I must indite a lay.
The subject of this short narration,
To be my name, and rank, and station.
So pretty Lu Lu, here I go,
To tell you almost all I know :
First for my name—stop, here's a blunder,
To find out that: you must look under
Where 'tis written in this way,
First Lieutenant, C. S. A.
And if you'd know a little more,
Why place me in the artillery corps.
Pray, now dear Lu Lu, don't you laugh,
This truly is my autograph ;
That ruby lip—nay, do not pout it,
I'm sure I've told you all about it.
And now I really am quite fervent,
In subscribing myself " devoted servant,"
One of the unfortunate men,
Captured with pa, at Island Ten.

Our Generals at Island 10, General Stewart came and left ; Generals Trudeau, McCown and Walker did the same. General Mackall came and took us with him (*to prison.*) Acting Brigadiers Alexander J. Brown, of Tennessee, a gentleman, and soldier ; and Colonel Gaunt, of Arkansas. The officers of my brigade were Alpheus Baker, of Alabama, a nervous, rash officer, with personal courage, generous disposition, but an indiscreet commander. Lieutenant Colonel W. T. Avery. I allude to Avery in another scrap, yet consider him entitled to a notice in two. Colonel Avery was a member of Congress from the Tenth Congressional district of Tennessee, was a prominent member of the House, having made the leading speech in support of the Administration, in the spring of 1860. Colonel Avery is not a tactician, but makes up in dash his deficiency in drill. There were no braver men in the army than Tom. Avery. His failure to advance in the line of promotion was his indisposition to sue for favors justly due him. Colonel Charles C. Henderson, commanded the 40th Tennessee. Henderson was socially a gentleman, yet tyrannical and unpopular with his command. Major Higgins, of the Fortieth, is an old veteran, having served through the Mexican war with much credit, is of pleasant address, and is one of the best officers in the division, highly respected by the entire command. Major Cansler, of my regiment, while endowed with personal courage, was not a disciplinarian or thorough tactician, yet made a pretty fair officer.

We give a synopsis of the evacuation and surrender: Sunday, April the 6th, 1862, we move from the front of the island, (as we were informed,) for the purpose of repelling an attack of the enemy, were halted at midnight, marched again the next day, lay in the mud all night in Reelfoot Lake swamp, and were notified on the morning of the 8th, that we were surrendered prisoners of war. While half buried in the mud and water, we were cheered by the presence of Captain Johnson, and Lieutenants John Kirk and Robert Malone, of Tennessee, whose gallantry was of no avail, as the passing gun-boat had annihilated their battery. The only escape of importance was Captain Wheeler, with his company of cavalry. The effective force surrendered was eighteen hundred (1800) infantry, the Point Coupe artillery, consisting of five brass pieces, commanded by that splendid officer, Captain Thompson, with his two chivalric and gentlemanly Lieutenants, D'Aubizne and Legendre.

After the surrender, we were detained at Tiptonville twenty-four hours in a drenching rain, barely anything to eat, and as most of us had eat nothing for two days, and had been marching and lying in the rain and mud without shelter of any kind, we were in a miserable plight. I will ever feel grateful to Captain Sterling, of the Twenty-second Illinois, Captain Lathrop, of Cincinnati, Captain Crittenden, of the cavalry, who accompanied us to Camp Chase, and who, with the officers above mentioned, were marked by kind and considerate treatment towards their prisoners. Captain Steiner, of balloon notoriety, and his amiable lady, of Philadelphia, are remembered for their courtesy to the writer. Major Nixon, of Ohio, who had charge of us from Tiptonville to Columbus, Ohio, while true to his flag, was one of the most humane men and perfect gentlemen I ever met. We were placed on board the " Emma," carried to New Madrid ; thence to Cairo and to Camp Chase. To sum up, we were sacrificed not by General Mackall, but by the government, for the purpose of holding in check the column of General Pope, to prevent his uniting with Halleck ; for had the gun-boats passed ten days before, the morale of our army at Shiloh would have been destroyed ; hence, in justice to General Mackall, we assert positively, that he was in no way responsible for the surrender.

We have omitted the floating battery in our mention of the guns. This impromptu affair was commanded by Captain Averitt, formerly of the United States Navy, an officer of nerve and intelligence. He had four guns. This, with the battery of the Southern Guards, and the five brass pieces of the Point Coupe Artillery, two small mortars, more ornamental than otherwise, make a grand total of fifty-three guns, the great portion of which were of light metal. The enemy report the capture of one hundred and twenty. We surrendered not exceeding twenty-six hundred men ; the enemy report seven thousand. They publish the capture of seven generals ; we had one, and two acting brigadiers. If there is any glory in such a capture, the bombastic Pope is welcome to it.

The above is furnished as a refutation of the many falsehoods that paid and partial historians are flooding the country with, and in hopes that the impartial historian will discriminate between the official report of a General who never won a battle, and the statement of the writer that will be endorsed by two hundred confederate officers captured at Island 10.

CHAPTER III.

WHO am I? a prisoner of hope? No, of war, not of "Chillon" or of "Ham," but of Johnson's island, three miles from Sandusky City, in the beautiful bay of Sandusky, the placid child of that angry mother, Lake Erie, and here I expect to remain, at least until I finish my story, as I am not a Leander, certainly too moral for a Byron, and Sandusky bay is wider and fiercer than Hellespont. How came I here? I answer *ala "Clive"* *Pecavi.* I have scinde (sinned). Why did I? I don't know. It may be because the sins of the fathers are visited upon their children, even unto the third and fourth generations, and this is my second or third, I don't remember which. Feeling informs me "I was brought here by certain officials, y'clept Federal officers." Judgment says, the law, evidence and fact was a strong incentive to the motive power that "boosted" "ye humble historian," and transferred him from Southern heather to the turf of not Yankee-doodledom, but the *terra firma* of the mighty West, the future base of the balance of power of the broad domain of the Continent of America, and as the equity of my case is in the military court, with a packed jury, I am condemned *de facto*, but not *de jure.*

In introducing myself so unceremoniously to my readers, I will endeavor in a short chapter, to make myself presentable, as a caterer to the literary tastes of our prison-pen, by drawing on my ancestry for present prestige, not that my grandfather was a wonderful man, but it is necessary in the chain, as proof of my existence. " It is a wise child that knows its father," it is a much much wiser one that knows its grandfather.   My grandfather, on my mother's side, was one of the largest planters of St. Domingo, having emigrated to Cape Francis, his town residence, from Nantz, in France.   'Twas a lovely spot of fruits and flowers, and balmy air, whose exhalations were as ecstatic as the soothing charms of hasheesh, or the opium of D'Quincy, whose sweet debility was enervating and charmingly relaxing, making the limbs flexible, the passions volatile, the physical seductive, all was warmth and electricity.   Humanity flourished at St. Domingo like some rare exotic on the banks of the Ganges, rich, luxuriant, tender and short-lived, such was the home of my grandfather.   For more evidences of the beauties of this boquet of earthly delights, read the works of Harriet Martineau, that fanatical, bold and impassioned writer.

The French Revolution sowed the seeds of disease in the body politic of this colonial dependence of " La belle" France, that eventually established social principles, which sapped the virtue of the Island.   Martial rights were disregarded, and the more congenial custom of placieing a connection of the sexes during compatability. A creation of the Indies was adopted.   The Creoles who placied with the women of the Island, many of whom were beautiful, sent their offspring in many instances to France, where they were educated, by which their crude ideas of liberty were directed to a radical change of the peculiar institution of their island home. This inoculation of new ideas of freedom developed sad results, a sharpening of the knife whose edge was destined to cut morally, socially, and politically, resulting in the loss to my grandfather, of all his property, and the massacre of all his relatives, save his wife and two children, with whom he escaped in one of the vessels. That enriched Girard, loaded as it was, with the freight of the wealthy islanders, consigned to him, they expecting to follow, a hope never realized. Thus enriching that wealthy citizen of the Quaker city, and enabling him to lay the corner stone of the mammoth fortune, which while its fruits beautify the city of his adoption,. and furnishes means for the education of the grateful youth whose orphanage was a blessing, under the auspices of Stephen Girard, it left a large relationship with shattered hopes.

My grandfather reached Boston, a city in the then United States, since familiarly known as the "Hub of the Universe," from the radical *felloes* in it, who never *tire* of *running* into extremes, and would like the car of Juggernaut crush their defenseless victims.

In time, the ancestral tree decayed and died, leaving my grandmother and eleven children; they lived and flourished, and like their parent stem have yielded to the strokes of time, save one, God bless her.

With the exception of one uncle lost at sea fighting the British, another going to sea and never being heard from; one aunt shipwrecked, another marrying a French colonel, son of one of the signers of the death warrant of Louis XVI., nothing has ever occurred worth relating in my family, except the following story, which is furnished the reader to prove that remarkable events will occur even in the most unimaginative families. Napoleon says that "two-thirds of the world is made up and controlled by the imagination," yet I never knew but one case in my family, which yielded to its potent influence. This was my aunt who flourished in the capital of the Bay State, A. D. 1812. She was then a frolicsome girl of fifteen summers. She was as fair a flower as decked the beautiful mall of Boston, and glistened amid the drooping branches of those venerable elms that stand sentinels to the curtain that separates the happy past with its patriotism, its honesty and its conceptions of liberty, nurtured under oppression and fledged upon Bunker Hill. From the flimsy present, with its anarchy, its devotion to self-aggrandizement, its polished chicanery, and its whitened

sepulchres of policy, whose emblems should be a cross
representing the religious fanaticism in the North, and
the raw-head and bloody bones of abolition hate—with
such a banner and with noisome influence as destructive
as the exhalations of the Upas tree of the desert, move
the elements of radical progression—yet the old elms
stand intact, moaning and writhing in response to the
whirlwind of passion, that fanaticism has sown in the
land, and the heart of the country is now reaping in blood
and tears.   The heroine of this chapter was buxom, agile,
and blithe, gentle, merry, and mild, a faultless figure, a
mass of golden hair, pearly teeth, and cherry lips, a laugh
like the gurgle of some limped, silvery crook, with a cin-
derella's foot, and you have the idol of the school room,
the pet of the household, and the brightest gem in the
casket of girl jewels, that sparkled in the solid city.

Why it was that nature intended something should
happen to this fair girl, out of the ordinary course of
human events, I know not; I only know that the story
is as true as strange, and is left to the consideration of
those who believe and accept the principle, that if mind
and matter are connected, action on the one superinduces
action on the other; and as the body anticipates its physical ills, in the aching bones or furred tongue, why not the
mind anticipate its ills by foreshadowings or dream-land
images?   The screen that separates the seen from the
unseen is of gossamer texture and invites the searcher to
an examination of hidden love, that stimulated the Chal-
dean and the wise men of the East to hope that occult
science and astrological scintillations would reveal a
golden sun of intelligence, in the clouded skies and un-
sealed book of nature.   All nature is mysterious, and we
are surrounded by an atmosphere of the supernatural.
At times we feel as if 'twere good to extend the hand of
fellowship, and to proffer the embrace of love, at others,
of " drawing our skirts around us as if the wing of some
offending angel were brushing by," and when catching
the eye, shrinking as from a basalisk.   It is a vulgar
saying, " speak of the Devil, his imps will appear," yet,
how often, when in a crowded assembly, some one is

6

named, and his character ventilated, and the subject barely finished, when lo! the owner of the cognomen appears. "We were speaking of you," says one, and all chime in with corresponding remarks. The electrical influence of the positive, has struck a negative chord, and the vibration is felt throughout the circle. The negative man approaches and mingles in the circle, attracts no attention, is unobserved, and his departure leaves no void, thus illustrating the mysterious influence of the positive, and negative influence in man. So much for the philosophy, now for the story itself. It was customary, in the good old days gone by, for fortune-tellers to wander round the outskirts of cities, erect little wigwams, and dispense the knowledge, gleaned from their inventive faculties of perception, for pence and shillings. These Gipsies were lavish of promises, to seekers after an insight into the misty future, and many a Miss has left the Sybil presence, with golden rays of imaginative light, shedding a halo around the future bride of Duke or Count, air castles, that toppled and fell from their airy height, erected by maiden's fancy meditation, at the fount of Gipsical incantation. The mechanical part of the trade, of those peregrinators was represented by a bottle, whose transparent proportion was supposed to reflect the destinies of those who sought its Delphic power. Into one of these bottles looked my heroine, and what did she see? Let the Gipsy tell us:

"So young, so bouyant, and so beautiful. Would that it presaged as bright a future! And, how pitiable, that thy rosy shadows should sink into the dark clouds of thy destiny; that innocent, thoughtless laugh, that brings dimples to the peach-like cheek; will be changed to a sigh, as ominous as that of the drooping willow; care will supplant thoughtlessness, and an early grave will receive the blossom, that will wilt and wither, before the keen blasts of winter. Shrinkest thou? 'Tis so with all the children of Nature, they lack experience. I have seen the snows of seventy winters; have blistered my feet upon the parched and burning soil of the tropics; have wandered among heartless crowds in the world's metropolis, and sought eagerly for the 'crumbs that fell from the rich man's table ;' have been buffeted and spat upon, as an out-cast. I have found that all nature is weak and wicked ; that it is susceptible to the touch of imagination's wand ; that the sciences seek their home only in the mind of the sufferer, whose disease is research, and whose lamp of life is cabalistic knowledge, incomprehensible only to the unitiated, and my experience has taught me, to shun, as I would a pestilence, that spirit whose soul and heart is engrossed with worldly cares, saying, ' Wherewith shall I be clothed ;' who never sees the beauties of the stella universe, and never realizes the fructifying influences of the solar system—their sun rising in the midst of daily cares, and its meridian splendor alone seen in the 'purple and fine-linen' of society, and whose setting is amidst frustrated plans, and disappointed hopes.

" Such is the life of those, whose opaqueness shuts out the light of wisdom ; such *their* end to whom the secrets of knowledge remain unrevealed. I turn from them— despairing of humanity—and hope in the study of Nature, to catch a glimpse of that religion, that emanates from God alone.

" But to my task : I see a strange vessel, from a distant land ; it nears the shore ; curious costumes attract the eye ; strange music is borne upon the breeze ; she reaches the wharf Lewis' ; a language, unknown to the mass, is heard on her deck ; she is moored ; the Supercargo* lands, and is received by a prince merchant of the city. 'Tis evening ; the scene—the drawing-room of the merchants house ; the Supercargo sits on the right of his host ; in his hand is a golden snuff-box ; as he takes a pinch of snuff, a fair-haiced girl, a sister by marriage of the merchant enters, and is introduced ; the Greek is fascinated, and in six months she marries the stranger ; time developes two pledges of affection ; she lives a period of time, bequeathed to flowers, droops and dies. Look into the bottle, and see—hesitate not—thy fate is mirrored in it. Thou hast courted the art of the wierd sister, and her oracles have been partially disclosed to thy inquisitive sense."

---

* The Supercargo was Nicholas Cicliteri, of Smyrnia, formerly Greek Consul to Gibraltar.

Eighteen months, from this occurrence, the first Greek ship, the "Jerusalem," that arrived in America, anchored at John Lewis'* wharf. Her Supercargo, Nicholas Cicliteri, formerly Greek Consul to Gibraltar, a gentleman of superior mind, was feated and feasted by the hospitality of the city. Among the most distinguished of his hosts was John Lewis, who gave him a reception; and was in the act of accepting a pinch of snuff from his guest, when all were startled by the fainting of the sister-in-law of the host, who had at that moment stepped into the room. Six months after, she was led to the altar, by the Greek. She lived a few short summers, faded into death, leaving a disconsolate husband, and two sweet children.

The above is true. It could not have been prophetic, but was simply an exhibition of that wonderful perceptive faculty, that draws heavily upon the marvelous, for its inspirations, yet is guided by the same mysterious and natural law, that, if studied by a devotee, will in time enable him, to give a spirit, interrogated language of his own creation, to respond. So keenly sympathetic will be natural, mental alliances. If you can look into a man's eye, and see, what he will do, why not look into the same mirror, and know, what he will say?

However, as I've given the history of the only remarkable member of my family, on the maternal side of my house, I now shift rapidly to the paternal. My grandfather was a Roman, and my grandmother a Genoese. They moved to Marseilles, France, a city settled by the Phocians, 2,600 years ago. My grandfather was one of the five hundred Marseillese, who marched five hundred and thirty-five miles on foot to Paris, and assisted in the grand denouement† of 1793. So much were they imbued with the spirit of "Down with the aristocrats," that the other Jacobin factions were compelled to quarter the dark visaged, more southern rebels, outside the city wall, to keep them from raiding on tamer rad's, so eager were they for blood.

---

* John Lewis, owner of Lewis' wharves, one of the most distinguished of the many solid merchants of Boston.
† Two-thirds of the author's relatives were killed during the massacre.

Coming from such a stock—one grandfather inciting the Revolution of '93 in France, that resulted to the injury of the other grandfather, in St. Domingo, who with the army of Lafayette, fought for American liberty at Yorktown. In view of the above facts, can you wonder, that your humble author should partake of that rebellious blood, that sparkled in the war of '61. I did not, when this inherited spirit moved me, feel that my destiny would be recorded in golden letters, *Veni*, *Vidi*, *Vici;* and if I did, I was sadly mistaken, as the following brevity, not as classical, but more applicable, has been forced upon me—Going—Gone—Gone up.

So far, you have had glimmerings of me and mine, and I hope you will pardon the egotism of the chronicle. And, thus I end the chapter, in which I have proved I am somebody, that my grandfathers were not "wonderful men," and, although not a Japhet, I knew my grandfathers a step beyond Maryatt. I have introduced much of the wonderful, have verged on German scholasticism, I have told nothing but the truth, which must be acceptable to the most opaque cranium, which is: that what is, is ; but how it is—why, that's the question.

Major W. S. Pierson, commanding post. Pierson says, he acts under the directions of Colonel Hoffman, general superintendent of military prisons, a lately released paroled prisoner himself, captured by General Twiggs. This may be so, but if so, we are deceived in the man, as Hoffman looks like a soldier, and could not countenance the doings of a subordinate, so inconsistent with the character of a soldier and gentleman. Major Pierson is of Sandusky, Ohio, owns several flouring mills, and, although he doesn't recognize them in the working up of flour for prisoners, highly recommends them. He is an arrant hypocrite, and would make an elegant lobby-member, if he had brains. His rules, as adopted and exhibited in this connection, were published, when the Rebellion was a thing of ninety days, and we were arch-traitors of the deepest dye. Events since, have placed us in a different position, and from rebels we have been transmognified into a million of Revolutionists. Even old Pierson appreciates the change; but the rules remain, and their barbaric letter has caused the murder of one officer, and the maiming of another. Pierson is a harmless individual, ostensibly, but is a dangerous man in the dark.

Captain Follett is of some fifty winters, stern, taciturn, and with little of the milk of human kindness in his composition; takes a delight in irritating those, whom the fortunes of war have thrown under his charge, and is a bear generally. He is sound on the punctillious of military etiquette, a great stickler for profound respect from his subalterns, and is a despot in a small way.

Captain Scovill is an officer that has the bearing and appearance of a soldier, and would pass for a gentleman anywhere but in Hoffman's battalion. As he who "toucheth pitch is defiled," so is he socially damned, who affiliates with Hoffman's battalion.

Lieutenant Benson is a forbidding character, but can't be held responsible for his personal appearance; with his red hair, and bow legs, he looks like a clown in his military habiliments. He is a shoemaker by trade, and had much better have stuck to his last. He has made himself obnoxious, to the entire prison community, by his boorish disposition, and his ruffian manners, and will catch many a castigation, if the chances of the field should throw him in the way of some of our gallant men, he has so often wantonly insulted. With little brain, and overweaning vanity, he is a patched up specimen of half shoemaker, and half "melish," he will never do anybody any harm, unless he should have a prisoner assassinated, which, 'tis said, he attempted. Benson is also from Sandusky, a city of ten thousand inhabitants, which, up to this writing, has sent but one company to the war, and outside of the infernal regions, is the blackest Abolition hole in existence.

Lieutenant Wells, post adjutant, performs his duties faithfully, and is a good officer, and a gentleman. Lieutenant Lennelle, is a negative character, yet is attentive to our wants, and makes himself acceptable to the prisoners. There are several other officers, whom I'll pass, to avoid the charge, of writing to fill up. Many of the officers have their families with them. To one of them, Dr. Woodbridge's, we are indebted for many courtesies.

After the capture of Colonel Battel,* (one of our most distinguished fellow prisoners,) he was first taken to St. Louis, and while on the boat, ascending the river, was anxiously hunted by the curious passengers, who had never seen a "secesh," and who were astonished at the hand- some and veteran-like appearance of the gallant colonel. Colonel Battel attempted to avoid them, but finding it impossible, retreated to the pilot-house of the boat, where he was soon followed by the eager crowd, among whom was a minister of the Gospel, who instead of preaching " Christ, and him crucified," was stimulating volunteers to fight their Southern brethren. This wolf in sheep's clothing walked into the pilot house, and with that indeli- cacy and effrontery, that could only emanate from a bad man, or fool, asked Colonel Battel, if he had any objection to kneeling, and uniting with him in prayer. " Of course not." The so-called saint offered up a prayer, for the United States, and for the destruction of all her enemies, and rebels in particular. On concluding, the colonel thanked him, and asked if he and the rest would unite with him in prayer, something, I am confident, Colonel Battel never did before in public. The response was in the affirmative, and at it the colonel went, praying with a will, for the Southern Confederacy, and the destruction of all her enemies, and Yankees in general ; and, rising from his knees, exclaimed with an air, as only those who know Colonel Battel, as we do in prison, can appreciate : " Now, I'll bet you, or any other man, a hundred dollars, that my prayer reaches Heaven first." The colonel assures us, he was not troubled by vulgar curiosity the rest of the trip.

I have seen Ely's book, and as those who read my " scraps," may say, " they are trashy," many of them at least, I, as a true historian, will pronounce a similar ver- dict upon Ely's, and state that, whereas, Tom Benton's book was one-third Benton's, and two-thirds Jackson's.

* Colonel Battel, farming in Tennessee.

Ely's is two-thirds the Honorable Alfred Ely, M. C., of New York, that many ladies sent boquets and writing desks to, (so he says,) and who made a great many speeches, during the ovations, offered up to his *royal highness*, on his release from durance vile.* He also refused audiences to petitioners, many of them the most distinguished men of the South, (so he says,) in fact they annoyed him, so great was the desire to see *Bull Run Ely.* The other third of his book is devoted to a wholesale abuse of Southern officials. The book is a humbug generally, which is easily accounted for, when we state that its author is originally from the *land of wooden nutmegs;* yet his books will out-sell my " scraps," because our people have been so accustomed, to being overwhelmed with the yellow-covered trash of the North, that it will take time to eradicate it. Ely places great stress on the style of sheets he received, (we have none.) He speaks of his treatment by Confederate officers : our rolls are called by a sergeant, of eighteen years of age, who, with an impudent air, orders, " Fall in, boys, I'm in a hurry," and this to his seniors in age, rank, position, and everything that constitutes a man, soldier, and gentleman. Ely, it is true, was a distinguished civilian, and should have had the fourth sheet, as, in my humble opinion, he was three of them in the wind at Bull Run, or he would not, with his Connecticut shrewdness, been caught napping. To close up, it is difficult to decide, which is the greatest humbug: Ely, or his book.

Most of us will remember old Moody; at least those of us that passed the ordeal of camp Chase, with its mud, filth, and disease. I could give this worthy's history in one word, as easily as it is stamped upon his forehead, but the application will do no good, and hence the long-eared allusion is left out. Colonel Moody was a preacher, a bigot, and religious humbug. If any being in the world has a respect for religion, or an appreciation of its disciples, and teachers, 'tis the author, but if any one is disgusted with the charlatanism of the profession, and the

---

* Ely has never been heard of since. " Alas! poor Yorick."

quackery of priestcraft, I am that man. I remember a
scene, that impressed me with the peculiarities of one of
the different sects. I was in Marseilles, France, on a
narrow street of stone, that one could jump across, tall
and frowning buildings of the same material arose on
either side, shutting out the fructifying rays of the God
of day. I sat at the window, of one of these buildings, on
the Mediteranean, five thousand miles from home. It
was twilight and the darkening shades of evening seemed
more sombre, and had none of the softness of the twilight
of a more northern latitude. I felt dull, warm, and unwell,
as I peered into the twilight shadows, from my little
casement on the *Rue Mauvestis*, No. 1. A dull, ominous
sound broke upon the stillness of the gloom, seemingly
an unearthly chant, doleful, melancholy, vocal rumblings
o'er the boulders of the narrow street. I listened nervously, feeling the weight of some pressure, as the mariner,
when the falling barometer indicates the coming storm,
straining my ears to listen, I could hear the tramp of
clogged feet, they came nearer, and a procession of
priests, like some dark cloud shadowing the street, turned
the abrupt angle of the corner, their long black skirts and
three cornered hats, heavy clogs, and black masks, from
which flashed the eyes of the fiery southern Frenchman,
was an impressive spectacle. In front of the procession
was a group of the same, carrying flambeaux, whose
yellowish, sickly glare, gave a deeper tinge of melancholy
to the moving column of sable-hued chanters, the hollow-
ness of their tread, 'midst the grim blocks of granite,
which seemed to shake their mossy locks with the rocking
arms and flowing skirts of the priests, seemed sepulchral
and unearthly. They disappear, and I asked the character of the procession. "It is an order of mercy, now on a
mission to a sick and dying brother; what do you think
of it?" In America a man is not asked, what his religion
or politics are; the question is, "Is he an honest man,
and a gentleman? (But it is not so to-day.) My private
opinion was that the leader of such a procession was of
the same "getting up" as Moody, either a knave, which
in parson Moody's case can be accepted if you will, or an

enthusiastic fanatic, a dangerous element in any circle. Moody inclines more to the latter class. Such men at the head of churches, with the *entre* of the family circle, create much mischief, causing irreligion in the former, and contaminating the latter. Moody, from ignorance, rather than indisposition, is not as dangerous as others of his class, but would be just the man to march down the streets of Marseilles, with about an American dollar's worth of hair, (in shape,) cut from his head, surmounted by a *chapeau*, and chanting some unearthly strain, particularly if a verse, could be brought in, anathamatising Dixie and Secesh generally. Moody would rob a church, maltreat a captive, (which he has done time and again.) To sum up, Moody is a long-eared individual, whose name is not allowed to sully these pages, and much taste has been sacrificed in introducing Moody.

Last evening, about 9 o'clock, a member of one of the messes left his room, to go after a bucket of water. He was a German, and did not know that two and two made four in English, and, of course, was hardly responsible for any act, that did not conform with the letter of the law of our prison rules, which forbade, under the severe regime at Johnson's island: going out after retreat, (as mentioned in scrap relating to the killing of Lieutenant Gibson,) he deliberately took his bucket, walked to the well, some forty or fifty steps from the building, and commenced pumping. It certainly did not look like an attempt to escape, but afforded a splendid opportunity, to a dozen warriors on the fence, who were ambitious for distinction, and burning with a desire to murder a rebel, thus placing themselves in the line of promotion. "Halt! halt!" was heard over the campus, but our Teutonic veteran did not understand, and walked quietly back to his quarters. Bang! bang! went the missiles, fired with a will, by a dozen sentinels, but without effect, as, most fortunately for the health of our comrade, it was dark, and the aim of our custodians erring. After passing through unscathed, the shower of buck and ball, that ricochetted, (much to the annoyance of the prisoners, who were protected only by half-inch plank,) over the campus. Germany was triumphant, drank his water, and tumbled into his bunk. In a few moments, the officer of the day came in, and was directed to the room in which the author of the alarm was quietly reposing, and on entering, inquired if any one was hurt.

"Ask the Dutchman."

"Well, sir, are you hurt?"

"Mein Gott! no, I vants vater, and den I vants sleep, you pe tam."

It was a narrow escape, and the poor fellow, who was one of the few private soldiers, who had not been transferred to another prison, barely escaped, having his name recorded in this book, as one of the prisoners at Johnson's island, who "*are so well treated.*" What reason our custodians can present, to clear their skirts of this cruelty, is beyond my comprehension.

An aged mother comes one thousand miles, to see her darling boy, a mere youth, who will be exchanged in a few days, and it is, possibly, the last opportunity he may have on earth, of receiving a mother's blessing. The mother prays to the relentless fiend in charge of us, to see her son but for one moment, but it is denied. Cut-throats of every character, and the vilest of criminals have had the boon granted them, of seeing loved ones pending trial, or prior to execution. In the Netherlands, criminals condemned to solitary confinement for life, are brought out once a year, and placed upon a platform, where relatives can see them, and they can breathe the free air of Heaven. It seems to be reserved for the United States government, through their instruments, to out-Herod Herod in acts of cruelty. The mother did not see her son, and returned home sick at heart, and disconsolate. The gallant boy loved his mother with a devotion, known only to the good and brave, but sacrificed the sweetest feeling of his heart, rather than take the "oath," and thus turn his back upon the glorious colors, he had sworn to defend. This is but another link to Pierson's endless chain of cruelties.

Fearing that the *one tin pan business*, to a mess of fifty men might, possibly breed contagion, which it has in some of the messes, as many of my comrades are aware, who have the singular disease, unnecessary to mention on this page, and which, I am confident, is from the effects of proper ablutions not being indulged in, in consideration of which, our dispenser of indulgences, has concluded to allow us the bath, not a "Turkish" one, with its experience of "tepidarium," "calidarium," "lavotorium," "spray douche," and "plunge," but a "Sandusky bay" one, giving each pore an opportunity of expressing its delight in a moisture of health. "Cleanliness is akin to Godliness," and there is a woful lack of the former in our prison, where "it is water, water everywhere, but not a drop to *wash*." But the great chief of our custodians is to let a few of us out this afternoon, provided that Colonel Battel, and a few other officers of regular habits, will guarantee that we will not attempt to swim out, and seize the little boat and twelve-pound howitzer, capture Hoffman's battallion, or do any of those desperate deeds, that have made rebels so famous. Colonel Battel has vouched for us, and six hundred of us, unarmed, are splashing, dashing, diving, and ducking, and a few disciples of old Isaac Walton, are fishing, and it is a piscatorial fact, that fish were caught by Confederates, in spite of the antics and noise incidental to the bathing of six hundred prisoners. A line of bayonets bristled at intervals on the beach, and now and then one would be lowered, and a bead drawn on some unwary prisoner, who had swam a little beyond the limits allowed. But bathing, as well as all material things, must have an end, and one by one the prisoners come out of the once limpid bay, arrange their toilet, and prepare for the inner walls.

Now the harpooning commences, the fun being strictly on the side of the guards. After all are in, as supposed, the sentinels, with their bayonets, walk leisurely along the edge of the water, and like the whaler, who longs for blubber, with harpoon in rest, launches it out at the mighty leviathan of old ocean, so do these harpooners of rebels, dash their bayonets into the weeds and brush that line the shore, certain to pin a poor fellow, should he be indiscreet enough to imagine he could escape in that way.

"Ah, I have you, you d—d rebel," says one of the Plutonic excrescences of the island, as he barely misses pinning to the bottom of the lake the form of an officer, who vainly attempted to escape in such manner, "get up and get, you are booked for the blackhole, d—m you."

I don't think any more of the officers will risk the bayonet of these military fishermen. This is the last of August; I have been out twice, but a thousand pores express their gratitude for that much indulgence. "Thou shalt be a Bishop," Pierson, aye, a Pope, Leo, if it please thee, for thy many indulgences, for the many *horns* thou hast stolen from us, will enable thee to issue as many *bulls*, as the energetic pontiff aforesaid.

In a former chapter, I reached from 1793 to 1812, in my chronicle. The want of connection, that I discovered, after reviewing it, did not dissatisfy me, because, as a prisoner of war, I have a consciousness, that could I have made the proper connections, and had my time-table been regulated, I would not have been in durance. But, as in the opening of this work, we have compiled a synopsis of the political history of the country, we deem our failure to connect, from 1812 to the present, a matter of no moment, as all deficiencies are supplied by the synopsis aforesaid.

Yet, to please my fellow prisoners, I will give a few private political histories, as lessons, for those who seek the "bubble reputation," in the whirlpool of politics. In the long line of distinguished men, who have filled the position of chief executive of the nation, General Jackson was one of the most prominent. His star appeared in 1828. He was Adamized and canonized, ran his course, yet left much for the future to war over, and work out. There is a bust of the General on Court Square, in the city of Memphis, an intense seceding corporation, with the magical letters: "The Federal Union must and shall be preserved." This bust was there, March the 1st, 1862, nine months from the vote, unanimously, save five, of the city for secession, as unterrified, and seeming as ready to swear, "By the Eternal, Tennessee shall not secede." Jackson's spirit still lives in his bust, proving the influence of his mind, over matter, as explained in the theory of forces.

The animal, vegetable, and mineral kingdoms, are the elements, that all our physical draughts are made upon, and into which we resolve, after we have " shuffled off this mortal coil." Man, in the flesh, is the acme of these three powerful forces. Having attempted to show, that the mind's forces have a chain of sympathy, uniting them, I will now ask, if there are not sympathetic influences, controlling the material universe? What is the impulse, that gives a being an irresistible desire to plunge over some precipice, that curiosity has invited him to its brink, and makes him shudder, while contemplating the dizzy depth, that seem to attract him, to take the fearful leap? This is the power of one force, too gigantic for the weakness of its miniature counterpart, in its fleshly tabernacle. Look at some mighty leviathan, of the deep, or some huge monster, upon the land, and you are startled, by an animal strength, that shows you so plainly your own pigmyism. Go into the regal woods, and hear the tempest howl, through the branches of the majestic oak, gaze out, upon the mighty ocean, wonder at the grandeur of all you see, and feel your utter insignificance.

It is rarely, that an excursion of pleasure, in which many healthy bodies partake, either by railroad or steamer, developing the hydrogen in man, expressed in an exuberance of feeling, but what some accident, too frequently happens. A public edifice is erected, some one is killed, or injured, during process of its erection. He, who habitually carries a pistol, is so influenced by its force, that he will draw it involuntarily. He, who constantly carries a knife, will, instinctively, clutch it in the same manner. Men, from infancy, prefer masculine toys, in opposition to the tamer selections of women, because they are more akin to their stronger natures. Men love the battle-field, the roar of artillery, the rattle of musketry, and the clash of swords, they are controlled by such forces, and yield to their irresistible influence, thus man meets his brother in mortal combat, and, it may be, that the force of " Old Hickory " has influenced his bust, that now stands frowning in Court Square, possibly proving, that forces of mind and matter, in the past, present, and future, are indissolubly connected. Forces, animal, vegetable, and mineral, are the same in origin, chaotic in the germ, intelligent in their forms, and susceptible of nothing but change, retaining, undisturbed, their elementary character, teaching us, we are superiors alone in the minute, but insufficient to cope with either element, in their separate strength, or might of combination. Referring to Jackson, reminds us of an incident, that came under our observation, showing how our great men are regarded in Europe, and what a poor opinion crowned heads have of the legal profession. While the writer was visiting Brussels, the capital of Belgium, (some time since,) it was his pleasure, to visit King Leopold, whom he considered the wisest sovereign in Europe. The estimate of this king's character, in Europe, may be judged by his marital alliances, his first wife, being the daughter of Louis Phillippe, and his second, the Princess Charlotte, aunt of Queen Victoria. To reciprocate the compliments, paid him, the king remarked, to the writer:

"I have just finished reading the life of General Jackson, of your State, and find, that he was a man of much character."

"Yes," replied General Fair, the American minister, "he was one of the first lawyers, in the State."

"A lawyer?" exclaimed the king, with evident surprise.

"Yes," says General Fair, "but one, who carries his briefs and challenges in the same hat."

The status of a lawyer, in Belgium, is that of a scribe, or clerk. The acceptance of such an error of opinion, in our country, would soon decimate the legal profession.

As I have introduced politics into this chapter, I will give a few more personal reminiscences, before closing the subject:

On the 9th of May, 1860, the Bell and Everett convention convened at Baltimore; the morning of the day of the nominations, the writer, who was a delegate to this last assemblage of the conservative element of the nation, was sitting at Guy's, the great Baltimore caterer, in company with the following distinguished gentlemen, with whom I had a julep acquaintance: John J. Crittenden, of Kentucky; Harris, of Maryland; Jerry Clemens, of Tennessee, and the veritable George Saunders, of New York; who was at that time, a part of the outside pressure, that New York had sent to Baltimore, for certain purposes that we forbear mentioning.

George Saunders remarked, "Mr. Crittenden, you will be nominated."

"No George, I am laid on the shelf, Mr. Bell will be the nominee of the convention, and a better selection could not be made."

"Well, what is your opinion, Mr. Crittenden, of the result."

"You are not of us, George, but we have confidence in your integrity, tell no tales, and I'll give you all a little advice. You are all younger men than I am, I am called a fossil, although at times I think I'm a "four-year old," but let me tell you it is probable the Democracy may elect their candidate, if so, they will want some honest men among them, (no exceptions, George,) swing together, and get some fat little offices. Yet, it is possible, the Republicans may elect their candidate, still swing together, your prospects will be still brighter, for the necessity for honest men will be even greater in that party,"

Thus spake that great and good Kentuckian, who had a keen appreciation of the spirit of the verse—

> "A little nonsense now and then
> Is relished by the best of men."

Mr. Crittenden's jocose prediction and suggestion, resulted as follows: He, himself, was no loser by the accession to power of the Republican party. Harris, of Maryland, remained in Congress, Jerry Clemens' head appreciated the situation, but the yearnings of his heart overcame the promptings of his policy; as for myself, not "swinging," I have "brought up" in prison. The night previous to the Convention, I was at a "blow out," given by the New York delegation, for the purpose of throwing a tub to the Southern whale, the occupants of the tub, Samuel Houston, of Texas, and Washington Hunt, of New York; the former, who, if he had had a few more workers with brains like his accomplished Secretary of State, E. W. Cave, and fewer like Girard, whose imprudence destroyed his prospects, he might have obtained the nomination. We did not swallow the tub and contents, but did the champagne. The light of the occasion, was Horace L. Day, of New York, to whose courtesy I could only respond, that should it ever be my misfortune, to be forced into Congress, I should vote for an extension of his patent. There were but few delegates to the convention, but who were aspirants for office, one of my friends in particular, a prominent Kentuckian, and certainly one the most "whole-souled," genial men I ever met, informed me, privately, that he was a candidate for the Vice-Presidency, and to secure my vote, would favor a bill for giving every thing to every body; based on such promises, the requisite number of votes were soon secured, but, unfortunately for the General, about eleven o'clock, the same night, he fell between the many planks of his platform, and, politically speaking, has never recovered. We lost a glorious candidate, and the State of Kentucky secured an incorruptible Adjutant General. Since the collapse at Baltimore, I have been the beneficiary of nothing but 228-pound bomb and percussion shells, with some 64-solids interlarded. I had hoped, the loss of a limb, or a flesh wound, might presage political preferment, as I know several colonels, who had horses shot from under them, and shortly after became candidates for, and were elected to, Congress, however, as "true nobility looks to the future," I will endeavor to forget the shadows of my past political, and military, history, and turn to the contemplation of a virtuous future, where the reflex of my past actions, particularly the time engaged, in writing this book, will afford me a solace sufficient. Like Cincinnatus, I will go "home to the plow," you may say, as a young lady, pert, pretty, and satirical, said, on my arrival, a prisoner, at Columbus, Ohio:

7

"While at home, you had better have stayed there, and then you woudn't have been here."

The true guide in life is "the lamp of experience," and if I am no better by its teachings, I hope I am wiser, and retire for the present, only willing to re-enter the arena, when, by a unanimous call of my fellow citizens, I may be selected to represent them in some of the many legislative branches of the country, whose tendencies are not toward a military prison.

CHAPTER IV.

WHY ARE WE PRISONERS.—MUGGINS' CLUB.—MISSOURI, AND HER
SOLDIERS.—DISTINCTION OF RACE AND SOCIETY.—DISSIMILARITY
OF THE SECTIONS, IN HABIT, ETC.—DEATH IN PRISON.—GENERAL
MURRAY DIED MAY 28TH, 1862.—YANKEE NEGRO PHILANTROPHY.—
SHAM FIGHT ON THE CAMPUS.—OUR PRISON MESS, AND CLUB.—
·NO. 2, BLOCK 8, JOHNSON'S ISLAND.—LOUNGERS' HEAD-QUARTERS.
—THE HASH QUESTION.—OUR MINISTERS IN PRISON.—THE CROWD
UPON THE CAMPUS.—OFFICER SHOT.—OUR PHYSICAL THERMOME-
TER.—ROUTINE OF PRISON-LIFE.—SHILOH PRISONERS.

SINCE my imprisonment, I have reflected upon the
chain of circumstances, that brought me here, and I
find, they are as much the result of incongruous elements
in man, as any thing else; a distinction of race, class,
and affinity. An American is not an American, the
popular theory of North, East, South, and West, one
and indivisible, is proved fallacious, by actions, that cause
the air to resound in the clang of arms. A man may be
born in America, and yet not be inspired with the spirit
of the genius of his birth-place, his blood may be of Turk,
Greek, or Gaul. Education, and social usage, may direct,
and habit may control, his character, yet the ancestral
blood remains undisturbed, and the volatile Frenchman,
phlegmatic German, or the stoical Englishman, are as
naturally true to their blood-instincts, even, though born
in the extreme North or South, as if fledged beneath the
air of La belle France, or amid the dense fogs, that are
broken by the chalk-cliffs of Dover.

In Belgium, you have, on the French frontier, the Wal-
loon; on the Prussian, the swarthe and frigid German;

on the Holland. the Dutch; in East and West Flanders,
the Flemings; here, in a small territory, one-fourth the
size of the State of New York, we find several distinct
races of people, it is the same with us, in Louisiana, you
have the Creole, in all his originality, the same to-day as
at the French occupation. Florida has flourishing traces
of her Spanish ancestry, and Catholic Lord Baltimore has
left a goodly descent, in the American Catholic population
of the banner city of the South, Baltimore. The other
extreme of the country, expresses the same fanaticism,
that landed on Plymouth Rock, to murder Indians, in
the three thousand clergymen, who signed the petition,
to abolish slavery in the District of Columbia, a document, full of the Round-headism, but void of the sincerity
of the clan, that supported the fanatical Cromwell. The
South exhibits, to this day, her descent from the cavaliers
of the seventeenth century, while the East exhibits a
Puritan descent, two elements, which are as impossible
to fuse, as oil and water. The habits and manners, of
the sections, are unlike. A Western man, he, who has
faced a thousand dangers, on the frontier, whose inspirations are from the broad and romantic prairie, and, who
with rifle in hand, sees his manly form reflected, from the
bosom of the mighty Mississippi, is as distinct from the
manufacturer of wooden nutmegs, as day from night.
The Northern, Eastern, Southern, and Western sections,
of this broad domain, are separated, by distinct natural
laws, incapable of early fusion, and which may require
generations, to harmonize. Railroad connections, causing a commingling of the people, and their interweaving,
through social, commercial, and marital relations, may
develop and cement affinities, thus brought together,
antagonism only widens the breach, and one of such
shocks, brought us here. My durance will widen a
breach, that time may heal, though the inherent principle
remains. The Tennessean is not homogeneous, with the
native of Maine, or New Hampshire, and I am a Tennessean, and time will demonstrate, that the natives of the
South, are as distinct from those of the East, as the
French from the English, they being separated by only

twenty miles of water, and they, with this close connection, bringing together large interests, in trade and
manufacture, the Frenchman is as much at a loss in Bir-
mingham, as the Englishman at Bordeaux. Then the
only proper course left to us, is to trust to the resolution
of society, which will regulate itself, by natural laws, as
the great " Daniel" said, " It is a question of soil and
climate." Society, like all streams, will soon find its
level, if left in its natural current, but if choked up in its
disorganized condition, will run madly over its banks,
carrying death and destruction in its wake. Fanaticism,
while knowing, that he and his neighbor are as separate
as the poles, would drag him to his political bosom,
regardless of the loathing and disgust, exhibited in every
natural and educational lineament. A disposition, to test
the truth of this "theory," brought me to Johnson's
island, and the coercive policy, that would amalgamate
discordant elements, has, by its madness and folly, detained me here, where I am likely to remain, at present,
satisfied, that blood will not come out of a turnip, and if
a man is born in a stable, it is not proof positive, that he
is a jackass.

The Muggins' Club was not inaugurated upon the basis
of the " Beef-steak," or " Crockford's," those famous
London clubs; they require means, or position, and an
initiation fee, of from fifty to a hundred guineas, before
you can enjoy the society of the " wits" and beaux, of
that great metropolis. Then again, these clubs have not
only a strong penchant for roast beef, and "'alf and 'alf,"
but they have the wherewith also, to satisfy the same,
and the fancy, that "mi" lord or lady has to wager a
thousand guineas, upon the turn of a card can be gratified. Per contra, with the Mugginses, their capacities,
as to imaginary investments, and fabulous winnings, were
as large, as "peer" or "potentate," and the greatest
wager ever made, in England, realm, was not as large
as the bet of a Muggins, (in his dreams.) One of their
largest bets, is of value in China, "one cash," another
the French "centime," the grand "pot" of the club, is of
value, English currency, "two-pence."

The following are the members of the club, who have been admitted to all its rights, and privileges, on pay-of the initiation fee, one cent.

"Captain Thompson, this gentleman, is one of our most erudite and finished scholars."

Captain Thompson, previous to his connection with the club, was engaged in teaching the "young idea how to shoot," succeeding so well in which, he concluded, to, teach the "old idea" the same principle, only varying the scene from the rude and happy school-room of the country, to the tented field of "blood and carnage." Thompson's name is spelled with a "p," yet he is not the Thompson of "Toodles notoriety," but a cheerful, pleasant gentleman, and president of the "Muggins Club."

Captain Frank McVay was formerly treasurer of the club, but unfortunately for the business wants of the society, he resigned, it being intimated by Lieutenant John Spain of his regiment, and secretary of the club, that there was a discrepancy of several cents in the weekly budget, and alluded to a brash game of "poker," in which the treasurer was known to risk a cent, on four kings, thus showing a recklessness, that would involve the society. By a vote of the club, the honorable gentleman was reinstated, and the resolution of Lieutenant Spain expunged. The Falstaffian treasurer accepted, with the following remarks: "I rise for information, you may say, 'no man needs it more,' it has been insinuated, that I have attempted, with the funds of the society, to build up an institution, approximating to the 'artificial rain water society,' a creation of 'oily gammon,' to ruin the Earl of Dredlington, it is said, I have grown fat upon the loaves and (not fishes,) but Pierson's 'blue beef,' of office. Fellow Mugginses, I deny the soft impeachment, and defiantly throw down my guage," (which happened to be a soiled sock,) the captain had put into his pocket, by mistake, for a glove.

At this crises, an irreverent member, under the influence of molasses and water, cried, "sock it to 'em." Nobody accepting the guage, that is, picking up the

disconsolate mate of a pair of half-hose, the honorable
gentleman proceeded: "I am here to night, (another
member,) "good, I'm glad to see you are not ubiquitous,"
"to give conclusiveness to my presentations," (a stolid
member, who has just awakened, "what's that? something good to eat?") But, in spite of these episodical
interruptions, the gentleman continued, and held the
audience for an hour, (one member by the tail of his
coat,) spell-bound, the whole speech was replete with
Demosthenic metaphor, and Ciceronian peroration, his
last remark, as he fell into the arms—of his chair, upon
the platform, in a state of exhaustion, was—"gas." The
society is now going on swimmingly, that is, most of
their heads swim. Lieutenant John Spain, lieutenant
Company A., First Alabama, Tennessee, and Mississippi
volunteers, was at the fight at New Madrid, where he
proved the working of an old rule, that if New Madrid
was not in Spain, Spain would not remain in New
Madrid, so he evacuated the latter place, with the Confederate forces, on the 13th of March, 1862.   He is quite
popular with the "club," with the exception of a little
bitterness, that has sprang up between a few members
and himself, a consequence of his boasting, of his being
exchanged for General Prentiss, an ebulition of pride,
that for a few days, made him obnoxious to the club, on
finding out, that some technicality would create delay,
and that the spelling of Prentiss by the Confederates, as
Prent *ass*, had been deemed objectionable by the "blue
bellies." The club met, and the offending member, who
had impugned the motives of Lieutenant Spain, in his
acceptance of an exchange, (thus quitting the society,)
was ruled out, and the lieutenant was reinstated, in the
good graces of the "Muggins Club."   Having gotten his
"rights in the States," at New Madrid, and in the
"Territories," at Island Ten, after a manful fight, he has
obtained full possession of all his personal and reserved
rights, as a member of the "Muggins Club," in good
standing, with the *cable tow* of jealousy removed from his
neck.

Another leading member of the club is Lieutenant

Darnell, of the Third Mississippi, who, without boister-
ousness, is full of vivacity, and a kind and considerate
gentleman. The club has honorary members, the best
men in it, Captain Burton, of the Twenty-sixth Mississippi, and Captain Saunders of the Third Mississippi,
the former a steady, firm, and honest man, of dauntless
courage, the latter an obliging, kind-hearted soldier
of the highest order of courage, proven on the fields of
Buena Vista, Monterey, Manassas, Shiloh, Donaldson.
The Captain lost an arm, some years ago, but it does not
disturb his active energies whatever. His bunk is a
perfect machine shop, a score of rings, walking canes, and
pipes, testifying to his industrious habits; for a perfect
model of a soldier, and patriot, with a disposition, as
gentle as *some* women, give me Captain Saunders, of the
Third Mississippi volunteers. I would say more about
the club, but they are now getting into a row, that requires
the interposition of the writer, as umpire. One of the
members has slipped a card up his sleeve, (accidentally,
of course,) while his opponent has grabbed stakes, and
"there's mischief *bruin*," (as the man said, when he shot
the bear," and an explanation is necessary, previous to
the retiring of the club, "from labor to refreshment."

The gallant State of Missouri, and her soldiers, under
the command of that great chieftain, Sterling Price, have
done, and suffered much, for the Confederacy, and she,
yet to-day, is one among the brightest gems in the Southern galaxy. My comprehension, of the military status of
Missouri, as reflected by the policy of the Confederate
States, is, I think, the correct one. It was supposed, that
the only way of testing the feelings of a citizen of a State,
was to leave them to their own free choice of expression,
the confirmation of which, would be their acceptance of
an appeal to arms.

The Confederacy placed a sufficient force in this gallant
State, to form a nucleus, for the brave sympathisers of the
oppressed South to rally around. The banner of freedom
was unfurled in Missouri, on the Missouri river, by a
steamboat captain, D. DeHaven, one of the State's most
gallant sons, and valley and mountain responded, inspir-

ing the citizens, of the down-trodden State, who flocked, enthusiastically, to the Confederate standard, but the iron heel of despotism, had been planted upon her capital, and marts of trade, and the facilities of her enemies, for transportation, and concentration, by land and water, rendered the continued occupation of Missouri untenable, and Missouri was left to her fate, yet thousands of her true men. as individuals, and in companies, left their hearths and fire-sides, and joined the organizations of other States, there were also thousands, who were intercepted, while en route for the South, with arms in their hands, and confined in the many military prisons of the North, many of whom are with us in Johnson's island, whose description of the massacre, by the "bloody Dutch," of St. Louis, is heart-rending, which satisfies the writer, that in a free country, (so-called,) "the people will submit to anything." The Missourians, in prison with us, have the reputation of being good soldiers, and have left their homes, with a burning zeal for independence, to follow the star of Missouri, (Sterling Price,) that now shines, undimmed, in the military horizon of the South, who, with his followers, have been driven from their State, by a spirit of fanaticism, stimulated by the "Devil," and the "Dutch."

William P. Clarkson, captain, Sixth Regiment, Missouri Volunteers, captured December 21st, 1861. Clarkson is a perfect specimen of human architecture, possessing the delicacy of the Corinthian, with the stength, and naturale. of the Doric, the quiet dignity of the Ionic, and the child-like manner of the Tuscan, reminding us of the times gone by, when simplicity of mien, was as much admired, as the antique Tuscan, in the present, forming a human temple, in the social world, that on can well nigh worship at.

> "With leave to write a stranger's name,
> A captive here—your father greeting,
> It is my fate, but not my shame,
> To give you this a prisoner's greeting.
> "WM. P. CLARKSON, Captain,
> "Sixth Missouri Regiment, Company H., taken prisoner near Sedelia,
> Missouri, while on special duty for General Price."

Captain J. P. Colwell, Porter's Regiment, Greene's Division, captured, January 8th, 1862, at the battle of Silver Creek. Captain D. H. McIntyre, First Regiment, Missouri State Guards, captured at Fulton, Missouri, December 25th, 1861. Captain Jno. G. Provine, same regiment, captured same time. Captain F. A. Rogers, Company C, Second Regiment, Sixth Division, M. S. G., captured at Milford, Johnson county, Missouri, December 19th, 1861. James F. Willhite, captured at same place, as were Captain Wm. E. Jamison, Adjutant J. Joplin, W. Singleton, Duncan, captured at Fulton, December 25th, 1861, Lieutenant P. F. Willard, Lieutenant Raines, Division M. S. G., captured at Kirksville, Missouri, December, 1862. Captain H. M. Salmon, one of the most thorough soldiers and gentlemen, from his State, captured at Versailles, Missouri, December 3d, 1861. Captains Weed, Hogane, and Fletcher, are mentioned in other " scraps."

The following lines are from Captain Simmons:

> " To ——.
>
> " I address thee—from a colder clime,
>   Than your own dear Southern land ;
> To prison consigned, to remain a time,
>   For daring to rally 'round Liberty's stand.
>
> " I write from a land where the pure holy fire,
>   In the lamp of Freedom grows dim ;
> To beg a kind thought, (as a friend of your sire,)
>   May be spared, from your thousand, for him.
>
> " And—I'll pray in return, that the rays
>   Of our rising Southern sun,
> The brightest and warmest, may meet thy gaze,
>   And cheer your path, in the years to come."

All natural convulsions are attended with more or less disastrous results, but the most terrible of all is—death—this is a convulsion that shocks the earth to its centre, affects all, levels all, and is a debt that all must pay, the interest of which is in the future, that to all is dark and impenetrable. Circumstances may modify the terrors of the grim monster's visitation, but the finale is the same, whether or not the struggle is ended in the quiet chamber, surrounded by the loved ones of the family altar, (and there amid groans and tears the spirit takes its flight,) or the fitful fever is o'er in the prison, or in harness upon the bloody field, the last gasp is the end. Although the desire to die at home is paramount in the human heart, yet there is a terrible disturbance in that society, of which the victim may be a member, disease has placed its iron hand upon him, and the icy chill of death is rapidly creeping o'er the once robust frame, the wail of the orphan children, and the expressed bursting of the widow's heart, is incense offered at the altar of the King of Terrors, to appease his wrath, but he is unrelenting, and the sufferer dies; then follows the gloom of the household, the horrid paraphernalia of the funeral cortege, and the blank despair in that once happy home, the roll of wheels is harsh, the laugh of the light and thoughtless is discordant, and the clock of the world for that day stands still, and life is a blank. This is death at home, a horrible shock, although at home.

Death rides his pale horse on the battle-field. Here amid the whistle of bullets, the shriek of shell, the fierce roar of cannon, and the yells of men drunk with blood, strikes down his victim, and the spirit wings its way to that bar, where its destiny is in the hands of justice, and not tardy, not bought and sold, and whose balances would break with a hair of falsity. The most solemn of all deaths is that within the prison walls, far from home, a chain of future subjects snapped in twain, hopes obliterated, deferred schemes rent and scattered, home and its happy associations, severed from living memory, the absent wife is in the mind's eye, the mother's nursery rhymes, (for it matters not how old the body, the soul of the child and the man are the same, and hence the mental recurrence to the circumstances of childhood.) The green grass of the meadow looks brighter, the running brook seems clearer, the laugh of your children ring in merry peals through the garden; he sees the thousand pictures of home-life, they become fainter, they are seen through a mist, (the film that looms round the death bed,) it is dark, the spirit has left its tabernacle of clay. Such a death in prison, died General Murray, of Warren county, Tennessee, on the 28th of May, 1862. A political prisoner, arrested and confined by order of Andrew Johnson, military Governor of Tennessee. General Murray was not much above the prime of life, fitted by nature, if spared to accomplish much ere the expiration of time allowed by the Psalmist, of high standing at home, the centre of a large and devoted household, he was cut down like a flower; he died as he had lived, calm and resigned. He was consigned to the resting place, that was to bear all that remained of him to his family and friends. The prison gates are opened, and the coffin disappears. Why is all this? Man's inhumanity to man. Does it not seem that God's vengeance will shower coals of fire upon the heads of this wicked generation. Chorazin, Babylon and Nineveh, were destroyed for much, for much less.

Colonel John Dorr, is a connection of mine, and overflowing with generous impulses, and is the soul of hospitality itself, yet is afflicted with the Abolitionphobia, that seems to strike him like St. Vitus dance, and, from having been an editor in good standing, of that sterling Democratic journal, the "Kenebec Journal," has sank into the abyss, created by rabid Abolitionism.

While on a visit to the colonel, in Augusta, Maine, he wished me to call upon one of her most distinguished colored citizens, whose cognomen was "Uncle Isom." I went, and was ushered into a neat cottage, that is, as much so, as the American citizens of African descent, are capable of keeping in such condition; the building had been erected at the expense of the corporation, and the ground donated quite philanthropically, by my African-loving connection, (possibly there were suffering whites about). Uncle Isom was glad to see me, as he was agreeably disappointed, anticipating seeing a slave-owner, (I owned one,) with a pistol sticking out of each pocket, and a bowie knife in his coat collar, a bottle of whiskey in one hand and a horse-whip in the other, a picture often presented to the gullible fanatics in the North. I was a modest looking youth then, and can appreciate his astonishment. I was also surprised at him, expecting to see "an ancient colored individual, with no capillary substance on the summit of his cranium," as from the donations made to him, made the presumption obvious, that he was superanuated, yet strange to say, he was a "big buck nigger," who had raised two trifling sons, that had ran off, much to the gratification of the citizens. He was perfectly able to work, but was taking advantage of the simplicity of his friends.

Our interview ending, I requested a glass of water; 'twas handed me in a tin cup, and had that de-decided flavor, that I have enjoyed so often, on a Missis-sippi plantation, in drinking out of a gourd, of a warm day, it was decidedly "Nigger." I drank with much gusto, and handed the cup to Dorr, who declined, remarking, as the door closed on us, "how did you manage to drink after that greasy old Negro?" I replied, with us, we are secure in our social position, and do not fear the trespass of an inferior race, you having elevated the Negro to the position of an equal, politically, you now fear a social trespass; the Southern man is the true philanthropist, and the best friend of the black man, if not from affection, from policy's sake. Dorr is a type of the New England fanatic, there is none of them, that will drink out of the cup of a Negro, and yet, are flooding the country with blood, to place him in a false position.

The amusement of the sham fight on the Campus, is one of the most exciting of the many efforts, to while away the time, and break the monotony of our confine-ment. The fortification consists of a wood-pile, with a crest of sticks, interior and exterior slopes of chunks. The rat holes are within the buildings, affording a secure retreat for the temporary vanquished. The engagement generally opens not by knocking a chip off an antagonist's shoulder, but by throwing several chips at the enemy, who is admirably poised upon a billet of wood, awaiting the attack and the opening of the foe's batteries, which are masked. The attack is frequently violent, and the character of the missiles effective, and if the shot are not hot, the work is. At the invitation of Lieutenant Watts, of the artillery, I had the honor of witnessing one of these combats from a secure position, behind some timber. The lieutenant is a polished gentleman, who flourished in the good old days of 1837, when Haskill catered at the Louisville hotel, and the Pearl Street house was in full blast, in Cincinnati, at either of which hotels at different seasons, Watts was the "lion" of all "hops," and the "mogul" of all dinner parties. Those fashionable resorts have long since *run down*, but Watts, like the writer, has *wound up* in prison. But our reflections are interrupted by a missile in the shape of a huge clod of clay, thrown with much vigor, by Lieutenant McWhorter, brother of Captain McWhorter, who is one of the most valiant of the combatants, and hurls his projectiles like he had a sling of the ancients, (not a gin sling,) and uses his forces with the power of Archimedes. Mac, as we term him, is a gallant young man, and the life of the upper part of the Faubourg, in Block 1. He is the most terrific of the battery corps, and is as good as a baker's dozen in the evening attacks, always sustaining his ground in the many combats in which he has participated. McWhorter is Lieutenant in the Forty-Ninth Tennessee, and is as pleasant, socially, as he is fierce in action. The clod happening to strike in our neighborhood, barely grazing the cranium of an officer on my right, Captain Erskine Joyce, of the Second Kentucky. Joyce is a desperately brave man, cares for nothing when aroused, and will fight under any and all circumstances. Bud. Joyce, like all the Louisvillians, is a good liver, and fond of good society.

If you want to pass a few days pleasantly, take any boat that Harry Spotts may command; who, with St. Clair Thomason, are the prince captains of the Mississippi, and take a trip from Louisville to New Orleans, and if Bud. Joyce is with you, a delightful trip is a certainty.

Joyce replies to the missile with a solitary *chip*, (in the language of Martin Van Buren.) The term *chip* is conventional, being used in fighting the tiger, as well as in sham fights on the island.

The combat is now waxing warm, the chips and clods are becoming more important in their volume. Lieutenant

Nichol, of Nashville, who has this moment entered the field, has barely escaped the odor of a shell, caused by displaying his handsome form to the enemy's batteries, exhibiting the non-chalence of a veteran. Nichol shows game and blood, rather impulsive, but it is possible, that dash, with nerve, may overcome cooler and calmer heads. Lieutenant Nichol shows good breeding, a requisite in joining Head's regiment.

Lieutenant James T. Kirkman, is of that celebrated Kirkman family, as well known in the history of Tennessee, as the Jacksons, Carrols and Polks. He belongs to the Tenth Tennessee. Lieutenant Kirkman is on the field, but is one of the lookouts, and is not much in danger from the shelling, yet is watching the progress of the fight, with much interest. Captain McWhorter, Eighteenth Tennessee, and Captain Henry Pointer, Third Tennessee, who are standing in conversation, with a *tout ensemble*, reminding you more of Broadway or St. Charles street, than the boulevard Beauregard. They are rather staid, not mingling in the rude sports of the Campus, which is attributed to their having fallen into the sere and yellow leaf, a period of life, when the failure of desire, gives man a reputation for virtue; I attribute their quietitude to the effects of sedentary habits at home. The shells come thicker and faster, and our two gallant friends retire. Captain G. R. G. Jones, of the artillery, is a son of George W. Jones, late Senator from Iowa, to the United States Congress. Jones deserves credit for espousing the cause of the South, yielding his prospects for place and preferment, to take up arms for his adopted State, Tennessee; he is an accomplished gentleman, and a versatile genius, being one of the best musicians in prison. In noticing Jones washing, some days ago, I was forcibly reminded of the fact, what creatures of circumstances we are, the elegant, and accomplished Jones, with arms akimbo, surveying the ressults of his labors in the soapy fluid, was a picture to be remembered. Jones sits at his window, quietly enjoying the sport, but keeping a sharp look-out for stray or spent balls. Lieutenant Rufus Polk, is passing, he is a son of the widow Polk, of

Columbia, Tennessee, and a nephew of James K. Polk, is one of the most gentlemanly, mild, handsome, brave boys, I have ever met. "Ruff." passes by, working on a ring, I suppose he is making for some loved one at home. He does not notice the projectiles, but moves unscathed. leisurely on. Captain McLaughlin, Tenth Tennessee, is sitting on a log, whitling, turning his head now and then, to see that no missile is in too close proximity, then returns to his whittling. The captain would make a fine executive officer, having splendid business qualifications, yet is a No. 1 line officer. Lieutenant Elijah Thompson, makes his appearance on the field. "Lige," is in the Tennessee Artillery service, and is the leader of fashion in the pen, there is no discount on Thompson's fighting proclivities, style, or taste, he calmly feels that he is a "looker-on in Venice," and is neutral. R. M. Southall, lieutenant, Tenth Tennessee, comes out with a dash, gives a nod of recognition to one, a grasp of the hand to another, and dashes back, as rapidly as he came, where he is happily, lost in "eucre," "cribbage," or the guitar, than in sham fight alarms of the Campus. "South" is a "taking man," in any circle, where accomplishments and address are at, or above par.

The fight draws to a close, with a single combat, between Captain Leslie Ellis, of the Tenth Tennessee, and Lieutenant Andrews, of Alabama. All others cease hostilities, and leave to these two representatives of the opposing hosts, the prowess of their respective allies, the Parthian mode of warfare is adopted, with varied success. Lieutenant Andrews makes a happy "hit," and the gay and gallant Ellis retreats, to a flight of steps, he again returns to the attack, anticipating a scarcity of ammunition, on the part of his adversary, who is beating a hasty retreat, the captain feeling his want of balls, is furnished by an ambushed friend, with a new shell, with which he now pursues his fleeing enemy, who seems aware of the character of the missile, brought to bear upon him, the combat now likened that of the Horaiae and Curaiae, the shells still flew around the head of the *merry Andrew*, until an unlucky one, with well directed aim, struck the devoted youth upon the most exposed part of his person, forcing an exclamation, faugh! as the odor from the shell threw its influence around him. He was seriously, but not dangerously, wounded, a few moments serving to recuperate him, and the attack was renewed. He was furnished with the same horrible missiles, this time, A well directed shot, from Lieutenant Andrews, struck the rear of Captain Ellis' fortifications, rendering him *hors du combat*, for the time being, an armistice was agreed to, the combat decided to be a drawn one, and the issues amicably adjusted, the wounded taken from the field, most of them *half shot*, a few in the *neck*, all of which was done rapidly, as the air was now redolent, with the scent from the exploded shells, satisfying the engaged, and unengaged, that the missiles were not only destructive, but were "bad eggs." I have met these pleasant and companionable gentlemen often since, and they unite in saying, that since the engagement, they have both been quite *eggotistical*. This combat took place, June the 25th, 1862, and as the Federals have, was planned by General McClellan, and the ball that *hit*, and *kilt* Ellis, was fired by a brother of Jackson.

To my readers, who have never resided within the precincts of a military prison, we give some observations on the character of a prison mess.

A prison mess is not like that of an army or ship's mess, of some few members, but contains from sixty to one hundred. They sleep in two large rooms, in bunks, called with us single, but in our prison two were forced into each; they are three tiers high, the uppermost barely permitting the occupant to turn over without brushing the ceiling. One dining-room, one side of which is arranged with bunks, which renders eating at times, disagreeable to a man of sensitive olfactories. In our room there are ten bare plank tables, each adorned with ten tin plates, an equal number of tin-cups, two-pronged forks, a dull knife, and an iron spoon, a chunk of bread about the size of your fist, to each plate, which allowance is all you get at that meal. In the centre of the table is the meat allowance for ten men, seven and a half pounds

8

of fat, if bacon, and twelve and a half pounds of mostly bone, if beef. Coffee is poured into your cups previous to meals, to cool, which it generally does quite effectually. You stand up to eat, and don't waste time at the table. breakfast at six, dinner at half-past eleven, and supper at half-past five, P. M. We retire to our quarters at "retreat," and blow out our lights at "taps," the former being beat at sundown, the latter at ten, P. M., and then all is quiet, until the treadmill of daily movements begins with the next day's sun.

A mess of one hundred men, representing different States, stocks, and peculiar characteristics, thrown together in a mass, furnish a fine field, for moral and intellectual dissection. I have studied the mess, and show them up in their true colors, and, as each mess is but a reflex of the others, the colorings may amuse the rest of my fellow prisoners. Our mess is a noisy one, a result of the influence of a noisy man in it, as, "he who toucheth pitch is defiled," so that he, who associates with a noisy man, soon becomes noisy, man being a ductile and susceptible animal. Our noisy man is D. Thaddeus Beall, lieutenant Twenty-sixth Mississippi Volunteers. Lieutenant Beall was mustered into the service of the Confederate States, August 20th, 1861, and belonged to that gallant State, Mississippi, whose people have rallied en mass, to the call of the South to arms. Among the hearts, that beat a prompt response to this call, was the gallant lieutenant, and, " with his soul in arms, and eager for the fray," he rushed, frantically, to the grocery, and there, amidst the cries of, " Put my name down," " Give me (not a horse, but) another drink," or a "Chew of tobacco," " Heard the news," " Lincoln 's going to arm the Niggers, and desolate our homes," " Who'll put his name down, in my company roll." " Mine goes on that list," says the chivalric Beall, and amidst, " Cheers for Davis," " Bully for South Carolina," and hurrah for the lower regions, Beall was elected lieutenant. The party were then treated, by the officer elect, who vowed, he never *retreated*, but that every private of his command should get into a condition, to appreciate his speech, which was entirely *original*, and summed up, as follows :

> "Strike till the last armed Yank expires,
> Strike for the green graves of your sires."

And etc. This was while the rank and file were joining in the chorus :

> "On the wings of love I fly
> From groceree to groceri."

Beall fought at Donaldson, and stood well, was taken prisoner, and wound up at this place, where he now is, and likely to remain, as his corpulence prevents any active exertion, by which his escape might be effected.

Our witty man is Hutton. Punning is a low character of wit, yet brilliant sallies, jokes, and bon mots, of the man of genuine wit, are acceptable to any crowd, therefore Hutton is popular with the mess. Our *jokist* sleeps in ths upper bunk, and says, it is "the first story coming down from the clouds," says, he is above the malaria of tobacco spittle, the noxious exhalations which do not reach him, and from the pure atmosphere of his perch, he expresses those sallies of wit, that has dubbed him, the Hood of the mess. Hutton was in the fight at Donaldson, says, it was a warm affair, and, at this fight, he realized for the first time, "the incapacity of legs, to sustain the emotions of a heart, to whose promptings a pair of flickering extremities could not respond, hence Hutton was bagged and bunked. His witticisms are often, and piquant, and although his jokes are sometimes broad, they are generally good, and he is still secure in his position, as the wit of Mess 2, Block 8. The Irish element of our mess, consists of Burke, Dwyer, and Fletcher. The former is a genuine Celt, full of expletive and nervousness, and is noted, for accepting a challenge, to fight at ten paces, with double charged muskets and fixed bayonets, is all impulse, and, like all Irishmen, is ready to fight, if you tread on the tail of his coat. Dwyer is a man of fine proportions, and my beau-ideal of a "bould soldier boy." He was a participant in the Rebellion of '48, in Ireland, is an en-

thusiastic follower of the banner of freedom, and will follow it to the death.   Fletcher was a commissioned officer,
in Tappen's Tenth Arkansas Volunteers, made his mark
at the battle of Belmont, and was taken prisoner, at Shiloh.   He is from St. Louis, Missouri, is a good liver, and
filled with the spirit of adventure, is a rigid disciplinarian,
an efficient soldier, and, like all of Celtic origin, is ever
ready for a discussion " with sthicks."   He takes his imprisonment cooly, and gives his own experience, as follows:
" I was born in the county of Tipperary, Ireland, December 14th, 1835, imported to the United States, March
7th, 1843, left the *fangs* of that government, at St. Louis,
Missouri, May 14th, 1861, for having whipped, on the
11th of the same, " Old Fagan," (the biggest miller and
Union man of that city,) for having upheld the shameful
conduct of the Dutch, who massacred the citizens, in the
camp Jackson affair.   I could add several minor fights, to
the list of those, in which I was engaged, in our espoused
cause of liberty, but do not think it necessary, to refer to
any, except the four *pitched battles* of Carthage, Springfield, Belmont, and Shiloh.   At the battle, last mentioned,
" killed completely," (to say nothing of several bad hurts,
whose marks I bear from the former ones,) was what they
put on the muster-rolls, opposite my name.   I was brought,
a corpse (to liberty) to this prison, having been *packed*,
without ice, *with* several others, dead, soldiers like myself,
in steamboat and car, and exposed, along the whole route,
to the rude gaze and gaping stare of the Union-shriekers.
I embarked in this, my military career, short, as it has
been, as a " private," under the " noblest Roman of them
all," the gallant Sterling Price, and when found dead, at
Shiloh, it was my boast, that in the lineal rank of our
" Grand army " I was next to that of my captain.   When
day of resurrection, for " dead soldiers " arrives, I trust,
that I may rank him, at any rate, I know that I will get
a " brevet," equal to his, for " services and faithful performance of duties," as a prisoner, for carrying water,
" euchreing" the Federal suttlers out of newspapers,
keeping out of the range of our sentries' guns, etc.   My

eyes fill at the thought of all these, and may this happy *day* of *resurrection* soon come to all of us prisoners."

Our quiet man, Dr. Warren,* is one of the most affable gentlemen of our mess. He is the great pacificator, is usually the referee, and one of the most placid of our motley group, and from his application to study and sedentary habits is very reserved, his urbanity of manner, has entitled him to the respect of the entire mess. He is from Kentucky, and like all her sovereigns, thinks there is no place like the "dark and bloody ground." The doctor volunteered from Mississippi, and as he is naturally proud of his native State, is equally as much so of his adopted one, that has done so much for Southern rights, and honor.

Captain James N. Bolen represents the cavalry in our mess. This gentleman belongs to the Kentucky cavalry, and was among those dashing horsemen, whose sabres are ever flashing, between the Ohio and Tennessee, and who, under the command of Morgan and King, are making havoc among the hordes of the enemy, who are scattered from Louisville to Corinth. Bolen is an off-handed, plain-spoken man, of force and character, satirical, and good at repartee, is a good soldier, and those who know him best, will admire his candor, and excuse his crudeness.

Lieutenant R. J. Moore, of the Twenty-sixth Mississippi Regiment, is the literary genius of our mess. In looking at Moore, I am impressed with the fact, how poorly we judge one another. Why is it? It is, because we accept, improperly, first impressions as lasting, and confuse the simple street introduction, or a night's acquaintance, with that of a few days, for it is only upon a cultivation of your new acquaintance, allowing a period of time to appreciate his or her attributes, you are not impressed by a passing glance, as it requires remarkable perceptive faculties, in such instance, to even approximate to the realities of your subject, you must examine each feature, you must hear the subject talk, must draw out idea after idea, and thus, by study, you can easily select congenial friends. There-

---

* Dr. Warren, physician, Friar's Point, Mississippi.

fore I believe first impressions *are* lasting, but it does not imply that the figure in the sand by the sea-side, that each wave destroys, or a handful of spray may dissipate, is lasting, but I accept rather the simile of the photograph, which shows, that while the operation is instantaneous, yet there are powerful combinations studied and used, to establish the impressions they impart to the subject. Lieutenant Moore would deceive you, at first glance, calm, and apparently unimpassioned, he is a Vesuvius, or Hecla, at rest, only awaiting a vent, that will allow the smouldering fires, to burst forth in resistless fury, with inspiration to have made him a crusader, who would have followed Richard, or Godfrey d'Bouillion, to the walls of Jerusalem, and yet but few men have more of the milk of human kindness in them, thon Lieutenont Moore.

The Boulevards of Paris, Savastopol Des Italians and Capucan, are among the principal lounging thoroughfares of that gay capital. London has her Pall Mall and Regent street, and New Orleans its Canal, St. Royale and St. Charles, New York its Broadway, and why not the denizens of this Confederate capital have our promenade and resort. Our principal walk is enjoyed by the figures of a thousand officers, who can boast as pure a descent as a Howard or De Courcy. The principal rendezvous of the bloods is in front of the post-office, which from the construction of the buildings, affords shade to the lovers of debate. Each of the thirteen buildings has a wood-pile, and here, with knives in hand, the sir oracles of the prison, will with Delphic mystery, explain while whittling the signification of the times. In other countries, little tables are placed before you with beer, and etceteras, but with us, conversation must be the production of the brain, and not of the *spirit*, however, a drop or so does get in some time, and ts potency is often felt, increasidg animation and boisterous conversation, the passers by are bitterly criticised, for men are, (if the truth must be told,) more garrulous than women. There goes a man with long hair, richly colored and luxuriant. "I'd cut that hair off," says one, " perhaps he told his gal, he would not cut it off until he came back," " he looks gay

and festive," says another. "Pea Ridge," as we call him, happens to fancy long hair, and such being the case, I think he has a right to wear it—it seems strange that men's peculiarities are not understood. One man wears long hair, and is a gallant soldier; another wants to be a tiger, shaves his head, and would jump out of his boots at the report of a six-pounder, in other cases, the long-haired man is an arrant coward—short-haired one, a Stonewall Jackson. Some men in our pen will wash out of a tin-cup, when they can buy a basin for fifteen cents, that is a peculiarity that does not unfit the man for the duties of life, yet subjects him to rediculous comment. I know other men in prison, who have the reputation of being gallant officers, with ample funds at their command, who will buy a five cent pie, go off to one side, and eat it, not in *peace*, for no man, so lost to generous impulses, could have a quiet conscience, but by the *piece*, that is their peculiarity.

"Well," says Lieutenant L. G. Brindley, of the Forti-eth Tennessee, "I wonder when we will be exchanged?" and so he asks every time he sees me. My answer is uniformly courteous, because I feel that Brindly wants to know—that's his peculiarity.

J. W. Kuykendall, captured at Mill Springs, belonged to the fighting Fifteenth Mississippi, takes a seat by me on a chunk, but does not criticise. He is a pleasant gen-tleman, was assistant post-master at camp Chase, at which prison I reaped the benefit of his agreeable manners. Kuykendall always wears his pants in his boots—that's his peculiarity.

F. M. Atkins is on the campus, playing ball. I can see him, in the distance, striking with one arm. Atkins joined the army with one arm, and is risking the other for independence. He could have remained at home, but that was not his peculiarity, or any of the Forty-ninth Tennessee, if I know them, and I think I do.

Captain McIntyre is retiring, it seems, to the casual observer, taciturn and sour. That quietude is his peculi-arity, and covers the brave man, as his wound in the face, at Springfield, Missouri, clearly shows.

Captain S. Q. Carey, who acted well at the battle of Booneville, is as sour, to all appearances, as a crab-apple, but Carey, when you enow him, is an agreeable companion. His peculiarity is bad health.

Lieutenant T. Johnson, of Nashville, Forty-ninth Tennessee Regiment, is seemingly puffed up, and consequential, but Johnson acted well at Donaldson. His peculiarity consists in weight, being rather *embonpoint*, for a young man, yet know him well, and you exclaim, a dev'lish clever American (not English) fellow.

Lieutenant-colonel Finney is a man, who must have an out-fit, to feel right. Put the colonel in old clothes, and he will be miserable; yet, with his vanity, he has nerve and polish, and wants the elegant things, because he has been accustomed to them.

Captain Joiner is a retiring, and one of the most modest gentlemen in prison, is generally in dishabille, and to look at him, it is difficult to realize, that Joiner, in his prison-quarters, and Joiner in the drawing-room, the pattern of a neat exterior, are one and the same person—but that's Joiner's peculiarity.

*Lieutenant W. R. Culvertson, Porter's battery, and P. K. Stankemitz, captain heavy battery. These gentlemen are knights of the sheares, and to see them cutting and stitching, you would not think, that so much fire and courage could spring from so quiet an appearing element. Yet it is so, they are as brave and dashing, as any in the service. Many a poor fellow is slandered, as he passes this or that group, about his peculiarities, if he has bad or good clothes, too many or too few stripes, no matter what color, he is sure to be subjected to the ordeal of the loungers: "There goes a chap, who wants to be major of his regiment, he can't drill a squad;" "There's a splendid field officer, I'll bet a hundred, I've a sergeant who can beat him manœuvring his own regiment." Mens peculiarities and eccentricities are not borne with, because they are not understood, and 'tis a good thing, that the world does not know, what is said of them, because if 'twas so,

_____
* Died in 1862.

there would not be four friends in it, 'tis to a great degree harmless, and much of it said thoughtlessly, not intending offend, yet if it should unfortunately come to the ears of the party, it was aimed at, possibly a false sense of shame to yield to truth, for fear of public opinion, the most relentless of all social tyrannies, would incite the offender, to refuse the *amende honorable*, and the result in many cases, the loss of friendship, and the engendering of hate, and in many cases, nothing but blood will atone for the idle expression. The tongue is an unruly member, and if it offends thee, thou hadst better cut it out. Twilight is taking her shadows with her, and the wood-piles are deserted, the sergeants are around, hunting up the six axes, with which the entire prison is furnished, to cut our wood during the day, and at night they are taken out, for fear we might use them, also our superintendent has several *axes to grind*. The departure of the sergeants from the campus, leaves the Boulevard Beauregard deserted.

(DEDICATED TO LIEUTENANT COLONEL W. T. AVERY.)

Those that have hash, have trouble about it;
Those that have none, have trouble without it.

Hash is to the denizens of Johnson's island, what the far-famed tongue of the peacock was to the Roman epicures or "lentils" to a distinguished foreigner.

There is an individual in our pen that has complained of the quality of "hash" furnished prisoners. The result was, the cook appealed to the mess, composed of some our most distinguished officers, who met in conclave, and appointed a committee to settle the vexatious question. The members of said committee were Colonels Baker, Avery, and Clark, Major Brown and Captain Dawson. By a unanimous call, Colonel Avery was selected as chairman, and after calling the meeting to order, remarked "That since he had forsaken the halls of legislation, and planted his stake on the tented field, he had ceased to declaim, and only presented or manipulated tangible subjects. Theory with him had played out, now he had espoused the practical duties of life, and to sum up, he would give in the morning, a practical solution of the 'hash question,' if the committee would trust him with the subject." A hearty concurrence was the response, and the committee retired to the hall, making a report in accordance with the facts elicited. Day broke in all its glory, and never did old Sol throw a brighter halo around a more anxious assemblage, than the mess in block one, as they nervously awaited the signal that was to announce to their all ready watering mouths and excited stomachs, that the great question of "hash" had to be settled ere the drum's martial beat sounded the breakfast call. We now return to the chairman, he whose assumption of the complicated and knotty question, had so relieved the minds of his associates. His pride had been touched with the insinuation that hash was not good enough for prisoners. His feelings naturally buoyant, were depressed at the ill-timed reflection of the favorite dish at the time of Johnson's island. What if Cleopatra did dissolve pearls upon bread, and make a breakfast of them? It was because she had no "hash." The Cafe de Mille Colon is famous for catering, but would be more so if it could make "hash." In Brussels they have an imitation called "bullet," but it is not "hash." Not on this green earth is there a place where you can get this grand mollifier in its perfection, but in the quiet retreat of Johnson's island. Knowing this, the chairman determined he would serve a dish, that would satiate even the great Handel, and one that would settle forever, the question, "is hash good for prisoners?"

Oily subjects are not of reputed tenacity, yet they have a tenaciousness of purpose and stick like glue, or "death to a dead Nigger," or "quills to a fretful porcupine." In their properties they seem to affect tin plates more than any other solids. Polished surfaces are easily influenced, and it is only by the severest action, that the feat of removing the slippery element is accomplished. Oil from the Polar whale; oil from the seal and walrus; petroleum or rock oil as oleagenous as they may be, have not the same stickitotiveness as the genuine oil from hash. Then again, plates are not easily handled; acrobatic feats, those of the Chinese jugglers, with feats by Hernandez and other wizards, have astonished the world; but had they the manipulation of prison hash plates, they would have signally failed. Hercules, when he attempted the cleaning of the Augean stable, had not half the difficulties to surmount as our chairman. If like Xerxes, lashing would have done any good, he would have vented his wrath on the water with his dish-rag, that now loomed up with its greasy surface as foul as the Styx appeared to Charon, when he took his first trip as a ferryman; and the shirt of Nessus never felt as terrible to its victim, as the influence of rag and apron upon the frenzied defender of the great and undying system of "hash," but with that stoicism that so distinguished the stoics that made Cæsar, while perishing, exclaim "et tu Brute," which many suppose alludes to his carniverous inclination, that held the Roman finger in the blaze until burnt off, that made the Spartan youth secrete the fox under his garment, 'till he eat into his entrails, and now will be calm and collected, while the streams of society are running knee-deep in gore, bloody hands are held up, and gory locks are shaking North, East, South and West, exclaiming, "thou cans't not say I did it." He looks at the mountains of plates, shining with some fatty substance, that tells of mutilated efforts to make "hash" visions of disjointed meats and particled grissels, seem to be heaped up like a volcanic eruption, in the place he had selected to open his new system. Pieces of bread lie scattered over the tables, grinning at the pigmy, who was to change them from their natural shape into a mass of what-not, a jumble of elements. Even the disintegrated meat seemed to offer up feeble petitions to the energetic artiste gastronomic, who, like Ajax, defying the lightning, stood boldly and bravely amid the wreck of the dinner of the day previous. He began his task, rushing here and there, pile after pile of plates sank beneath his gigantic rag; meat and bread were buried promiscuously in the vortex of the loud-mouthed cauldron. He waxed warm, large drops of sweat ran down his cheeks, but he felt triumphant, the pot was closed, the committee entered, it was then opened and a specimen served on a plate and

tasted by Colonel Baker, who with an expression, that
would have electrified even that stupid Horace Maynard,
of Tennessee, "Avery, d—d if you can make hash." One
howl went up from the committee as the report was made,
which was as follows :

> "Those that have hash are troubled about it—
> Those that have none are troubled without it."

Since his discomfiture, Colonel Avery has confined himself to the more congenial pursuits of "hewing wood and
drawing water," and may be seen, of a pleasant afternoon,
after the duties of the day are over, strolling about the
campus, feeling like Othello, "that his occupation's
gone," and in his musings and often soliloquies, indulges
in the reflection, that if Alpheus Baker is not a prophet,
or the son of one, he is a good judge of 'hash.' His experience has done him much good, and he is tranquil and
happy, only when reminded of his failure, then merely
giving vent to his feelings in the quaint remark, "d—n
the hash."

> "Religion is the chief concern of mortals here below."

In the endless variety of human nature, within our
precincts, are our ministers of the Gospel, some of whom
are men of much character.   It is an unquestionable and
incontrovertible fact, that every man has some semblance
about him of the christian; he may not be Methodist,
Presbyterian or Catholic, but his sympathies are with the
sufferings of our Savior; he has a dormant realization of
the great sacrifice for man, and his innate promptings are
to accept, as messengers of mercy and types of their
Master, those men, who, if necessary, are to take neither
purse nor scrip, but to go into all the world and preach
the Gospel to every creature ; even should the man not
sensibly realize his situation as a sinner, and feel his need
of a Savior, he may, perhaps, be impressed with the
purity of that worthy representative, a true minister of
Christ; halt and consider, and the proper appli-
ances, the wooing and the storming, if necessary, of his

heart by the preacher of tact, he may become a disciple
of the meek and lowly Jesus, but whether he be so or
otherwise, the man, unless a brute, is influenced by a
Divine of piety and judgment, of whom we have several
in prison, and their influence is wonderful. On the
Sabbath, many of which the author has passed in
prison, the thousand officers retire to their rooms, or
promenade, no cards or ball-playing, no rioting, nor
shouting, but regular and full attendance at the morning
and evening services, and a universal reign of quiet and
decorum. This is as it should be, and shows the influence of these ministerial aids to the Bible, in dissemi-
nating its holy teachings, and diffusing the cheering rays
of christianity, with all its concomitants of peace civilization, and humane progression. Captain A. J. Witherspoon, chaplain of the Twenty-first Alabama Regiment;
this model of the ministerial profession, is a gentleman
I have become warmly attached to, he is mild, quiet, and
affable, and an orator, of persuasive style, with much
perspicuity, and to whom I listen with pleasure; not
to his bold and vehement flights alone, but to his chaste
and concise sentences, clothed with humility of mien, he
is one of the gentlest and kindest men I ever met, yet the
compressed lips show determination and courage, when
occasion calls for it, which was well exhibited on the field
of Shiloh, where his attentions to the wounded, under
the terrific fire of that Sunday struggle, marked him
most eminently as one whom the terrors of the battle-
field could not deter from performing the duties of his
profession. Dr. Witherspoon is a protege of the great
Thornwell, of South Carolina, and takes much of his
ministerial inspiration from that able divine, whose
sermon of June 3d, 1860, on board the steamer Adriatic,
still remains in my memory.

William H. Adams, chaplain of the Forty-third Tennessee Regiment. Captain Adams is a firm and good
man, of some ability, and much force of character, is on
the Cromwellian order, and would carry the sword in one
hand and the C___ ' in the other, who preaches a good
practical sermon. naple

E. Hogue, Eleventh Arkansas, J. B. Overton, Second
Kentucky, H. H. Robinson, Third Mississippi, A. G.
Taylor, Fourteenth Mississippi, J. F. Walker, Fifty-third
Tennessee, and A. A. Wilson, Fiftieth Tennessee.
These gentlemen are all reputed good men, and are
certainly zealous in the cause, ; the two latter I have
heard preach.   Captain Wilson is a man of much genius,
and quite a pleasant delivery.   These are the eight
righteous men here, I hope they will save us, yet ten was
required in Sodom.

> " Now the brooding silence deepens,
>   And the scene is one of rest,
> While the wrecked day drifts down gradually,
>   To be stranded in the west."

Aurora is gathered to her fathers, and her radient train,
with their peerless influence, are seeking the realms of
night, there to repose 'till the call to orisons is heralded
by the lark.   How beautiful the prismatic colorings of the
robes of the etherial throng, as they sink beneath the
blushing horizon;   the crimson intermingling with the
cerulean depths of Heavens space, the glittering spray
reflecting a myriad of colors, from tinted cloud-banks.
'Tis beautiful, but transitory ; they gather their skirts,
their drapery dips into the silvery lake, they lave their
shining faces in the limpid waters, their gossamer robes,
spangled with the glittering spray drops that have nestled
in their laps ; they sink into the vast deep, and the sire
of them all, twilight, closes the portals of day upon their
fading shadows.   'Tis a pleasant melancholy, that steals
o'er the senses during this period, when the great struggle seems to take place for supremacy, between the going
and coming powers of day and night.   Like all natural
convulsions, they startle and impress, the day is dead to
all, and the eye that scans the horizon, to witness the
last effort of the mighty power, as he sinks into the abyss
of night, turns away conscious of the vacancy in
nature.   The approach of night is soothing, but not as
cheering as the lively morn, yet the calm of the one,
and the exhilaration of the other, commingle, and exert

a charming influence in the deepening twilight. The
groups that have been playing and frisking on the sward,
have resolved into contemplative sets. There goes a
squad of the boys of fifty years ago, they are the men of
the progressive present, and as they saunter along, discussing the merits of this or that strategic movement of
our different commanders; one wonders how the times
and fashions change. They are Lieutenants Samuel P.
and John Walker, Kirtland, Kelsey and Duncan; the
first two are sons of Samuel P. Walker, of Memphis,
Tennessee, nephews of James K. Polk, formerly President of the United States. This family influence, has
given the young Walkers many advantages of society and
purse, that they show marks of, in their gentlemanly
bearing, and general urbanity. They are lieutenants in
the Fortieth Tennessee, commanded by their uncle
Colonel (now General) Marsh Walker. Lieutenant
Samuel Walker is a fine tactician. John is younger, yet
a quick student. Lieutenants Kirtland and Kelsey, are
residents of the city of Memphis, young men of intelligence, but as their connection with the army was only
of a few weeks previous to their capture, I know but
little of their military ability. Lieutenant Greene Duncan is from Kentucky, and a promising officer. Lieutenant McKay, is also a Kentuckian, one of those
desperate men, who figured in the Walker expedition in
Nicaraugua, and followed the grey eyed man of destiny,
until his star set in the night of an unsuccessful Revolution.
During that terrible campaign the lieutenant lay upon the
brick floor of a cabin, with a block of wood for a pillow,
suffering for thirty days with yellow fever; he is one of
the best disciplinarians in the service. This group has
scanned the horizon, as the sun has left its last ray upon
the blue vault above, and with a few straggling expressions about exchange, and the future of the Confederacy,
they wend their way leisurely back to their quarters.
Another group passes conversing with much animation.
There is genius and wit in that circle. Captain Jesse
Taylor, of the artillery, a regular navy officer of the
United States, is replete with sallies. Captain Weed, of

St. Louis, Missouri, is an officer of merit, he was formerly
of the house of Abbott, Johns & Co., of Philadelphia,
but has espoused the cause of the Confederate States,
with much enthusiasm.   Captain Simmons, of Missouri,
of the editorial corps, was early connected with, and was
a great friend of General Jeff. Thompson, in the
struggle in Missouri, at the opening of the war.

Captain Wash. Gordon* is passing, apparently musing
upon the reign of terror that afflicts his family at home.
He is a middle aged man, of piety and fearlessness, and
an honest man, "the noblest work of God," of mild
manners, with many christian virtues.   He is a
shining light in our circle.   He is a firm and decided
sympathizer with the down-trodden South, and will rot
in prison, rather than his government shall abate a jot or
tittle of her just demands, for an honoreble exchange of
prisoners.   We all love Captain Gordon, not alone for his
gallantry in the field, but for his consistent walk and conversation in durance, and as he leads the evening prayer
meeting, with the fervor of a zealous christian, showing his
faith by his works, we can't help regretting, that there are as
few such men in our distracted country.   Captain George
W. Gordon is the father of nine children, two of his sons
now in the service of their native State, Tennessee.   He
was captured at Fort Donaldson, and bears his imprisonment with patience, he is of a family of patriotic men and
women, one of whom alone is known to me personally.
His sister, Mrs. Sarah C. Law, of Memphis, Tennessee.
This estimabie lady is one of the old time matrons, keenly
alive to the woes of suffering humanity, she has not neglected a mother's duty, as her dhildren are remarkable
for piety and intelligence.

Mrs. Law is one of the originators of the most perfect
systems of hospital treatment in the South, she has been
unsparing in her efforts, her energies have never relaxed
in assisting and soothing a sufferer, and is of vigorous
sympathies, great strength of character, and a beacon

---

* Captain Gordon died at Vicksburg, Mississippi, September, 1862, from
disease caused by exposure, incidental to that tortuous trip of thirteen days
on the river.

light of the Presbyterian church community of her city.

Captain Meadows, of the First Alabama Regiment, while passing within the line of stakes, (laid by our captors,) and totally unconscious of any danger, was shot and badly wounded in the leg, by a buckshot, discharged by a cowardly sentinel upon the wall. The wound is severe, but not dangerous. The act, the superintendent says, he " does not justify," as it displayed a feeling of brutality, as a brave man seeks revenge, for a supposed insult to his flag, by enlisting in a safe place for ninety days, to murder a prisoner. He is an arrant coward to the core. Captain Meadows is a man of nerve and courage, and bears his sufferings with much patience. His gentlemanly deportment, and indisposition to offend, makes his case a sad one, yet, we hope, he will speedily recover, and live to perform gallant deeds for the cause of his country.

The following are the resolutions, drown up in accordance with the facts elicited :

" JOHNSON'S ISLAND, June 14th, 1862.

"At a meeting, held in Block 7, Mess 1, on this day, at 10 A. M., of the representatives of the different messes, on motion, Captain G. W. Gordon, of Tennessee, was elected chairman, who explained the object of the meeting, as follows : 'To consider, and take some steps, concerning the firing upon our unarmed fellow prisoners, by the Federal sentinels on guard over us, and for the better protection of our lives, whilst prisoners of war, in the hands of the authorities of the United States.) Captain Frank. Jay McLean, of Tennessee, was appointed secretary.

"Captain Moss, of Kensucky, moved that a committee of four be appointed, to see Major Pierson, and confer with him, and ascertain whether the prisoners, who have been fired upon by sentinels, were so fired on by his orders, and especially the one fired on last night, and so seriously wounded, was shot by his authority.

"Lieutenant Watts, of Tennessee, offered a resolution as a substitute for Captain Moss, to the effect that the chair appoint a committee of four, who are requested to report

9

in writing, to this meeting at three P. M., this day, what communications, resolutions or remonstrances they propose to make to the commander of the post, concerning the conduct of the sentinels, and that this meeting confer with, and if necessary, advise with said committee. After discussion, the substitute was adopted, whereupon the chair appointed the following committee: Colonels Battle, of Tennessee, Simonton, of Mississippi, Baker, of Alabama, Smith of Arkansas. On motion, the names of Rev. Mr. Witherspoon, and the chairman of the committee, were added.

"On motion, this meeting adjourned till three P. M., this day.

"Three P. M. meeting met, pursuant to adjournment, Captain Gordon presiding. The committee, appointed by this meeting, through Colonel Battel, of Tennessee, presented the following remonstrance, to be presented to the commandant of this post, which, on motion, was unanimously adopted.

"Colonels Baker, Battel and Simonton, and Rev. Mr. Witherspoon, having made some remarks, the secretary was ordered to copy the remonstrance for Major Pierson, presenting to him the original.

"On motion, the meeting adjourned *sine die*.

"GEORGE W. GORDON, Chairman.

"FRANK JAK. McLEAN, Secretary.

The following is the remonstrance, which is accepted in letter and spirit by every prisoner in the pen, and expresses their feelings, in relation to the attempted assassination of Captain Meadows:

"JOHNSON'S ISLAND, June 14, 1862.

"SIR:—As a committee, appointed for that purpose, by the prisoners of war, contined on this island, we respectfully address to you this communication, in respect to the shooting of one of our fellow prisoners. Last night, by the sentinel upon post No. 13, Captain J. D. Meadows, of the First Alabama Regiment, a gentleman of most amiable character, and correct habits, whose whole deportment here has been unexceptionable, and faithfully observant of all rules, was by that sentinel shot down, in the path-way, while returning from the sinks to his quarters. The statement of Captain Meadows himself, and of other officers, who witnessed the occurrence, shows that there was no shadow of justification for this atrocious brutality. In stepping from the sink, Captain Meadows had stopped, for a moment, in the path-way, to arrange his clothes, the sentinel, who was very near him, on the wall, speaking in a voice, so quiet, and, apparently, kind, as to afford the unfortunate gentleman no warning of his cruel purpose, said to him, "You musn't stop there." Captain Meadows immediately moved, when, without another word or warning, after he had made one or two steps towards his quarters, in obedience to the order, and with his back towards him, a fact incontestibly shown, the sentinel shot him down. It is now the third time, that prisoners have been fired upon for very slight offences. Heretofore we have submitted without murmur, fully aware, how entirely we are at your mercy, we have endeavored, with scrupulous care, to observe the regulations, posted upon our doors; we are taught, by these cruel lessons, that even this is no security, against mutilation and murder. We hesitate how to act. Are we, sir, to obey the rash instincts of despair? or may we trust, as we once thought, to your sense of justice and humanity? We claim the right, to be treated as prisoners of war, and not as enemies, and claim this right with a deep sense of injury and unprovoked wrong. We appeal to you for justice. If Captain Meadows was in error, we have not a word to say; but if, as is believed, this sentinel has shot him down in cold blood, we call upon you, to see that he receives the punishment his crime deserves, and we be secured against similar outrages."

If the sentinel is punished, it will be a new chapter in our prison history.

The grape-vine line has at last succumbed to the genuine article, and the fact being a fixed one, that we are exchanged, Othello's occupation on the grape seems gone. Yet there are spasmodic evidences, of the leavening influence of grape, on the minds of some of our prisoners, and in spite of the absorbing news that we are exchanged, and that on the 31st of July the Fort Warren prisoners, including the glorious Buckner and heroic Tilghman, had left for Fortress Monroe, arriving August 1st, and the forwarding of the Confederate prisoners, confined at Washington, still there is some little pulsation in the grape-vine line. Captain Scovill says, he thinks we will go via Buffalo, and New York. Lieutenant Lytle says, he is not particular as to route, and with his sprightly, nervous manner, that he would go without his unmentionables, any route, to get out of old Pierson's clutches. Lytle belongs to the Eighteenth Tennessee Regiment, and is one of its most popular officers. Lieutenant D. S. Martin, of the Third Tennessee, is more staid, and as he joins our group, says, he wants to get out, but waits the moving of the waters. Captain Peacher, Forty-ninth Tennessee, is a matter-of-fact man, not influenced by passing remarks or events, and as yet the grape has had no effect upon his calmness. Lieutenant Berry, of the Tenth Tennessee, is a brave young officer, by birth a Virginian, yet with a great influence with the command, raised in his adopted State, with that enthusiasm so natural in youth. He is ever ready to hear the latest news, and is as anxious now, as he was before hearing the confirmation of our exchange.

Captain J. G. Sharp, Company E, Twenty-sixth Mississippi Regiment, has an enviable reputation for courage, fine personal appearance, quite a lion among the ladies, 'tis said, and what you would call a *taking* man, is ever ready for fun of any kind, and were it not for his efforts, aided by Lieutenant Isham G. Randolph, (Red Shirt,) and Lieutenant Murphy, from Mississippi, with the few other spirited officers, I am afraid the grape would not keep our spirits up. Sharp in his exuberance, vows the *grape* shall not play out, the fun must go on. Captain Joe Hubbard, of Tennessee, seems pleased with the news.

Lieutenant R. Hyde Dick is the general thermometer of the island; good news, Dick's eyes get as large as saucers; bad news, his face assumes the weazen, and the once full and ruddy countenance is corrugated by despair. Lieutenant John Douglas, although quite young, but one of the best drilled officers in the service, appears unconcerned on the subject of *grape*, trusting his material future to the rising star of the Confederacy. Lieutenant Hiram Lewter, from Mississippi, is one of my messmates, and is the most jovial youth in the room, he is quite seriously affected with the exchange fever, and only accepts consolation in whortleberry pies, and sundry games one cent *poker*.

All our prisoners are affected by the news. Some express their feelings in excess of sobriety, others of hilarity. Yet as we judge the entire campus, by the characters given, it is seen how the news of exchange affects a prisoner.

Among the arrivals, to-day, are three officers, who distinguished themselves at the memorable battle of Shiloh, fought April the 6th, 1862, Captain Palmer, formerly of the "Crocket Rangers," one of the gamest companies ever organized within the bounds of the Confederacy. Palmer is a regular *game cock*, always *spurred* for a muss, no matter how questionable its character. Lieutenant Shep. Webb, First Lieutenant of the Beauregards. Lieutenant Webb, with this company, was in the battle of Shiloh, and performed the duties assigned him, with nerve and ability. At the time he was captured he was acting upon the staff of General Nelson. Lieutenant Webb is a citizen of Memphis, Tennessee, respected by all who know him, is an efficient officer, and considering his youth, one of the best in the service. Lieutenant F. D. Moore, of McNairy county, Tennessee, One Hundred and Fifty-Fourth Sen. regiment, Tennessee Volunteers, is a spirited young officer, of much wit and humor. He was captured while in company with his sister, driving within the enemy's lines, while on leave from his command. Lieutenant Moore bears his imprisonment well, solacing himself with his violin, on which instrument he performs admirably. "Foss," as he is familiarly called, is popular at home and abroad, and as a brave soldier, is missed by the service, that he, by his good behaviour and soldierly bearing, reflected credit upon whilst in the front rank at Shiloh and other fields.

Breakfast, six A. M., tin cup of water and coffee, and a piece, too frequently, of sour bread, in a tin plate, and the boiled meat of the day before. About this time, the ice man comes in; the milkman, who rarely gets in until after breakfast. This arrival creates some excitement, as the supply rarely equals the demand, and all those who desire the fluid, are compelled to place their vessels in a line, beginning at the post at the guard-line, in front of the big gate. The vessels present an amusing spectacle, canteens, preserve jars, bottles, jugs, cups, pitchers, bowls and crocks, of all shapes and size; each officer on the alert to see that some other individual's vessel is not slipped nearer the milk-cart. At 8 A. M., the vegetable man comes in, with a dray load of onions, beets and potatoes. He is immediately surrounded by the prisoners, who have the money to buy with, and sells out by nine. Then the newspapers come in, the " Sandusky Register," a dirty, falsifying sheet, as black with Abolitionism as Erebus; " New York Herald," and "Cincinnati Enquirer," the latter having claims to gentility of journalism; the former a time-serving engine, mighty for evil, but powerless for good. The rush for papers is quite exciting, several hundred prisoners at *double quick*, yelling out, papers, cursing the vendor for his slowness; the lighted up countenance on the receipt of good news, the blank ones when it is bad, or the dull ones when it is indifferent, is an excitement that amuses us 'till the mail comes in. At twelve M., the mail-boy arrives, then all are keenly alive to hear the news from home and the *loved* ones. Some are made happy, *others* go back to their rooms disappointed. The chief of each mess receives the mail for his mess, and as he stands at the foot of the stairs, calling out the letters, with the anxious faces above peering into his own, the scene is an interesting one. The sutler comes in twice a day, morning with clothing, etc., in the evening with edibles. These are the only excitements furnished us by our enemies, (shooting excepted.) Our own excitements, ball playing, card playing, whittling, and reading, those who have books—sleeping, filling up the intervals.

CHAPTER V.

EXCURSION *ala* AFRICANA.—ANNIVERSARY.—EMANCIPATION IN WEST INDIES.—FUNERAL IN PRISON.—THE DEAD LINE.—PETTY MALICE. —REGULATIONS OF THE PRISON.—LONDON PHILOSOPHY.—INCIDENT OF BALAKLAVA, BY A PRISONER.—DEATHS IN PRISON.— POETS AND POETRY.—THE WRECK.—THE LAKE STEAMER.—THE ROLL-CALLER OF OUR MESS.—ST. CLAIR MORGAN, OF TENNESSEE. —OUR BUSINESS AFFAIRS.—GENERAL JEFF. THOMPSON.—GRAPE-VINE LINE.—GOOD NEWS.—MAN A CREATURE OF HABIT.—OUR MILK MAN.—JACK HANDY.—OUR POST SURGEON.—CONFEDERATE SURGEONS.—PROMENADE REFLECTIONS.—NEW ARRIVAL.

WE were made aware, to-day, by the odor borne upon the lake breeze, from a passing steamer, that something unusual was agitating the atmosphere, on inspection with an opera glass, exhibited a motly grouping of black kinks and ugly specimens of the "pale face," something like the display of currants in a plum cake. 'Tis true that all the extracts of Lubin, Bazin, and Phalon's rarest compounds, were scenting the air, yet the sweet perfume of Afric's fairest flowers expressed through their excretories, annihilated all opposition, leaving the smell of "Nigger" triumphant, as they passed the island, the wool of Nigger kinked tighter, the sleek face shone sleeker, and the scent rose stronger, and Nigger was Nigger, at least for one day, in Sandusky bay. They had a band that discoursed Yankee Doodle, they waved highly scented handkerchiefs, and passing slowly out of sight, leaving us to our reflections. The Federals have Cuffee, they are welcome to him and his exhalations, there is no legislation, or social regulation, that will change the African, or his descent. Nigger will be

Nigger, the world over; he is destined to fill the positions of boot black and scullion, and at any intellectual employment, he is at sea. He cannot comprehend intellectual effort and how the professional can ride in his carriage, without exhibiting any physical attempt to earn his wealth, is a mystery, and arouses within him, that radical Abolition emotion, "Down with the indolent aristocracy," not willing to accord to them the credit of the years of intellectual toil employed, to attain the position that alone can fit them, for the walks of their calling. The line of demarkation, has been drawn by nature, between white and black society, and is as impassible as a gulf of fire. Northern Negro philanthropy is reaping its reward, and like the man who won the elephant, they have got Cuffee, now what will they do with him? The boat is out of sight, with its freight of sables, who are suffering from both friend and foe. Alas! poor African, an object of pity and commiseration, thou mayest well exclaim, "Save me from my (so called) friends."

A funeral at sea is a melancholy spectacle, the gloomy looks of the crew, the dejected air of the passengers, and the agonized expression of weeping relatives seem to fill the imagination with all that is distressing and heartrending, yet the freshness of the ocean breeze, new scenes, the excitements of storm, and "sail ho!" with the whirl of life midst the hundreds on shipboard, softens, if not efaces, death's shadows at sea. 'Tis not so in prison, the soldier dies and is confined in a common pine coffin, a little wagon is sent in, that is daily used by the sutler, the coffin placed in it, the driver cracks his whip, as if his animal had stalled with a load of wood, and the vehicle rattles over the ruts and clods of the campus. To-day we buried poor Hodges. He was from Memphis, Tennesee, and died from a wound received from a copper ball from a Mexican escopet, while acting gallantly in Mexico, which the irritation of his imprisonment, added to a fall, caused to break out afresh, resulting in death. The death of Captain Hodges has been alluded to in another "scrap," yet mention is made in this connection, as addi-

tional evidence of the inhumanity of our custodians, his
friends requested to attend his funeral, but were denied,
the reply, as mentioned previous, being, that none,
excepting those belonging to his regiment, could attend
his funeral.   We were not of the number, and the tortur-
ing Pierson let his cartman drive out the body, without
the attendance of his friends, an unheard-of barbarity, for
which there is no excuse.   It was a sad sight to see all
that remained of our friend driven out, like the carcass
of some dumb brute, and buried without the ministration
of friends, all of this under the eye of that eagle whose
wings are supposed to enfold the "best government the
world ever saw," with the most damnable representatives.
Pierson's *trestle* board is discolored by dark and treacherous spots, and how he can serenely stand beneath the *arch*,
without viewing it as the sword of Damocles, is beyond
the comprehension of a *pillar* of the arch, but his temple
will be one of Babel, and not of Solomon, as his moral
tools are rusty, and as "he soweth, so shall he also reap."

Thirty feet from the wall around the entire prison, is
an imaginary line, called the dead-line, yet on one side the
sinks are not ten feet from the wall, and it was while
going to his quarters from one of them, that Captain
Meadows was shot down, an account of which is given in
another "scrap." To step across this line is death, a heavy
penalty for a slight offence.   Genghis Khan, or Timour
could not have been more severe; only the sack or bow-
string is more revolting to the feelings, and is not as
prompt as a quietus, as the old "Springfield," with its
charge doubled, and the finger of its merciless (because
cowardly) owner upon a trigger, itching to respond to the
call of the sentinel' sheart, that secure in its home-guard
battalion, burns, to gloat over the murder of a rebel.   If
the war continues, and we are held in durance, we may
have yet to choose between the "gnout," "bastinado,"*
or "ropes end," for slight dirclections, and between the
garote, gallows, or musket, for graver ones.

---

* They are now whipping negroes in the free State of Illinois, (see scrap),
and why not apply the lash to white men, which they will surely do, if fanaticism triumphs in the present struggle.

Captain J. P. Colwell, Captains Cary and F. A. Rogers,* with Lieutenant Josiah Joplin;† these four officers were notified this morning, that they would not be exchanged. They were gentlemen, and influential citizens at home before the war, and have served their flag faithfully since. They had made ready, anticipating the call of their names, when an official announced they would be detained. It is difficult to imagine the feeling of despondency felt by them, as eleven hundred of their fellow prisoners filed out of prison, into the free air beyond the walls. Each heart beat in sympathy with them, but we could do nothing but surmise as to the cause of their detention, they had been the most quiet and orderly soldiers in prison, men of education and refinement, and true Confederates. Old Pierson is up to some Devilment, and we would not be surprised, if our Missouri friends don't suffer many hardships in addition to those already endured. Every device is used to annoy gentlemen, by the curs in charge of us, the ingenuity of the Devil is invoked to create disappointments for us, and to see if we cannot be killed by worry, and the mental tortures, to which we are daily subjected. "Curses, like chickens, come home to roost," and when the finale comes, Pierson will be as thoroughly sifted, as the article connected with him in our note.

In connection, we append the following from Captain F. A. Rogers,‡ of Coalbank, Cooper county, Missouri, whose veracity and integrity, none will question.

"After our exchange, December 15, 1862, two and a half months after your release, Joplin and myself went to Richmond, Virginia, and there for the first time learned from Mr. Seddon, Secretary of War, that I was a bushwhacker, bridge-burner, and out-law, and that Joplin was accused of holding a commission under the United States government, and at the same time serving in the Confederate States Army. The truth is, it was all a lie, and

---

* Captain F. A. Rogers, Coalbank, Cooper county. Missouri.
† Joplin resides in Myrtle Springs, Bowie county, Texas.
‡ The paragraph in relation to Captain Rogers, received since the war, is inserted for uniformity rather than noted.

only a pretext to hold us, to please some good Union man or personal enemy. Old sand sifter, had still a hankering after the almighty dollar, after you left, and at the time I left the island, he confiscated ten dollars, all the money I had, and positively refused to give it up; also some clothing, sent me by my friends in Baltimore. All the money passed through Pierson's hands, and he invariably retained a portion at the time. As to Pierson, I think a more contemptible scoundrel never breathed than that wretch. Captain Clarkson died in Texas, in the Fall of 1863. He was never well after his exchange, he was a noble man, and killed by *long confinement on Johnson's Island.*"

Regulations of the United States Military Prison, at Johnson's Island.

HEAD-QUARTERS HOFFMAN'S BATTALION, DEPARTMENT OF PRISONERS OF WAR, NEAR SANDUSKY, OHIO, March 1, 1862.

"*Order No. 1.*—It is designed to treat prisoners of war with all the kindness compatible with their condition, and to other ends, as few orders as possible will be issued respecting them, and their own comfort will be chiefly secured, by prompt and implicit obedience."

"*Order No. 2.*—The quarters have been erected at great expense, by the government, for the comfort of prisoners of war, the utmost caution should be used against fire, as in case of their destruction, the prisoners will be subjected to much exposure and suffering, for want of comfortable quarters, *as others will not be erected,* and rude shelter only provided."

"*Order No. 3.*—All prisoners are required to parade in their rooms, and answer to their names, half an hour after reveille, and at retreat."

"*Order No. 4.*—Meals will be taken at breakfast drum, dinner drum, and half an hour before retreat."

"*Order No. 5.*—Quarters must be thoroughly policed by 10 o'clock, in the morning."

"*Order No. 6.*—All prisoners will be required to remain

in their own quarters after retreat, except when they have occasion to visit the sinks, lights will be extinguished at "taps," and no fires will be allowed after that time."

"*Order No.* 7.—Quarrels and disorders of every kind strictly prohibited."

"*Order No.* 8.—Prisoners occupying officer's quarters in blocks 1, 2, 3 and 4, will not be permitted to visit the soldiers' quarters in blocks 5, 6, 7 and 8, nor go upon the grounds in their vicinity, nor beyond the line of stakes between the officers' and soldiers' quarters; nor will the soldiers be allowed to go upon the ground in the vincinity of the officers' quarters, or beyond the line of stakes between the officers' and soldiers' quarters."

"*Order No.* 9.—No prisoner will be allowed to loiter between the buildings, and the north and west fences, and they will be permitted north of the buildings, only when passing to and from the sinks, nor will they approach the fences anywhere else nearer than thirty feet, as the line is marked out by the stakes."

"*Order No.* 10.—Guards and sentinels will be required to fire upon all who violate the above orders. Prisoners will, therefore, bear them carefully in mind, and be governed by them, to forget under such circumstances is inexcusable, and may prove fatal."

By order of
WILLIAM S. PIERSON,
B. W. WELLS, LIEUT. AND POST ADJT.

(FOR THE AMUSEMENT OF MY FRIEND, COLONEL R. T. JOHNSON,* ONE OF TENNESSEE'S MOST DISTINGUISHED SOLDIERS, AND AS GENIAL AS HE IS GALLANT.)

"London befogged, drizzly London," have exclaimed all writers, since time immemorial. I had left the city of Brussels, on the 4 P. M. train, passed through Ghent, made famous by Froissart, and by the celebrated treaty at that place; thence to Calais, where I crossed the channel

---

* Colonel R. T. Johnson, (now 1868,) with Jno. K. Smith & Son, 47 Broad street, New York city.

to Dover, at this point twenty miles wide, always with a chopped sea, caused by the water from the Atlantic ocean and North sea commingling, a commotion that will make one sick, even has he passed the ordeal of an Atlantic voyage. Nauseated and wet Dover is reached, eighty miles, in two hours time locates you in London, and if you prefer it, at Morley's hotel, on Trafalgar Square, where the writer stopped. Morley's reminds one of a first class private residence, on Fifth Avenue, New York, and is far inferior to any of our leading hotels. After staying at this hotel a few days, you are satisfied, that while an Englishman's house is more home-like than an American's, they " can't keep a hotel." To form an idea of a stream of humanity, you must stand on London bridge, and see the moving mass, that rushes by like some mighty river. I gazed upon the current, my mind reverting to the nursery riddle, "As I walked over London bridge, etc." And while many, in wandering through Pall-Mall, and Oxford street, would dwell upon serious reflections, as o'er these same stones walked the bloody Richard, here strode the gallants of the rival houses of York and Lancaster, good Henry IV., or the lewed Henry VIII. I felt no such emotion, my thoughts were of Dickens and Oxford street, connected with the strand and Ludgate hill, wealth and poverty, State and dependence. Warren's "Ten thousand a year," with its Oxford street hero Tittlebat Titmouse, M. P., Dick Turpin and his many haunts, and his mare " Bess," flash over the mind, showing the effects of early reading upon the youthful imagination. From the bridge you pass to the tower, visit the cell of Sir Walter Raleigh, whose confinement lasted twelve years, depriving England of the services of one of her wisest citizens. There are many stories related of Sir Walter, only one of which we will relate in this connection. Being asked the weight of smoke, that had escaped from his cigar, he promptly called for a pair of scales, and weighing the ashes that had fallen from the tobacco and the part unsmoked, exclaimed, " the difference is the weight of the smoke." There are many cuttings on the walls of the cell, in Greek, Latin, French, and English,

in prose and verse, illustrating incidents in the lives of
the writers, who for centuries have been incarcerated
within its gloomy walls.   You slip a six-pence into the
hand of a burly English usher, who promises to show you
more than any one ever saw in the tower, directs you to
the spot where the Princes were found, murdered by the
bloody Richard; the "Traitor's gate," through which
prisoners were brought from the Thames to the tower;
you see the block the Queens were executed on, and
headsman's axe, the instruments of torture, etc., and wind
up, by visiting the crown jewels, the most prominent of
which is the "Kohinoor," or "Mountain of light," and a
world's wealth of various other gems, all encased in glass,
surrounded by an iron rail.   The female in charge, ex-
plains to you, and moves you 'round this vast treasure in
quick time.

   After sight-seeing until fatigued, you find yourself
outside the gate, and all your dreams of the past of the
tower's history, interrupted by the hoarse cry of "here's
your fresh fish," as the street, contiguous to the tower,
has many fish houses on it.   Even the tower, and its
associations, are lost in the din of trade.   St. Paul's
cathedral, and other sights are visited.   At last you con-
centrate on Westminster abbey, and here we meet another
incident, that seems but to have been one of many that
have encountered us all through life.   On approaching to
within some few hundred feet of the venerable pile, we
received the profound salutation of an individual, dressed
in a seedy suit of black, that had that powerful faculty of
reflection, so often seen in the habiliments of the professional man, whose briefs and prescriptions are limited.
A cap of the same transparent texture, sat jauntily upon
his head, his coat was buttoned close to the chin, not to
hide the absence of some garment, as vulgar curiosity
would suggest, but it seemed the style of the man.

   "You seem, sir, as if you would wish to examine the
noble building, that stands so eloquently before us, speaking with its ivy, and moss-covered turrets, in melancholy,
yet deeply interesting tones, as it refers to the past memories, to the hallowed associations, of church history, that

have cemented the past and present, in this hoary creation of past architectural solidity and taste, grace, and grandeur."

"You seem to be enthusiastic on the abbey, sir."

"Yes, sir, it is owing to my appreciation of the glories of Westminster abbey, that the corporation of London have made me the *outside* usher, to show strangers the beauty of the edifice, and as I daily examine its interesting details, I am more deeply impressed with the sublimity of the clouds of historical incidents, connected with the mortality, whose bones lie mouldering in sepulchres, that have leveled all distinctions, that finds the crown and coronet in close companionship. In that corner of the building reposes the remains of Queen Elizabeth, who with all her foibles, did much for "Merrie England," and although 'tis said she persecuted the beautiful Mary, it is possible that the sympathy of historians, for the peccadilloes of the Scottish Queen, enlisted them in her defence, and have done injustice to Queen 'Bess.'

"In that chapel lies Henry VIII., the English 'Bluebeard.' Yet he had his virtues. The place is full of memories, hallowed more by their historic associations, than by the impress they make on the fancy or imagination of the stranger. Now, sir, we are at the door of the abbey, and within you will find those who will show you the beauties of this ancient book of tomb histories, a description of which I have attempted from the *outside.*"

I hesitated a moment, and handed him a penny, at which he seemed delighted, and making a bow, that would have honored a prime minister, disappeared, leaving me impressed with the idea, that I had been taken in by a chevalier d'industrie, whose daily bread depended on tricks upon unsuspecting travelers. He took a bee-line for a gin shop, and I sought the damp retreats of Westminster abbey. I paused at the "poet's corner," and as that quaint inscription, "O, rare Ben. Johnson," attracted my attention, I could not but think, that in spite of fulsome epitaphs, all prose and poetry find a common grave. One chiseled effort of the sculptor, is a representation of the capture of Major Andre, by Paulding, Williams, and Van

Wirt, as we saw them in our school-books, in the act of examining boots, and etc., with the inscription beneath : "Beloved by his friends, and respected by his enemies." There is much to be seen in the old abbey, and one is puzzled to comprehend its vastness of past teachings, written in marble and stone, with decay palpably marked in their monumental records, as the end of all humanity, in their epitaphical vanities.

These slabs teach us that the man is dead. Philosophy, that he is not lost, but changed. How do we know but that in the transmogrification of particled humanity, that the decomposed matter of the Patriarchs may not now be the wealth of our gardens, and that the beet or cabbage may not once have entered into the composition of our ancestors. We leave the abbey and its curious collections, wending our way to our hotel, passing through the living stream, elbowing fish-women and shop-keepers, students and professors, all intent upon their own advancement, all with hopes of profit or preferment, all looking to the future; in many hearts that paints the "cottage by the brookside," the "old oaken bucket," and a quiet sleep 'neath the "drooping willow," when life's fitful fever is o'er. There are but few, however, who realize these fancies, perfect happiness is not decreed to man, he is to "earn his bread by the sweat of his brow ;" and when he does attain a day of peace, he "is cut down like a flower." I have rarely known a man to reach great pecuniary success in life, but that he was to suffer by family affliction. If a successful political gambler, he is apt to be poverty stricken. One is elected President, and loses an only son ; another is similarly elevated, a daughter perisheth. Men become suddenly rich, when some counteracting visitation, mars their joy.

Philip of Macedon understood this theory, who, on hearing of the success of Alexander, at the Olympic games, and his mounting Bucephalus, exclaimed: "Oh, that the Gods would make my afflictions light," for he knew that his joy must have some reacting sorrow. Families have their rise and fall, they have their periods of affluence, as well as decay. It is said, "the sons of the

rich die poor, those of the poor die rich." In view of all
these mutations of sense and time, with these evidences
that man is but a dreamer, and nine in ten are mono-
maniacs, for when one sees beyond the comprehension of
the mass he is insane to them. Why do we live so much
in the past, and court the fickle future, with its great
expectations? while we lose sight of the only reality in
life, the practical present. Living in the past, and a
hopeful future, are absurdities, and it is only in the
present that we can hope to accomplish the true object of
our being. Let us leave the past with its buried
memories, trusting the future to that Great Being, who
alone comprehends the mystery that envelopes the system
of which man is the representative head.

*Lieutenant Seymour, Tenth Tennessee Volunteers,
relates: "I was a commissioned officer in the British
army, and formed a part of the advance, that landed at
Eupatora, fifty miles from Balaklava, on September 14,
1854. The troops were debarked in five days, and on the
19th the line of march was taken for Balaklava. The
enemy were formed of an outpost of cavalry, supported by
a troop of Cossacks, and some heavy cavalry in their rear,
behind a range of hills. The Earl of Lucan, the General
commanding the entire brigade of cavalry, took some of
the Eighth and Eleventh Hussars, and Thirteenth Light
Dragoons, and moved towards the hill-top, where they
met heavy columns of the enemy's cavalry, with their skirmishers thrown out, awaiting their attack three-quarters of a
mile in front. The British advanced eight hundred yards at
a trot, halted and waited until their infantry came up, who
soon approached at double-quick, and formed, two hundred yards in rear of the cavalry, who advanced, throwing out skirmishers. The Russians had doubled their
numbers, and commenced firing. Our cavalry out of
range, did not reply. The enemy then advanced ten
guns, and opened on us at nine hundred yards. We lost
five or six men, before our horse artillery replied. Lord
Raglan did not wish to use his artillery at that moment,

---

* Tennyson has given the poetry, Seymour the prose of this action.

10

for fear of bringing on a general engagement, but it was
unavoidable, and the reply was made, upon which the
enemy retired behind the hills, extending their wings,
evidently attempting to out-flank us ; but in this manœu-
voring they used no guns, and our artillery opening on
them, after a few discharges, that went through and
through them, caused them to fall back to the next ridge,
and finally leave altogether. The next day was the
"Alma," they were intrenched fifty-five thousand strong,
with one hundred and ten guns. The cavalry did not participate in this action, it being left to the infantry to haul down
the old " Red Cross," or sustain it, which latter they did,
seeing it flaunt defiantly the next day three miles from
Sevastopol, on its victiorious way to Balaklava. We
camped in the valley of Kadokoi, about two miles from
Balaklava. We opened the first guns on Sevastopol on
the 17th of October ; on the 25th, it was rumored the
Russians were advancing in force by the Tada road, upon
Balaklava. The Turks had charge of the redoubts, and
I don't think they fired a shot at the advancing Russians,
who took the fort, and turned the guns upon our rascally
allies. Their cavalry, a dashing body of five thousand
horse, flushed with their success, came whooping and
wheeling o'er the plain, and right at the Ninty-third
Highlanders, under Sir Collin Campbell, the then only
regiment to dispute their advance, to the capture of all
our military stores, perhaps shipping, the certain occupation of Balaklava, and shutting us up in the plain, with a
mighty enemy in front, and on both sides, and the Black
sea in our rear; had they succeeded, the British army
were prisoners. On came their lances against the Nine-
ty-third, and when within pistol range, in went the front
rank fire of the Highlanders ; they reeled, and many a
saddle was emptied before they knew they were hit; in
went the rear rank volley, and before its smoke was lifted
off the regiment, our cavalry was at them by squadrons
of divisions, and after successive charges, they were forced
back. The Second Dragoon Guards and the Scotch
Greys, especially distinguished themselves, bravest where
all were brave. During the charges, Captain Lewis Nolen, of

the Fifteenth Hussars, brought an order from Lord Raglan,
I don't remember its precise tenor, but we were ordered
to retake the batteries lost by the Turks; they were
retaken. First Regulars, Scotch Greys, Enniskillen
Dragoons, with the Twelfth and Seventeenth Lancers,
formed the Light Brigade, the Earl of Cardigan at their
head. The Russians were retreating, but on discovering
our advance, formed line, and unlimbered their guns.
On dashed our light division, until they met the Russian
cavalry formed in four lines, but through them we went,
breaking line after line, and as their last line was broken,
our trumpets at this instant sounded the recall, giving
them time to reform their line, and at them we went
again, and now a murderous spectacle was witnessed:
the Russians seeing their splendid cavalry in a fair way
to be destroyed, let fly their artillery into the mingled
mass of friends and enemies. French troops were now
appearing on the field, and what was left of our fellows
responded to the recall, and rejoined our comrades; we
rode in seven hundred and four strong, and came out one
hundred and ninety-eight, but the guns were retaken.
Captain Nolen was killed early in the fight.

As an indication, of the courage displayed on this
occasion, I will relate an instance of individual heroism,
in the person of a soldier of the Twelfth Lancers. He
was surrounded by twenty Russians; they were in each
other's way, and couldn't catch him; somehow they were
thinned around him until five or six were left; he killed
them all; the last one was so near, he could not cut him,
so leaning back in his saddle, with his bridle-hand, hit
the Russian in the face, threw him backward in his saddle,
then gave him his point. He joined his regiment with
seventeen wounds."

The above charge, as related by Lieutenant Seymour,
is historical. The lieutenant is still an honorary member
of the regiment, and bears upon his person, many scars,
as proof of his participation in that terrible engagement.
With becoming modesty, like all brave men, he has not
alluded to himself, but the medals he wears are so many
evidences of the appreciation of his services and gallantry

in the Crimea, by the French and British governments. Lieutenant Seymour is a soldier, scholar and gentleman. The charge at Balaklava has only been equalled or excelled by that of the Punjaub, where they went in twelve hundred strong and came out seventeen.

I deem it due the connections of the poor fellows who have "shuffled off this mortal coil," leaving this busy and wicked world, and who have gone down to the cold and silent grave, amid the confusion, thoughtlessness, and devil-mi-care of prisoners, whose clammy brows have not been smoothed by the hand of affection, and whose visitation was not soothed by the presence of mother, wife, or sister, to relate the time and manner of their death, who died martyrs to liberty, the very Heavens must be amazed at "man's inhumanity to man." The poor prisoner, pining and agonizing on his couch, hoping a respite from the persecutions of his enemies, in one breath of the pure air of Heaven, without the cursed walls of his prison, is told no paroles are given to the sick, sinks back in anguish on his bed, that has now nearly worn him to the bone, and with his feelings lacerated, in his heart consigns to endless torment the oppressors, who in the name of liberty, are committing crimes that would put the savage to the blush. These men have died for their cause in prison, far from home and family, they have sank to rest with the restless waves of the fretful lake, lashing the shore of their resting place, and the sighing breeze, dirging sadly to their memories, as it disturbs the leaves of the scant forest, that barely shades the barren-looking grave of a gallant soldier, and a martyr to liberty.

Lieutenant R. M. Ray, Eighteenth Regiment, Tennessee Volunteers, died of typhoid fever, was an officer in good standing.

Private Wood was a member of Colonel Battel's Twentieth Tennessee Regiment, and brought his death by exposure, while attending to his sick comrades, at Mill's Spring.

Lieutenant Samuel A. Pearson, Company B, Thirtieth Tennessee Regiment Volunteers, was admitted into the hospital, June 23d; died July 6th, 1862, of typhoid fever.

Lieutenant R. A. Crow, Company B, Eleventh Arkansas Regiment, died in hospital, July 22d, 1862, of typhoid fever.

Captain J. R. Hodges, Fifty-first Regiment, Tennessee Volunteers, was admitted into the hospital July 6th, 1862, died July 24th, from inflammation of a wound in the leg, received in the Mexican War.

Captain L. M. McWhorter, of Company I, Third Mississippi, died July 29th, in hospital, of typhoid fever, after an illness of eighty-six days; his case was an extraordinary one, symptoms not well developed, suffered much.

The death of General Murray has been alluded to in another " scrap."

The above has been kindly furnished by Dr. H. L. Ray, assistant surgeon of our hospital.

THE BEST PIECE OF BAD POETRY EXTANT, BY LIEUTENANT BILL RUPERT.

(These lines were composed by a lieutenant of infantry, after much laborious investigation of the causes of his incarceration. The style is peculiar, pungent, and original. I give them unextolled, with all their beauties of metre and orthography.)

> "I John Chandas an English Knight
> Seneneshal of all Poictou
> Against the French King oft did fight
> On foot and horseback; many slew
> Bertrand du Guesclin prisoner too
> By me was taken in a vale.
> At Sussac did the foe prevail
> My body then at Mortimer
> In a new tomb my friends inter
> In the year of grace divine
> Thirteen hundred sixty-nine."

(SOMETHING LIKE THE LINES OF SIR JOHN CHANDAS.)

1

> " composed by a Renegade
> of the age of Twenty & Three
> who in the South drew his glittering Blade
> to fight for cotton and Liberty

2

" here is the story I have to tell
    it is of a Tremendous Bombardment
    whear meany Bums fell
    upon & around our encampment

3

" when the fight first begun
    the federals fired the first gun
    Dark and gloomy was the morn
    when comder foote blew his horn

4

" when the gun boats passd
    we thought it was our last
    Stormy & Dark was the night
    but we Brave Boys stood to fight

5

" our general thought it was no fun
    so he started on a run
    when w e Surrendered Island Ten
    the federals had ten Thousand men

6

" when the federals came on land
    they took in hand our little Band
    But we could not give them Bail
    So we were lodged in the Cairo Jail

7

" now the war has Just Begun
    I tell you Boy tis no fun
    But Brave comrads have no fear
    although we are pointed at with many a Jeer

8

" for our honest Jeff of the Southern clime
    will come with might & mein combined
    and with a strong & powerful hand
    he will lead us back to our native Land

9

" we Traveled to columbus
    by rail and umnibus
    then Col Moody a hard case
    closely confined us in camp chase

10

" from there to Johnson's Island
    where the winds are howling
    here we are a Thousand in all
    one rebel fell by a musket ball

11

" Old Major Pierson
a man without reason
Justiffed the Sentinal in his cruelty
for shooting a rebel for his Disloya'ty

12

" now Boys this will not Doo
friend ' Tid ' is it not True
it is a horrable Shame
for the feds a prisoner to mame

13

" if the federals will come South
many a one will bite the Dust
they will finde it is mighty hard
for them to conquer our Boregard

14

" now Boys I have finished my rime
I will tell you my name in good Time
It is a reble Bill Rupert
after this you will not consider me a fiert

15

" now my song it is complete
Gentlemen it is your Treat
my Drink it is of Brandy Sling
But I can Drink most anything

16

" Now we lye and wallow
But I am a Verry poor Scholar
But we will leave soon I am thinking
then we all will do our own Drinking "

The above, on the Sir John Chandas style, is presented in justice to its originality, as I feel there is but little
of our poetry that is genuine, it is mostly tributary to
the brain, and but little gushes from the fountain of true
and genuine poetry—the heart. I have known poets to
descant upon the virtues of society, and make appeals for
sobriety, and get intoxicated the same night. I have
known them to write the most moral lines on honesty,
confident at the same time they would rob a church. I
have seen their versification in print, on woman, as the
"fairest of her sex, "the weaker vessel," "soother of our
cares and sorrows," and yet stand the self-same day, on

a crowded thoroughfare and indulge in vulgarisms at the expense of the subject so colored in verse, of their brains creation. There is too much brain, and not enough heart, in modern poetry, too much of the huskster of song, and too little of the "troubadour."

The "Soldiers Tear," "Alice Gray," in song, are tame to-day, and Goldsmith and Gray are lost in the sensational steam-poetry of the hour. (These remarks don't apply strictly to the above poetry.)

Standing at my window, looking at the vessels moving to and fro, upon the broad bosom of the lake, with their treasures of cargo and life, their prows directed to the wild waste of waters, trusting to the same Providence that protects those on land, I often wonder why the same Providence has left the old Ship of State to the mercy of the surging waves of Abolitionism. Onward moves a splendid craft, the dim outlines of frowning clouds are ominously moving, yet the apparently staunch craft rides nervously on, rougher and fiercer become the billows, more threatening the thunder claps, the blast strikes her, she will not answer the helm, drags her anchor, and in a few moments more is upon the reef, it grows dark, she is no longer discernable. In the morning, what is left of her, is a wreck, the breakers madly leaping, with their white caps high in the air, against the shattered sides of the once strong vessel, that now creaks and strains, as each successive attack is made upon her now dismantled and helpless form, by the angry waves of the lake.

How much is involved in that little word—wreck, hopes, dreams, expectations, prospects, and schemes half accomplished, are buried with the wreck. The Union is a wreck, and the once noble ship, with its richly laden freights, has drifted into the sea of vicious politics, and been wrecked on the reefs of fanaticism.

St. Clair,* as we familiarly call him, is one of the most finished scholars in the pen; is a constant reader, and of much taste, is charming in conversation, and edifying in his literary offerings to his friends. Captain Morgan is a

---

* St. Clair Morgan was killed at Chickamauga. He was the son of Colonel Samuel Morgan, of Nashville, Tennessee.

gallant soldier, and a graduate of West Point—fired the first gun at Sumpter, since credited to Ruflin, of Virginia; was wounded in a duel at Pensacola, from which he yet suffers; was struck with a shell at Donaldson, at which engagement he was taken prisoner, carried to camp Chase, and from there to this pen, where he is the life of the campus.

The tailoring department of our prison, is an extensive one. We have two shops. Number one is presided over by Captain Samuel Graham, Company D, Fiftieth Tennessee Regiment, Lieutenant W. W. Wilson, Company F, Walker's Fortieth Tennessee Regiment, J. C. Walters, Company F, Twenty-Sixth Mississippi, First Lieutenant D. H. Hannah, Company D, Third Tennessee. The old saying that it "takes nine tailors to make a man," has been entirely disproved in this war, for some of our most gallant officers are of this department, and have proven themselves equal to nine Yankees, in all arms, cavalry, artillery and infantry. The business of this department amounts to about fifty dollars per day. There has been twelve hundred dollars spent for buttons to make rings, which are sold to prisoners as high as one dollar and a half each. Our shoemaker shop turns out three pairs of boots per week. The barber shop is constantly filled. We have an ice cream and lemonade establishment, whose net receipts are six dollars a day. Two pie establishments, and a ginger-cake department, under the control of a captain, who seems more affected by the fluctuations of flour, than the fortunes of the Confederacy. Two laundries, price of washing five cents per garment. The business of the post office, nine dollars per day. The entire summing up of our expenditures, four hundred dollars per day, quite a business tone for a population of one thousand one hundred and fifty souls.

The "Cincinnati Enquirer," of to-day, states that General Jeff Thompson sat upon horseback, in front of the Gayoso hotel, at Memphis, witnessing the naval engagement at that place. General Thompson was formerly Mayor of St. Joseph, Missouri. His Southern proclivities drove him into the swamps of his State, and with a command of

some hundreds of desperate Missourians, did much execution, and annoyed the Federal armies to a great degree.
He would make an excellent ranger-chief, but as to
generalship, he is too impulsive for a division commander.
The General is known by a yellow hat and white plume,
and a big Indian, (his aid,) always with him.

General Jeff Thompson is charged with being too
boisterous and hilarious. He may be, off duty. He is a
splendid judge of human nature, and understands how to
use it, as well as "oily gammon." In justice to the
Missourians in the pen, we must say that we know the
slur on General Thompson, in the "Cincinnati Enquirer,"
(in allusion to his sitting on horseback, while the fight
was progressing, if it questions his courage), to be a
puerile attack on a gallant officer, who has no ambition
but to serve the South.

This is the 26th day of June, 1862, and as per the daily
Sandusky papers, the "Island Queen" would, with a gay
party, steam around the bay slow, so as to give a fine view
of the prisoner's quarters. She is now passing, crowded,
with both sexes vieing with each other in displaying their
contempt for prisoners, whose fault has been opposition
to tyranny and despotism; for which so-called offense we
are brought here to be gazed at by a vulgar rabble, as if
we were caged hyenas. They would even stir us up with
a pole, if they dared, to see us growl, (perhaps bite.)
What a commentary on frail humanity, showing the utter
depravity of the human heart, the entire surrender of all
that is manly and generous in the soul, to gratify a mere
idle curiosity. Woman, she whose mission is one of love and
mercy, also throws her influence into the scale, and jeers
at the distressed. They are certainly not christians—if
so, I don't understand what it is to be a disciple of Christ.
If such people go to Heaven, the Universalist is correct,
there is no h—. The whole Abolition North is mad, and
will only awaken to their senses, when the South takes her
place through Democratic principles, as an independent
element of the country.

The "Island Queen" is passing out of sight, and
"Doodle" and "Columbia" are faintly heard in the

distance; as an Englishman says about the latter, I would not give a glass of "'alf and 'alf for an ogshead of 'ail Columbia.

Captain Graham, of the infantry, an aged rebel from Nashville, Tennessee, for many years chief of the tailoring corps in that city, proposes three groans for Beast Butler, which is promptly responded to with a will. They are out of sight, and the "Island Queen," with her living freight, is homeward bound for Cleveland. They will never see us, nor we them again. They will marry and die, and a majority of them may possibly go to the d—l.

It seems strange that a boat load of men and women, should consider it a pleasant excursion, witnessing the afflicted of humanity in some of their ("favorite acts.") Retreat sounds, and we go in.

The "Grape-vine line" of Johnson's island, alluded to in another "scrap," is one of the most remarkable on the island. It is under the control of men, whose reputation for creating expedients, are of camp-wide notoriety. They build up the most wonderful stories of speedy exchange, of paroles, of great victories by the Confederate arms, utter annihilation of Federal hosts, and the taking of thousands of prisoners. It has an agent in each mess, whose arrival with the latest news, is received with strained eye-balls, and palpitating hearts, every word of which is eagerly swallowed, because the wish is father to the thought, and hope is the strongest element in our nature, "lasting beyond the grave."

I think, the "grape-vine" line was a powerful agent, in assisting in developing the slumbering elements, that burst upon the country, with the inauguration of war. Legislatures were influenced by its action, it said that things were done, and said by whom, or for what. We will not say, but we can say, that the "grape-vine line" did much in bringing this bloody and fraternal strife upon the country. There are Southern, and true men, who know this to be a fact. The sutler, "Joe," is the Sandusky agent of the line, and is quite a character in his way. Captain Wiley is the chief, but "Joe" is the Friday of the establishment. "Joe" winks at you, and says, "It's all right," smuggles in a drop of the "*crater*," (an article that attracted the Irishman to the apex of Vesuvius,) and charges you double-price. But it's clever in Joseph. The sutler is the most important man on the island. He is required to sell at certain figures, which he does, but they are not low figures, (as figures don't lie.) "Joe," however, under their influence fibbing a little, but he is a clever fellow, (American,) and, for a sutler, is as honest as a sutler well can be. He has been kind and obliging to us, and has our heart's remembrance.

Adjutant G. M. Parker, of Mobile, the "roll-caller" of our mess, calls our roll for the purpose of facilitating the sergeant, who acts in that capacity; it is preferable to have it done by one you know. Heretofore, at roll-call, we all fell in line, in two ranks, a boy sergeant steps up in front of the line, and in a brusque manner, addressing a hundred gentlemen, "fall in boys, I'm in a hurry," showing a great wantof breeding. We are glad he has left us. Parker is ever in a good humor, and as chief of our mess, keeps posted on the details of daily labor, which is made daily from the rolls; four officers as cook and assistants, one to cook, one to bring water, and one to wash plates and cups. The keeping of colonels and other officers in proper domestic trim, is part of our adjutant's duty, and a gratuity on his part. Lieutenant Parker is a resident of twenty-five years standing, in Mobile, Alabama, of unquestioned integrity, of fine practical ideas, and withal, somewhat of a poet.

"To ———

"Were I but gifted with poetic fire,
    For you, dear ——, I would tune my lyre,
    And sing in Scott's or Milton's lofty strain,
    The scenes of death on Shiloh's bloody plain;
    Where the calm quiet of a Sabbath's morn
    Was startled by the battle's iron storm:
    Where Southrons fighting for their sunny land
    Met, and o'erthrew the mercenary band;
    Where many a hero found a bloody grave,
    And yielded up the life he freely gave,
    To check the hireling and to stay the tide
    Of hated Yankees, who in dreams of pride,
    Had thought to subjugate our people free,

Our happy land, the home of flowers and thee.
But —— mine is no poetic muse ;
It plods along, nor soars beyond the views
Of common mortals ; so in *rhyming* prose
I'll simply tell you I was one of those
Who 'gobeled up,' when fighting at the worst,
(Lieutenant in the glorious ' Twenty-first.'
Of Alabama's sons) have learned to feel
How sad—far from thy scenes-beloved Mobile
Is exile in a foreign—hostile land,
Far from the sorrowing, loving household band,
Who wait my coming, may it not be long
Ere I and your loved Father hear the song,
'Our country's free and ceased, rude war's alarms,'
Of joyful welcome to the loved-ones arms.

. Adjutant Parker has two mess-mates, his table being separate from the grand dining-room of the Hotel de Beauregard. Lieutenant Trepagnier, of the guard Francaise, of the Crescent city, who was captured at Shiloh, is like every pure blooded Frenchman I ever met, agreeable, witty, and courageous. Lieutenant John Daily, of the Thirteenth Louisiana, is the other member of the table. Being an associate of Parker's, is a sufficient recommendation to any circle, stamping him as an intelligent gentleman.

"Hark! what's that?" says an eager listener, as the deep bay of a blood-hound is borne to our ears, by the breeze from the lake. It is echoed in the yelp of the fox-hunter, until we almost cry "tally ho." Again the mew of a monstrosity of the feline species, in unison with the whine of its mate, now the bray of a long-eared animal, nearly breaks a pane of glass in our window, with its sonorous strength. Chanticleer is exhuberant, while his " better half " clucks. Braying, yelping and screeching, crowing and hooting, interspersed with cheering is making night hideous to our custodians, who, alive to any opportunity that will furnish them an excuse for shooting some of us, have sent in an officer, who, in gruff tones, orders the noise to cease, or the sentinels will be instructed to fire into the building, as the sepulchral voice of a sentinel near our window, has repeated the signal, " half past nine o'clock, and all's well," reminding us that in thirty minutes, "taps " will warn us to put out our lights.. This, in conjunction with the imperative orders of the officer, closes the jubilee, and the expressions of joy at the good news, is checked for the time being. The sentinels call the half hours, for the purpose, I presume, of keeping awake, which, if ineffectual, operate successfully with us. The prisoner's pulse has beat high to-day, a consequence of the supposed good news, letters from Washington. Reports relative to amicable adjustments, all tending to fasten this fancy upon the prisoner's mind, and bid him hope soon to be in the "happy land of Dixie." Bouyancy and exhilaration have been the order of the day ; the oxygen of the camp was as stimulating as a victory to our arms. Officers bought nick-nacks, satchels sold well. There was much talk of the difficulty of obtaining stationery in the South, and all were for taking a large supply. One selfish individual, who had purchased a quart of molasses, not being liberal enough to divide it, and too economical to throw it away, drank it all up, and a pain under his apron, was a consequence. The man subdued under the influence of his incarceration, and who has been on the penitential stool, now under the influence of speedy exchange, begins to allow the outer world to engross his thoughts. Magnificent schemes are dwelt upon, the deception of attempting to smuggle goods through that would sell at the South, at enormous profits, was canvassed. Glimmering of future military distinction, loomed up in some minds. Many took the "flattering unction to their souls," a speedy termination of the war, and a return to the communion of their household Gods. I hope all will realize their dreams, and that we may soon be exchanged. Good news is as a medicine, bad as depressing as disease. We have had good news to day, and new new life is infused into our heretofore despondent hearts.

There are long faces in prison to-day. Rumor states there is a hitch somewhere in the exchange business, that Wool and Huger have misunderstood each other. I look around the mess, and find the blue faces catching. Lieutenant Gassaway, of the Twenty-third Mississippi, generally in the best of spirits, and one of the best fellows in prison, has a countenance as long as the moral law.

Lieutenant Roberts, of the Third Mississippi, is sitting, pensively bent over his chair, with his chin resting on his hands, wanting to know if the Yankees havn't quit lying yet, and if the exchange business is all a humbug. J. C. Turner, of the Third Mississippi, is quite sober-sided, is pulling his beard with one hand, and holding a newspaper with the other, a fit picture, like many of us, for a comic almanac. Lieutenant Donoho, of the famous Tenth Tennessee, has taken his thoughts and gone to bed with them. Donoho is one of our geniuses, having a great amount of versatitity, being thorough in engineering and infantry, and has served an apprenticeship in some half dozen different pursuits. His associate in the mess, Lieutenant Barrett, of the Second Kentucky, is sitting by his bunk, whittling, and damns everybody that says a word against S. B. Buckner, and is confident that exchange will turn out all right. Lieutenant McAlpine has dropped in, for sympathy, and finds it in a game of "old sledge." Lieutenant J. Y. Moore and Captain Garrett, of the Third Mississippi, two of the best behaved gentlemen of our mess, are brooding over the bad news in a game of "draughts," and in their alternate successes, forget the checks to their speedy exchange. Other members of the mess are sleeping off their anxieties.

> "Nature's sweet restorer balmy sleep."

This great restorative is our only restorative, when all others fail. Lieutenant Daisey, of the Third Mississippi, one of the most sonscientious men we have in the mess, is nodding, with that great soporific, the New York "Herald," in his hand. Lieutenant Coleman, of Tennessee, our dry humorist, is not affected either way, says, he never will believe he is exchanged, until his foot presses the soil of "Dixie." Lieutenant A. B. Lewis, of the Third Mississippi, one of our most intelligent members, with a manly, yet unobtrusive manner, is solacing himself, in attempting to make a large ring out of a small button, a task as difficult as "squaring a circle." The member of our mess, who takes the news the most philosophically, is

Captain Grace, of the First A. T. and M. Regiment. He doesn't trouble himself in any way about exchange, he is taciturn, and a little moody, but not disagreeable. Grace is every inch a man, and has the respect of the mess. We are all blue to-day, and while condoling with each other, Lieutenant Duncan, of Grace's company, comes in, (having lately recovered from a severe illness,) remarking, "gentlemen, we have much to be thankful for; to-morrow the news may be better."

"'Tis education forms the *common* mind."

Man is a creature of habit, a victim to surrounding influences. Put a man in prison, and if it is his first experience, he is outrageous, that cure-all-time, gives him power to resolve into his former condition, habit, and he is resigned; but let the cause that produced the effects, that wound him up in prison, be brought to bear upon his apathetic condition, and his torpidity changes into restless energy, and if rebellious, becomes dangerous. In mess number three, in our prison, there is much of this rebellious element, that only requires exertion to arouse to a Vesuvian excitement, scattering plates, if not destruction, around; break up cups and saucers, if not the waters of the mighty depths of passion. The elementary character of block three, is combustible, being composed of electric *sparks*, (so the women say.) It has much dash, and is violently nervous. The mess has made character in our pen, by the somnambulism of one of its most active members, Captain D. T. Campbell, who has come nearer than "any other man," in the pen, in demonstrating how much a man can sleep without it's killing him. While Campbell has not invented perpetual motion, he has accomplished its "atipodal," perpetual sleep. But he may be like the Irishman's horse, who died from starvation, on the termination of the effect to live without eating. There are many visitors to see him daily, whose presence don't seem to disturb his somnolence. Campbell is the chief rebel in the mess, and is the father of the "*mess rebellion,*" agitating the question in his somnambulistic

moments, as well as in his somniloquistic. The cause of
the trouble in the mess, in which Captain Campbell and
Lieutenant McCaul are so deeply interested, is a supposed
innovation upon the rights and privileges of prisoners,
not laid down in "Vattel" or "Puffendorf." Our mess
has likewise caught the contagion, and there is a suppressed
grumbling. Two threatening faces look daggers at federal
officers. Lieutenant J. A. Connors, Twenty-Sixth
Mississippi, and Lieutenant R. S. Cox, same regiment, are
intensified by the news. They are amiable and modest
gentlemen, but decided in their characters, contemning
any action that cuts short their privileges, even in prison.
Unless the cause of the excitement abates, we will have
trouble. The cause being nothing more or less than an
embargo on spirits, our alcoholic imbibations had been
interdicted at camp Chase, by the terrific Moody, he,
who would, with the

> "Aid of God,
> And Governor Todd,
> Carry his flag to Dixie."

Moody suppressed our stimulants, yet we made no demonstrations. But it in this damp and heavy atmosphere,
stimulants had been a necessity, and the deprivation has
been a source of irritation and annoyance, culminating in
a disposition to "revolute." Education forming the common mind, reminds us that it is only on such minds, that
its potency is felt, as the world over "blood will tell,"
and the same rebellious blood, that makes a man a sinner,
that causes him to take up arms against "that old flag,"
and makes him rebel in prison, is proof that Nature will
express herself in spite of educational forms or checks.
The "common mind" only is developed by education;
education may assist it, but not remodel it. 'Tis only
the great mind that properly receives educational impressions, to all others, the acquisition is as useless as the
prattle of the parrot. The palaver about school and college, making mind, is all humbug, 'tis the same as the
tailor making the physique; the close observer easily
detects the padding in the ill-shaped form. Great men
are great, regardless of education or adornment.

11

A collegiate course seems to be a necessity, cramming and gorging, thus choking the brain. giving us weeds with the growth of intellect, causing the mind to be derivative, rather than original, as the student who is a slave to the ideas of others, finds them an absorbent of the few he may possess. Like most musicians, they are not composers, (although they think so,) they but arrange, taking one eigthth of Mozart, a sixteenth of Strauss, and a sixteenth of Handel, or fractions of other masters, whose ideas they have drank in during their course of study, and present the world, with what is supposed to be, an original effort. The same process of arrangement applies to all —literature, art, and science. There is not one artist in a host of so-called—he who creates, is one. The imitator is a mechanic, he who adds a shade or color of his own conception, should be classed among the former, while the exact imitator of the most beautiful specimen of art, should be classed among the latter. Art, as an original, is superior to mechanism, as a derivative, giving to the latter the benefit of educational forms. We call art beautiful, because the beautiful does not awaken desire. M. Cousin defines: "To desire the subject is proof that it is not beautiful. as 'tis only material and derivative, subjects that invite sensual desire, the beautiful is beyond the reach of vulgar emotion."

Education does not create Revolutions; they are the result of natural laws, one of which has been disturbed by the refusal of old "sand sifter," to allow spirits to come in, even for medicinal purposes, and my two gallant friends are morally in arms, indulging in the refrain-song of yore, by an old Negro, "Kit," of Memphis celebrity, who would drink a pint at a draught, enthusiastically singing:

> " Oh, whiskey, oh, whiskey, you very well know,
>   You have kicked, you have cuffed, you have laid me so low."

"'Nother drink, please, master."
There are not, in Tennessee, two more agreeable companions, than Messrs. Campbell and McCall, both being pre-eminent for courage and gentlemanly deportment, and

Arrival of Milk Man.

when they, chiefs of mess 3, say revolute, the "sans culotte" without the walls, had better rescind the order that is tending to promote discord, or Bacchus will be once more enthroned upon the debris of Johnson's island grapes, a cheaper process, than paying our meek and rascally steward two dollars a bottle for swill.

"Sourkrout's" arrival is heralded with unfeigned pleasure. He is our milk and vegetable vender. "Dutchy" has had the trade of the prison since our arrival, and, of course, is feathering his nest. I don't know that his milk is like the Dutchman's, who made his fortune selling half and half, and on his return to the Faderland, while counting his money on shipboard, the bag was seized by a monkey, and carried aloft. "Jacko" taking out the coins, and dropping one into the ocean and one on the deck, alternately. The Dutchman, when sympathised with, replied, "dat ish right, what come from the vater, he give to the vater."

This milk question reminds me of an incident, related to me by that prince of good fellows, and greatest living wag, Henry Dollis, of Memphis, Tennessee. A milk man, who furnished the steamboats with the lacteal fluid, was remonstrated with, on the thinness of his milk. He would hand the steward ten or twenty dollars, and the milk next day was thinner. At last an inspector came around, with a hydrometer, testing all milk sold on the river. The steward excitedly informed the milk man, that his milk only raised twenty-three—"what is requisite," twenty-seven. The next day the test was applied, it rose to thirty-two. "The heaviest milk I ever tested," says the inspector. "How did he do it, Dollis?" "Simply added one pint of molasses and another gallon of water, to the can that held four gallons mixed, with an additional twenty dollars." How can a man buy hay, and haul water, to dilute with, and sell pure milk? 'Tis impossible.

Our Dutch vender doesn't pour water in his milk, but milk in his water. He remarked to us, a few days ago, that his cow had calved the night before : dat de milk vas goot and strong for soltiers dis morning. "Hans" was in great distress on yesterday. He understood we

were to be exchanged, and with frantic ejaculations exclaimed, "Mein Gott, mein Gott, vat can I do if dese
brisoners leave; I usht gone and buy twenty more cows.
Mein Gott, mein Gott." I believe the old scoundrel
would keep us here for ten years, if he could make fifty
cents a day selling us milk. These Dutch are pretty
heavy on suffering humanity, particularly on secesh prisoners. Our Dutchman will get rich, selling us strong milk,
go to the Faderland, become a Burgmaster, and look upon
all milk venders with suspicion and disgust.

"Cans't thou administer to a mind deceased."

A good physician should know the power of mind over
matter, and treat the former as carefully as the latter.

When Jack Handy[*] goes into a sick chamber, with
his irresistible manner, he places his cane carefully in
the corner, his hat is then handed to the servant, his
gloves are carefully drawn, and if unexceptionable, are
placed upon the chair or stand, then the gay, yet accomplished Jack, shows his fine teeth, shakes his luxuriant, really handsome head of curly, coal-black hair, and
with a smile, the well dressed and fresh looking Jack
Handy approaches the bedside of the sufferer, who by
this time by the physician's tact has had time to recover
from his nervousness, caused by the announcement of his
arrival. The pillows had to be arranged, the coverlid
respread, a little cologne spread here and there, the relatives or friends take position near the patient, all is ready,
and when Jack reaches the patient's pulse, his little
studied arrangement has given him time to settle down
his pulse to a beat conformable with the action of the
disease. Jack looks at the patient's tongue, feels his
pulse, comprehends the diagnosis in an instant. If a
purgative is needed, he finds out whether the subject is
accustomed to calomel, oil, jallop, or magnesia, and then
if either has been the habit, the other acts more ready;

[*] Captain Handy died on his plantation, in Mississippi, 1867. Our friend is
gone were the stern alarm of war no longer affrights, nor the sound of "big
gate' attracts to the window, yet his ringing laugh is even now vibrating
through memory's corridors.

some are monomoniacs on " blue mass," others on salts. Jack Handy is *aufait* on these distinctions, and from the fact of being a fine judge of human nature, is a fine physician, can tell a yarn with a better grace, and laugh more heartily at its detection, than any man living, is one of the proprietors of the " grape-vine line " and " prison telegraph." He was captured at Fort Donaldson.

Dr. Woodbridge, although a loyal citizen of the United States, is worthy of remembrance by myself and fellow-prisoners, as a kind, considerate and humane officer, and like his good wife, has much of the milk of human kindness in his composition. He has been quite attentive to our wants, and has our grateful acknowledgments.

Some eschew medicine, and take their text with Shakespeare, " throw physic to the dogs, I'll none of it." This is well when men are in good health, but when ill, obtain a good physician, a man of science, not a charlatan or quack one, of will, strong perceptive faculties, tact, and address. "An ounce of prevention is worth a pound of cure," is trite, but does not justify an individual in continually dosing himself with ounces, aforesaid, hoping thereby to ignore a necessity for pounds. The Italian tombstone has it, " I was well, wanted to be better, here I am." It is like a man beginning with *scruples* and winding up with *drams*.

Many depreciate the use of medicine. This is wrong. If we lived like the Aborigines, hunted, slew, and cooked, the food we eat, drank of the limpid stream, and were in constant action, then we might have no use for medicine, but when we live artificially, eat late suppers, surfeit on grand dinners, make swill-tubs of our stomachs, dram-shop signs of our proboscees, all tending to keep our minds constantly irritated by ideas foreign to our happiness, it seems plain enough that these artificial diseases require artificial remedies, hence the necessity for the physician. of which class, we have seventeen in our prison, many of whom are among the most eminent surgeons of the South.

Dr. J. M. Jackson, surgeon of the Forty-second Tennessee Regiment, has immediate charge of the hospital, and is a man of great force of volition, and of a high order of surgical talent, a deep thinker, and of strictly temperate habits.

Dr. Joseph E. Dixon, of the Tennessee Battalion, is of much nobility, acts and thinks simultaneously, of unflinching nerve, a polished gentleman, showing the usage of good society.

Dr. F. Grant, Thirty-second Tennessee, is a quiet gentleman, and from his care and nicety of arrangement, will make an excellent family physician, one who will inspire confidence in a sick chamber with his calm presence and positive treatment.

Dr. A. H. Voorhies. Nature made Voorhies a surgeon and physician. Education and commingling with the best society has formed him a gentleman. His quiet deportment and impressive urbanity, would assuage much of the severity of his patient's affliction.

Dr. J. M. Taylor, Twenty-sixth Mississippi, an able practitioner, and well-informed gentleman.

Dr. O. Becker, a gentleman of versatile accomplishments, a fine musician and composer, and a man of science. Dr. Becker, although a foreigner, is enthusiastic in the support of the Confederate cause.

Assistant Surgeons, Thomas M. Nichols, Ninth Battalion ; J. J. Dumont, Fiftieth Tennessee ; W. B. Mills, Fiftieth Tennessee ; J. J. Mills, Twentieth Mississippi ; M. S. Neely, —— Tennessee : N. J. Rogers, Twenty-sixth Mississippi ; W. G. Owens, Graves' Battalion, Tennessee : H. Griffin, Fiftieth Virginia ; B. M. Croxton, Graves' Battalion ; C. H. Edwards, Thirtieth Tennessee. The above surgeons and assistant surgeons are men whose proclivities for the excitement of camp and field have led them to enter the army ; a fine opportunity being thus furnished for the development science. A large number of amputations, and the various characters of wounds and contusions that are under constant treatment, are fine subjects aiding the cultivation of new systems that will tend to the amelioration of pain, and present more cases and experiences to the world of medicine. It is a melancholy spectacle presented to the world—the present war—the meeting of Greek with

Greek, yet "it is an ill wind that blows nobody any good," and amid all the sufferings and horrors of war, the field of medical science is being opened and expanded, thus benefitting future generations. Yet I question very much, whether the returned surgeon from the field of quick and, too often, careless amputations, is as fit as the regular home practitioner, to attend the duties of private practice (for the time being.)

To-day we learn, the surgeons are to be released unconditionally. This is a move in the right direction. Although a deprivation to us, 'twill be but a sheer act of justice to them.

In walking along the street, how frequently one becomes lost to the external world of sense and materiality, and feeds upon his own thoughts, how often in stepping on a pebble, you have felt an irresistible desire to kick it ahead of you, and if it should fall towards the curbing, a feeling of anxiety springs up, to keep it in its place on the pave, and you will follow it up, kicking at it until an unlucky kick sends it into the gutter, then you feel an indiscribable relief, and your ideas become more alive to passing events. Have you not, in promenading, musingly began to count your steps, guessing how many it would take to reach a certain point, and on nearing the goal, seeing you have improperly guessed the distance, rushed eagerly forward, lengthening the steps, or if you to near, shortening them, with as much interest as if a kingdom was at stake? The illustration is simple, but is given to show the perfect simplicity of that mind, so much boasted of by the "lords of creation, its imperfections, and one-ideaism.

We are all weak by nature, and the boasted individual strength is not the result of acquisition, but a constitutional virtue, and much to be pitied, are the unfortunate, who have suffered from poverty and pernicious example. The Cyprian on the one hand, and the Roue on the other, are objects of commiseration. Much of the opprobrium and epithetical denunciations hurled upon the erring, by those who circumstances have placed them above the want of vice, will, like most curses, (chicken-like,) come home to roost. We should pity and reclaim, not decry, and give up : should sympathize with and protect, not "turn the cold shoulder" to the weak and guilty, but take them by the hand, in the bonds of friendship, love and truth, knowing the mutability of man, and his many frailties.

In ruminating on our promenades, with the great volume of the "genus homo" open before us, we are forcibly impressed, with the spirit of the musings spoken of, and are not disposed to "crowd." Now there passes a soldier from a certain village until he left it, it supplied his conceptions of all that is beautiful ; he goes to a larger place, and finds, alone by comparison, the insignificance of his former home, and feels that he has reached the Mecca of his hopes ; thence to a metropolis, again his ideas change, and he conforms to the tastes and habits of others—proving himself an inconsistent creature of change, not realizing, "that pigmies are pigmies, tho' perched on Alps, and pyramids are pyramides in vales." Such a man is the creation of the hour, was my enemy of yesterday, perhaps my friend to-day, and possibly my reviler to-morrow. He became a soldier because Jim and John joined, is burning for distinction, but when in close quarters, thinks it judicious to retreat ; when captured, gets intimate with the enemy, will soon take the oath, go home, and in a week afterwards, would desire to be in the field again, from habit, to which all common minds bear slavish allegiance ; he is not to be blamed, but he with others such in prison, are weak brothers.

The Catholic church comprehends this weakness of man, and startles the imagination with its pomp and pageantry. The Methodist church follows, with the enthusiasm of its revival. France understands the susceptibility of man, and touches with its military wand, the pride and circumstance of war : and a magnificient army, with its splendid paraphernalia, strikes with wonder, the imagination of the gazing multitude. Since time immemorial, the world has studied to impress the imagination of man, as 'tis one of his weakest points. Columbus broke his egg for effect, so did Alexander cut the "gordian knot," as he also rode "Bucephalus." The

"tub" of Diogenes was also of similar device, as were the
Delphic oracles. The Persian poet, Sadi, went bare-
footed to accomplished the same end, and like our chief
custodian, wears a white cravat, to impress with his
sanctity, while he maltreats prisoners, 'tis all a
species of quackery, reminding us of the anecdote of the
quack, who, while riding in his carriage, was accosted
by an eminent surgeon of the old school:

"How is it you succeed by imposture, while we of the
regular profession, well nigh starve?"

"Easy enough, forsooth; do you see that crowd of a
hundred persons? In it there are ninety fools, and ten
wise men, the former are my patients, the latter yours,
and as a rule, the fools have the most money."

Placards and the teeming columns of the press, attract
the attention, and the bumps of the marvelous and
imaginative are tapped, and success follows. Barnum is
a practical illustration of what use can be made of man's
imagination, as he has humbugged them from "mermaids"
to "gorillas." In church and state, social and political
life, it is all the same, all action seems predicated on the
weakness of humanity. The true secret of happiness is
to accept these truths, but not to abuse the knowledge
they impart. Don't force your weaker brother into forbidden paths, be kind to him, and if he wont conform to
you, do like Mahomet, "if the mountain will not come to
Mahomet, Mahomet will go to the mountain." Let us
emulate that part of his wisdom, even if we cannot accept the romance of the Koran.

"Kick not against the pricks," but be susceptible, be
"taken in" once and a while, you will feel better, have
confidence and faith, and as you pass your erring brother
or sister, have compassion, let mercy linger 'round your
heart. Flee bigotry, that most abominable of sins, that
seems to be enthroned in the very soul of Abolitionism,
so graphically described by Charles Phillips, "The Abolition preacher or bigot:"

"He has no head, he cannot think,
  No heart, he cannot feel ;
  When he moves, it is in wrath,
  When he pauses, 'tis amidst ruin.
  His prayers are curses, his communion death ;
  His decalouge is written in the blood of his murdered victims ;
  And if he pauses, for an instant, in his infernal flight,
  It is to whet his fangs upon some kindred rock,
  To prepare for some more sanguinary desolation."

How much happier is that condition, where the people
are influenced by teachings of "peace and good-will to
all mankind," who evince a superiority of soul in bend-
ing to the necessities of man's defects ; that feels that as
the man allows his attention to be engrossed by the
pebble on the pave, so will he be sensitively alive, to the
externals of kindness, charity and affection, he will be a
child, acting and thinking like one ; make him so, and you
prepare him for Heaven, for such is the kingdom, and
thus win a Heavenly crown for yourself.

We call some thirty-five or forty, (it may be fifty,)
prisoners, a batch ; one or two hundred would be an
arrival, a squad we hardly notice. The prisoners alluded
to, of North Carolina and Georgia volunteers, was quite
an event, and we compliment them with the title of an
"arrival." They came in, attracting much attention, by
their fine bearing, handsome uniforms, and general
martial appearance, and as a whole, are the best looking
"crowd" that have honored us with their presence.
Among them we notice some of the best blood of the
Carolinas, and brightest intellects of Georgia, whose
gallantry on the field—if we had space for incidents—
would cause a glow of pride to rise to the cheek of every
lover of the South, and heroic deeds. As in all wars,
where renown is to be gained by acts of chivalry, so in
this, the Celtic element is found, one of whose brightest
ornaments stands before us, six feet, two inches in height,
standing as firm as Roderick Dhu, is Lieutenant Christopher Hussey, of the Montgomery Guards, of Savannah,
Georgia. He was born in Ireland, in 1820, arrived in
Georgia, 1841, became thoroughly Southern, and entered the service of the Confederate States, to aid in

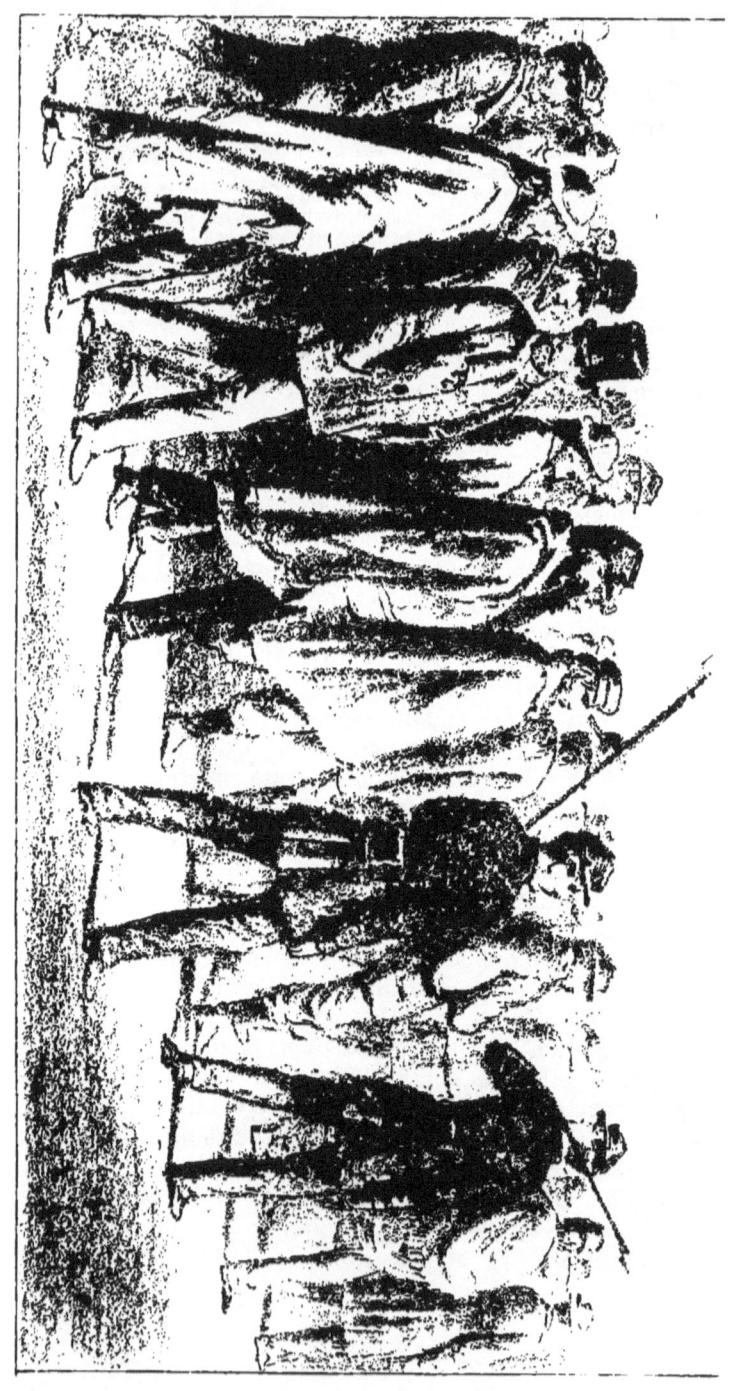

checking the encroachments of a fanatical domination, whom, he says, will entail the same miseries upon the South, that their parent, that accursed despotism, has inflicted Ireland with. Lieutenant Hussey was captured at Fort Pulaski, April 11th, 1862.

Colonel H. Olmstead, First Volunteer Regiment of Georgia. This gallant officer's defense of Fort Pulaski, is a matter of history; he is a gentleman, in or out of prison; like all brave men, he is a lamb in peace, in war, a lion. Colonel C. M. Avery, Thirty-third Regiment, North Carolina Troops. Colonel Avery is one of your grand, old-fashioned North Carolina gentlemen, representing a large landed estate. He espoused the Southern cause, strictly in a spirit of patriotism, and one can see from his manly appearance, the stern and inflexible patriot. He is resigned to his situation, yet is anxious to be once again at the head of his regiment, that is now with North Carolina, gallantly assisting in driving the invader from their hearths. North Carolina may well be proud of her representative in prison, as few circles are adorned with a brighter social element, than the noble Avery.

Major John Foley, First Georgia Volunteers, is a native of Ireland, and having suffered from English oppression in that country, has drawn his sword in defense of the South, to save her from the degraded condition of his own down-trodden "Green Isle." He is a gallant Irishman, with the generosity and courage so characteristic of his race. Captain F. W. Simms, of same regiment. Captain Simms is one of the most sprightly intellects in prison, has been connected with the press of Georgia for years, and to his pen we are indebted for many substantial articles, in defense of Southern interests. Among the other distinguished officers present, are H. C. Freeman, first lieutenant, Oglethrope Light Infantry; J. D. N. Sutton, second lieutenant, Wise Guard, formerly of Wise Legion, transferred to the Twenty-fifth Regiment, Georgia Volunteers, December 7, 1861, thence to First Volunteer Regiment of Georgia, February 11, 1862; Second Lieutenant A. G. McArthur,

Washington Volunteer Regiment, Georgia: George W.
Tennet, engineer corps, Confederate States Navy;
Lieutenant Charles H. H. Umbrock, First Georgia;
Lieutenanant John J. Symons, First Georgia; Captain
Robert D. Walker, Confederate States Army, of Georgia;
Captain R. W. Brown, Eighteenth North Carolina,
captured at Hanover Court House, a gentleman whose
heart is in his hand, and one of the best behaved gentlemen in prison, an ornament to the service, and a social
treasure to his friends. Second Lieutenant B. Werner, .
First Georgia. Werner, like our friend Umbrock, is
German. The Americans are too prone to call every
German a d—d Dutchman. The Dutch come from a
very small district, whereas Germany is composed of
thirty-eight States, that have given us a host of eminent
painters, lawyers, theologians, historians and mechanics,
comprising a citizenship, that we are glad to welcome to
our own shores, among which class, our two friends occupy
an enviable social position. Mathew H. Hopkins, First
Georgia; Robert Erwin, captain and quarter-master,
Confederate States Army; John A. Blaine, second lieutenant, Twenty-fifth Georgia; T. W. Manniford, same
regiment; Samuel D. Zane, lieutenant, same regiment,
captured at Hanover Court House, May 27, 1862; N.
Bohannon, first lieutenant, Twenty-eighth Regiment,
North Carolina Volunteers; J. W. Vinson, second lieu-
tenant, North Carolina Volunteers, captured at New-
bern, North Carolina, March 14, 1862; Lieutenant R.
L. Steele, Thirty-seventh Regiment, North Carolina
Volunteers; J. N. Anderson, second lieutenant, Thirty-
third Regiment, North Carolina Volunteers; Lieutenant
Christopher Murphy, Captain J. M. McMahon, First
Georgia, captured at Fort Pulaski, April 11, 1862;
Captain T. W. Mayhew, Thirty-third Regiment, North
Carolina Volunteers; S. W. Stowe, captain, Twenty-
eighth North Carolina Volunteers; Captain Oscar R.
Rand, Twenty-sixth North Carolina Volunteers; M. T.
Farthing, captain, Thirty-seventh North Carolina Vol-
unteers; First Lieutenant R. C. Hauser, Thirty-third
North Carolina Volunteers; Lieutenant J. S. Eggars,

37th North Carolina Volunteers; Lieutenant William A. Stewart, Thirty-Seventh North Carolina; Lieutenant C. Scott, Twenty-eighth North Carolina Volunteers: Lieutenant John Baily, Company B, Chalmette Rifles, Fifth Louisiana Volunteers, captured on the Chickahominy, May 24, 1862. I have given an extended notice of the gentlemen mentioned, having been attracted to them by their high-toned deportment, and soldierly bearing.

Our prison has seemed more cheerful, since their arrival. They have an excellent club of amateur musicians, who enliven our moonlight nights, with the guitar and flute. Their good behavior is of general comment, and they are welcome to our pen.

CHAPTER VI.

_____

CROSSING from New York to Brooklyn, some years
ago, I met with one of those incidents, that often
occur to travelers, and by which they are taught to see
the necessity, for always being on the look-out for swin-
dlers. The incident, however, to which I allude, was one
of much service to me, and by which I acquired more
information, at less expense, than is usually the fortune
with susceptible gentlemen, who too frequently travel with
more money than brains, and who are generally genial
and familiar, not realizing that familiarity with superiors
is indiscreet, with inferiors to suffer an indignity, and it
is a difficult matter, to select your equals in a jostling,
moving crowd. I had reached the middle of the ferry,
when a venerable looking gentleman, encased in a seedy
suit of black, with white cravat, and a portfolio under his
arm, accosted me, in a bland, persuasive manner:

"Lovely day, sir."

"Yes."

"Ah, from the South."

"Yes, sir. Why do you think so?"

"You speak broader than we do, sir. I hope, sir, you
will excuse this intrusion, but knowing the literary taste
of the South, I always endeavor to make my largest list
of subscribers represent that section, which we of the

North, who are debarred its enchanting domain, look upon as the promised land."

" You are complimentary, sir."

" Ah, no; the South is the future base of operations, for this progressive continent. She has an area of territory, less some few hundred miles, equal to our own. Look at Texas, six times larger than the State you are now in. Can you imagine the future of such a territorial power? Give her the ratio of population to the square mile, that we find in Belgium, four hundred, and what an empire you make of the 'lone star State.' Of the three thousand millions of production, forty-five per cent. is Southern, sixty per cent. of the exports of the country are from the same source. The importations of the country, a great part of which is for Southern consumption, only ten per cent. of it is introduced through Southern ports. We in the North have everything in our own hands. We import for you, and export for you, make your wardrobe and your toilet, which should impress you with the fact, that producing regions are always in a state of vassalage to their trading neighbors, of amanufacturing, shipping, and mechanical interest North, as is exhibited in revolutionary Mexico, the West Indies, and Brazil. And it seems strange, that with so complete a theory, as when you bring the producer and consumer together, you realize the last, which is the greatest price, to the former, the latter obtaining his supplies at the first, which is the least price, that your section will not endeavor to establish a commercial chain, uniting you to the continent of Europe. You have had the political influence of Congress, of the Cabinet, and of foreign representation, and you have accomplished nothing, and why? because, while you have had power, you have not preserved its balance, which is trade, which resolves into interest, and ultimately into a balance of political power. The sails of England dot every collection of water between the poles. Her commercial drum follows the sun. Look at her efforts in our own country, granting subsidies to steamship lines, for trade purposes, one item, in particular, of eight thousand dollars per trip, to the Montreal and Liverpool line of steamers. The legislation of the English government, is identical with the commercial prosperity of the country, the strength of her monarchy, the wisdom of her aristocracy, are united with her honest democracy, on trade questions, if no other. She has profited by the experience of the 'Hanseatic League,' and other past lights of the commercial world, and is now reaping the benefits, derived from a proper consideration of this powerful element, in a nation's prosperity.

"In 1820, we inaugurated a system of manufacturing, that has grown to a consumption of nearly a million bales of cotton, thus driving out the English supply of heavy cottons. Our 'Globe,' 'Dunnel,' 'Sprague,' 'Merrimac,' and other prints, compete successfully with those of Great Britain. John Bull is aware of our competing progress, and trembles for his prestige on this continent.

"England is a great power, and must be watched, as the influences of Exeter Hall lights, that shine in the befogged atmosphere of London, will spare no means to accomplish the object she has in view. She has no attachment for America, her sympathies are with the North, through commercial alliances, and she will sacrifice all, North and South, to benefit her trade. Proving to us, as she has to the rest of the world, that she is the commercial Jesuit of the nineteenth century. Let us see what this most christian nation, "so called," has done to attempt the destruction of our country, she emancipated the slaves in the West Indies, not from the mere considerations, but for the effect it would have upon the institution in this country, in attracting the masses of Europe to a contemplation of the subject. Finding that this process was too slow, she attempted the destruction of our cotton interests, by introducing its cultivation in the East Indies, hoping that cheap labor would equalize uncertain crops and defective staple, and by underselling dethrone King Cotton in America, in all of which she has signally failed. I have the proof that every pound of cotton, raised in the East Indies, from 1840 to 1850, cost the British Government one guinea per pound, yet she continues her efforts, and from the year 1800 to the present time, no half dozen successive, regular crops, have been produced in the East

Indies. One season 35,000,000 pounds, another 80,000,000 pounds, another 240,000,000 pounds, then back to 120,-000,000 pounds, then again up to 400,000,000 pounds, until at last she has attained 1,500,000,000 or 2,000,-000,000 pounds, (these figures are approximating ones.) With such an irregular production, it is impossible for her spinners to anticipate orders, and they must wait until the crop of the Indies is ascertained, and hence must look to the South for their regular supply. All political economists know that the cotton area is within parallel, 30 and 35 degrees, is a belt 2,000 miles long and 240 miles wide, extending from the Atlantic to the Pacific, and out of these limits cotton can not be raised in perfection. Indian, African, and Brazilian efforts will prove fruitless, and the whole world must ultimately look to the South for its supply of cotton. It may seem strange at first glance that cotton is so local in its attachments, but the same rule, it will be found, will apply to all valuable products. Tea comes from China, the best coffee from Java, Mocha, and Rio, the best wines from France, a peculiar kind from Madeira, Holland for gin, England for beer, Brazil for diamonds, Mexico for silver, California for gold, each in their places, have their own specialities of production and manufacture, convincing us that it is the object of creation, that all shall be dependent, yet harmonious, and that the demand of one shall be answered by a supply from the other. We see it in our own country, certain States produce cotton, Louisiana produces sugar, South Carolina produces rice, and Virginia produces tobacco. It is strictly a law of nature that makes man a dependant, either as an individual, or in a national sense, and this dependence is most palpable, when affected by the laws of trade which are as fixed as those of the "Medes and Persians." Cotton is not King, but trade is, and until the South takes the commercial interest of her people more to heart, ceases to think of political progression and the self-aggrandizement of leaders, she will never compete with the North, who have the numerical strength, and balance of trade, which you now understand is the balance of power, and if the South does succeed in

12

breaking the chain, that now binds her, she will be merely transferred to another state of vassalage, having her commercial shackles forged by the hands of France and England. The South can only escape these dangers, by wise and prompt commercial legislation. Am I right, sir ?"

I answered, "Yes, to a certain degree," somewhat impressed with the old gentleman's reasoning, but the South has ever looked to New York city, as the "Mecca" of her merchants, Saratoga and Cape May, have been her "Spa," and "Baden Baden," and so potent are these influences when exerted on our people, that should a war break out between the sections to-morrow, and continue five years, one year after its cessation southern merchants would buy dry goods in New York or Philadelphia, brogans in Boston, soap, whiskey and candles in Cincinnati,* all owing to the capital of the North, which enables them to grant long credits. The planter makes a good crop, his surplus is invested in Negroes, the northern man places his profits in trade, and holds the lever, by which he moves the commercial interests of the country, to his own enriching. The south is not energetic enough, she is too much afraid of stocks and improvements, and does not seem to study political economy as faithfully as she does political histories, however, better days may come, when the South, true to herself, she will arise from her lethargic state, and occupy the true position nature has intended her, that of an independent producing region, and if dependent, it is from choice, not from necessity. At this point in the conversation we neared the wharf, when the old gentleman renewed his original subject, informing me he had expended, and the greater portion of his life, in compiling the work aforesaid, that he was so zealous in distributing, and he felt confident, that from his past success, he would meet with sufficient patronage in the future, to justify his efforts,

He referred me to his list of subscribers, in which figured foreigners of distinction, senators, and diplomats, and hoped to have the pleasure of adding my name to the

---

* The war is over, and the author's prediction is verified. "They" do buy soap, whiskey, and candles, in Cincinnati. The laws of trade are among the most immutable of all material matters.

list. I responded, by ordering two copies, which seemed to please my venerable book-agent, who remarked, as we stepped upon the shore, with a smile, that seemed to indicate an innate virtue in the man, "Shall I mark you paid in advance." I was dumbfounded, and could not avoid the not classical answer, "nary time," and we both disappeared in the crowd. Suppose he tried one hundred persons a day, and met with one success, it was ample remuneration, as the subscription price to this mythical work was five dollars. He taught me much in relation to the duties of the South, and, I think, he deserved the five, although his object was to swindle me.

The Zouave squad, at Johnson's island, was composed of six of the most chivalric denizens of that lovely isle. It was the intention of the gentlemen, comprising the nucleus of this formitable coalition, to have organized a corps, rivalling Billy Wilson's "*Roughs*," or Ellsworth's "pets" in drill, but circumstances have altered the programme. As comparisons are odious, I will not accord to any individual, the distinguished honor of fathering this organization, but merely give the names of the members, as I found them. M. Burke,* (spoken of in another "scrap,") whose war-cry was "Faugh, a ballah." Lieutenant John Morton,† of artillery. Lieutenant Morton is

---

* M. Burke, the last I saw of him was on the deck of a Mississippi steamer, amusing himself in assisting to "wood."

† Captain John W. Morton, from his release to the close of the war, performed the part of a gallant soldier. Modest, unassuming, and courageous, he was the most perfect specimen of the soldier and gentleman, the war produced. The following letter, from one who *knew him well*, is attached to show, that "Bedford" Forrest never mistook his man:

"HEAD-QUARTERS, MILITARY DEPARTMENT FORREST'S CAVALRY CORPS.}
"GAINSVILLE, ALABAMA, May 10, 1863. }

"DEAR SIR:—It affords me pleasure, to report the following to you of the conduct of your son, Captain John W. Morton, Jr.

"He was ordered to report to me for duty by General Bragg, to take charge of my Horse Artillery, in November, 1862. His appearance was so youthful, and form so frail, (wishing stout, active men for my service,) I at first hesitated to receive him, but coming so well recommended by Colonel Hollenquert, General Bragg's chief of artillery; Major Graves, General Breckenridge's chief of artillery, and others, I concluded to try him; having learned he was first lieutenant of 'Porter's' famous Tennessee battery, which surrendered at Fort Donaldson, February 16th, 1862; was highly complimented by General Buckner in his official report, and received from General Buckner the high appallation of 'gallant Lieutenant Morton, our heartless boy.'

"I gave him command of a section of artillery, and moved with my first raid into West Tennessee, in December, 1862, and soon captured other guns,

from Nashville, Tennessee, son of Dr. Morton, a most distinguished physicians of that city. He is one of the most perfect gentlemen in prison, the soul of honor, and one of the most promising officers in the army. The Zouaves supposed that "Johnny Morton" would make a good member. Sanders Sale is also of the artillery, was wounded at Donaldson, is a brave soldier, and of a character to make friends and enemies. Captain A. S. Levy is a South Carolinian, whose character is given in another " scrap:" Captain Farabee, who is also mentioned in another " scrap." The above gallant gentlemen, with the author, formed the Zouave squad.

We began our first offensive operations, on the night of the 27th of May, 1862. The night was happily adapted to our peculiar performance, the rain poured, the darkness was profound and impenetrable. Our uniform and out-fit was characteristic of the night's movements: three coats, to keep us dry ; crackers, to appease the stomach's cravings : a hatchet, to keep off " cerulean apparitions," that might confront us ; and with a saw, rope, and a bottle of cognac, to fortify with, we moved to the front. But, to be serious, our little party of six were in prison, and anxious to escape. We had prepared to saw out, and had, as we supposed, arranged things to perfection. Our programme was, as follows : Burke took the lead, with the saw, having us in communication, by a rope, which he was to pull, as soon as the sawing was completed. The cause of our being called Zou-zou's, is attributed to John Morton, who, on being instructed by his uncle, Lieutenant Banks, (a highly

---

and placed him in command of the battery; and during this expedition, the gallant and efficient manner in which he handled his guns, won my confidence and esteem. He has been constantly with me since, in all my engagements, never absent from his post of duty, apparently happier when in the thickest of the fight. He has held with great credit, for twelve months past, the position of chief of artillery of my corps. By his soldierly bearing, generous disposition, affable manners, strict attention to duty and the welfare of his men, uniform and true gallantry on so many fields, has made him many friends, and you may justly be proud of such a son. He was with the troops of this department, surrendered his 'old' battery, one of the best equipped and finest in the service.

"I deeply sympathize with him, and wish him much success and happiness in any vocation in after life.

"Yours, most respectfully,
"N. B. FORREST, Lieutenant General.

"Dr. JOHN W. MORTON."

esteemed officer, and whose absence from the army will be sensibly felt,) replied, " Never mind me, I'm a Zou-zou, and aufait on scaling, climbing, or leaping." In proof of which, the enthusiastic Zouave commenced sprawling, squatting, finishing *volite a la Mobile.* The writer, with a hatchet, was to exercise in the " parries," in prime, in second, in right, high prime, and left ditto, thrust, lunge, and etc. But again to facts. We crawled one hundred and fifty yards, through the wet grass, in a drenching rain. We crawled breathlessly, as the sentinels were ordered to fire on any one seen out after retreat. Nevertheless—" faint heart never won fair lady," much less escaped a prison's bounds—we moved on, dreading our attack on the fence, that loomed up in our front, a regular " buncombe" one, (" bull strong, horse high, and pig tight,") and felt, " we fain would climb, yet fear to fall," and as it was high and studded with nails, the feat of gaining the crest might *entail* the loss of our nether garments, and remembering the advice of Elizabeth, " if thy heart fails thee, climb not at all," and being afraid of slips, as the boy at marbles says, when he misses the big middler, concluded to call a halt, rallying on Sale, who was secure behind his fortification of " Martel's best," half of which had been demolished during the attack. The night was intensely dark, but our wily captors had placed reflectors on either wall of the prison, whose rays converged, forming an unbroken line of light, and we felt that to cross it would be worse than the Rubicon, and instead of the Pontine marshes, swamping us, we would have been inevitably *swamped.* The grass was high, and wet, and we were becoming quite uncomfortable, having lain in the grass three hours, awaiting a favorable opportunity to cross the line of light, when a snakish form wriggles through the grass, and the pate of Captain Farabee glistens in the rays of the two converging reflectors. " Hush, the sentinel sees us." " The devil he does; what shall we do ?" " What do you say ?" " I am willing to do as they say." " Don't tell me what '*they say,*' (Aaron Burr.) You are in the lead, you say advance, advance it is ; retreat, we'll follow." " Then leap to the rear," which we respond to, by a right, rear, vault, at a " 2.40" speed, reaching our quarters, soaked to the skin.   Our expedition was a failure ; the writer being accused of having gotten the affair up, for a sensational article. The night was one to invoke the pen or pencil of an artist. The wind howled, the lake-waves lashing the shore with fury, the lone lights from the light-houses, flitting like spectres, athwart the dark interval, the white breakers rushing madly upon the reef, the noiseless figures in the grass, the solitary sentinel in our front, the quick tread of the officer of the day, as he made his round, all combined to make it a worthy subject for *record* or *canvas*.

The next day, we were all sore, and suffering from bad colds, excepting Sale, who had so well fortified himself, that he seemed exempt from all external impressions. The signal failure of the Zouave squad, has shown us the difficulties in the way of making an escape, and we have concluded, to wait for the development of other means, that may tend to deliver us from bondage, and rehabili- tate us, and then, in the exercise of those inalienable rights of an American citizen—trial by jury, and *habeas corpus*—we may again breathe the pure air of Heaven without these prison walls, and feel that all the crimes are not committed in the name of Liberty.

The real cause of the failure of our many attempts to escape, is owing to the system of espionage within the prison, and that our custodians *without* were fully posted as to our movements *within*.

It is ten months, this the 22d day of May, 1862, since I entered the army, and became acquainted with, and was initiated into, the military system of log-rolling and wire-working, from the start.   The thirst for office was as inordinate in military circles, as in the tamer atmos- phere of politics.   The organization of regiments was in this wise: A, who has been in Congress, or who has held official position, obtains permission to raise a regi- ment, promises B a lieutenant-coloneicy, if he can control four companies; another, captain, a majority, for three companies; furnishing three other unambitious captains, with the compliments of supplying his staff department, from their companies, all of which generally culminates, in the command being dissatisfied, with the officers thus log-rolled upon them; however, A is excusable, as all men are, more or less, ambitious. I remember my friend General Leslie Coombs, who is a brave and generous man, but has some vanity, and is a little ambitious himself; he it was who told John C. Breckinridge, "I have done more for my party, and received less, and you have done less and received more, than any two men alive." The General and myself were promenading Chestnut street, in the Quaker city, some years since, we stopped at Jones', a famous hotel at that time, to take a smile of "old wheat," a beverage for which this caterer was celebrated. After testing the article, the General became communicative, and gave me to understand, that the failure of the conservative ticket, at Baltimore, was owing to the absence of his name from the ticket. I think his ticket was Sam. Houston, of Texas, and Leslie Coombs, of Kentucky. This was all the result of ambition and vanity, yet there are few men who occupy a higher niche in the hearts of their friends, than this venerable soldier and politician of Kentucky. Associating with such men as him, Brownlow, that political Barnum of the South, and in sitting in the same pew at Baltimore, with that nondescript, Horace Maynard, of Tennessee, I possibly have become inoculated with that disease—ambition.

Andrew Jackson Donaldson* was another one of my political friends. I introduced the major once, to an old friend of mine, from New Hampshire, who had read law with, and been an intimate friend of, Franklin Pierce.

"How do you do?" says the major, "From New Hampshire, the same State that d—d rascal Franklin Pierce is from?"

"I beg pardon, Major Donaldson, I know Franklin Pierce well, read law with him, and am assured he is an honest man."

"Well, Mr. Merriam, I may have been abrupt. I can't

* Major Donaldson is planting in Mississippi; Merriam practicing law in Chicago, Illinois.

swear that he ever stole anything, but you must admit that he was a d—d fool."

"No, no, sir," exclaimed our friend, "I esteem Mr. Pierce as a man of mind."

At this juncture, several friends coming up, the conversation closed.

The major told me, the next day, over some "anti-Buchanan spirits," as he termed them; "I was rather severe on your friend yesterday. Say to him, that I didn't wish to hurt his feelings; but I can't withold the expression of my detestation of Pierce." I felt sorry for Merriam, as he was one of the few Yankees, in the many I have met, who could pronounce C. O. W. as we spell it. Franklin Pierce had his faults, but was one of the most consistent politicians the country has produced. It is said, that while a member of Congress, at Washington, he and a friend were returning to their hotel, in the "wee sma" hours of the morning, when an unlucky trip sent his friend into the ditch, "who exclaimed, "Frank, help me out!" "I can't do that," says the generous and gallant Pierce, "but I'll come down and stay all night with you." After his elevation to the Presidency, among a series of entertainments was a private dinner, given to a score of personal and political friends, to which his old companion in arms in Mexico, Jere Clemens,* was one of the most distinguished guests. A few hours, previous to dinner, Clemens and Pierce were closeted. They had not met since a certain convivial night in the halls of the Montezumas, and for several hours "fought their battles over again," over porter. This being too weak, a little cognac was added. Six P. M. approached, the dinner hour, still no abatement, and the guests were waiting, the President summoned his private secretary, Sydney Webster, excusing himself on the plea of illness. He requested Mr. Webster to assume *his* place, at the table. I asked Clemens, to whom I am indebted for this incident, how *he* came to be senator from Alabama. "Plain enough. I was in Mexico, colonel of infantry fifteen

---

* Jere Clemens, deceased.

months, and on my return, my friends found I was fit for nothing else, and sent me to the United States Senate."

But, to return to my being mustered in. I had seen so much of the above doings, that I thought my experience—with a flesh wound—would give me promotion, but have been cut out, and lost my reckoning, by being taken prisoner, and while here, have discovered, that ambition is a great humbug, and like the boy with the alphabet question, " whether it's worth while to go through so much, to learn so little." A man, to rise above the mass, or to retain marked individuality, must be a giant in some world, moral, physical, or intellectual ; must be saint, or sinner ; Bonaparte, Cæsar, or Wellington ; Calvin or Voltaire ; Hippocrates, or Valentine Mott. And these men ventured health, life, limb, time, fortune, and their soul's salvation, to reach the eminence that made them great. There are but few men who are remembered, even by their grandchildren ; and I will venture to state, that those of my readers who know theirs, are in the minority. The discovery of mine has been a matter of research. Step into a grandchild's room, twenty-five years hence, and ask, whose portrait is that on the wall ? " That's my grandfather ; mother says he fought in the Revolution of 1861, and was killed at the battle of Shiloh." Ten years afterwards, the same portrait may be in the garret, to make room for a modern styled one, of a new member of the family ; and even you, my reader, if an officer or soldier, may be killed, and if so, let your ghost visit that little cottage a few years after your demise, and in the hall, upon the rack, that once held your tile, you will discover another chap's hat, stick and umbrella, it being possible, that your wife has consoled herself with number two. The reflection is not an agreeable one, but natural ; for what a widow can't accomplish, is not worth striving for. "That's so," and "beware of them," says old Weller ; another argument, (the above,) against seeking the "bubble reputation at the cannon's mouth." As for myself, I am satisfied, and have arrived at the conclusion, "I had rather be a live jackass, than a dead lion."' Therefore, I feel that my imprisonment is of real benefit, for while it has brought time for reflection, it has also enabled me to discriminate, what was worthy in the past, and what should be left to the gullibility of the present. I shall, in future, try and be politically honest, and retire from the scenes of this busy, pseudo, political, whiskey-headed, card-playing, theatre-going, late-supper-eating, humbuging, outer world, that is, when I get out, if I'm not corrupted from within. Well, you may say, "that's vanity," so say I, so says the preacher, 'all is vanity."

Speaking of vanity, reminds the author of some little of his own. In 1850, while James C. Jones* was using his efforts to have the Memphis and Charlestown railroad built, aided by James Robb, of New Orleans, I happened to meet him while in that city, he there for the purpose of making one of his railroad speeches, my ostensible object in visiting the Crescent City, was to hear the world-renowned Jenny Lind, the Swedish nightingale. I had listened to the trills and cadences of Pedrioti and Fanti, Bishop Hayes, Biscacianti, Cariadora, Allen, Parodi, and a number of others, and having a passion for song, traveled twelve hundred miles to hear "Lind." I can never forget my feelings of satisfaction, after having breakfasted at Moreau's, lunched at Bonifan's, dined at Victor's, quaffed little potions at Sazerac and the Gem, and then having been tonsorially prepared by Rollins, I stepped into the lobby of the St. Charles theatre, the scene of many a star's triumph, before the exquisite taste of the Creoles of Louisiana.

I soon found myself in the "pit," which was a jam, as was all parts of the building. I sat in salmon tie, unblemished vest, and spotless kids, with an elegant opera glass *in rest*, and felt that I had the "world in a sling." In gazing round the dress circle, at the beauties of a dozen States, who had traveled by every conveyance, thousands of miles to pay homage to the *northern birdling*,) it suddenly flashed o'er my mind, that I was the centre of attraction, and the objective point of hundred leveled glasses. I

---

*Governor Jones died at Memphis, Tennessee.

could not make up my mind, whether it was my good
looks, or style, as I could not attribute it to anything
else, not being old or wise enough, to have figured in the
many worlds of fashion, science, politics, or religion. The
supposed triumph was too much for me, and I retired, to
recuperate with a "brandy smash," after which I resumed
my seat, inflamed with self, puffed up with vanity, feeling
like Alexander, when he had conquered his last world.
But it was a delusive wand that had touched me, the
enchanting one of vanity, and it turned my transparent
head around, where sat immediately in my rear, "Lean
Jimmy," formerly governor, senator, and one of the
noblest men in the South, the observed of all observers,
in company with Colonel David Leatherman,* one of the
handsomest men in the South; my feathers fell in a trice,
and I have been a modest man ever since. Speaking of
Leatherman, reminds me of one of his eccentricities. On
remarking he would stump the State of Tennessee, from
Shelby to Carter, during a late political canvass, he was
asked upon what issues. "Ah, that's the question," says
the prudent politician, a non-committal position that he
still adheres to. All great men are not modest, who
would imagine that Cobden, the great English statesman,
with white cravat, and eyes as meek as a child, to be a
joker. Some time since, we met Cobden, in Paris, at one
of Charles J. Faulkner's receptions, at which there were
the Persian ambassadors, Commodore Stewart's widow
and son; W. P. Smith and bride, representing the elite
of Philadelphia; the Emory's, of Cincinnati, a charming
family; Miss Preston, of Kentucky, forming with Miss
Goodrich, of New Orleans, a galaxy of fashion and beauty,
unequalled in any of the salons of Europe. C. J. Faulkner was a Virginian of the old school, and knew how to
make "apple toddy," to which I paid my devoirs, assisted
by Judge McKinstry, of California, and Major Brownlee,
St. Louis, since dead, "peace to his ashes." He became a sympathizer with the South, was banished St.
Louis under a vandal order, with only four days' notice.

*Leatherman is, as usual, anticipating a happy political future, yet a most
companionable gentleman.

This great grief, added to a feeble constitution, killed one of the best men that ever adorned the commercial circles of that city. While the "toddies" were flowing, I was introduced to Mr. Cobden, who was "pleased to know that I was from the West."

"You Western people are wild speculators, your whole system of hypothecation on land is dangerous, you have invested largely in them, with credit as a base of operations, and your crops having failed for several years, you are bankrupt, and in fact," says this model of the stoical Englishman, this mild and urbane Briton, "you remind me very much of a gentleman caught out, without his unmentionables."

I was astonished, and felt conscious that all men are fond of quaint expressions, but this quaint expression is like much of our modern prose and poetry, borrowed.

By referring to the files of old newspapers, or the original works of original authors, you will be reminded of the resemblance between the literary treats of the present and of the past, changed, and garbled, so that the originators would not know the sermon, while they created the text. There is very little that is original, "except original sin," and I much prefer simplicity and some little impurity of diction, with not so much perspicuity, and more originality. Stephen A. Douglas, was an original thinker, and deep as the ocean in his political subtleties, yet as artless as a child, in his impulses. In a conversation with him once, at Washington, I remarked,

"Your Squatter Sovereignty, Mr. Douglas, has cast a fire-brand among your Southern friends."

"It was not my intention, sir, I am for peace."

"Yes," I replied, "you would conquer one."

At that moment some one beckoned to him, from the other side of the Hall of Representatives, (where we were conversing,) and excusing himself, skipped off like a boy. I am not much of a politician, but if the much mooted question, that brought Stephen A. Douglas before the country, was not understood by the people, it was simply because they had no confidence in the judgment of Daniel Webster, who resolved the whole question into one of soil and climate, showing that where the soil was susceptible of slave labor, there it would naturally go. After leaving Douglas, I was introduced to Roger A. Pryor, of Virginia, now one of our Generals, a polished hot-housed political plant, with much brilliancy of classical lore, and urbane deportment, and if restrained, opportune circumstances may afford him a chance to *properly* employ his talents. The laudations of a crowd, who barely understand his trophies and figures, and the enthusiasm of his friends has nearly ruined Pryor. In America, a man is not born with political character, neither must he seek it, rather let it be thrust upon him. But all, I repeat, is vanity. I have it in writing this book, and like Cinna, I may be injured by my bad verses, but I hope not badly *kilt*.

I have amused my "mess" with an adventure in London, now they claim another from Paris. In 18— I found myself on that splendid effort of the lamented George Steers, the peerless Adriatic, en route for France: a parting tear, an embrace, the wave of handkerchiefs, a few puffs, and we steam out, in a few hours we are off Sandy Hook, a few more, and the wide expanse of water encircles us, we cast one long, lingering glance, at the trackless waste behind, compress our lips, and with a sigh, turn our head to the East.

Sea voyages have been described so often, that we will not bore our readers, with a repitition of description. We were sea-sick, had good and foul weather, and arrived safe at Southampton, landed the English mails,. and passengers, then turned our bow-sprit towards Havre, which we reached after a run of seven hours. We leave Havre for Paris, passing through Normandy, one of the finest farming regions on the earth. They have no rugged fences to mar the beauty of the landscape, a simple stone marks the boundaries of estates; vast masses of foliage, added to the crimson of the fields of dotted poppies, the richly laden cherry trees, with their sparkling fruit, peeping from the midst of emerald leaves, seem like some old painting. Then the little villages, that looked a thousand years old, whose people appeared

as if they had slept centuries, and had awakened to continue their same routine of daily duties, as of yore.
They wear the same costumes as those of their patriarchal
ancestry, but if they retain the quaintness of the antique
past, in relation to style and habit, they seem to have
attained the perfection of economy, in its application to
farming. You will not find a rock, or stick, beneath a
fruit tree, the smallest cherry is picked from its stem, and
carefully gathered, without bruise; the limbs of fruit
trees are trained upon walls of houses and courts, thus
economizing space; the vegetable is not pulled from the
soil, as we would jerk up a radish, but a sharp instrument
is inserted in the ground around each, so as to loosen the
soil, thus avoiding lacerating the tender fibre of the half
matured vegetable attached. All is attention and care, for
while labor is cheap, the laborer receiving from 30 to 40,
and the women from 25 to 30 cents per day, while land
rents, in some instances, as high as sixty dollars per acre;
the women do the digging, and watering, the men the
residue. The most remarkable perfection is attained in
the production of beets, some weighing as much as eighty
pounds, the sugar produced from them is universally
used on the continent.

We leave Normandy, with its famous old towers, and
its beautiful scenery, described by a myriad of writers of
all kinds of fry, a majority of the small fry order. Therefore, not wishing to be rated with the latter class, we pass
on to Paris, where much is to be seen. To find Americans,
you go to the Grand Hotel, the most magnificent, and the
worst kept in Paris. For elegance and comfort, we go
to the Grand Hotel d'Louvre, on the Rue Rivoli. You
leave the hotel, drive out the Rivoli, cross the Place du
la Concorde, look at the site of the guillotine, now surmounted by an Egyptian obilisk of Luxor, of the time of
Sesostris, 3,000 years ago. You leave this beautiful
square, and continue out the champs Elysees, to the Bois
d'Bologne. Here you have some of the most magnificent
works of art, to be found upon the globe—lakes, cascades,
a miniature Niagara, artificial banks of roses, which fasci-
nate you, even to wearisomeness ; and you turn to gaze upon

the brilliant scene of vehicles, comprising phœtons, car-
riages, *voitures remises,* filled with the beauty and fashion
of Paris, from mi Lord and Lady to the Lorettes and
Grisettes. Here comes the Emperor, Empress, and Prince
Imperial, and in a few moments, followed by a butcher in
his cart, the Bois d'Bologne knows no social distinction,
and Louis Napoleon is a better democrat, than two-thirds
of those gentlemen at Washington, who are "ringing
little bells," and having honest men dragged from their
beds at the dead hour of night, and sent we know not
where. For amusement, you can go to the opera, or to
the jardin—Mabile or the Chateau d'Fleurs, and a hundred places, useless to mention

There are a thousand sights to be seen in Paris, to see
either of which, is worth the trouble of an Atlantic voyage.
We saw many of them, and returned to our hotel, fatigued
and thirsty, and while recuperating, under the influence of
some of Martel's best, we were approached by *another strange
gentleman,* this time in brown. He took a seat vis a vis,
and also called for a glass of cognac, as in Europe you
are not expected to invite every gentleman who sits near
to drink with you. The same rule applies at a restaurant.
If you invite a person to dine with you, it is understood
that the expense is divided. This is general; there are
special cases, however. You frequently fall into conversation with gentlemen sitting near you, as I did in this
instance; thence into an argument, he assuming the negative, to my positive assertion, of the superiority of the
nineteenth century.

"The world is not fitted for progression; a principle
of truth and virtue, which as yet have not been cardinal
points in the world's history. In this sphere all forms
may change, but the original substance remains the same.
In one era, you dwell with wonder upon the art that created the "hanging gardens of Semiramis; in another, the
world looks on, in amazement, at the apparently super-
human efforts that raised the Pyramids. The baths of
Caracalla were marvels of genius in one age; Gallileo
brings out the telescope, thus extending man's vision into
the mysteries of the stella universe. Where do we get our

architectural beauties; the simple and massive Doric: the severe beauty of the Ionic; the elegant Corinthian, and the Italian, Tuscan, and Composite, with the grandeur of the Gothic, but in the past? The Archimedean screw and burning reflectors; the triumphs of skill, in engineering, and chemicals of one period; the Chinese wall, and other wonders of the genius of the past, applied to different ages, satisfy us, that in those fields of inventive and mechanical genius, the nineteenth century finds an unquestioned superiority. Homer flourished in one age: Solon of Athens, Periander of Corinth, Bias of Priene, and Lycurgus, had their periods of poetry, philosophy, and law-giving; Æsculapius and Hippocrates initiated the science of medicine; Xenophon made the most memorable of retreats; Cesar, Pompey, Hannibal, Scipio, Atilla, Alexander, and Xerxes, distinguished themselves as warriors, at different epochs, and have left perpetual monuments of the generations that produced them. Woman has added the genius of her nature, and has contributed to make remarkable, the eras that have sank into the oblivion of the past. Semiramis Cleopatra, Joan of Arc, Cornelia, Charlotte Corday, and a host of famous authoresses, poetesses, and amazons of power and talent, have illumined with their greatness, the generations in which they flourished. The Iron, Brazen, and Golden ages, have all had their periods of Rebellion and Revolution: of men, and women, great and small; of Bonaparte and D'Stael; of Washington and Hemans, and in our day, of Howard and Nightingale.

"As to any great men in politics of to-day, there are two, Napoleon and Bismark, in America none. In military circles, Bazaine, who sacrificed himself rather than disturb the prestige of his Emperor; George B. McClellan, whose military genius would have adorned any period, and Robert E. Lee,* the master military spirit of the age, heroic even in his defeat.

"We are not benefitted by the light of the past, as is usually accepted, nor by the experience of others, there-

---

* Robert E. Lee, (is now 1868,) President of Washington College, Virginia.

fore the wisdom of nineteen centuries is lost upon us, and we are indebted to the intelligence furnished us by that Great Being, who gives to us, as to each other century, things agreeable to His will, and adapted to the wants of each. Were it not so, Mexico would profit by her fifty-six Revolutions, and the many different governments of Europe, by past political convulsions, that have cost millions of treasure, and the sacrifice of a myriad of lives, and in America, our system is the result of success, obtained through the murder and robbery of the red man. All human government is imperfect, the most perfect organized society is not secure, the dearest of ties, domestic, social, political, or religious, are disturbed and broken through man's incapacity to control his passions, all of which proves to our mind, the fallacy of that theory of human legislation, which proposes, by its workings, to insure the greatest amount of good to the greatest number, and satisfies us, that government is not the result of Revolution, but Revolution is a consequence of government, and as long as the world stands originals will exist, while derivatives may change their forms."

"You have satisfied me, sir, the negative has it, with this exception, that the 'bad whiskey,' sold in the caffes of Paris, and represented as the best 'Old Bourbon,' has never had, nor never will have, its equal, in any century."

13

CHAPTER VII.

THE "LONE STAR" STATE.—TURCHIN IN ALABAMA "OUT-HERODING" BUTLER IN LOUISIANA.—WM. G. BROWNLOW, THE "BARNUM" OF THE SOUTH.—GRAPE-VINE LINE ACTIVE.—THE "FOURTH ESTATE" IN PRISON.—HOW WE OBTAIN STIMULANTS.—GREAT EXCITEMENT IN CAMP.—CONFEDERATES REPORTED VICTORIOUS.—THE MUNIFICENCE OF OUR CUSTODIANS.—OUR LAUNDRY.—HUMAN NATURE IN BREAD CHUNKS.—EDWIN M. STANTON, SECRETARY OF WAR.—ARRIVAL OF CIVILIANS.—MURDER OF A PRISONER BY A SENTINEL.—BIG GATE.—THEY STOLE MY WHISKEY, AND ROBBED PETER TO PAY PAUL.—JOKE ON OUR CUSTODIANS.—PICNICIANS ON THE RAMPAGE.

WE have thirty-two officers in prison from Texas. To the traveler, who has been in the wilds of Texas, the distinguishing of these brave and daring men from the natives of other States, as he traverses our campus, is no difficult task. One of the most remarkable characters from Texas, with us, is Lieutenant D. P. Gallagher. He has held his own, in every circle in which he has ever figured—California, Nicaragua, thence into the fields of Texas, then a soldier, now a prisoner. "Texas," as we call him, is as little susceptible of change as any prisoner in the pen; has a head and hand shaped right, for "poker," of which game he is the acknowledged chief; and he is a perfect specimen of the men of that soil, that has been watered by the blood of Crockett, Travis, and Bowie. The other Texans with us are a distinguished body of officers, who will make their mark, whenever time and place offers an opportunity.

The following are those personally known to us: Sergeant S. F. Moody, Captain W. S. Moody, Lieutenant C. F. Moore, Lieutenant W. McAlpine, Lieutenant J. C. Lowe, Lieutenant G. B. Lipscomb, Lieutenant J. D.

Henderson, Robert H. High, Wm. T. Harris, Lieutenant
A. Ford, Lieutenant J. H. English, Lieutenant S. P.
Donnelly, Adjutant W. D. Daylen, Lieutenant J. H. Col-
let, Lieutenant J. H. Coven, Lieutenant J. M. Craig,
Lieutenant Thomas B. Camp, Captain J. W. Brown. Cap-
tain H. M. Bradheart, George A. Blain, George F. Boley,
Captain E. F Broughton, Lieutenant E. Ballinger, Lieu-
tenant T. J. Bell.

We have sad news in prison to-day from Alabama,
relating to abominable atrocities, committed at Athens,
in that State, by a horde of barbarians, under the immediate command of Colonel Turchin, the same miscreant,
who disgraced the name of soldier in Missouri, committing
excesses, that the soul of civilization revolts at. Let this
officer and his command be remembered by the gallant
sons of Alabama. Let them inscribe upon their banners,
" Victory or death, over all such murderers as Turchin
and his command, those violators of children, robbers, and
assassins, authors of crimes so monstrous, that human
nature revolts at their recital, Butler, the 'beast,' and
Turchin, the 'American Haynau.' " (The Austrian tyrant
merely lashed women; this would be a mild offense
for Turchin.)

William G. Brownlow,* the " Barnum" of the South.
This arrant " humbug," now perambulating the gullible
North, is hardly worth a few lines; but as he has attracted
some attention, by the publication of a huge volume of
blackguardisms, and vituperative falsehoods, it would seem
vain to overlook him. This blasphemer is politically
what the French call a "charlatan," good society a "blackguard," the rabble a "brick." He says, he never took a
" drink" in his life. His little, weazened and cadaverous
features show the absence of that soul, that incites a man,
to indulge in a "little wine for the stomach's sake." He
says, he does not use tobacco. This we also believe, as

* No greater scoundrel than the present Governor of Tennessee ever disgraced the gubernatorial chair of any State. This agrarian is a curse upon the
soil; and there can be no relief from his putrid carcass, until the Father of
lies claims his son—W. G. Brownlow, the blackguard, incendiary, and blasphemer. His book, *Chitls*, of the Philadelphia " Ledger," gave him $15,000
for; to help him, 'tis said.

he is too mean to buy it.   I met this clerical hypocrite
at the Baltimore convention, where I had a fine opportunity, of listening to his ribaldry and cant.   He has no
talent.   His reputation, as a writer, is based upon the
same capital that built up Bennett—a sort of " stingare."
Brownlow has some nerve; as he fears no Hell, conscious
that no element has more fire in it, than his own bad passions.   The Revolution has thrown him to the surface,
as it has other scum ; and failing in his attempt to impose
upon the South, he has sold out to the North, whom he
is now "Barnumizing."

To-day, Sunday, July 21st, 1862, is the most violently
active one we have had.   Grape-vine has been startlingly
alive, to the merest rumors.   Slips from ancient papers,
with letters from hopeful and confident Fort Warren
prisoners, were eagerly scrutinized, and in some instances
severely criticized.   One letter from Colonel Cooke, of
the Thirty-second Tennessee, one of the most popular
officers in the army, reads, " Be of good cheer, we will
be out in a few days."   But unfortunately for the reliability of the colonel's judgment, he wrote the same thing
two months ago, proving our Fort Warren friends to be
as credulous as ourselves.   The letters, however, from
all quarters, are more cheering, and we are more hopeful.

The father of Captain Hedden visited us yesterday, an
intelligent citizen of New Jersey, who is sanguine of our
speedy exchange.   Some one has a letter from Colonel
Lyon, who has one from Colonel Kenly, of Baltimore, who
saw Stanton, who said, that the only impediment was Buckner ; but that the Federal government had agreed to
give up this noble Kentuckian,; and that General Dix
had been authorized to accede to the demands of the
Confederates, and arrange as per cartel of 1812 ; all of
which makes a pretty good chain of circumstantial evidence in exchange, which has carried the stock up to-day,
" higher than a kite."   May the stock still go up, up, up,
until we go down, down, down, to Dixie, where, " With
a bottle of whiskey in each hand,

> Many will make their gallant stand
> In the happy land of Dixie."

The press is the most powerful of all the moral engines in the world; it has more influence upon the mass, than all other forces combined. The press, with the powerful influence it wields, is not always the leader of popular opinion. It usually feels the public pulse, and taking its direction from their impulses, leaps to the front of the progressive element, and becomes its champion; too often assuming any expedient that may give it prestige with its "drawn in followers." The press, under the control of a badly balanced head, is mighty to do evil; directed by the power of a bad heart, is a dangerous weapon, and powerless for good; but in the hands of wisdom, the press is the most beneficent creation in the physical world. The "New York Herald." This sheet comes out after the battle of Fair Oaks, (which is claimed as a brilliant victory by the Confederates,) and says in flaming capitals, "Glorious victory for the United States forces under McClellan, our loss 200." A few days afterward, in small print, "200 typographical error, loss supposed to be 3,000." A week afterward, in still smaller print, "real loss about 7,000." But the aim of the "Herald" is accomplished, the first impression upon the public mind is lasting, and the after corrections are of little importance until the developments of time prove the "Herald's" falsehoods, and then, the articles are only remembered by a few, as the mass, in the exciting present, lose sight of the past, and the "Herald," with the independence of impunity, goes on lying. The "Tribune" says "A or B, is a great scoundrel," in large type. A hundred thousand readers pore over its slanders, and believe them. The following day, the *amende honorable* is made in small type, and is read by (possibly) one half of those who swallowed the slander of the previous "issue." Thus fifty thousand persons remain under the impression, for the balance of their days, that the man is a great rascal. All papers have a weakness for puffing Adams' Express. On the sea-board and river towns, steamships and steamboats. Editors, in general, are fond of whiskey. Writers for literary weeklies, of women and the twist of their moustache. Political editors yearn for fat consulates.

Printer's devils are really impish, follow copy if it goes out the window; criticize the chirography of correspondents, and curse the want of brain that presents unintelligible manuscript, yet emanating from the genius of an individual who loans the editor sufficient to meet composition bills. Carriers are in ecstacy when the "New Year's Address" is profitable ; too many of them chew, smoke, and swear, and if you don't watch them, will sell you a paper a week old. Like the Gamins of Paris, they look upon the world as their victims, outside of their own craft.

I was standing on Lafayette Square, in the city of New Orleans, some years since, witnessing a review of the "Louisiana Legion," by Major-General Lewis. I was anxious to hear Jordan, the famous old drummer of New Orleans, and Mexican war notoriety, and to see the evolutions of the " Louisiana Grays," a celebrated company of the Crescent City. Being a stranger, I interrogated one of two little news-venders standing by, as to the position of the company in the line ? The little fellow looked me right square in the eye, while he expectorated a quid, with the nonchalance of a Jack tar, answered, ask Bill, I don't study *geography*, then opened a battery on the passers by, " here's your Crescent, Picayune, Bee, and Delta." The boys always take to the political tenets of their paper, and discuss the " why and wherefore," with as much enthusiasm, if not with as much ability, as their wiser " bosses." Papers, like theories, have their day, flourish, decay, and die. The smart ones, who control theirs, get rich during the sunshine. Philadelphia papers were once potent ; they yielded to Boston, and now New York bears off the palm. Bonner, with his blood and thunder stories, having trotted (Dexter-like) over the field of weekly journalism. He, as others before him, will live a few years, and Bonner's "Ledger" will be among the things that were. Before the innovations of the telegram, and the retirement of Kendall, the " Picayune," of New Orleans, was *par excellence* the journal of the South, and was to that section, what the " New York World" is to the North ; the "Boston Post" to the East, and the

"Louisville Journal" and the "Memphis Avalanche" are to the West, what the "Picayune" was, the "Crescent" is.

The press of to-day,* is in a position to take its stand as the great mover of the moral world, or to ruin it by vacillation, pandering, and falsity, and thus reduce itself to a state of negativeness, that will demoralize its efficiency, leaving us nothing but rags, ink, and bell-metal. We have many journalists of rare ability within these prison walls, whose names are known to the country as being among its most distinguished writers, to whom the Southern people can look as the proper custodians of the interests of the "Fourth Estate":

Captain Beaumont, of the Nashville press; G. W. McCraine, that fearless writer and courtly gentleman: Ward, that chaste writer of the Tennessee press; Hogane, of the Missouri; Lipscomb, of the New Orleans; Whitfield of the Alabama; and Simms, of the Georgia—the latter one of the most brilliant writers in the country.

Army officers, no matter of what clime or caste, have a strong *penchant* for alcoholic beverages, most particularly when absent from the excitements of camp and field. Imprisonment begets thought, then *ennui*, then we need some little reactionary fluid to partially destroy, if we can't drive "dull care away." But the officials of this point of land, (I wish it was a neck instead, attached to a goodly bottle,) have denied us the invigorator, so we have resorted to all kinds of tricks to get a "drop o' the crather," in (an article that attracted the Irishman to the summit of Vesuvius, learning that at this point alone, there was a superabundance of the "crater.")

A trick at camp used to be, steal a barrel from the commisary, bury it, and play "mumble the peg," over the bung-hole, each man mumbling in turn, sucking at a quill, rather than pulling at the peg; it has been done within ten steps of the officer's tent. Some would introduce it in coffee pots, the jaw of the spout filled with dough, the mouth with buttermilk. Some few days since, Captain Morton was inclined to imbibe a drop of

---

* The great paper of America to-day—1868—is Brick Pomeroy's, in New York, because fearless and honest.

the ardent, and conceived the happy expedient of feign-
ing sickness, so we put him in bed.   Jake Morton is one
of your melancholly looking men, deep black eyes, very
nervous, and can feign a shake, like a man with the ague.
As soon as we got him up to a good shaking point, we
sent for the post surgeon, who prescribed a quart of
whiskey and an ounce of Peruvian bark, to be well
shaken before taken, and drank *ad libitum.*

Jake had read of the entire exemption of the workers
in Peruvian bark from fever, and as a sanitary measure,
concluded to put the bark in his pocket, and take the
whiskey plain. There was one drink around, for when it
comes, seldom the potations are large.   Jake's disease
kept us in spirits some time.   Jack Handy has reported,
that there is a jug of good whiskey in the hospital, "how
to capture it," is the unanimous expression.   We got a
jug, sealed it with wax, and arranged that Captain Palmer and T. Saunders Sale, should take a loose linen coat,
secreting the jug beneath its capaciousness, get some of the
boys to raise a row in front of the hospital, which would
attract the inmates to the front, thus enabling the two
juggists to make the change at the back door.   Unfortunately for the plot, so well laid, the owner came for his
jug, and we lost the spirits, since which time, we have
suffered the pangs of the victims of the *jug or not*, (Juggernaut.)   Our Georgia friends have smuggled in some
Otard, in bottles labelled, "Allsups."   Some has come in
false bottomed buckets, and by the use of other means,
not mentionable.   We manage now and then, to keep
our spirits up, by pouring a few drops down.

To-day, the sutler brings in a bundle of extras.   They
announce in ambiguous language, it is true, yet unmis-
takable to us, that we have won a great battle at Richmond, June 30, 1862, and the enemy has found our last
ditch.   Many brave and gallant soldiers have bitten the
dust, many households made desolate, yet a thousand
voices, in our prison to-day, are expressing their joy at
the victory.   One of our most staid prisoners, ever dignified and reticent, Captain Walker, of Tennessee, has
thrown his hat away, and is carried off by his friends.

Lieutenant C. H. Stockdell, of Nashville, Tennessee, one
of the most intelligent and sprightly gentlemen in prison,
is quite carried away by his feelings. The news has
reached the hospital, and acts like a charm on the sick.
Good news is a fine curative, tattling and prison duties
are forgotten, all play is suspended, the buildings are
deserted for the campus, and all join in the general
rejoicing. Our custodians can't stand the disappointment, now comes their turn.

" Stop that yelling, you d—d rebels, and clear the
campus, or we'll fire upon you."

" We are not disobeying orders, or breaking rules."

"Clear the campus, and dry up, or d—n your rebel
hearts, we'll give it to you."

" Go to the front, you cowardly scoundrels," mutters
each Confederate, as he enters his room, " where you can
have a chance of facing men with weapons in their hands,
a more dangerous business than threatening, and murdering unarmed prisoners."

The hospital has been alluded to before, but will bear
repitition, as it has changed hands. The release of our
surgeons unconditionally, thus leaving the sick without
medical attendance, has made a draft upon some of our
line officers, who were practicing physicians at home, of
the first order of ability. Captain Allen, of the Fortieth
Regiment, Tennessee Volunteers, is now in charge of the
hospital. He is a calm, dignified gentleman, skillful in
his profession, and quite popular with the sick. Captain
Ray, of Lauderdale county, Alabama, is an assistant, and
adds to his medical knowledge conversational powers, and
gentlemanly bearing. Captain McNutt, and Lieutenant
Coppice, of Tennessee, also aid in the dispensatory ; are
very attentive, confine themselves strictly to their duties,
which are quite arduous. Their untiring efforts, in
connection with their chief, Captain Allen, to administer
to the sick, entitle them to the grateful acknowledgments
of the entire prison.

On entering the prison a sergeant approaches the
"mess," and desires to know if any are suffering for
clothing, and if a candidate responds in the affirmative,

his breeches are critically examined by the energetic non-commissioned officer, who, if the breach be a wide one, furnishes a new pair of pants, a light blue blouse, a little cap, a pair of drawers and shirt, and one blanket for two men. There were but few of us who *got* the *blues*, in this particular, as many did not need them, and not over a half dozen became ornamented with what *we* deemed badges of servitude. One blanket for two men would be sufficient covering in Calcutta, but in Johnson's island it is for those to determine who have tried it. Our commandant says, that if we lose our buildings by fire, we will suffer; it is possible with one blanket to two men: however, the issuance is on a par with the other brutalities extended. Did we depend on our custodians for necessaries, much less superfluities, we would have a sorry time on Johnson's island. We have expended $60,000, since our arrival, the greater proportion of which has been devoted to supplies, as the chunk of fat pork that adorns our mess-table, is not sufficient to make Falstaff's of any of us. We have had many friends among the humanitarians North, to whom we are indebted for many comforts, that have gone far towards soothing the rigors of our imprisonment and the asperities engendered by subordination to Pierson and his *braves*.

Solomon, when asked by the Queen of Sheba, to select the boys from the girls out of fifty equally divided, as to sex, but all dressed alike, as boys, ordered water for ablutions, and discovered that the females rolled their sleeves to the elbow, the males to the wrist. Solomon's wisdom answered for those days, but he would have been sadly at fault had he visited our laundry at Johnson's island and seen the spectacle of four confederate officers, with coats off and sleeves rolled up, not only to the elbow but the arm pits, manipulating socks, handkerchiefs, and unmentionables generally. The establishment of our laundry by the four officers aforesaid, resulted from capital: they having means sufficient to buy soap, and wit enough to borrow tubs, in consequence thereof they do a "land-office" business. Monday morning is the time for delivering your articles, as the chief

of the establishment is positive and despotic, (capital
ever is,) and will not receive garments after *sharp* four P.
M., Monday, and will only deliver up to *sharp* dark,
Saturday. We patronized the establishment, as having
attempted the washing of a doughty shirt at camp Chase,
that like the Gascon's, had been changed in two months,
and then inside out; he it was who said "what a filthy
fellow he must be who changes his garment every day,"
and found ourselves unequal to the task. We soaked it
and wrung it, and tried to dry it on the stove-pipe.
After three days it was still wet, and on being transferred to this island, we nailed it to the wall, where it
still hangs, as a wet memento of the writer's failure as a
washerman. Our laundry on Johnson's island has
system. A cigar box is nailed to a tree, and in which are
found pieces of blank paper, the executive head of the
establishment retaining his pencil in his port-folio; not
that he feared its disappearance surreptitiously, but
pencils were pencils. Each patron of the firm wrote his
name, and number of articles—the latter not a difficult
task—on his bundle, and turned joyfully away hoping
that a mistake would occur on delivery, he getting some
one's article for his own, knowing he could not be
worsted. Each thinking so felt safe as to the return of
their articles. It is a curious sight, a hundred bundles
strung out under the eyes of the managers, who were
buoyant in anticipation of the returns, at the close of the
week. The charge is five cents per piece. The prisoner
who has more than one shirt, is a *Pacha* with three tails,
to his shirts.

"He who steals my 'rank,' steals trash;" but he who
filches from me my chunk of bread, robs me of that that
will not satiate him, and I am not much the worse, as the
United States commissary's flour, at this post, is mene,
mene, tekel, upharsin. Tell it not in Gath, but 'tis even
so, a brother officer, who was honest at home, watching
a favorable opportunity, to-day at dinner, exchanged his
chunk of the staff of life for mine—having an eye to
quantity as well as quality. 'Tis said, human nature is
made up of chunks; but a hungry man is averse to hav-

ing the individual representative of nature made of huge
proportions, at the expense of his stomach. Man is a
queer animal; some are born great, and don't know it.
Like English Hobson, who, in letting horses, forced each
comer to take the one next the stable door, little dream-
ing, that "Hobson's choice" would become a common
proverb, and thus be notorious in a certain sense. So
with my chum; the greatness, that I envelope him with,
will descend to posterity, as a "commissary's choice."
My fellow prisoners can see the point. We make history
for the pilferer, but on the bread question we lose avoir-
dupois. "Necessity knows no law;" but when a man
slips up on a friend, on the subject of bread chunks, and
in a season of good wheat crops, in a fraternal sense, we
place him beyond the pale of—communion.

It is not exactly the province of a prisoner of war, to
say much about outside barbarians, but as Edwin M. Stanton, Secretary of War, the barbarian aforesaid, has placed
himself in a position to be shot at, why it is but fair, we
should make him a target; and if we don't knock the
black out, the arch military fiend of the war department
of the United States will, if the North whips the fight.
Until the world in aghast at the atrocities, that in such
an event will ensue, will exclaim, not as of yore, when
the Puritans were robbing and murdering the Indians,
"Lo! the poor Indian!" but with ejaculations of horror,
"Alas! the poor African!" He bid Godspeed to Senator
Brown, as he was leaving the senate, to unite his fortunes
with the South. He was also Buchanan's legal adviser,
when the struggle was fermenting. He earnestly advised
and commended the course that Breckenridge pursued;
and look at him now. I have examined the record alpha-
betically of all great men, both good and bad; and of all
the bad men, not one but has had some spark of manhood,
some devotional instinct, or some humane inspiration.
Robespierre signed death warrants with one hand, and
stroked a poodle with the other; Marat left intelligent
works of science, although a butcher of his kind; Nero was
fond of music; Caracalla had architectural tastes; Xerxes
and Alexander could weep; but poor Stanton is *sans*

soul, *sans* heart, *sans* taste, *sans* everything that is noble and true.   I had asked a parole, for the State of Ohio, knowing they were granted in a score of cases, and it had been strongly recommended by that polished gentleman, and humane Union soldier, Inspector General Wright, of the State of Ohio, and approved by Governor Todd, of the same State, whose consistent kindness to prisoners is proverbial.   And on being transferred from camp Chase to this prison, I had forwarded the parole to Edward Everett, of Massachusetts, for his influence, as the superintendent of our prison would not honor any recommendation of Governor Todd, referring me to the Secretary of War.   In a few days, I received the following from Mr. Everett :

"CHICAGO, May 14th, 1862.

"DEAR SIR :—Your letter, inclosing General Wright's parole, having been forwarded to me at this place, was received by me this evening.   I will, by the next mail, address a letter to the Secretary of War, inclosing General Wright's parole, and requesting the Secretary to ratify it.

"Respectfully Yours,
"EDWARD EVERETT."

The immaculate gave an equivocal reply.   Again the honorable gentleman applied—and a similar answer from the scarecrow of the war department.   The third time the kind-hearted Everett asked for my release, and the final answer of the *bear* was : " No special paroles granted until the rebels lay down their arms, as the arrangement for a cartel has been broken by their bad faith, by thus telling a lie; and snubbing the distinguished son of Massachusetts, whom he detested because he was a gentleman. , Were it not so, the favor would have been granted, out of courtesy to Mr. Everett's eminent position, and even if a political opponent, among gentlemen, the courtesy was doubly due—little points, however, that Stanton is not supposed to know anything about.   It was not a fling at me, for I am too small a fish for this mighty Leviathan to swallow,   Plutarch said : "the difference between a man and a beast was, the latter had no knowledge or feeling of a Deity." If Stanton felt or knew there was a God, he would act differently, "the Beast."

Of all the damning outrages committed by our enemies on the Southern people, one of the most high-handed, is the arrest of private citizens, of whom several hundred are driven into the pen to-day, like sheep led to the slaughter. Some taken from their beds, others from their desks, and ploughs, and some from the bar, and pulpit, hurried off, half clad, without warning or a suspicion of a charge against them. I asked one, of the several old men, in camp Chase, a man at least seventy-five years of age, with hoary beard and tottering steps, as he was wandering listlessly around the prison yard : " How came you here ?" " I can't tell. I was taken from my home and brought here, I don't know what for. I did no one harm, and am very much distressed about my people; they will not know what has become of me." Others did not know why they were similiarly treated, nor could any of us tell them. Among the arrivals, this morning, is the distinguished Dr. Hobson, of Kentucky, one of the most eminent divines of that State, who preaches us a sermon to-morrow.

Lieutenant Gibson, of the Eleventh Arkansas Regiment, Volunteers, was murdered to-day by a sentinel, whom, I learn, did the shooting wilfully and maliciously. An order, that would have put a Caligula or Nero to the blush, had been published by the hypocritical and contemptible Pierson, to the effect, that all prisoners should retire to their quarters at retreat, which was at sundown, the only period of the day, that it was possible to be comfortable, crowding us into a suffocating room, to the number of fifty in ours, three bunks high, and reaching to the ceiling, two in a bunk. One tin pan for us to wash out of; and the straw of our beds changed, not at all in our room. I don't know of other messes. Yet they say we are well treated. Lieutenant Gibson, as all of us, obeyed the orders of the petty despot ; yet this poor fellow fell a victim, as some one must be shot, at intervals, to advertise the crew, (a majority of them) of that Hessian battalion (Hoffman's,) so they could play the feather-bed

Murder of Lt Gibson

warriors, while the gallant soldiers of the United States were at the front. It may have been different at other pens, but *I never knew an old soldier to maltreat a prisoner.* Courage and humanity, are synonymous, and the coward is always cruel. Lieutenant Gibson had been spending the afternoon with a comrade, some twenty steps from his quarters, and on hearing the signal for retreat, hastily returned to his room, and had one foot on the threshold, when the assassin hailed him with the expletive, "You d—d rebel, go back to your quarters." "I'm going to them now: these *are* my quarters," stopping for a moment to answer the sentinel, who had his gun leveled at him. "Go back to your quarters, I tell you, you d—d rebel." Lieutenant Gibson, whose body was inclined towards the sentinel, turned to step in, and without warning, was shot down; the entire charge, a *double* one, entering his body. This act of cruelty and crime, places the miscreant, who has proved himself a willing tool, in the line of promotion.

Since writing the above, we learn that the author of this damnable outrage, has been promoted to a sergeantcy. And they say, we are well treated. Heaven save the mark!

There are but few of my fellow prisoners who are not interested, when the sound of "big gate" attracts them to the doors and windows. It may admit "fresh fish," an appellation given new comers, or the wood wagon: possibly some angel in female form, that comes to administer to the wants of the sick and dying. The sutler, milk and ice men all come through the big gate. We came through it, and we hope soon to go out through it's portals, as 'tis the living alone who shadow this gate: the dead are hauled out the side gate. The grass seems greener beyond the big gate than within, and we would risk our blood upon its lintels, to once again taste the air of freedom that so invitingly bids us make the attempt without the prison walls. The mail with its letters and remittances from loved ones: the newspapers with their many fictions, all come through this opening. And now, while writing this, the stentorian announcement is made "big gate," and we go with the rest to see what comes next.

They stole not "my purse," nor "my child away," nor
"o'er me gently," but with malice aforethought against
the peace and dignity of our mess, they purloined my
spirits, presented with other good things by that most
estimable woman and humane dispenser of the charities
of life, Mrs. H. I. Spotts of Kentucky, and added insult
to injury, by sending in the bottles filled with water.
The prisoner can imagine the look of disappointment
that clouded the brows of the mess, with whom I had
proposed enjoying the et ceteras, on the discovery of the
fraud.   I appealed to Major Pierson, whose answer was
laconic:

"I can't help it, sir, the boys will steal whiskey, and
besides, sir, it is contraband."

"Well, major, if the article is contraband, confiscate
it in a legitimate manner, but don't allow your rascally
subs to practice their little tricks upon us."

"Never mind, captain, I'll send you a bottle of
whiskey to-morrow."

The morrow came, and in came the bottle, and while
preparing to open it, our gallant friend, Captain Hooper
Harris, passed the window.   "Come in, Harris, and join
us," which was promptly responded to, as the susceptible
Harris had sniffed the odor of the beverage as the war-
horse the battle afar.   Courtesy prompted offering the
captain the first smile, which on raising to his lips produced an exclamation of wrath:

"Confound old Pierson B—, he has sent you a bottle
of the twelve stolen from me.   Robbing Peter to pay
Paul.   Chorus—let's swallow the insult."

And we did, but the palliative was not sufficient to
make us forget the peccadillo of the cerulean individual,
who threw cold water, by the bottle-full, on our hopes of
a social re-union with spirits, not of the Fox-sisters.

Personal difficulties among brother officers, are the exception; yet at times they will occur, and our custodians
being aware of it, pay but little attention to the confusion
incidental to a "*set to*," that after a few blows, is usually
terminated by the interference of the friends of the parties.   Last Sabbath morning, the startling announcement

was echoed through the pen, " man killed. "When?" and "who by?" was the general exclamation, as all rushed to the spot, where a large crowd had assembled, in front of the building where the gunboat-men quartered, one of the most rollicking messes in prison. It being a lovely morning, Hoffman's battalion, in their Sunday uniforms, prepared for inspection, were covering the roofs of all buildings outside the walls, with their "cerulean abdomens," anxious to see what was going on—yet in dread of a stray shot from an officer of the guard. One of their officers, more courageous than the rest, stepped up, and the familiar sound of "big gate" ushered him in.

" What's the matter, boys?"

" O, nothing ; but a man killed."

" Who was he, and what was he killed for ?" said the nervous lieutenant.

" O, *dog-on* him ; he was a traitor, going to take that oath, that old Pierson says some four hundred of us will take—so they told him. Even old Pierson himself had to whistle when he told that *whopper ;* and the boys are so disgusted with the traitor, they thought they would kill him ; 'that what's the matter.'"

" Why, that's awful. This thing shall not go on. The entire power of our force shall be called in requisition, if necessary, to check such outrages."

" O, *let em rip*, lieutenant. Don't you know, that traitors don't do any good ? Kill 'em lieutenant, kill 'em—that's the document."

" You are savage, sir. I will examine into this matter at once," says the now really excited lieutenant, moving quietly towards the front.

On reaching the margin of the crowd, he discovered traces of unfeigned vengeance on the lineaments of each Confederate, and asking, tremulously, " Where the body was ?"—was answered, in the house. At that moment, a mournful procession was seen issuing from the building : six officers bearing the body upon a board, that served as a mess table ; a slouched hat covered the face, and a blanket, marked U. S., gave it a national winding sheet. The horrified officer could stand it no longer ; but rush-

14

ing into the circle, demanded the name of the murderer ;
and placing his hand upon the board, with the air of
" Richard," " Put down the corpse ;" upon which a loud
cheer burst from a hundred throats, as the two sticks of
wood, blanket, old hat, and plank fell, nearly rendering
the lieutenant "notocrious." The lieutenant turned away
chop-fallen, with the remark : " You boys will have your
fun ;" and the gun-boat mess always did, and ever will, in
prison or elsewhere.

If there ever was a more devil-mi-care set of men in
the world, than the mess, in which figured Tom Kirtland
and Harry Hedden, they are found out of Johnson's
island. The dinner hour, of this mess, is frantically announced by each member rushing to an outlet, and with
the aid of tin plates, in the absence of tom-toms and
whang-doodles, proclaim, not like the Khan of Tartary,
"I am finished, the other kings of the earth can dine ;"
but like so many howling dervishes, yell out grub, and
with a clamor that would do justice to an army of China-
men, whose prowess is in their lungs and gongs, wind up
with a deafening "*tiger*;" then take their stand at the
sumptuous repast. But with all their *jocoseness of jocu-
larity*, there is not a more subordinate mess to prison
rules in the pen, nor a mess where the social amenities of
life are better comprehended, and in the instance we
speak of, no harm was dreamed of, much less intended.
It seems, one of the gentlemen had placed his best coat,
(a black one,) against the window, to protect the occupants of the room from the rays and intense heat of a
summer's sun. The coat was pendant about ten minutes,
when crash came a stone against the window, another,
and another, followed by a volley ; and amid the racket
of the missiles, could be heard the voice of an irate Teuton ; " Mein Gott ! dat ish te plack flag ; down mit de
repels, and tree cheers for te Onion." The uproar soon
became of a character to excite apprehension, as the valiant Sanduskians knowing us to be unarmed, had made
daily threats to mob us, and, I am confident, they would
have done so, had they the courage. After finding,
that the noisy crowd in their front had taken their coat

for a black flag, the mess hauled down their colors; on which the firing ceased, with a wild huzza for " de stars ant stripes, dat bully old 'rag," as viewed through a glass for the tenth time of *zwei lager*.

After this emeute on the part of the picnicians, black coats were at a discount on festal days.   The impression of the mess is, that the attack was an exhibition of drunken spite, rather than loyalty; and the black coat was used as a pretext, by ruffians, to stone unarmed and defenseless prisoners, which, had they numbers and spunk, might possibly have terminated in murder.

CHAPTER VIII.

NAVAL ENGAGEMENT AT MEMPHIS.—LIST OF OFFICERS AND BOATS.—
COMMAND UNDER COMMODORE J. E. MONTGOMERY.—"LOG" OF THE
GUN-BOAT "PRICE," BY L. F. DELISDEMIER.—THE WOMEN OF LOU-
ISVILLE.—MRS. H. I. SPOTTS.—MRS. DAVID LOONEY.—ANDREW JOHN-
SON.—CAPTAIN J. M. WINSTEAD.—CAMP CHASE, OHIO.—AN INCI-
DENT AT CAMP CHASE.—ATTEMPT TO ESCAPE AT CAMP CHASE.—
OLD MEN AT CAMP CHASE.—CAMP CHASE—HOW SITUATED.—MRS.
JUDGE CLARK, OF OHIO.—DR. CLIFF.—MRS. HARRY H. HEDDEN.

OUR gun-boat flotilla arrived at Memphis,* on the evening of the 5th of June, 1862, to await the arrival of
the Federal fleet, which came down about 9 o'clock of the
same evening, and laid on "Paddy's Hen and Chickens,"
in sight of Memphis. On being informed of this, our commodore sent up a small tug, in charge of Captain Bennett,
as a picket. By some mismanagement, she got aground,
on the foot of the island, and she could not be got off
with her own power; consequently the torch was applied,
and she was left to her fate in flames. Nothing more
of importance happened during the night, but the general
understanding with all the fleet was, that we would not
make a stand.

After daylight, on the morning of the 6th, we could see
by the movements of the enemy, that they were making
preparations to come down, for the Heavens were one
solid cloud of black smoke. In the meantime, we were
not idle in making preparations to back out in the stream,
which we did, one after another, until our whole fleet,
eight in number, were drawn in line of battle. It was

* The account of the naval fight at Memphis, is from the hands of the gallant Captain J. Henry Hart.

here we received the first intelligence, that we were going to make a stand. The enemy was now in full view, coming down in line of battle. The following boats were sent up, to draw the Federal gun-boats off of the bar: General M. Jeff Thompson, Sumpter, General Beauregard, and Colonel Lovell, from the fact that they had sixty-four-pound guns mounted on their bows. The fire was opened by the Thompson, but not until she had fired three rounds, did the enemy make any reply. The fire on the Federal side was opened by the flag-ship Benton. The fight now became general. Brisk firing from both sides, was the order of the day. It was while the battle was raging with intense fury, between our rams and the Federal gun-boats, that their rams made their appearance; first came the Queen of the West, which made a bee-line for the Colonel Lovell, which tried to back out of the way, but in so doing, got in such a position, as to show her opponent a broad-side, when she run into her, and sunk her immediately, in water her hurricane deck, in the channel of the river. Life-boats were immediately dispatched from the Little Rebel, to assist her crew in getting ashore. Before the Queen of the West could regain her position, the Confederate ram Sumpter struck her in midships, sending her ashore, during the balance of the engagement. Next came the Switzerland, bearing down on the Sumpter. The Beauregard next in turn singled out the Switzerland, for her antagonist. The Federal ram, seeing her intention, drew off from the Sumpter, and headed down on the Beauregard; they struck head on, but glanced, placing the Switzerland *hors du combat*, knocking down her bridge-tree, when she had to go ashore, where she threw out her sharp-shooters as pickets. Next came the Federal ram Monarch, in chase of the Jeff Thompson, she at the same time rounding to, head up stream, followed by the Monarch; here the General Price was put under a heavy head of steam, to overtake the Monarch, which she did, striking her a heavy blow in the starboard quarter, driving in her hull, and rounding her to, after which she stopped to back around and give her another blow; but, unfortunately, the Beauregard had made a dash at the Monarch, and missed her object, and striking the Price on the port-side, completely disabling her. During this, with only one wheel left, she managed to get ashore, but too late for the crew to make their escape; disabled as she was, the enemy kept up a constant fire into her; for humanity's sake, the "stars and bars" were hauled down. It was about this time, the Beauregard got headed up again to meet another of her adversaries, when a shell was shot into her hull and burst, damaging her boilers and hull; killed one engineer, and wounding three others, and scalding three firemen. She was unfit for duty, floated down the river about one-fourth of a mile, and sunk in twenty feet water, face to the enemy, and colors flying. It was about this time, the Little Rebel made a dash at one of the rams; but before she could reach her, received a shot in her boilers, when she kept her course into the shore, where all but three made their escape. In the meantime, the Sumpter had been run ashore, and crew all escaped; also the Thompson was run ashore, and burned to the water's edge. The General Bragg stood off and looked at the fight, likewise the General Earl Van Dorn: neither offering any assistance. The Bragg, in attempting to round to, to make good her retreat, was run into by one of the Federal rams, which drove in her side. The crew of the Bragg nearly all made their escape in yawls and life-boats. The Van Dorn, handling much better than the Bragg, was fortunate in making good her escape. Thus ended one of the hottest naval engagements ever fought in the Mississippi.

The following is a list of the principal officers, as far as we can ascertain:

Earl Van Dorn.—Captain, Isaac Fulkerson; Purser, Charles Reynolds; First Officer, John W. Jordan; Second Officer, John Mardis; Chief Engineer, Wm. Hurst: First Assistant Engineer, John Swift, William Camon and William Molloy.

General Sterling Price.—Captain, Thomas E. Henthorn; Purser, L. F. Delisdemier; First Officer, N. J. Henthorn; Second Officer, George L. Richardson; Chief

Engineer, William Branden ; First Assistant Engineers, William Orin, W. W. Hayden and Oscar Postall.

General Beauregard.—Captain J. Henry Hurt; Purser, J. C. Haynes ; First Officer, R. D. Court ; Second Officer, John Rawson ; Chief Engineer, Joseph Swift ; First Assistant, Edward Connolly; Pilot, J. Pope Altram.

General Bragg.—Captain W. H. H. Leonard ; Purser, William Riply ; First and Second Officers, names unknown ; Chief Engineer, John Porter ; First Assistant Engineer, Henry Sisson ; Pilot, James Russel.

Sumpter.—Captain Wallace W. Lamb ; Purser, John Wilbanks ; First Officer, Lemuel Murray ; Second Officer, name unknown ; Chief Engineer, Robert T. Patterson ; First Assistant Engineer, John Ramsey ; Pilots, Thad Siederburg and Moses Gray.

Little Rebel.—Captain J. White Fowler; Purser, Chas. Smedly ; First Officer, James Wall ; Second Officer, name unknown ; Chief Engineer, Gus Mann; First Assistant Engineer, William Reeder ; Pilots, Newton Pue and John Bernard.

General M. Jeff Thompson.—Captain, John Burk ; Purser, James Bissell ; First Officer, Louis Camfield ; Second Officer, Henry Moore ; Chief Engineer, Thomas Mitchell ; Pilots, Barney Arnold and Daniel Thomas.

General Lovell.—Captain James C. Dellancy ; Purser, Hardy ; First Officer, Thomas Johnson ; Pilot, William Cable.

Commodore of the fleet, J. E. Montgomery.

The Federal fleet consisted of sixteen mortar-boats, six rams, and eight gun-boats, besides any number of tugs and transports."

The cause of our disaster at Memphis, was from a series of incidentals to the campaign on the Mississippi. The original occupation of Columbus, was a stragetic stroke of policy. The advance of the gun-boats did not intimidate, and we continued to hold Columbus. The advance of the enemy's land forces, on the opening of the Tennessee river, by which Columbus would be outflanked, compelled the evacuation of that point. We fell back to Island Ten, to there check the gun-boats, while our land forces, assisted by gun-boats, held in check General Pope's grand army, at New Madrid. The occupation of Point Pleasant, and its fortifications, by the enemy, by which transportation was cut off, and our gun-boats would be compelled to go below, involved the evacuation of New Madrid, which was a good movement in its conception, but badly executed, in a slovenly manner, ill becoming the commander that directed it. But instead of falling back, we advanced into the enemy's lines, and we were all moved to Island Ten. This we continued to hold, although outflanked by the enemy, on both flanks, and it was held until the battle of Shiloh, when we were surrendered. This gallant little band, after suffering many privations, had to yield to a military necessity, and were given up. The surrender of Island Ten compelled the Confederate forces to fall back to Fort Pillow, so as to keep up a corresponding line with their land forces, as all armies, when occupying positions, if a flank is thrown forward, hold theis position, until sustained by the other flank or the centre. This is a rule, advancing or retreating. When our army withdrew from Corinth into the Mississippi, our fleet should have retired to Vicksburg, and thus under its guns sustained the line of defense. The battle of Memphis ought not to have been fought, and when it was, it ought to have had the presence of the entire Confederate fleet; and as it was badly managed, defeat was a consequence, and the brave and gallant men, many who are in prison with us, and whose names I have given, suffered a defeat that there was no necessity for. The boats were manned by daring crews, commanded by hardy officers, as dashing men as we have in the Confederate service, and they had every element to insure victory, in an engagement with an enemy upon equal footing, and would have been willing to have fought them with one to two; but they could not fight a fleet of (16) mortar-boats, (6) rams, and (8) gun-boats, and innumerable tugs and transports, opposed to some half dozen gun-boats and rams successfully. It was a terrific fight, and right gallantly did our heroes of the Mississippi sustain their reputation for chivalry; for in spite of the great disparity

and the fearful odds, they went in, death staring them
in the face. Yet they were not conquered, for there were
no dastards there,—and the brave fellows, who went down
in the grand struggle, we can say in the applicable lines of
the author of the eulogy on Lawrence: " If the Phaeton
and horses of fire had been destined for their translation,
they could hardly have departed in a brighter blaze of
glory." But they have been sacrificed to appease the
wrath of the God of war, and to show the bad management of an affair so nobly and obstinately fought, yet for
no purpose, unless to show the Federals, how the gallant
South can fight, can suffer, die, for Liberty and Independence.

I have formed the personal acquaintance of several of
the officers of the fleet, who are as courteous and as soci-
able as they are fearless: and to I. Pope Oldham,
one of the most popular officers in the valley, and to Captain Hurt, a polished cavalier, I tender my thanks, for
their information so kindly furnished.

(LOG* OF THE "PRICE," FROM NEW ORLEANS TO MEMPHIS.)

March 25th, Tuesday, 1862.—Left New Orleans at 9
P. M., with the following officers: J. H. Townsend, captain ; T. E. Henthorn, first officer ; L. F. Delisdemier,
purser; George L. Richardson, second officer; William
Branden, chief engineer ; J. H. Frobees, Assistant do.

March 28th.—Laid up last night, on account of fog ;
left Red river at 10 A. M. ; passed the General Bragg
to-day.

Saturday, 29th.—Arrived at Vicksburg, at 4 P. M.,
and found the Bragg had stopped here ; left at 5.30 P. M.;
found no iron there. Weather pleasant.

Monday, 31st.—Arrived at Eunice, at 8 P. M. Informed the railroad agent, that we wanted some iron.
He said, he had none. Our captain then told him, he

---

* Written by L. F. Delisdemier, purser of the General Sterling Price. The
Log of the Price and the engagement is published complimentary to the boat-
men of the Mississippi, many of whom composed the officers and crew of the
flotilla, whose gallantry on the 6th of June, 1862, is historic, proving that
steamboat men, as a class, are the most chivalric men in the world.

would have to tear up his track, and set the men at it, and soon had some three miles torn up and ready to carry on board.

Thursday, April 3d.—Left Eunice yesterday afternoon, after getting on board all the iron that we wanted to finish the Price and Van Dorn. Arrived at Memphis at 3 P. M.; found the Bragg had arrived yesterday afternoon. At 4 P. M. the Van Dorn came up. Captain Townsend, being senior captain, set all available men at work, to finish the boats as soon as possible.

Friday, April 11th.—Weather rainy. Received order to leave for Fort Pillow. Got two pilots to-day, viz: W. W. Hayden and Oscar Postall. Left Memphis at 6.30 P. M.

Saturday, April 12.—Arrived at the fort, and reported to the General at 6.30 A. M., and then dropped down to coal. Orders were sent down, for us to escort the transport Lockland up the river on a foraging expedition. We started at 5 P. M.; left orders for the Van Dorn to follow us. Those of Hollins' fleet went up ahead of us; passed them at 11 P. M. at anchor near Island No. 25. As soon as we rounded the bend saw a United States transport, and gave her chase. She either heard us, or saw our smoke, and started up the river. We chased her about eight miles, when she met the Federal fleet, at the mouth of the Obion river.

Sunday, 13th, 1 A. M.—Sent a note to Captain Huger, flag officer on the McRea, notifying him of the presence of the enemy. At 5 A. M. received his answer, that he would be along after daylight; 8.30 the look-outs report the fleet coming up; dropped out into the stream, and formed in line of battle, and stood up to meet the enemy: and when within three miles of us, the United States gun-boat Benton opened on us; her shot fell short. The Confederate States gun-boat Maurepas replied to her from a nine-inch Dahlgreen, also falling short. The Federals now showed their whole fleet, consisting of eleven gun-boats and eight mortars. So Captain Huger, knowing it to be folly to contend with them, left us alone with them. We then rounded to, and waited until the enemy came within two miles, and let them have the contents of our stern guns, and then we went after the balance of the fleet. The Yankees followed us, and kept up a running firing, but without any damage. We arrived at the fort at 11.30, and reported the fleet coming down. The guns were immediately manned, and all waited for the appearance of the fleet. At half-past two they made their appearance, but only exchanged a few shots, rounded to, and went up the river about six miles.

Monday, the 14*th.*—This morning the Federals opened fire on the fort, end every fifteen minutes they gave three shells. The bombardment was kept up till 9 P. M. A scouting party from our boat and the Van Dorn, under command of First Officer T. E. Henthorn, went out this morning on the Arkansas shore, and went within six hundred yards of the Federal fleet, and report them forming in line of battle and dropping down stream, stern foremost.

10 P. M.—No demonstration been made by the fleet as yet.

April 15*th, Tuesday.*—First Officer T. E. Henthorn, with a party of thirteen men and officers from the R. D. fleet, have gone out again this morning. The bombardment was renewed at an early hour this morning, and has been kept up at regular intervals of ten minutes. They have three mortar-boats in position, at the distance of three and a half miles, and lay around a point opposite the fort.

10 P. M.—The firing ceased at 8 P. M. The scouting party have just returned; report three men captured at Mr. Lamies', by Federal mounted infantry; were chased by a party, but made their escape.

Wednesday, 16*th April.*—Went down to Mr. Lamies. and moved him and family on board of steamer transport Charm, and sent them below, under convoy of the Bragg. A party of fifty " Feds " came down last night, to capture one of our boats, but not finding us, they returned at daylight. This morning, a party of United States soldiers appearing in sight, gave them a few rounds of grape. Scouts report fifteen men killed and wounded;

burnt ninety bales unginned cotton, and thirty bales of cotton.

April 17*th*.—Went down and moved Mr. Morgan to a place of safety.

*   *   *   /   *   *   *   *

May 8*th* (*Thursday*).—The bombardment has been kept up day by day, but no damage done ; loss two killed. This morning, the Sumpter, Bragg and Van Dorn were ordered to go up and cut out the mortar floats. Arrived at the field where they had been posted, but found they had been moved up to the fleet. The Sumpter remained there until 9 A. M. ; the Federals firing a few shot at her, but did not come down. She returned at 10 A. M. The mortars were then brought down, and commenced a furious bombardment, throwing over two hundred and fifty shells, but most of them fell short.

Saturday, May the 10*th*.—Agreeably to the decision of the council of war, held yesterday, the fleet left their moorings at 7 A. M., and the several positions in line of battle, as follows : The Bragg, Sumpter, Sterling Price, Van Dorn, Jeff Thompson, General Lovell, Beauregard, and Little Rebel. On rounding the point, the Federal fleet was plainly visible in " Bulletin Bar," with the exception of the Cincinnati, who had come down as a protection to the mortar, but made (as soon as we appeared) for the balance of the fleet. According to orders, the Bragg immediately gave her chase, and soon overtook her, striking her a violent blow on the larboard bow, dismounting one of her forward guns and slewing her round. The Cincinnati fired a broad-side into the Bragg, one shot going through her, killing a cook. The Price next in turn started for her, and at the same time delivering an effective at the mortar, silencing it. The Cincinnati kept a running fire, as the Price kept away from her, soon overtaking her, and struck her oft a little starboard of midship, carrying away her rudder and stern post disabling ; the Sumpter came up soon after, and also struck her, and she then drifted on the bar and sunk. The Van Dorn in the meantime had come up. Those of the Federal fleet came down to the assistance of the Cincinnati, and surrounded the Van Dorn, who made a sudden dash at the Mount City, striking her a midships, driving in her hull about six feet, causing her to leak badly; but as the Federal gun-boats are all built in water-tight compartments, it was some time before she sank; she was able to make the bank. The United States gun-boat Pittsburg was disabled, by getting between the fires of the two fleets. The firing between both fleets was rapid and heavy, and our boats were struck several times, doing some damage to the cabins, but only one was damaged in the hull, and that was the General Price, who received a shell (128 pounds) between wind and water, cutting off the supply pipes and causing her to leak. As the "Feds" had drawn off in to shoal water, where we could not reach them. Commodore J. E. Montgomery signaled the fleet to retire, which was done in good order, all dropping down stream, below the guns of the fort. The total loss was two killed; but several firemen were wounded with splinters, and one man had his arm broken. The only damage was the upper works of the Van Dorn and Price, with the exception damage done the Price reported. As soon as we arrived at Fulton, commenced to repair damages.

Sunday, 11*th.*—All damages on our boats repaired, and all ready for another engagement with the enemy. At 4 P. M. scouts came in from Osceola, report the loss of the enemy to be three boats sunk, and several killed and wounded. The enemy are hard at work raising their boats. The Little Rebel went up on a reconnoissance to-day. On her appearance, the Yankees took their mortar floats and started up the river.

* * * * * * *

Tuesday, June 3*d.*—The bombardment has been kept up, but no damage done to the fort. Second Officer John C. Rawson, and a party of seven men, went after ice, and were captured. At 3.30 P. M., two gun-boats and three rams, came down to cut out the Jeff Thompson, but the fort opened on them, and they retired. The Confederate States' fleet then went up to the fort, and were

actively employed in taking on shot and shell, and
commissary stores, as the fort is to be evacuated.

Wednesday, June 4th, 1862.—The fort being completely
demolished, the fleet started down the river. At Randolph,
the Van Dorn, got aground, and had to send men in
the woods to cut spars and spar her off.

June 5th.—Arrived at Memphis, at 1 P. M.   9 P. M.
all were aroused by the report of a cannon, and a rush
was made to find out the cause, and found the General
Lovell out in the stream, dropping down.   Passing us,
Captain Delancy reported the fleet in the bend above,
coming down.   All then dropped out in the stream, in
line of battle, but the "Feds" not making their appearance, returned to our anchorage.   The tug Gordan
Grant, was sent up as a picket boat, but grounded, and
had to be burnt.

> " Oh, woman, all must own thy magic power !
>   The sternest sages at thy altar kneel ;
> And, from the natal to the final hour,
>   Before thy beauty bend, and deeply feel
> The essence from on high.   Though skies may lower,
>   And earth and heaven conspire against his weal—
> Alike unchanged by happiness or grief,
> Man ever from thy soothing finds relief."

Mrs. H. I. Spotts, is a true friend of the South ; is the
wife of Captain Harry Spotts, well known to the denizens of the Mississippi Valley.   She was a Miss Jane
"Jennie" Tunstall, of an old Kentucky family, of
sprightly intellect, and of extraordinary beauty, being the
belle of Mississippi, where the author had the pleasure of
meeting her, in the days of Auld Lang Syne.   Mrs.
Spotts is a charming lady, and by her sympathies, and
substantial assurances, has given ample evidence of her
appreciation of the virtue that exists in the Southern
struggle for independence, and we rank her in the list of
the true women of the second Revolution.

Mrs. David Looney,* is an estimable lady, is a daughter
of the late James Roland, formerly of Kentucky, late of

---

* Now (1868) residing in New York.

Memphis, Tennessee, and the wife of Colonel David Looney, of Louisville. She has given a great many evidences of her sympathy with the South, is a thorough lady, and in every way fitted to take her place and have her name enrolled upon the tablets of history, as one whose name is worthy to be recorded, as one of the women of the second Revolution. The ladies of Kentucky, in spite of the distraction of their State, have stood firm, and by their example, have incited their fathers, husbands, brothers, friends and lovers, to deeds of valor, and stimulated them to enter the field, in the defense of the down-trodden South. Yes, all honor to the fair women of Kentucky. They have stood by us in all our distress, and are justly entitled to our grateful acknowledgments for their resolution and faith. We take much of our inspiration from fair woman, she who is an incentive to gallant deeds, (her smiles and her approvals,) then let us honor her, and be true to ourselves, and all will be well.

Several of our prisoners have appealed to the military governor of Tennessee, for a release from durance, promising not to take up arms again during the war. It has been done under excitement, and in a week, they will regret it, (which they have,) and as they are heartily ashamed of it, we withold their names. However, the military governor of the volunteer State will not pay any attention to their application, as he is relentless in his determinations.

Since hearing of Andrew Johnson's* appointment as military governor, our Tennessee prisoners have been rather nervous, it being rumored he would demand us from the United States' authorities, and transfer us to the Nashville penitentiary, and there attend to us at his leisure. As for myself, his elevation has given me an attack of dyspepsia; added to the homœopathic treatment of the prison, yet in a few days, I hope to regain my wonted vigor, as I am now in the middle of my book, and it's

*The bold stand taken by Andrew Johnson, in defence of the Constitution, in 1868, has placed him in the highest niche of the Southern heart, and what evil he afflicted us with in 1862, is erased from the tablet of memory, leaving stamped upon our minds Andrew Johnson, the greatest living statesman, the unflinching patriot, and the model President.

necessary to keep a clear head, as the modern reader must have fresh "scraps." Then again, I am on the margin of a large body of water, where there are many shoals and quicksands. I must be careful of my literary boat, as all small boats should keep near the shore. Men, too often get beyond their depth, and in attempting to sail in fathomless seas, are overwhelmed and wrecked. One aspires to the legal profession, whose proper employment should be "mauling rails;" another has, by a few years of speculation, accumulated some thousands, and now burns to become a candidate for popular suffrage, is defeated in his aspirations, becomes a political loafer, spends his money for whiskey, and is lost in the whirlpool, filled with political pot-house heroes, he is out of money, won't work, has lost his influence, and has become an object of loathing to his once warm political friends, who could use his money for bands and banners and such like, but now being useless, is kicked out of the circle, and goes down while the sharp ones go up.

Another man comes down the river on a flat boat, (like old Cobb, of Jackson county, Alabama, with a load of salt. Many years ago, when "*salt was salt*," it was *non commatod*, nobody could buy it. Old Cobb, with that strong generosity which he has so frequently exhibited since in his sixteen years in Congress, told the people to take his salt at cost, they were made happy, and Cobb went to Congress, thus virtually *salting the district down.*

It is said of him, (when accused of having voted on both sides of a question, by an opponent, who had the temerity to oppose him,) that he "acknowledged the corn," but retaliated by charging his opponent with "always voting wrong, while by his principles, he was sure to be right in one instance or the other.")

But in this instance, ties up, at the wharf of a Mississippi river town, sell his onions, apples, and whiskey, at handsome profits, and after a term of years, is successful beyond his most sanguine expectations; he is uneducated, and of coarse manner, but honest and happy. He becomes ashamed of his boat, and rents a store on the batture, at last gets upon the hill, becomes a commercial fixture of the city, takes stock in everything, dabbles in cotton, and finds himself in the centre of a social circle, which is a cold bath to him, and he is unequal from a want of education to the requirements of that society; sighs for the poor, yet happy past, and yearns for that circle, that frolicked on the deck of the old "Broadhorn," "Ohio Belle," or "Western Queen:" he becomes morbid, and an habitual drinker, and winds up too often broken in spirits and purse, having quietly killed himself drinking "old rye" in his private parlor, or out of the barrel in his back office, which is the rendezvous of bank and insurance officers, who receive his deposits and take his premiums, laugh at his coarse jokes, and drink his liquor. The poor fellow is out of his depth, and is lost amidst the breakers of a society that he has not been fitted, by nature to enjoy. Another man curses the West Point graduate, and insists that to the people should be left the choice of their leaders. This popular doctrine of universal suffrage, is readily accepted by the masses, in military as well as civil life, and the man formerly a shop-keeper, is made a colonel, the result being, in many cases, his regiment is cut to pieces. This is no slur upon the volunteer system of our country, as I accord to our volunteer officers, (hundreds of whom are gallant and meritorious,) their full meed of praise. But am firm in my belief that education is as necessary in this department as in other schools, and that the oblique attack of Frederick of Prussia, that of seperate columns, by Napoleon, and the arrangement of Xenophon's retreat, are as much subjects of study, with Scott and Hardee's tactics, as is Bacon and Locke to the philosopher, Shakespeare to the actor, Blackstone to the law student, Scott or Henry's exposition to the young theologian.

If men, in all the relations of life, would but realize that "discretion is the better part of valor," and that the hotspur is sure to be circumvented by the oily gammon, that to go to sea, like the wise men of Gotham, in a bowl, is not as secure as a staunch vessel, they would be saved much vexation, and find out that opposition to the true

15

laws of society, is as Quixotic as dangerous, and a being who throws what little brains he may have, into the public chaldron, without discretion, or studied purpose, as to their innate properties, is like the man "carrying coals to New Castle," or the "Dutch taking Holland," proper illustrations of the above truths.) They are little boats, and like my "scraps," should keep out of deep water, for no matter how much temporary success they may meet with, in taking "the flood that leads on to fortune," they will ultimately be swamped, for once a traitor* to their own people. they will ever be traitors to any cause they may espouse.

Among the hundreds of officers captured at Fort Donaldson, Captain Winstead is one of the most marked; tall, with much *distingue*, classical features, elegant manners, with a vast amount of *bonhomme*. Winstead is acceptable to the men, and agreeable to the ladies. I became acquainted with Captain Winstead, at camp Chase, in prison number 3, mess 46, composed of a splendid set of fellows, or "chaps," as Moody politely calls Confederate officers. The mess gave me a grand dinner on my arrival, Captain Winstead presiding. The cards of invitation were playing cards, with the names of the guests on the backs, and were distributed through the agency of a tin plate, as a waiter, in the hands of George Diggons. The writer will wager a bottle of "cliquot," that there are not a dozen young men in the "City of Rocks," (Nashville, Tennessee,) but who know "George," one of the most rollicking, generous, dashing, fighting, good fellows, in or out of a military prison. He is as gleeful as a lark, but get his "dutch up," and he is for a strike "from the shoulder," or "ten steps with a musket."

Diggons was assisted in his efforts to get up a dinner in style, by Lieutenants Harlow and Morton. Harlow is a pleasant gentleman, of an amiable disposition, with a warm temperament, yet pre-disposed to take the world and all things, easy, believing (like the predestinarians,)

---

* The mass of traitors to the South in Tennessee, Stokes, Maynard and others.

that what is to be, will be, even should it never come to pass. The great interest I took in mess 46, was owing to a dream I had months previous to my capture; and on my honor, as a faithful chronicler of human odds and ends, what I relate, are facts. In September, 1861, in camp of instruction, at Germantown, Tennessee, whose leading citizen, Judge Petitt, that honest man and able jurist, and Mrs. Cornelius, that most estimable woman, and their attentions, I will never forget, I dreamed one night, and related it to my mess next morning, composed of Lieutenant U. J. Brooks, of Georgia, a man of courage and decision of character; Captain A. S. Levy, and Colonel W. T. Avery, (I give these gentlemen as proof of my statements, in this particular,) that I was taken prisoner and carried to the North. On entering the prison yard, I saw many faces I had seen in the Confederate lines, and thought it strange they should be there, and not prisoners. I inquired of them the reason of this, they replied, "they were recognized as good Southern men in the South, but were true to the old flag, and their services were then engaged by the United States government, to communicate useful information concerning the movements of the rebels," while at the same time, the Confederates were giving them the heaviest contracts in their gifts. I remarked, "it was very strange." Yes, but you know "a prophet is hardly without honor, save in his own country and his own house," and a man from the North, stands a better chance to obtain employment in the South, than he "to the manor born." In the South, your churches, in a majority of cases, are controlled by Yankee elders and deacons; your bank stocks, to a great degree, are owned in the North, thus controlling your bank officers; two-thirds of your insurance companies are under the same control; the great mass of your railroad employes are of Northern extraction, and with this Northern influence entering into every crevice of the many ramifications of your social, financial, religious, and other circles, how can you expect to succeed in your present struggle for political independence.

"We know and understand these truths, and while we

are trying to make all the money we can out of the South, we are still faithful in our allegiance to that old flag.

"I moved on, and was taken into a room, filled with bunks. Feeling sleepy, I asked *which was my bunk*, and getting into it, woke up."

I never realized this dream until April, 1862, seven months afterwards, (when I met several of these traitors, who had been "running with the hare, and pulling with the hounds." One of them I saw on a Federal gun-boat. General McCown had employed him at Island Ten, to watch the movements of the enemy, giving him a thousand dollars for the service. He accepted the money, and gave the Federals his information in regard to our condition,) when on entering prison number 3, mess 42, camp Chase, I was requested by Captain Frank McLean, to make myself at home. Bed-time approaching, I surveyed my apartment, and asked the courteous captain, *which is my bunk ?* Like a shock, it flashed over me that I had seen the same bunk in my dream, and I got into it a strong believer in dreams. The members of mess 42, were Captain Frank McLean, a gentleman of much polish and solidity of character—he is of the cavalry, and a brave soldier; Lieutenant Porter is a modest, intelligent gentleman; Captain Bob Moore is a hearty, out-spoken, generous soldier; Dr. Dixon is an able physician, thorough gentleman, of gentle mien, yet with sufficient vigor to make his mark in the scientific world; Captain Joe Walker is from Columbia, Tennessee, is a good liver, a genial companion, and although with some *mauvaishonte,* has quite a pleasant address; Lieutenant Joe Irvine is an agreeable, obliging gentleman. These gentlemen formed a pleasant society, and although comparative strangers, we lived like brothers, while tabernacling in mess 42, prison number 3, camp Chase, Ohio.

To say that Moody, that fanatic had charge of the pen, is enough to convince all who know him, how "well we were treated." We were searched on our entrance, from hat to boots, as if we had secreted stolen goods. Eighteen of us confined in a room about fourteen by eighteen feet and our cooking and washing to be done in the same

room, and by detailing, eighteen of us wedged into six bunks. In our prison, number 3, containing nearly a thousand prisoners, we had two sinks, about ten steps from the cabin; they were uncovered, about ten feet in length, five in width, with a pole on each side, two inches in diameter. The depth of the sinks, I am happy to say, I was not so unfortunate as to fathom, which some poor devils did. The cisterns were below the cabins, in the centre of the muddy street, and below the grade of the sinks, consequently, upon the principle that all fluids will find their level. The water of prison number 3, was not as good as *Marah's* wells. In the second cabin from ours, there were several cases of small-pox, and I am constrained to say, remained long enough, (in spite of our appeals to our custodians to remove them to the hospital,) to spread infection, had not an order of the government removed us to Johnson's Island, where we had better scenery, with rations of an umbelliferous nature, (food, physic and poison,) in Pierson's blue beef and sour bread.

One day, Moody exhibited his carcass upon the walls of our pen, and with stentorian voice, yelled "men," to which we responded by going to the doors of our cabins, when lo! "another Richmond" appeared upon the field, in the shape of Brownlow, the irrepressible; he, who while he was willing "to fight rebels until Hell froze over, and then fight them on the ice," yet never drew a sword or shouldered a musket, but made collections of sympathies and substantials, all over the North, and played his financial cards, all trumps, the Federals paying him as the British did Arnold, while they despised him for his ingratitude.

The prisoners, who were present that day, will remember his looks, cadaverous and sinister; his hat pulled fairly down over his eyes, he looked, in the presence of those gallant Tennesseans, the abject creature that he has proven himself to be. He made a speech, and we gave him a patient hearing, on finishing which he stepped one side, to make way for Moody, another light and " specimen brick" of the church militant, which has lost so much caste during the war by its patronage of such "wolves in sheep's clothing," as this patent prea... "Men," says the immaculate, "do you want to...ar preaching next Sabbath, there is a powerful good pr...her from Columbus, who will preach to you, next Sabb...if you are willing?" (Old Brownlow still looked on, gr..., gloomy, and peculiar, with knowing thoughts, an...villainous expression.) "Come, what do you say, me...are you willing?" exclaimed this clerical charlata... A general response, "aye, aye," with one negative fr...an unconverted sinner in a distant cabin, whose idea...ere on a ring he was making, who exclaimed, "no."...immediately jumped upon a stick of wood, and rem...ked, Colonel Moody, excuse that gentleman, he thou...the invitation to preach was to Brownlow. The s...t wilted, Moody's face grew blacker, the prisoners che...d, and I had invitations to dinner for a week.

One of the...ndsomest men in prison, attempted his escape, but fa...d. He shaved off a magnificent beard, and trimme...head of luxuriant, ambrosial locks, and in citizen's cl...nes smuggled in, with a colporteur's pass, purchase...started for the gate with a basket of tracts on his arm...he remainder of the numbers supposed to have been d...ributed to impenitent rebels. Had he moved five minu...sooner or later, he would have been under the bro...canopy of Heaven, without the walls, but as G...eral Prim has it, "inflexible destiny is stronger than t'...will of man," and old Moody happened to pass the ...ate as the guard ushered the pretended colporteur out.

"Good morning, my christian friend."

"Good morning, Colonel Moody."

"Have you a pass?"

"Oh, yes."

"Let me see your pass. I'm in hopes you will convert these rebs. Your name is—"

"It's in the pass, colonel."

"I asked you your name, sir."

"Well, colonel, I told you it was in the pass."

"Well, sir, what is it?"

This was too much for reb, and his patience giving way, the rebellious spirit broke out.

"D—n you, can't you read?"

"Hallo, guards, gobble this reb," which was done, and we dubbed the gallant fellow, "Moody," ever since.

Moral. It is bad enough to forget your own name, but unpardonable in prison, to forget an assumed one. Our friend lost his whiskers and hair, and as a *quid pro quo*, received a punch and reprimand. It might have been worse.

There are in camp Chase, several old men, with hoary locks and tottering steps, (civilians,) who were dragged from their beds, at the dead hour of night, without trial or legal form of arrest, but the "get up, d—n you, we will give you rebels h—l;" and here they are, barely able to keep soul and body together, a sad commentary on the policy of "the best government the world ever saw," while under the control of Yankee Abolition fanatics. It was a piteous spectacle to see these infirm citizens making their way through the mud, which submerges camp Chase, when it rains, to obtain a cup of water from a cistern, foul with the influence of the sinks above them, and all this among a so-called free people. There stands a man on the wall, whom a recruiting sergeant enlisted one month ago, as his foot pressed the shore of America for the first time. He can barely understand the word of command, yet at a signal from the wretch Moody, would murder citizens whose fathers fought for the independence of these sovereign States. The world has never seen so horrible a moral picture as this. There stands the miscreant Brownlow, worse than Arnold. The latter was a traitor from necessity, the former from choice, with his hat over his eyes, gloating over the misfortunes of his fellow-creatures, and as we take our departure from camp Chase, we can but offer a prayer that the poor old men may yet live to see these miscreants meet the fate of Judas. Men seventy and eighty years of age, dragged from their homes in Virginia, and incarcerated in a filthy prison, for what? No charge, no form of law, but to gratify the malevolent hate of that spirit that would murder, rape and rob, in the name of the Federal Union.

Oh, for a Jupiter, to knock such fellows into Hell, as he did of yore.

Camp Chase is situated in a flat, four miles from Columbus, Ohio, with a high board fence around the cabins, which are one story high. There is an elevated plank walk within the yard, to keep us from floundering in the mud, while making the circuit of the prison. It is one of the filthiest prisons of the many pens assigned for the confinement of Confederate prisoners. The sutler has his supplies without the fence, and is approached by a "pigeon hole," in which you insert your hand, drop the money if any is in it," and you obtain the purchase through the same channel. "A little hole in the wall," is at the entrance, where prisoners are searched, and if you have anything valuable, you are sure to lose it. One individual, on searching the writer, attempted to take a small empty flask, when another "fine young thief, of one and twenty," with more of the milk of human kindness, said oh! let him keep it. Falstaff would have gone into ecstacies, could he have recruited from the "fine young thieves of one and twenty," who examined prisoners, in 1862, or part of that year, at prison number three, camp Chase, Ohio.

There can be nothing said that can add to the character of Mrs. Clark, who is a true Southern woman of soul and heart, with an energy that carries our minds back to the women of the first Revolution. She has worked and traversed the four sections of the country, to assist in alleviating the sufferings of prisoners, that the fortunes of war have thrown into the hands of the Federals. She has played the part of mother and sister to the heart-sick soldier, whose face brightens at her coming, confident she brings good tidings. She has never tired, but has struggled and toiled for privileges for the sick and suffering prisoner, and her importunities have rarely been refused. With a powerful family influence, she has been able to do much in substantials, shown in the many little comforts and delicacies that daily find their way to the prisoner, reviving and invigorating him. Mrs. Clark's cheerful face and sympathizing heart is known to thousands of imprisoned soldiers of the Confederate States, who now fill the many prison-pens of the North. This estimable lady is from Virginia, sister of R. W. Moon, Esq., of Memphis, Tennessee, and wife of Judge Clark, of Ohio. She is no fanatic, but is to this continent what Florence Nightingale is to the Old World. God bless her, may her children and her children's children never suffer, and " as the sins of the fathers are visited upon the children, even unto the third and fourth generation," so may the virtues of the mother be visited in drops of mercy, upon her children even to the third and fourth generation.

Dr. Cliff, of Williamson county, Tennessee, late surgeon of Colonel Battel's regiment, the Twentieth Tennessee, who was taken prisoner at Mill Springs, has taken the oath, visits us to-day, and advises all to go and do likewise, but none of us will take it, as we cannot consistently, after the oath we have taken to the South as Confederate officers. We respect Dr. Cliff as a gentleman, but as to the necessity for our taking the nauseous palliative for our supposed offence, if any exists, " we can't see it."

Among the many Southern women who have endured privations to accomplish the darling object of their heart, the independence of the South, and to commune with loved ones in camp and prison, none can be more highly spoken of than that estimable woman Mrs. Harry Hedden. Fragile as a flower, yet with nerves that duty has strung up to a steel hardness, she ran the gauntlet of offensive subordinates, (who are always pushed forward when the duty is unpleasant,) risked life, health and comfort, to visit her gallant husband, Captain Hedden, as splendid a fellow, and chivalric an officer, as tabernacles in our prison home. On arriving, she requested permission to see her husband, but was sternly refused. She plead, her hundreds of miles of travel, her anxiety, but her pleadings were all in vain. Pierson denied the privilege, as the souless wretch is not alive to any emotion of sympathy for the sick, weary or distressed. However, in a lucky moment, the Captain was taken quite ill, and our generous Post Surgeon Woodbridge, swore he was going to die, thus forcing Pierson to admit the wife. Harry got well, was soon after exchanged, and his courageous and lovely wife accompanied him to Dixie. I don't think the captain would have died, but it was a ruse, dictated by love, "which laughs at bolts and bars," and hence was successful.

CHAPTER IX.

NEW ACQUAINTANCES.—CAPTAIN LOW.—LIEUTENANT BOWERS.—CAP
TAIN O'NEAL.—FAITH AND DESTINY.—THE RAFTSMEN OF JOHN
SON'S ISLAND.—THEIR INVENTIVE GENIUS, AND ACCEPTANCE OF
EXPEDIENTS.—CAPTAIN HAYDON, OF TENNESSEE.—FOURTH OF
JULY IN PRISON.—GENERAL FAIR, MINISTER TO BELGIUM.—MRS.
FAIR.—MISS ROSE WYATT.—MRS. BASS, OF LOUISIANA.—J. HUNT
STROTHER, OF MISSOURI.—MISCONCEPTION OF CHARACTER.—COL
ONEL JABEZ SMITH, OF ARKANSAS.—COLONEL CLARK, SIXTH TEN
NESSEE.—CAPTAIN BLAKE, OF KENTUCKY.—A CHALLENGE HAS
PASSED IN PRISON.—A QUIET MAN ON THE CODE DUELLO.—LIEU
TENANT D'AUBIGNE.—MRS. COLONEL BRYAN.—ICE-CREAM SALOON.
—A SQUAD OF PAROLED PRISONERS.—THE FOUR TRAITORS WHO
TOOK THE OATH.

IN forming new acquaintances, one must remember
that first impressions are lasting ; that each word,
each expression, has its weight, and although lost sight
of for the moment, leaves an indellible stamp upon the
memories of both. I always refuse an introduction to
new acquaintances, unless my mental and physical are in
happy unison to produce felicitous effects. This is why
nature assumes the tidy or dashy in the fair sex, or the
exquisite and ponderous, or the elegant substantials in
the males, in their *entre* into each other's society, creating favorable impressions, which are so lasting, that
future years' slatteringly and slovenly manner and dress
fails to eradicate, although it may more or less pall. You
must either storm your new acquaintances, by an overwhelming dash of conversational powers, or solemnly
measure your words, as if announcing profound ideas,
often obscure to yourself, or you must by a certain degree
of *manvais honte*, be an eager listener to the supposed

intellectual pearls, that are dropping from the mouths of
your new acquaintances.   I dropped into a new set to-
day.   I found Captain Low, a modest, intelligent gentleman, full of nerve and resolution.   I like him as a new
acquaintance very much.

Lieutenant Bowers is a man of much thought, and for
his age (twenty-six) developes the facial corduroy of thirty-five.   He is a gentleman, and, I am confident, a good
officer.

Captain O'Neal, of the Thirty-second Tennessee Regiment, I am much attached to.   He is one of your whole
souled fresh men, ever ready to do a generous deed, and
whose every pulsation and innate promptings are of disinterested politeness and friendship, a genial companion,
intelligent officer and good man, full of confidence in
his kind.   'Tis a blessed boon to have such a nature, and
Captain O'Neal is a happy man.

General Prim, of the Spanish forces, writing from
Orizaba, Mexico:

"Inflexible destiny* is stronger than the will of man."

I remember once, as I was wandering over the memorable field of Waterloo, to be impressed with how much of
human happiness and human success depend upon faith,
and how impossible it is to anticipate a Heavenly future
without it.   The ancient philosophers, either Bias or Pe-
rander, I forget which, said, 'twas hope that was the
strongest thing in nature, because it lasted beyond the
grave.   But I differ; for what is stronger than faith?
and what has more buds of promise to the hopeful?   I
think, they are indissolubly connected, but if there is distinction, I think the inclination is to faith.   The farm
of Hougmont, the celebrated farm house, occupied as a
stragetic point by Wellington, on the field of Waterloo,
has two large gardens, separated by a brick wall, the
entire grounds being surrounded by a wall of the same
material.   The buildings were also brick, as well as a
chapel, as in Europe, (i. e.) upon the continent, the sur-

* Reflections upon the death of that great chieftain, Albert Sidney Johnson,
who seemed fated to be cut off before his time.   'Twas his destiny.

rounding tenantry have no village church, but attend at
the chapel of the estate. This farm was taken and
retaken, by the contending hosts, three times. During
those fierce encounters the buildings caught fire, and
were only extinguished upon reaching the feet of an
image of our Savior, which in all Catholic countries is
always behind the altar of every chapel. (I saw the
image, and with the exception of a little char on its feet,
it was not disfigured.) Was this faith, or was it not?
These Catholics, in spite of the hew and cry of Know-
Nothingism,* the accusation of dissenters, and the male-
volence of many rival sects, have much of the spirit of
faith. Their physical peccadilloes do not seem to disturb
the channel of their devotion to the church, her glories
and her virtues. There may be some discrepencies
—there are some in my own church—but I have traveled
in Catholic countries, and in all of them I have not seen
any more display of the dangers of confessionals, than I
have in the private parlors of Protestantism ; I have seen
no more licentiousness in Catholic courts than in the lob-
bies of Washington, and seductions and murders are of
more frequent occurrence among the Lazzaroni of Italy,
than the roughs of the oyster-cellars of the Points ; and
to-day the only conservative element in the country is
Catholic. It was something saved this image. The
death-dealing missiles were hurling destruction upon all
who attempted to quench the flames, and the chapel was
left to be destroyed. The flames raged until they reached
the feet of the image of our Savior, and then, " I say,"
not " they say," it stopped, and the image stands to-day,
as it stood then. untouched. The chapel is visited by all
the curious of all nations, and as the field of Waterloo is
the Mecca of English travelers, the crowd is numbered
by thousands, that pay their annual pilgrimages of worship at the shrine of the allied successes upon this field of
blood. Of course, as each man is anxious to carve his
name upon some .tablet, that may bequeath him by his
initials to an admiring posterity, I was anxious to impress

* A Yankee trick to divide the Southern Democracy.

upon the same, when I was there, at least, how I spelt
my name, and was making an effort to place my letters
upon the wall, that was literally covered with a thousand,
when a gentleman suggested, that his guide had informed
him that the wall was whitewashed every spring, to make
room for new names.   One visitor, who was up to Waterloo tricks, for fear of this process, stole a brick, by picking
it out, that Byron wrote his name on.   So I declined,
and left the field, after purchasing some Waterloo canes,
from the forest of *Soignes*.   The relics of bullets and
eagles are all manufactured, and I took no interest in
them.

Predestination is a belief, this is not a *concio ad clerum*,
but to prisoners, and is not to force my belief, which is
strong in foreordination, I look upon destiny as a concomi-
tant of faith, and as in the latter, the inspiration incites, so
incitation moulds the subject into such shape as destiny
will accept, and the man of faith becomes the child of
destiny (paradoxically speaking).   Napoleon remarked to
the soldier at his side, who dodged from a passing ball,
"Mind it not, if it was intended to kill you, it would do it,
if you were two hundred yards under ground."   The great
Emperor was a great believer in destiny, and had perfect
faith in his star.   The Sun of Austerlitz, in all his glory,
was an omen to him of a glorious success, and a harbinger
of victory.   Richelieu had faith; so had Wolsey.   The
former's enthusiastic reply to his bearer of dispatches,
when questioning his own success, said, "What if I should
fail?"   "Fail," said the brilliant cardinal, "In the bright
lexicon of youth, that faith reserves for a glorious manhood, there is no such word as fail."   This was faith.   "I
go from a corruptible to an incorruptible crown," said
the heart-crushed Louis.   Here was a faith, that looked
beyond the present sphere, and hoped for a realm where
Revolutions cease to corrupt, and where the thirst for
blood, that men's hands were reeking with, would be as-
suaged, and where Yankee Abolitionists are not known,
not even living in Boston, can save them, even under the
shadow of their deities, that dirty dog and fanatic, Wen-
dell Phillips, the Negro thief, and slanderer of Southern

people, and that old humbug, that keeps the Boston museum.* Charlotte Corday was a child of destiny, when she stabbed the heartless Marat. What but belief in their destiny stimulated the Girondits, and made the "mountain"† feast, the day previous to their execution? Washington bore to the savages a charmed life, as they often said they had him in point blank range to their unerring rifles a hundred times. It was destiny, and Washington had faith in it. Faith as a commander, stimulates armies to deeds of valor. The cry of a Richard, the flash of the steel of a Saladdin, were as inspiring as the bold charge of Boabdil el Chico, and the resistless dash of the gay cavaliers of Spain, under the walls of Granada, to their inspired and enthusiastic followers. Mahomet, although accused of charlatanism, had much faith. His calling the mountain to him, was an evidence, and he displayed his good sense, when finding that the mountain would not come to Mahomet, he said, "Mahomet would go to the mountain." In all ages, and among all men, sects and societies, faith has been the motive power, that has given propulsion to the wheels of the energetic world. It is the incentive to study, and action develops each resource of the finite being, and when united to belief in destiny, prepares us to accept the fiat of that Great Being, who arranges the application of both principle to the *true believer.*

> "Loud roared the dreadful thunders,
> The rain a deluge showers,
> The clouds were rent assunder,
> By lightning's vivid power."

And so raged Sandusky bay, on the night of May the 30th, 1862. The lines above, alluded to the famous bay of Biscay, off the Spanish coast, but they apply with equal force to Sandusky bay, when considering the difference between a full-rigged Queen of the Sea of some

---

* Kimball, whose entertainments are as flat, as his character is negative.
† Let the Southern people do the same, bide their time, which will surely come, and then, when the South is redivivus, take your true position, as rest assured that the South and West will control the country, but at present you can't make the mountains come to you.

two thousand tons, and the delicate limbed and canvassed yachts of the bugs of "Bay City," whose occupation is adapted to the elements they adorn.   In a former
"scrap," I alluded to the formation of a Zouave corps.
The brilliant movements of this gallant battalion has
stimulated others to achieve notoriety by chivalric deeds,
and another organization of some of the decided braves
of the prison was effected.   Their incitation from the
wants of success of the Zouaves led them to adopt a different procedure.   Their war cry, "Arrah, arrah," this
although misunderstood by the sentinel on the watch
towers, would be magical, as the chief was a Celt, genuine and full, but he was much affected by the "Swiney,"
which prevented too rapid locomotion, and thus was calculated to retard the velocity of the manœuvre; this was
obviated by the agile capacities of Captain Thompson,
the Blondin of Johnson's island.   It is to the latter gentleman, we are indebted for the conception of crossing
the bay on a rope.   Thompson, who vowed "he knew
the ropes," would attempt the feat, but one difficulty
seemed in the way, the want of a bottle.   "Herr Cline,"
the famous rope dancer, would take a bottle and sit upon
it on a slender cord, and Blondin would also perform
similar tricks.   This seemed quite an acquisition, and
Captain Thompson was heralded as the apostle of
prisoners desirous of escaping.   The ropes and bottle
were obtained, as Captain Thompson had built up much
prestige upon the peculiar performances, and to be satisfied that all was ready for the hazzardous enterprise, a
rope was stretched across a room in one of the buildings,
and the bottle was produced.   The performance began.
The bottle presented, when by some mistake, (not of the
printer,) but of the Post Surgeon.   It was found to be
full of whiskey.   It had to be emptied.   It was a pity to
waste it, and it was intended that the chief of the corps
should drink it, he did so and the manœuvre opened, but
much to the surprise of the rank and file, the bottle
holder had neglected to tighten the slack-rope, and the
result was a depression, and the chief was on his head.
This not being in the bill, and the attempt having sig-

nally failed from the derangement of the *head* of the column, the ropes were abandoned, and the rafts were
adopted, hence the term raftsmen, and the use of this
means to effect the escape of the disappointed five. The
getting out was not considered, as all said, " *getting out
was nothing*," leaving the island was the rub. The party
comprising the raftsmen corps consist of Captain Jessie
Taylor, Lieutenant Sweeney,* Lieutenants Thompson,†
Stockdell, and Cainpbell, *five trumps, a good haul* for
any enterprise.

The arrangements completed, another difficulty seemed looming up in hideous proportions in the distance,
and to all appearance, it was the fact of the amount of
paper money in the crowd being too large to risk, in case
of a warm or cold bath, if you will, in the bay; and all
seemed desponding, because the party had experienced
much difficulty in obtaining the money. The law of the
prison being such, that the prisoner is only allowed to
buy what he wants, and give checks to the sutler. At
camp Chase they were allowed five dollars at a time, so
as to allow change to buy sundries and papers. Therefore, all kinds of tricks were resorted to get to the money
inside. Some would buy five dollars worth of postage
stamps, and then retail them to the officers, and by " hook
and by crook," our gallant corps obtained a goodly sum.
But the money must be placed in some secure place, it
being paper, and getting wet, would become ruined and
worthless. A bright thought, however, flashed across
the mind of the susceptible Thompson; and seeing the
bottle, drained of its contents, lying in bold relief, on
the bare floor, like some ancient grave yard, "the place
of departed spirits," he grasped it eagerly, and presenting
it with that impulsiveness, that so characterizes the
house of Thompson, exclaimed—"this is the bottle!"
and suggested the happy idea of placing the roll of bills
in it, and then corking it, trusting it to the water,
attached as a caudal appendage, if need be, by a cord to
some one of the party, and on reaching "*terra firma*," to

---

* The gallant Sweeney was killed while nobly performing his duty.
† Lieutenant Thompson had his foot shot off.

16

have the satisfaction of having not only obtained their freedom, but in the possession of ample funds, would hie them to their happy homes, in the land of "Dixie." All seemed delighted, and each extended the hand of congratulation, while the left was elevated by the assistance of the forearm to the auricular extremity of the head, which was the signal agreed upon, "all right." All seemed jubilant and sanguine, but there was one clouded brow, in that brilliant circle, it was ominous of shadowed thought.

"Oh! cast that shadow from thy brow," all exclaimed, but there it was, on the massive forehead of the sprightly Sweeny. The veins upon his brow seemed to swell like the bounding billows of the "Mad lake," whose surface he intended to bare his manly breast to that self same night; those eyes, that when influenced by heart emotions of pleasure, seemed to sparkle like some diamond buried in one of the catacombs of Egypt, or like the application of castile soap to the cranium of some ancient Zouave, whose capillary substance has yielded to the stroke of time, that unrelenting destroyer, and expose from some dark corner, its shining surface, but to be more strikingly like the reflection of a smooth quarter in a rat hole. The hue of his formidable moustache darkened with those sad features, and like some frowning promontory, added an eclipse to the usually happy expression of a mouth wreathed with smiles, that now compressed its lips like the door of the cave in "Ali Baba's" time, when the magic word "Sesame" had been pronounced in commanding tones. In this case 'twas bottle, the clenched teeth gritted together like the shock some closing fissure of some convulsed system, and he came out with his pent up feelings barely restrained, in one loud acclaim, "How can the money be gotten out of the bottle?" The crowd of anxious friends, who had awaited the results of the mountain in labor, felt like an Ateas, or the old man of the mountain, had been removed from their shoulders, and the sunshine of satisfaction illumined the countenances of the re-assured crowd. It seems that the history of the "apple dumplings" had not been imparted to the youths in their early course of studies, and therefore the abstraction of substances from vacuums as imbecile, as one of the merry monarchs said in Merrie England, when presented with the mysterious compound, "y'e clept apple dumplings," "Pray good dame," quoth he, "how got the apples in?" But with Sweeny, the problem that required solution, was, "quoth he," how will you get the money out? Excitement was depicted on each rueful face, as they thought of the danger they had ran, and all looked upon Sweeny as the discoverer looks upon a Kane, a Marcapola, a Columbus, or a Bilbo; and never did as much consternation exhibit itself than on this occasion, when they awoke to a perfect realization of the dangers they had escaped.

Mutual congratulations ensued on the narrow escape of the party from pecuniary annihilation, and the entire party concluded to retire for that night, with a consciousness, that some other plan must be adopted to effect their deliverance, as the failure of the Zouaves, and the risk of getting their money wet, disturbed their raft evolutions, and they retired to their cubby-holes, satisfying their intellects, that getting out was not what it was cracked up to be, and that scaling, sprawling, or squatting would not pay. They felt, that to cross Sandusky bay on a raft might do for a seal or walrus, but not for a Confederate, and to land in the North without a cent, Stockdell says, is the next thing to supping with Pluto; and Jessie Taylor being a man of sense, he added his voice, and the raft was abandoned; Campbell determining he would *humph* himself off, in some *dryer* way—such as reading my account of it.

Captain Hayden, of Tennessee, sits at his window, and as he sees the boats come in view, says, as he retreats from the window, "Don't look, boys, treat them with silent contempt," and all drew back. It seems magical, the campus that a few moments before had been alive with Confederates, seem to catch the inspiration, and all rapidly withdraw to their quarters, leaving the vulgar curiosity of the insulting songsters, with their "Stars and stripes," and "The red, white and blue," to luxuriate in ·

full view of a tamer heather in the plain walls of our
quarters. It was a good joke on the *small fry quill
drivers* of the nine-inch sheets across the bay, in trying
to drum up customers, for a pleasure excursion on an old
hack-boat, to enlarge upon the "sight," on Johnson's
island.

Captain Hayden is in the engineer corps, is an experienced engineer, and one of the best informed men in the
"bull-pen," a deep thinker, a careful reader, of much of
the German scholasticism about him ; a great believer in
the mysteries of nature, like your humble author, and a
man whose mind seems to accept all outward natural
influences. I like to argue with the captain, as he has
much of that courtliness of the Virginian of the old school,
he being a native of the Old Dominion, although a Tennessee volunteer, and this, with his travels and his deep
researches, makes him a reliable companion, as well as a
pleasing one. If he does oppose my theory of "like be-
getting like," in figure and mind, but more particularly
in complexions and outlines, I argue that constant associations with any or each element in the physical world,
produces a likeness in each, that attracts a close observer
to the strong assimilation even in ideas. I believe, the
man or woman, who lives constantly in the woods, with
no companion but the brave old oaks and the tight bark
hickories, and the rude and compact cane, will ultimately
become hard in visage, rude in manners, and partake of the
humaness of the wild nature they associate with. Contact with the animal, constant seeing and rubbing against
the crudeness of the tangled forests, or the dense and regal
woods, is as effective in forming not only physical traits,
but also physiognomy, as the power of education or association forms the personelle and the manners. Did you ever
see people who looked like animals? I have. Some
people look like the bark upon the forest trees, and their
manners are like their countenances. Captain Hayden
says, 'tis the result of impressions, produced at certain
seasons, upon certain parts of the human family. I don't
think so. I look upon it as the result of associations.
Cities give polish; there is much corruption in their pur-

lieus, but it is refined; you are murdered with a smile, and robbed with a salam, yet enjoy it more than the "stand and deliver of the road." In speaking of the woods, I don't mean the country entire, with its honesty and candor, its soothing influences of quiet and contentment, but I allude to the wild woods.

The Fourth of July was decorously observed, and in a manner becoming officers on such a day and in such a place, upon the soil of our forefathers, where we are now victims of the most abominable despotism in the universe, resembling more the terrorism of the Visigoths and Vandals. The Fourth of July, two years ago, I passed a happy one in Europe, as a representative of the happiest and the most powerful government in the world; to-day I am a prisoner of war, held by the fiat of a kingdom, a usurper, one whom the Almighty seemed to have placed at the head of a government destined to destruction. No great man would have been allowed to have occupied the seat of the head of such a corrupt dynasty, and it seems a part of the Divine wisdom, to have put the right man in the right place. All are quiet, it seems, like the Sabbath. I repeat it, on this the 4th day of July, 1862, in prison on Johnson's island, the Confederate officers acted well. I have episoded on this chapter, but if you are willing to put up with the literary crumbs, that fall from the tin-plates of my oaken, greasy table, why, you will be compelled to accept my " scraps" with a good grace, as stated, two years ago, I passed a Fourth July in Europe, and being honored by the receipt of an invitation to dine at Brussels, from the American Minister, General Fair.

General Fair, Minister to Belgium, is an honest, hospitable gentleman, gave good dinners, and always had on hand a bottle of " eye opener." His office and drawing-rooms were always open to his American friends. He is a true Southern man, and deserves well of the South.

Mrs. Fair is polite, fragile, but with a great spirit, and any quantity of active energy. Mrs. Fair, in fact, is one of the best feminine diplomats I met in Europe, is an esteemed friend of the Duchess of Brabant, and has the *entre* of the best society in Europe.

Miss Rose Wyatt, Mrs. Fair's niece, is a beautiful girl of sixteen summers, accomplished and intelligent. The above were the family, to whose courtesy I am indebted, for much of the pleasantness of my sojourn in Brussels, the beautiful capital of Belgium. The General and family are residents of Montgomery, Alabama. I took a dinner on the 4th with this agreeable family. ·

Mrs. Bass,* of Louisiana, is an elegant woman in carriage, a *tout ensemble* of Parisian mould, the result of constant attendance in the best society of the continents of Europe and America, superb taste, and an inexhaustible supply of this world's goods. You have before you the widow Bass, of Louisiana, one of the most stylish women I met in my travels in Europe. Her brother was on my left, quite an agreeable young man, now in our army and a good officer. Judge Cobb, of Georgia, a delegate from the cotton planters association, a man of venerable appearance, and much information.

J. Hunt Strother,† of Missouri, a gentleman who is connected by marriage with some of the nobility of Austria, was one of my personal friends, and a whole-souled gentleman. A residence of twelve years in the capitals of Europe, had made him *aufait* in all that appertains to the first order of society. I'll never forget an incident that occurred in Brussels, in which he figured. The "octoire" duties had been abolished by the representatives in Congress, and approved of by King Leopold, and was to go into effect by a popular demonstration of the Burgeois of the city and environs. This "octoire"‡ duty was a special tax on all liquors and meats that came within the barriers, (i. e.) the corporate or municipal limits. The tax was about one cent per pound, on meats,

---

* Wife of the Italian Minister, (1867,) to the United States.

† Hunt Strother's sister married the Baron Fahrenburgh. She is one of the handsomest, and most hospitable of the nobility of Europe.

‡ There is no octoire duty in America, but ladies were searched during the war, by many of the defenders of the "old flag," bureaus broken into, work baskets examined for bombs,hells, and everything stolen—old Butler the Beast—that could be laid hands on ; no privacy respected, missionaries to foreign lands forsooth. There is not a mother in the world who would be guilty of the excesses of the miscreants who plundered Selma, and sacked Columbia.

and about twelve dollars on a cask of wine; and as a
city improved, and the residences went up in squares,
outside the prescribed limits, their female occupants were
liable to be searched for anything possibly contraband in
satchel or redicule. Of course, although the loss of
revenue was some three millions of dollars, yet the abating
of the nuisance was hailed with unfeigned delight by the
class alluded to, particularly aided in their expressions of
joy by the Burgeois, who anticipated cheap meats and
wine. "Hunt" and myself, concluded as our residence
in Brussels had as yet produced no uprorious results, we
would engage in the rejoicings of the good Burgeois of
the city, and give them a touch of western hilarity.
The clock struck twelve, and the day that was thus timely
ushered in to herald the going into effect of the freedom
of outside productions in their transit, was made wild with
the cheers that greeted a wagon loaded with beef, mutton,
beer and wine. The crowd numbered thousands, and
they gave vent like most of foreigners, to a sort of growl.
I have said cheer; 'tis not on that order. It is to the
cheer of an American, like the war-whoop of an Aborigne
was to the early settlers upon Plymouth rock. We passed
to the front and commenced a series of whoops; the
sensation was electric. We still continued. Like a host
of fiends were after them, they took up the cry, and not
since the departure of the crusaders, or the finding the
mannikin, did the streets of Brussels ring with the vo-
ciferations of the aroused and excited citizens. We
thought the storm was at its height, and left, going to the
Prince of Wales' coffee house, and taking—a glass of
"'alf and 'alf." This was my only spree in Brussels
with Hunt Strother, or " any other man."

Corr Van Damaren sat opposite to me. This gentleman
was judge of the tribunal of commerce, president of the
board of free traders, and the Cobden of Belgium, an
able exponent of the system he advocated. Speeches
were made, and all were gay. This gentleman alluded to
an audience I had with the Duke of Brabant, one of the
most thorough gentlemen I ever met, and a fit scion of

that astute King Leopold,* and remarked, looking at the hand the Duke had removed his glove to shake, said to me, " I'd never wash that hand again, as long as I lived." It was a pleasant gathering and characteristic of General and Mrs. Fair; but this *Infair* of the ever memorable anniversary of the independence of the United States of America, although more festive, is not of as much moment as the day itself in prison on Johnson's island. "A long way round, you will say," I've no doubt, but as I started out to write as I felt, as I wished, and as I know how, I am going to do the same in this and all succeeding "scraps." We drink no champagne here. Some messes, I believe, had whiskey. The sick in the hospital, had some "knick nacks," puddings perhaps.

Our next Fourth of July, I hope, will be in the happy land of Dixie. I have closed this chapter. It has been called watery by Captain Jones, of Kentucky, a splendid fellow, a staff officer of Tilghman's, and a dashing soldier. Jones is with us daily, and we take liberties, (at times, something else.) Jones says it is watery, but if so, 'tis variety, and as variety is the spice of sublunary things, I have concluded to put it in the bunch or bundle of "scraps" I offer to a nation of epicures. It is growing dark, and the Fourth of July is lost in the sultry retrospection.

Prison life is the best index to the character in the world, and if within the reach of all, students of morality would be the graduating class, for school hours, those devoted to tare and tret, and the syntax and prosody, "*Ego amo*," declamation and composition, are the preparatory ingredients to form the man; but the moulding is by contact with the outer world, and it is only by rubbing against the various phases of society, that the mind is matured and fitted for the active duties of a deceptive world, filled with every incentive to err, and alive with vice in a myriad of shapes and fancies. Our youth have an entire misconception of life, its aims, its demands, and its obligations; the effects of which want of information shows disastrous results all through life's journey. I've

---

* The present King of Belgium, Leopold, is the most intelligent gentleman I met in Europe, having a quick apprehension, and comprehensive conception.

seen and mingled with all grades of society, and have seen much of *that* class, vulgarly called "big men," and like all hills that seem green and grassy in the distance, or like huge mountains, or deep vales, encountered in the path, seem small when you approach them, and the mass of "big men" I've seen, are quite common when you approach them, and if half the youth of our country could be taught the habits and different usages of first-class society, after they are on the way, or have attained the full zenith of their ambition, they would, (if moral,) cease to have that reverence for legislators, and that awe of "big men," statesmen and warriors. Much of the dignity and pride you see in men is assumed; 'tis a false key played upon; it is the same disguise used by the actor, put on to suit his role; frequently like the clown, so flimsy as to be penetrated by the child. How many men are to the world what they really are in their natural selves? About one in a hundred. Frederick the Great, was an intelligent monarch, yet would get upon his all fours and play horse for his children. Napoleon cooked omelets, Webster had an uxorious love of stock, and one of the last acts of his life was to have some *Ayrshire* cattle brought to his window to gaze upon, with a mind and heart free from anxiety, and full of innocent amusements. 'Tis true that these men of great intellects are the effects of a reactionary influence, like that great void or hollow-ness after too much laughter, the nervous depression after excitement, or *vice .versa*, calm and sadness will be fol-lowed by storm and hilarity. But few men live one life to themselves and the world. The mass of great men put their manners and feelings on like they do their cloaks.

Colonel Jabez Smith,* of Arkansas, is a quiet, mild gentleman, one you would take for a draw-back upon enterprise, from his easy and loose manner of quiet, and his reserved style generally, yet stir up the inner man of "Jabez Smith," and you have a lion in the path.

Colonel Clark, of the Sixth Tennessee, is a gentleman

---

* Necessity for a knowledge of the world to Colonel Jabez Smith, one of the best judges of human nature in the pen.

of pleasant and agreeable manners, has a large quantity of the "man of the world" in him, an officer, I am confident, who is loved by his command ; yet Colonel Clark is a quiet man, nothing of the braggart, but on the field, I'll wager, is full of metal.   You would, if a casual observer, misunderstand him.

Major Brown, of the Fiftieth Tennessee, is a modest lawyer, (i. e. if there is such an animal,) a thorough gentleman, and one of the mildest men in prison, but if I am any judge of character, he is one of the firmest in our circles, and one to whom the most dangerous enterprises could be entrusted.   I like Major Brown; he is a christian gentleman, a cool, calm, kind and generous officer.   I have simply touched these characters off, as they are in prison, and as, I think, they are at home.

Captain Blake, of Kentucky, is the hospital steward, and is confined strictly to the hospital and its duties, is a good liver, and is quite faithful in his attentions to the sick.   Blake looks more like a festive and gay man of the world, fond of a "smash" in the morning, and the opera at night, than an attentive and kind man to the sick and needy.   I know the character of Captain Blake, simply from a little occurrence.   I was indisposed, and there was an embargo on spirits ; Blake administered a brandy-toddy; it cured me.   I don't know where Captain Blake obtained it, but as the Nigga said, "'twas powerful good." Blake, like many of us, in prison is natural, out of prison we are artificial.   I know some individuals here that, when they get out, will, if asked, if they knew so and so, as a seedy personage passed, who has nodded, " Oh ! yes, slightly, a mere watering-place acquaintance, not at Saratoga, Cape May, or Biloxi—no, Johnson's island."   "Ah! ha!" says the stranger, as he walks off.   "Snob," the leaver of outdoors has worked, and the natural man of Johnson's island becomes the artificial scrub of Canal street.

I would ask my readers, to take a careful survey of prison life.   Study man in his two lives, the inner and the outer, and he will learn much.   Man's study is man. There are many influences that may tend to warp a man's

natural instincts, and avocation may change him unbe-
known to himself; yet this is the exception, not the rule.
The man is a victim of society, and with all its despotism,
he is held under its tyrannical rod by iron hands, in spite
of himself, and while conforming to its rigidity, he licks
the rod that chastises him. So to avoid the seeming des-
tination of youth, let him read his history of the world
early, not pore over them in old age, instruct him in
character, and teach him that the world is a great volume
in paragraphs, illustrated with its plates, highly colored,
whose attractions are apt to attract from more sedate
colorings, and as he turns over each new leaf in the wonderful book, see that he leaves no thumb-marks, and don't
let him suffer, as many do, by a sad experience, that says,
well, I'll profit by this example, and be instructed for the
next emergency. But, unless schooled, the student is
never profited, but is attacked by new issues, until experience comes too late. If you want your boy to have
the instincts of a man, bring him to Johnson's island, and
let him study human natural nature.

I am, in this "scrap," on another tack, as I found out,
upon a critical analysis, that I was getting prosy; and
then again, I find it difficult to adopt any singleness of
style, for instance: it would not do to attempt a novel,
because you will say, Bulwer, James, Scott, or Maryatt are
good enough for you; nor a history—McCauly's or Pres-
cott's works will suit; and as to the blood and thunder
of periodicals, why Emerson Bennett will answer. So
what should I write? Anything I please! Just exactly
what I have done, what I am doing, and what I intend
to do. I have in some previous "scraps" alluded to
various subjects, such as forces, politics, connection between mind and matter, and etc.

I will now present a peculiar theory of mental disease,
believing as I do, that there are periodical mental visita-
tions, as well as physical epidemics: that "free loveism"*
is a disease. Abolitionism and Mormonism, and all

*Turkey is called "the sick man," because politically diseased. As the cru-
sade against the South in 1862, history will prove to be as fearful a political
and moral disease, as the plague of London in the seventeenth century.

influences that tend to revolutionize society, is as much
a disease as the small-pox or yellow fever, and the mental
powers can be easily caught by the infection that a
man can imagine himself ill, (like the old man in the field,
who had put on his son's vest, entirely too small for him,
imagined himself bit by a snake, and that he was swelling
under the influence of the poison, was only relieved on his
son arriving with his father's vest dangling around him;)
the mind contemplating, makes it susceptible, or like the
passage of the angel of the plague into grand *Cairo*,
when asked how many he intended to destroy, replied
3,000; on coming out was informed 15,000 had died,
retorted, I only killed 3,000, the rest died of fear. The
fright was as much an epidemic as the loathsome disease
itself. The mind is delicately susceptible, and assisted by
the imagination; then reflected to other imaginations,
inspires enthasiasm or inflicts despair, and there has not
been an age or even a year, but some disease, social or
political, has run like wild fire through society. 'Twas
the case in the South, and particularly so in the State of
Mississippi, from 1831 to 1842. Much of the effects of
this epidemic that was called the "Duello," was witnessed by the author. Randolph and Tom Benton, had
their opinion of the "code." Randolph changed his
opinion three times in his life; once strongly advocated
the principle, then condemned, then again became a
supporter. During a latter stage of opinion, he fought
Mr. Clay, Randolph's argument, was "Duelling" is individual war. I will give an instance of the feeling existing at
that time in Vicksburg, Missssssippi, the rendezvous of
such men as S. S. Prentiss, McClung, Robbins, and a
host of others, gallant men, whose bravery was made the
avenue to *mislead* them to (what is deemed by many)
barbaric encounters. I was at the school of an old
gentleman whom we all loved and feared, for he did not
spare the ferule or the birch. It was 1838, when, one
bright morning, all Vicksburg was crossing the river to
the "battle ground," as the encounters were all in one
place and of frequent occurrence, as any stranger who
visited Vicksburg, contemplating settlement, if a pro-

fessional gentleman, had of necessity to fight a duel, to establish his claim to gentility. The river was covered with skiffs or canoes, (usually called *dugouts*,) as it was always a gala day, and witnessed with as much gusto as a "bull-fight" in Spain, or the old English and French tournaments of the good old day of legalized chivalry The duel came off at 7 A. M., between Judge Lake,* and Tom Robbins ;† the former killed twenty years afterwards, in a duel with rifles, (not long ago,) the latter, a distinguished Mississippian, but a native of Pennsylvania, died in the insane asylum, 'tis said, at Philadelphia, the place of his nativity. I, with the other boys, crossed the river to see the fight, anticipating to get back in time for school hours, 9 A. M., but the duel was postponed until 10 A. M., and we feeling disappointed, started back and darted into the school yard as the bell rang, much excited by our race to get back in time, as boys will loiter, and we were boys.

" Where have you boys been?"

" To see the duel."

" Did it come off?"

" No, sir."

" Well, when is it to be decided?"

" Ten, to-day, Mr. Lewis."

" Why you young rap-scallions, why didn't you stay and report the results? School is dismissed, you have been good boys and shall have a holiday. Bring me my pony, (which as he was lame he always rode,) and I'll go and see the fight."

He did go, saw it; his pony strayed off, and our good old master was three days finding him, and of course we had a jolly good time. So much for the duel fever of 183-. Judge Lake's gun snapped, (they fought with double-barreled shot guns,) the latter lowered his gun magnanimously, and shot him in the knee. Sargeant S. Prentiss came from Portland, Maine, to Mississippi; a quaint, mild, gentlemanly master of the ferule. In five years he was the "Ney" of the State in the "code."

*Judge Lake, one of Mississippi's distinguished sons.
†Tom Robbins was a Pennsylvanian, and the soul of chivalry.

You see at once how catching the disease was, and in spite of the many flings at the "Yankees," they seemed to have been more violently attacked than the denizens of the fighting latitude themselves. Prentiss' life has been written, and I shall briefly allude to a man that I loved, "They say," and as "Burr" said, witheringly; "don't tell me what they say," that the brilliant orator drank, that he gambled; well, so he may have done, and how few great men but do. Nine men of brains out of ten, are men of sensibility, of ambitious hopes, of great nervousness, and in ninety-nine times in a hundred, are men of disappointed aims and desires. Again, men who attain a position in the world, do it at the sacrifice, (in a large majority of cases,) of the physical man; the intense application of mental, the continued strains upon the nerves, require artificial stimulants. Some fly to the card-table, some to the bottle, and others to other sources of dissipation. Men of mediocrity seldom drink, (of course I leave out the church,) it is only the two classes; the blackguard in the gutter, or the man of genius of high tone, who feels that the world is selfish, that dollars are almighty with the masses, and the plating of society silvered by peculation, is fastened upon a corrupt system, that, like a corporation, is soulless, and is represented by the "Hickmans" and McFlimsys of society. The man of heart and soul feels all this, and is driven to some excitement to quell the emotions of disgust, that rise in his heart when contemplating society from such a standpoint. A society that will say to the soldier,* who perhaps after suffering for months in camp, from disease and exposure, comes home maimed and broken up in constitution and in purse; and after the war is over, and trade has resolved into its original channels, and preferment is in the current of peace, when war is forgotten by those who did not go into it, and those who did, have no power to do good, he asks a pittance, it may be he has imbibed too much,

---

* In the South he has but little advantage, and in the North he may be seen the recipient of coppers, as he handles the organ's crank in the place of the musket.

what matter, he is broken down and feels sick at heart, when gazing on the tinsel of society, that glitters past him, unconscious of the suffering he has endured for his country and his flag, and he is desperate and asks for help, the reply is: "We have so many calls of similar character, it is impossible to supply the demand ; George, give this man a dollar." The money is thrown upon the counter, by a sleek young gentleman, whose future is in the color of his meerschaum, and the gloss of his hair, with the expression, "These *fellars* are very annoying." He takes the dollar, and unless he wants a drink badly, throws it at his head, damning the world by sections, and feeling that ambition and patriotism are the results of the ideal and imaginative, and not intended for practical life, unless their votaries are the children of property. Prentiss saw things in this light. He was disgusted. Then he loved certain society, he was in bad health, and then, what if he did drink, so did Webster, so do most all great men. The author is no apologist for this vice, believes in the use and not abuse, and only drinks upon two occasions; one is, when he is invited, the other, when dry. The duel and street fights of those years would fill a score of volumes, therefore have no place in this work. I have merely alluded to the principle, and only partially to the actors in the drama.

Duelling is not the proper settlement of difficulties, out of the army or navy, there where men have united themselves to make a business of fighting. The "code," ought most certainly to be accepted, but I ignore it in civil life, as barbarous in the extreme, as there is no equality between the good and bad shot, the splendid and indifferent swordsman, or the athletic and the pigmy, (with the bowie,) you can't place men upon an equal footing in the field, and when they are, it makes no difference, because they *seldom fight.** I speak of the

---

* One of the most ridiculous customs, is that of field arrangements. Settlements should be made before they reach the ground. A good business for a tactician in the "code" would be to open a broker's office, charging a per centage, to make honorable adjustments.

rule, not the exception. I must admit, I have been nearly drawn into rashness, which might have resulted in a duel, but if so, had I escaped, would have felt that I had abandoned my principles, and sacrificed my moral worth to the severe demon of a false sense of honor, formerly called the "code," by a false society, that has for its stand point, punctillio, that only a fraction comprehend, and they mutilate the part they pretend to accept. I see that I am compelled to start on some other subject, as details of men, and their actions become tiresome to the reader, where there are so many men of genius and note in the land, and if I am wearying my reader, why I feel sorry for it, but he or she will pardon this apology and digression, when I tell them, that in this "bull-pen," there are some thousand Confederate officers, possibly eight hundred of them under thirty years of age. These men are, some of them at least, men of the first order of talent, and with the world before them, many of them will make their mark, therefore I deem it may be interesting in after life to read them, and know who they are. Now, there goes Captain Vance Thompson, of Columbia, Tennessee. He passes by with a light active step, and a certain *suaviter in modo*, showing the careless and easy man of the world, yet Vance Thompson is one of the most brilliant speakers in the State, and formerly beat one of our ablest men for a seat in the Legislature, and you would not think it to look at him. Men become creatures of habit, and like all men of talent, Thompson conforms to circumstances, and yields to habit.

Speaking of habits, and brilliant men, and how men under the influence of this force will exhibit it, I remember being at a dinner in Paris, given to Americans by Charles J. Faulkner, assisted by some liberal Americans, Monroe & Co., the celebrated bankers, and several others of the wealthy Americans, residents of the city. "Dency," the liberal French millionaire, whose wine cellars in champagne, had three millions of bottles at that time. "Dency," with princely munificence, furnished the wine, and with generous politeness, assisted in dispensing and discussing it. It was a Fourth of July affair, and promised to be grand. Among the guests present, was "Big Beverly Tucker," consul to Liverpool, who had come to Paris, (he said,) for his rheumatism, I thought, for the frolic. Beverly Tucker, is a good liver, like all of our foreign and consulor agents abroad, and when the Southern Confederacy is recognized, Tucker will get something. I'm sure he is the man for a fat office, and I think he deserves it. "Gus" Conover, of New York, was there. It is this gentleman that allowed himself to be caught in the net of the *Fowler*, to the tune of some $50,000, when said Fowler was postmaster of New York city. I look upon Conover as a man of fine character. George Law's son, of the same city, a pleasant young man of good manners, not spoiled by the immense means his father's fortune furnished. The author's secretary was there, Lush Taliafero, of Newport, Kentucky. This young gentleman, now a lieutenant in the Federal army, has at least one virtue, that of being the son of Mrs. F. M. Parker, one of the best women of Kentucky. "Lush" is a lion among the ladies, and of a *tout ensemble* that would stamp the child of fortune, (born with a gold spoon in his mouth.) I again met Mr. Cobden at this point, and he had the same placid smile, ready conversation, that discovers so easily, to even a casual observer, the politician. There are some three hundred more, whose names would not interest any one, and in fact I don't know that these will, but it is in the bill, and I am compelled to go through with the performance, but I'll make it short.

I intended to state, that man is a creature of habit. Now amidst other festive demonstrations, it was necessary to have a speech ; so the Honorable Charles J. Faulkner was called upon. It must be considered, that it was getting late in the day, and that wine had been used *ad libitum*. The courteous Minister rose, and said : "Fellow countrymen, upon this anniversary of our national independence, we feel that it behooves us to celebrate it in a manner becoming worthy sons of those noble sires, who fought, bled, and died, in Freedom's cause—*and stand-*

17

ing, as I do, here beneath these wide-spreading elms—." Here I left, as there was not a tree in a half mile, and I felt satisfied, 'twas the force of habit, and nothing else, showing the influence of Fourth of July orations, at points where there were *wide-spreading elms.*

There goes another officer, passing my window as I write, always grinning, ever humorous, and constantly in fun or frolic, ready for cards, ball, fight, or a foot-race. Who is he? *The Blood Hound.* Yes; that agreeable looking individual is Captain Harris, called, by common consent, the "Tennessee Blood Hound." It is hard to realize, that a man can smile and kill; yet they say Harris will take a chew of tobacco, and draw a bead upon the enemy's eye with equal non-chalance. There is something in the depths of that man's flashing eye, that reveals the unrest of ill-restrained passion, that like the snake, charms while it stings. I don't like to fight men like Harris; you are hurt before you know it; a laugh one minute, and a death-blow the next.

This is a great place to study human nature—this prison. Look at Lieutenant-colonel Wood, of the famous Natchez troop of cavalry. There he goes, coat off, hat in hand; he is playing town-ball, running and cheering as lustily as the youngest player in the party—the entire set looking like the boys upon the college campus. And yet see Colonel Wood in the fray, amid the clash of sabres and shriek of minies, and he is a tiger, a brave, gallant, dashing soldier. Lieutenant-colonel Wood is a son of the surgeon-general of the United States army.

There goes a Texas Ranger; buckskin hunting-shirt, and leggins of the same material. If any man has read the tales of our borders, Texas and her conflicts with the Mexican and the savage, he has not failed to feel interested in the history of these rangers. Recklessly brave, splendid horsemen, (as they ride like the Commanches, while the animal is at full speed, picking a coin from the ground, while they retain the saddle,) and of great power and endurance, they are formidable enemies. Captain Austin is one of these, and is a man of fine physique and prepossessing manners. A good idea suggests itself to me for cavalry; it is the ranger's.   Take a cup, fill it with all kinds of spices, take a peck of corn-meal, swing it in a bag over your horn or crupper, and when hungry, take a tea-spoonful of spice, half a cup of corn-meal, mix with water, and 'twill satisfy you for the day in an emergency.   The above quantity will sustain life in a nourishing manner for twenty days.

In looking out of my window, at the few representa-tives of that famous battery, the Point Coupe artillery, who are with us in prison, I am forcibly impressed with the fact, that some of the best blood of America is con-fined within these prison walls.   Lieutenant Legendre, a young Creole, of New Orleans, and a cousin of General Beauregard, is now promenading the campus.   He is one of the most courtly looking gentlemen in prison; his face alternating in flashes of pleasant thought and clouds of present troubles, expressed in the glittering eye, and frowning brow; he is possibly thinking of the Crescent City, of Royal street, and the St. Louis, and of his pleas-ant home; which thoughts are broken by the reality of his foul imprisonment, and the fiery Frenchman frets. They are a great people, the Creoles of Louisiana; and among the most distinguished soldiers in the Confederate service, are those who have been fledged under the wing of the pelican.

Lieutenant D'Aubigne is a descendant of the great writer of that name, and to look at the pensive cast of features and thoughtful brow, you can easily discover traces of the author of the history of the Reformation. These young Frenchmen are disinterested patriots, having left affluence and position behind them, to face disease, death, or imprisonment, for the cause they have espoused. In them we see the days of chivalry revived, and they should feel, that it is no disgrace to be a prisoner.   Lafay-ette languished in prison, so did the present Emperor of France, and so have the great and good, of all ages, and we are but mortal, and must bend to the fiat of destiny. Yet our motto is, *nil desperandum*, which will sustain us, until we leave these quarters; after which we hope to have a better appreciation of the troubles of those who have suffered before us, and may come after us.

To-day, prison life was illumined by a female form, one of grace and elegance, Mrs. Colonel Bryan, who visits her brother, Captain Sam. Thompson, a prisoner with us. Her appearance infused new life into our prison circles. It seems, as if there is something more soothing and refreshing in the rustle of female garments, than in any of the other modifiers of the prison worry ; the step of a gentle, loving woman, with her winning smile, and cheerful presence, are well-springs of joy to the sufferer. Mrs. Bryan, as she visited the hospital, conscious of nothing but woman's duties and her mission, seemed like a fairy visitation, to the sick and weary soldier, as she moved over the campus, the thousand prisoners thought of home, and their loved ones. This lady traveled thousands of miles, without an escort, subject to the inconveniences and exposure, incidental to such a trip, for the purpose of assisting in ameliorating the condition of the sick in prison, and provide for the comforts of her brother, one of the truest soldiers in the service.

An ice-cream saloon has been opened under the cheering auspices of a warm day, and twelve hundred panting prisoners. The conception of the institution, originated with Lieutenant D. B. Griswold, of the engineer corps ; who argued, that the prospects for getting out were rather slim—so he concluded he would try and *freeze out*. Lieutenant Griswold makes cream for the sick, for which they seem quite grateful. The proprietor of this establishment is assisted by Lieutenant William Swiney, of Memphis, who is a brave and faithful soldier. Lieutenant Griswold has much humor, stands his imprisonment better than the best of us ; his spirits never flag, is always disposed to be accommodating, makes pies for others to eat, and rings for others to wear ; is always on hand at base-ball or cribbage ; in fact, I don't know what we would do without " Griz." I first met the lieutenant at camp Chase. If it was wet, he was pleased ; if it was dry, it suited him as well ; hot or cold, it was all the same ; and with this happy faculty, for adaptation to circumstances, Lieutenant

Griswold is enabled, to make himself one of the most agreeable gentlmen in prison.

A squad of prisoners, who have been on parole, are now entering the "big gate." This arrival is attracting more than ordinary attention, as they have been on parole, and are supposed to bring us news. Captain Morton, of the Thirty-second Tennessee, steps in; he is immediately surrounded by a crowd of prisoners, and is distributing the latest papers to his friends. Captain Morton has the reputation of being a fine officer. Lieutenant Weller is of Taylor's battery; also an accomplished and energetic officer, is receiving the congratulations of his friends. Captain T. Wood and Colonel Steadman pass in, and the " big gate " closes. Colonel Steadman is one of the best soldiers, Alabama has sent to the field. Captain Wood is eminent for courage and judgment.

In spite of the superintendent's falsehoods, threats, and misrepresentations, only four men have taken the oath; and to show the class of men, who are faithless, I will state that one is the poet—Bill Rupert; his taking the oath is to be expected, when one refers to that *chandoic* effusion. Lieutenant Rupert is a native of Illinois, and was an assistant in a Southern restaurant. Another is Colonel Smith's ostler, who was allowed to come with us. He is a Swiss, and very ignorant. The other two are natives of Pennsylvania; one of whom made a speech in Sandusky, the night of his release, in which he stated, he had been forced into the Confederate army. The Sandusky " Register," (that filthy sheet,) was honest enough to rebuke the author of this falsehood, in a well-timed article, the spirit of which was, that while they welcomed the traitors to their ranks, it was the first time they had ever heard of officers being forced into the army. Not one of these traitors was a Southern man. Placards had been posted in prison, inviting us to take the oath, which were torn down by the prisoners in five minutes. As the traitors went out, they received a succession of groans from the friends of the cause they had deserted.

CHAPTER X.

ATTEMPT TO ESCAPE.—SIMPLICITY OF A PRISONER.—NERVOUSNESS
IN PRISON.—LIEUTENANT RANKIN AND HIS CAT.—MRS. BATTEL.—
A SINGLE ARRIVAL.—THE ABOLITION DEITY—ABRAHAM LINCOLN.
—NOT AN ENGLISHMAN IN PRISON.—MEMPHIS "GONE UP."—MILI-.
TARY DISTINCTION.—"PETTY THIEVING."—FIRING BY PLATOONS.
—"ARREST OF CIVILIANS."—WINDING UP OF "SCRAPS."—"TRIP
TO DIXIE," ETC.

LIEUTENANT Green Duncan having heard of the
brilliant exploits of Dick Turpin, also of the present
puissant Emperor of France, Louis Napoleon's (the
greatest statesman, with one of the most comprehensive
military minds, of this, or any age, and whose history of
Cæsar stamps him as a profound thinker, and ripe scholar,)
hegira from Ham, concluded that nothing is impossible,
save the preservation of the republic of the United States,
man having a capacity for self-government, having been
proven an hypothesis of error, and in a few years, the
sleek bell-ringer of the star chamber at the Federal Capital
will accept peaceably, the robes of royalty, that a people
(tied hand and foot) will tamely submit to see thrust
upon him by his usurping colleagues ; and the little stars
(those military satraps,) who float in the circle, (some of
them in whiskey,) of their lord and master William
H. Seward, will be as ready to imitate in this particular,
as they have the excesses of the powers that be, in their
crusade on the South, among the most prominent being
William T. Sherman* and Philip Sheridan.† The night

---

* General Sherman ordered thirty families out of Memphis, in 1862, as retaliation, (so he said,) "your guerrillas firing on our transports." Why did he
order out of Memphis, women and children, innocent of any participation in

was fearfully stormy, yet Duncan, with that intrepidity so peculiar to the citizens of that State that furnished the great Breckinridge, the most perfect gentleman, erudite scholar, and gallant soldier, that this century has produced. Where is the compeer of John C. Breckinridge of Kentucky?—left the building, and groping his way to the open field, crawled to the fence, passing the stream of light that crossed the path from the reflectors, undiscovered, as he had taken the advantage of a drain, which ran to the lake, and which was covered with grass. He commenced sawing one of the posts that supported the fence, when he struck a nail, and becoming excited, (and possibly a little vexed,) rather than wait until the tramp of the relief would deaden the sound, pulled at the plank, and it came off with a ripping sound, that vibrated from one end of the wall to the other, and most unfortunately, a sentinel whom he had not discovered in his eagerness to saw out, was on the wall immediately above him, who exclaimed, " halt," and lowered his musket. Duncan seeing the polished bayonet in the gloom, hallooed, " Raise your gun, you yankee scoundrel, or you are a dead man." The sentinel obeyed orders either from habit or imagining that the rebel had a torpedo in his pocket, and Duncan taking advantage of his surprise, ran like a turkey, and was soon too far in the murky gloom, for the balls (a score of which were fired at him,) to do any damage. The Lieutenant lost his saw, the Yankees some

---

the so-called offences of their male relatives? Why did he not rather, send out his *gorrillas*, selecting them from the Eighth Missouri, where they could have fought men, instead of burning down houses, murdering inoffensive citizens? (as they did in the case of that esteemed citizen of Memphis, Columbus Alexander, Esq.) The reason he vented his spite on these defenseless families (the writer's being one of them,) was to carry out his doctrine, "that war is cruelty," a policy to which he faithfully adhered at Memphis and Atlanta. His boasted march to the sea, has been beaten by Weston, as it was only a feat of pedestrianism, there being no enemy in front of him. As a marauding expedition, it was a human sirocco, leaving nought but desolation in its track.

† Sheridan boasted of having destroyed two thousand well filled barns in the valley Shenandoah; Sherman left nothing of the property of their *fellow-citizens*. Let the civilized world take these men, (with Butler, the beast; N. P. Banks, a nobody; Schurz, a blasphemer; Pope, the braggart; that *Munchausen* Kilpatrick; that English adventurer, Wyndam,) and compare them with John C. Breckinridge, Robert E Lee, Joseph E. Johnson, Stonewall Jackson, Leonidas Polk, G. T. Beauregard, and Kirby Smith, and discriminate between the vandalism of the former, and the forbearance of the latter

ammunition, and the author obtained a sensational paragraph.

As we moved from the depot to the boat, at Sandusky, Ohio, a densely packed crowd surrounded us, many of whom were women ; some of the latter abusing us in unmentionable language, and going so far as to spit at us, and it took the united efforts of the guard to prevent their mobbing us in that most damnable of all places, that sink of Abolitionism, where they mob defenceless prisoners, but don't send soldiers to the front unless they can find some poor Irishman* or German, who they can get drunk, enlist him, and then steal his bounty.   While the rush of prisoners and of guards was making to the boat, one stalwart Confederate, with an immense overcoat enveloping his person, had lagged behind, but on noticing the last prisoner file off the gangway, and fearful of being left, rushed eagerly on to the stage-plank, where he was suddenly halted by the guard.

"Get off this boat, we don't want any of you fellows talking to rebel prisoners."

"Let me pass, I am a rebel ?"

"Get off, I tell you, or I'll stick about an inch of this bayonet into you."

" If you don't think I'm a good reb, look at my buttons," (unbuttoning his overcoat, displaying the well-known Confederate uniform to the astonished guard,) who said :

" Get aboard, you're a d—d fool, than *Thompson's colt.*"

" That may be so, Yank, but Jim P. never deserts his crowd."

The Lieutenant could have made his escape easily, by the aid of his citizen's coat, and if he had known as much as he does at present, it is probable he would, but as we only learn from experience, the Lieutenant may profit by

---

* The United States Army was composed as follows : Germans, 176,800 ; Irish, 144,200 ; British Americans. 53,500 ; English, 45,500 ; other foreigners, 48,400 ; nationalities unknown, 26,500 ; of the colored troops, (who fought nobly,) 200,000. Total, 694,900. Add to these, twelve or fifteen thousand officers, nine-tenths of whom were Americans ; the host of provost guards, teamsters, ambulance drivers, hospital attendants, assistant quartermaster and assistant commissary departments, and the other bomb-proof estab-lishments, all filled with native Americans, and we find that of the thou-sounds who have been offered up to appease the thirst for blood of Yankee Abolition fanaticism, about seventy-five per cent. of them were foreigners.

his lesson, and may not be so enthusiastic in his devotion to his crowd, the next time a Yankee guard attempts to change his front to rear, while moving towards a Yankee bastile.

'Tis passing strange, how nervous one gets in prison. There goes Colonel John Minter, of the Fortieth Tennessee, as brave a man as ever drew a sword, yet John is dreadfully nervous in durance; he walks to and fro, beating his breast in the region of the heart, until one could imagine he would loosen its pericardium. He imagines he has heart disease. Not a bit of it; it is only pulsating in response to the beat of it's better half that is palpitating in unison, in the cheerless solitude of the colonel's old home in Dixie. There passes another nervous individual, Captain Humes; he stalks about the Campus, brooding in nervous silence over his misfortunes. The captain is a man of mark, a one-idea'd man, who loses sight of all, but his objective point would make an enthusiast or a fanatic; is of that class of men who make magnificent failures or achieve great results. I hope the latter, for the brave captain. The "Tour d'Auvergne of the army, Colonels Baker and Avery, are decidedly nervous. When the news is favorable in relation to exchange, they dance and leap, and beat their heads against the wall; when 'tis bad, they are among the most despondent. In applying the term nervous to these gentlemen, I use it in a double sense, colloquial and otherwise, for while the officers mentioned, are susceptible to nervous attacks, they have strong wills and resolute action. The writer, colloquially speaking, is nervous, and will continue to be so until he gets out of this pen, as no man of sensibility, can be calm under the abuse to which the prisoner is subjected. Nervousness, however, is not peculiar to the prisoner; all men are nervous and imaginative. Colonel George H. Monsarratt, a distinguished officer of the Confederate States army, with one of the most comprehensive minds I ever knew, said, " I asked Graves, whom I had visited a short while prior to his death, (and who was as true and brave a man as the State of Kentucky ever produced,) how he felt." "Ah, Monsarratt, my pain is all here," said the sufferer, pointing to his groin, the place where he shot Cilley, of Maine, in that celebrated duel, in which General Webb played so *distinguished* a part. Graves was nervous and sensitive, yet of dauntless courage. The Honorable Solon Borland told me that on one occasion, a cannon ball passed near him, producing such an effect on his nervous system that he felt as if losing half his dimensions in his involuntary shrinking, and Colonel Borland was a man of unquestioned courage. I have known Alexander McClung, the great duellist, to pace his room the entire night with the candle burning, and McClung had the courage of a lion. Ergo, nervousness is admissable in Johnson's island. I remember that gallant officer Lieutenant Samuel L. Cowan, who became so nervous in camp Chase, that he contrived to get out. A frigid individual would never "have made the trip." I believe the most of us are nervous, yet all don't show it. My accomplished friend, Dr. Becker, is passing under my window, humming a line from Goethe—

"Kennst du das Land wo die Zitronen bluchen."

When the Doctor gets nervous, he goes to his fiddle, which furnishes him with a pleasant auxilliary in warring against ennui.

Lieutenant Rankin has a cat, (I do not give a history of Whittington and his cat,) the male of the story, i. e. the *genus homo*, (or possibly the cat may be a *tommy* for all I know,) who thought he would find the streets of London paved with gold, was mistaken as Rankin may be, if he thinks the paths of a prisoner are strewn with flowers. However, from his own standpoint, the *cat*-astrophe of his finale is not yet fully developed, as the gallant lieutenant thinks he may get out ; *but*, (that is a great word, it signifies a great deal, much depending on the application of the parlance,) Lieutenant Rankin has found a cat, and sits smoothing its glossy back, as happy as a mother with her first hopeful. I wonder if he thinks that the nature of this animal assimilates much to our own, rub a cat one way ninety-nine times, and it will purr, then tread on it's tail, and 'twill scratch ; do most men ninety-nine favors, and they respond amen, refuse their demand in a solitary instance, they forget the favors and abuse you. Lieutenant Rankin, however, intends to retain the cat, yet his delicate form leads us to believe that he will not get pussy.

In addition to our cat, we have two ducks, two dogs, (I mean four-legged ones,) one hen and brood, and are beginning to feel quite domesticated, concluding to make a virtue of necessity, and if we can't get out, we'll raise stock. Lieutenant Rankin is a pleasant gentleman, remarkable for his great conversational powers and gallantry in the field, is a native of Kentucky, and one of the first volunteers from that great commonwealth, to respond to the call to arms to repel the vandal invader.

Mrs. Battel,* the widow of the lamented son of that noble Tennessean, Colonel Battel, visited us to-day. It was a sad sight to see this young and estimable woman, in her mourning weeds, cut off from her protector, and compelled to buffet a heartless and pitiless world; yet with her crushed feelings and her delicate constitution, she has passed the ordeal of insulting guards and wearisome travel, to visit the suffering and lonely, in prison. The visit of Mrs. Battel teaches us a lesson, that our mothers and sisters, wives and daughters, are displaying fortitude and courage, that would, if needs be, (like the Hindoo widow), mount the burning pile for our glorious cause.

Lieutenant-colonel Bennett, of the Sixth Mississippi, arrived to-day. The arrival of one officer is barely noticed, yet Colonel Bennett being a positive character, did not fail to have his arrival heralded by a half dozen stragglers who had been watching the "big gate," wishing

---

* The war exhibited to the world, the virtues and courage of Southern women, in action, prose and poetry. The energy and courage of Miss Belle Edmonson, of Tennessee; Belle Boyd, of Virginia; Mrs. Matlock, of Mississippi; Miss Ann Nelson, Miss Nettie Coleman, of the same State, are a part of the history of our late struggle. The author well remembers the risks ran by these brave women, in assisting our cause. Compare their actions, and the soul-stirring poetry of Miss Ready, L. Virginia Smith, of Louisiana, Estelle, (Mrs. Brown, of Memphis, Tennessee,) and a hundred others, famous in our sunny land, with the fanatical, heartless Harriet Beecher Stowe; the strong-minded, ugly, weak-headed Anna Dickinson, and a hundred others of such wishy-washy advocates of women's rights, and Southern ladies lose nothing by the comparison.

for the magical words, "*Open, sesame,*" (which are as distant in reality, as the forty thieves of Alababa are to the same ilk in Hoffman's battalion, *not duces,*) or for the strength of Samson to lift the gates as he did those of Gaza. However, as wishing could do no good, they wisely concluded to wait the moving of the waters, (of exchange,) and while waiting, Bennett came in, and was immediately surrounded by the curious. The colonel being a man of good judgment and observation, we accept his news as the most reliable or any received since our incarceration.

It is amusing to witness the efforts of the Abolitionists to deify their master, Abraham Lincoln, the "jokist." Is he as strong as the elephant? Has he the courage of the lion or the tiger? Can he run like the ostrich, or leap like the kangaroo? Has he the cunning of the fox, or the agility of the monkey? Can he crawl like a snake, or climb like a squirrel? Can he dive like a duck, or swim like a fish? He has brains, so has a hog; he can talk, so can a parrot. Can he fly like the eagle? Has he the gratitude of a dog? Can he see like the owl, in the dark, or a hawk, in the light? When he was an infant, if placed on the edge of a precipice, he would roll off, while a kitten, a week old, could hardly be pushed from her hold; and yet, these ignorant fanatics worship man, and that man Abraham Lincoln. Man is inferior to the brute creation in the physical world, as a rule. The exceptions are as follows:

Butler is king of beasts; Lincoln was fleeter than the ostrich, (in passing through Baltimore;) Stevens, of Pennsylvania, more venomous than the snake; Turchin, fiercer than the hyena; Logan, of Illinois, is a greater spouter than the whale, and equally as watery; Brownlow, of Tennessee, the hoggiest of all wallowers; Horace Maynard, more stolid than the jackass.

None of these political scavengers have the respectability of the elephant, as he always carries his trunk, while they are nothing but *carpet-baggers.*

It is a remarkable fact that we have not a representative of "perfidious Albion," in prison. We have the sturdy

Teuton, the chivalric Gaul, the gallant Celt, but John
Bull is not with us. "Where the carcass is, there will
the eagles be gathered," and as the surly Briton believes
in the heaviest artillery deciding the gage of battle, and
the North being the possessor of this force, he casts his
lot with the superior power, in the endeavor to sack the
South and enslave a free people. Since time immemorial,
England has been a nation of territorial robbers; she has
oppressed mankind in the East Indies, making the excesses of Clive historic; in China, in the West Indies, and
America, North, East, South or West, 'tis all the same.
Wherever the beat of a British drum is heard, or the
British flag unfurled, there stalks oppression and violence.
One of her victims is Ireland, the down-trodden and oppressed Green Isle, the land of that immortal patriot, Em-
mett. When will she take her place among the nations of
the earth? Only when her people are united, and then
let them wipe that political blot from the map of Europe.
Treacherous to her enemies, faithless to her friends, (she
caged the great Napoleon, like a wild animal, who had
trusted to her generosity,) she[*] has has aided in bringing
on the unhappy strife in our own land; as where governments are to be broken up to benefit English commerce,
she spares neither blood nor treasure in accomplishing
her unholy purposes. The English politician prates of
England and her past history. What is it? A bastard
aristocracy, composed of natural sons of merry monarchs;
a line of kings, whose history is written in blood. (As
to monarchy, the author does not object to it.) Oneness
of power, in all material matters, is the best conservator
of law and morals. The most despotic governments are
recognized in the Old Testament, and in the New our
Saviour said, "Render unto Cæsar the things that are

---

[*] England has furnished the North men, (nearly 50,000 Englishmen were
enlisted in the Federal army,) and the South, munitions and vessels, to aid in
our destruction as a great nation. An Englishman, an office-holder in the oppressed South, one of those political waifs that the war has thrown to the surface, (the South being the carcass for all such eagles,) says to the writer, "The
Radicals have elected me to office, and I have accepted, and a pretty d—d fool
I'd be to refuse. I don't care a d—n which side whips. Your country's gone
to h—l, and if there are any loaves and fishes comeatable, Johnny Bull comes
in. It's a fat carcass, and I am a first-class eagle."

Cæsar's. Each circle must have its centre, and no corporation can be permanent without a sovereign head. Since the organization of society, governments when bereft of the strength of a monarchy, even though despotic, and the wisdom of an aristocracy, although licentious, have ran riot with the anarchial excesses of democracy, showing the incapacity of man for self-government. The world, for thousands of years, has witnessed repeated trials of this fallacious system of self-government, all of which have proven failures; and the conflict in America, to-day, for a *sentiment*, is a useless waste of blood, as the days of the republic are numbered, and there may be those living who will see kings enthroned in America, not from any desire, but from one of those natural laws that seems to decree that as a man is made in the likeness of his Creator, the comparison shall apply to all the details of his action, while carrying out the object of his Being.

Kings are feeble, yet true representatives of this singleness of administration, that is a reflex of the God-head, and which is ordained to rule in the world, and any change in the character of this delegated power, from the Great Author of our being, to the anointed on earth, will be attended with disaster. The true theory of government is supreme power in the chief of the nation, the subordination of the people, to human strength, prepares them for yielding obedience to their spiritual heads, as in all democracies, there is a tendency to infidelity, and it is alone to despotic governments, that we are to look for religious subordination. The settler on Plymouth rock is a fit descendant of the English politician, for while their forefathers were murdering East Indians, they were imitating them, in destroying the aborigines of America, despoiling them of their lands, and seducing their women, and as Black Hawk said, poisoning their hearts with fire-water; and now, their descendants are causing rivers of blood to flow through the land, and the Negro is meeting with the fate of the Indian. The murderer and despoiler, who is he? The author of the war, who is he? The plunderer of homes, and the destroyer of household-gods, who is he? This

besom of destruction, that is sweeping all—liberty, peace,
and prosperity, from the country, leaving nought in its
track, but the wail of the widow and orphan, no light
but burning homesteads to show the traveler, where once
stood the homes of a free and happy people; from
whence cometh it, who is the author of all this hellish-
ness, that has made a saturnalia for the North; and
David said unto Nathan, "Thou art the man;" you, the
mean, whining, prying, hypocritical, white-livered, Negro-
stealing, fanatical Yankee, a fit shoot of the round-head
English politician, that sang psalms and cut throats, and
who would enchain the world, and make it bow the knee
in homage to the British lion and Yankee eagle, who
alone seek and destroy their prey, when it is defenseless.

"Tis reported in prison to-day, that Memphis has surrendered to the Yankees, and those that are prisoners,
hailing from that place, have the " blues."

Captain Jeannett, who resigned a handsome field position, to accept one in the line, where he thought he
could be more useful to his cause, is a fine drilled officer,
and an ardent supporter of Southern rights.   Captain
Hall, captured at Fort Donaldson, a thorough gentleman,
with one of the best legal minds in prison.   Captain
Hugh Bedford, a thorough-bred soldier, in bearing, information, and courage.   Captain Abe Levy, one of the
truest men living, and a score of other Memphians, whom
the fortunes of war have cast into prison, are condoling
with each other.   My friend Lieutenant Jack Wright, of
Alpheus Baker's* regiment, "drops in," and says to con-
sole us,

"Well, Memphians, if old Memphis has gone, 'let
her rip.' "†

Jack Wright is one of my warmest friends, full of generous promptings, true as steel to his friends, and as
they say, "never flickers" under fire.   The surrender

---

* Alpheus Baker, was one of the few officers who improved in his continued
service, he was promoted for gallantry, at Baker's Creek, (where he was
wounded,) and in his new position as "brigadier," made a gallant fight, to the
close of the war.

† The "let her rip" (letter) of America, is the theta of our language, showing the anarchial tendency of our times, towards violence, rapine and abandon.

of Memphis, has produced one good result, it has placed us in communication with our loved ones, and furnished us an opportunity to add to our stock of " filthy lucre."

Some one has said, " Generals say, go on, Captains say, come on ; the Generals gather laurels, the Captains cypress ; the former become candidates for the Presidency, the latter for the grave." There is much truth in this, and it does more to demoralize an army, (this withholding of the award of merit from line-officers,) than the influence of o'erwhelming numbers of an enemy. There are four important officers in the service—Generals commanding, colonel, captain, and orderly sergeant ; the others, unless on detached duty, are to a greater or less degree—file-closers. In many instances, the advancement of general officers is promoted by intrigue ; line-officers overlooked through the same influence ; merit is not considered, and the "come on" of the captain is followed ordinarily by death or wounds, rather than promotion.

It takes a man of brains, of vast comprehensiveness, and stoical courage, to make a General ; and you may obtain such characters from the " cloister," (as in the case of Bishop Polk, of Louisiana, now one of our most distinguished Generals,) from the "bar," (as in the case of Preston Smith,* of Tennessee,) or from the plow, loom, or anvil, shown in a score of military lights, representing these different interests. A ten year old boy will make a drill-master, but he would not be prepared for the emergencies of the field, while there are many officers, who would be equal to almost any occasion, yet are sadly defective in the details of drill ; yet of the two evils, the judgment of the one, without drill, is preferable to the knowledge of an expert in Scott or Hardee, without judg-

---

* General Preston Smith was killed near Atlanta, in one of those series of conflicts, between a vastly inferior force of the Confederates, under that great commander, Joseph E. Johnson, (who alone could have managed that wonderful retreat, in the face of an overwhelming foe, from Dalton to Atlanta.) Preston Smith, although educated to the bar, was born a soldier, a strict disciplinarian, courageous to rashness. As an organizer and leader he had few superiors. He was one of the few Generals, who risked the "cypress" to deserve the "laurel;" and in his death, the Confederacy lost one of her staunchest supporters, and the army one of its most valiant soldiers. His last words were : "I have tried to do my duty."

ment. There are few officers, who are blessed with the happy faculty, of combining these two virtues, so necessary to success in military life. Yet, I believe, we have one exception in prison, Lieutenant John Childress, of Murfreesboro', Tennessee, who, while having one of the best balanced heads, in our pen, and every mental requirement for a commander, is one of the best drilled officers in the service; a gentleman in deportment, genial in his companionship. He is a worthy representative of that distinguished family, from which he sprang.

The meanest trick, of all the rascality of some of our custodians, is the purloining of rings, buttons, and other souvenirs, for friends and loved ones, that are daily mailed, and as they pass through the hands of the "sifter's," subordinates, many are extracted before the letters are forwarded. This little, petty thieving is too contemptible for notice, but as a faithful chronicler of the Sir John Froissart school, who says, "In such a grand and noble history (as you like it) as this, of which I, Sir John Froissart, am the author and continuator until this present moment, through the grace of God, and the perseverance he has endowed me with, as well as in length of years, which have enabled me to witness abundance of the things that have passed, *it is not right that I forget anything*," and as an humble imitator of Sir John, I must not forget any of the many rascalities of our custodians.

We have had firing at us by companies from the walls, also individual firing, (at will;) last night it came by platoons. A few officers engaged in playing cribbage, were so unfortunate, as to neglect putting out their lights the moment "taps" sounded, not imagining, that the dereliction of a few moments would be attended with the danger, which they found it was, as a volley came in at the window. Fortunately no one was hit; but the lesson was heeded, as no mercy could be expected, from men who are merciless. It has been a timely warning to other messes, to furnish not the slightest pretext to our barbarous guard to find fault, with our want of prompt and punctual observance of the severe rules of our prison, as

18

all they desire, is any excuse to murder us, individually or *en masse*.

The arrival of three hundred civilians in prison, has been alluded to in another " scrap." This is another one of those high-handed outrages, that has made the cabal at Washington more notorious, than that lawless ministry of Charles II. What right has that miscreant at Washington, that party ghoul, Edwin M. Stanton, to arrest citizens of a sovereign State, and confine them on the stale bread and blue beef of a prison? All over the land, American citizens are torn from their hearths and firesides, from the communion of their household Gods, their houses searched, no privacy respected, and incarcerated in foul dungeons. Captain T. Harrison Baker is in one of these, (at Fort Lafayette,) manacled. The capitol, at Washington, is filled with the best men of the country, who have been brought there through the instigation of Stanton, and the tinkling of Oily Gammon's (Seward's) little bell. Fort Warren and other bastiles are filling up rapidly, all in the name of Liberty. The three hundred gentlemen, driven into our pen, are among the most distinguished citizens of Kentucky ; Dr. Hobson, Colonel Murray, and other citizens, eminent as ministers of the Gospel, lawyers, physicians, merchants, and farmers. All grades are taken, none spared ; no matter the health, condition, or sex, all must be victims to this infernal tyranny, that is causing the name of American to be looked upon among civilized nations as the synonim of savage.

Four months experience in prison, has produced this collection of "scraps," thus conglomerated from the prison table—'tis true they are not so rare as those that would fall from the china of serves, and I hope my readers will make allowances for tin plates, boiled beef, and sour bread. You can't expect tit-bits from such a source, and if you do, and are disappointed, why, 'tis your misfortune, and want of forethought, not my fault. I expect the work will be run down by its readers, all works are, in fact, there is more matter in it already than I would read of any one's else—therefore, as it will be *run down*, I'll

give it a good *winding up.* Then, again, everybody is
winding up—the suttler, the vegetable man, the milk
andice man are all winding, and so by way of following their illustrious example—I'll wind up. Not that
I expect half the running down that will be accorded
to these honest men, for that would take centuries to
wind up, as to their faculties to wind up their affairs, the
deponent saith not. I have written the above "scraps"
because I have had nothing else to do. I tried to make
a ring, and failed, but would have commenced again, (but
after looking at a box and a set of chess-men, exquisitely
carved and designed, that would take a prize at any fair
in the world, made with a file and knife by Captain
Winn, of the Fourteenth Mississippi Regiment, who made
it as a souvenir for his mother,) I concluded that talent
must be inherent, and I had no talent, mechanically
speaking. Captain Winn is a fine officer and a polished
gentleman, yet I think he had better turn his attention to
the chisel, as his conceptions are wonderful, peculiarly so,
when 'tis known that he never had an instrument in his
hands before. Finding I could not make anything
mechanical, I wondered what I would do to amuse myself. 'Twas possible to get up a newspaper. Captain
Provine, of the "Fulton Telegraph," Fulton, Missouri,
and Captain McCranie, of Jackson Parish, Louisiana, both
sprightly writers, were willing to join, and with the press
gang already alluded to, would have formed a corps that
could have entertained, as well as instructed; but no one
led off, and I thought 'twould be no go. So in self-defence,
I was compelled to write "scraps," and offer the accumula-
tion to the public, as a memento of how we did, and felt,
in prison. I think, 'twill be interesting for future reference for ourselves, because if we get out, (which I hope
we will in a short while,) in a few years, we could hardly
remember a score of our fellow prisoners, and this little
collection will remind us of scenes, and refresh us with
more vivid recollections, of what we were in prison. It
will also be interesting from the fact that the best blood
of the country is within these walls, many men of note,
whose names will shine upon the pages of history, in

time to come. Lieutenant Colonel Wood, (a relation of President Davis, and a son of the surgeon general of the United States,) of the Adam's cavalry, a fearless officer. Captain McDonald, of Nicaragua fame, and a rebel from boyhood. Here we have a nephew of D'Aubigne, a cousin of Beauregard; Lieutenant Legendre; the Polk's; the Pillow's; the Overton's, of Tennessee. Lawyers and Divines, Senators and Congressmen, are all represented, and as their future will be more or less interwoven with the history of the Confederacy, I feel that as a book of reference, this little collection may be of some value. I often think, in looking out of my window, seeing men like Major Kavanaugh, stern and inflexible, while engaged in youthful pastimes, how strangely we all act while in prison. Kavanaugh would march on a battery with as much non-challance, as he would light a fresh Havana. It will be interesting, to follow these officers in their future career, and see what becomes of them. They say we will be exchanged in a few days, and then, Ho! for Dixie. I hope 'twill be so, and that we will all arrive home, safe and sound, that I will publish this little work to the satisfaction of my friends, and delight of my enemies. (Oh! that mine enemy might write a book,) and the twelve hundred Confederate officers, who have endured the past incarceration with me, and now with the disposition to get away from this "lake-girt isle" as soon as possible. Accept the salaam of the author, and allow him to say, not "finis," but in prison slang, "well, a good evening."

We leave this day, September 1st, 1862, our "lake-girt isle." The guards are coming in, the roll is being called, "Captain B., company A, First Alabama, Tennessee and Mississippi Regiments." The writer responds, and thanks to a kind Providence, steps clear of the "big gate" and stands without the accursed walls of a prison—

> " A prison, heavens! I loathe the hated name,
> Famine's metropolis—the sink of shame,
> A nauseous sepulchre—whose craving womb
> Hourly inters poor mortals in its tomb."

A free-born American citizen, confined in a loathsome
prison, as a punishment for fighting for freedom and
"State rights,"* rights that the intelligent North must
admit as the true theory of a republican form of government. We board the little boat, the line is cast off, and
we are once more upon the bosom of Sandusky bay, free
from the foul air of a prison, rid of the presence of the
miserable wolf of a custodian, and his heartless subordinates. It is a glorious feeling to be free, known alone
to those who have suffered imprisonment. The sensation
is exquisite, and is expressed in laughing eyes, and glowing cheeks. My friend, Captain W. R. Butler, of Murfreesboro', Tennessee, usually calm and reticent, one of
the most accomplished soldiers in the Confederate army,
is alive with the joyousness of the occasion. Standing, as
many of us are, near the "taffrail," gazing at the island
that is now receding rapidly from view, having no regrets,
but those engendered by the thought that we leave our

---

* The author is still firm in his belief in the integrity of the principle of State
rights, while a republican form of government exists in this country, and if
might does make right, in the policy of the fanatical "powers that be," it cannot change *one* Southern man's opinion, who, while submitting to brute force,
and accepting the issues that defeat has forced upon his devoted land, (the
South, the Mecca of carpet-baggers and thieves, the scummiest of the scum of
the North,) still firmly adheres to not a sentiment but a principle, true and
fixed, the sovereignty of the States of a confederation, not a nationality, and in
spite of imprisonment, or other degrees of punishment, that the vultures of
fanaticism would fasten upon a citizen of this confederation—(such as the
hanging of the innocent Mrs. Surratt; the manacling of Jefferson Davis; the
arrest and ironing of Ryan, of Arkansas; the slow torture of American citizens on the Dry Tortugas; and every other conceivable mode of punishment,
known to a barbaric tyranny, the writer will ever rigidly adhere to a principle
that involves the rights and liberties, not only of the so-called unreconstructed
States, but of each and every State in the Union.

Messrs. Jacobins, be honest for once, show the cloven foot entire, and give
us a monarchy, the term "Republic" is a mis-nomer. You have the despotic
disposition, the rapacious desire, the cruel conception, and criminal action of a
Czar's government, without its expressed honesty, you have stamped out with
the iron heel of brute force, the liberties of millions of your fellow citizens.
Oppression rules the land; the whistle of the bullet, and the glisten of the
knife of the assassin are the only sound and lights, that reverberate and flash
o'er the South, a land more pillaged than the historic ravages of the Palatinate.
Desolated hearths, fatherless children, outraged women, ignorant and besotted
Africans placed in power, the sanctity of the ballot-box invaded, law and order
derided, in the name of a republican form of government. Fie, fie, ye Marats
and Robespierres, come down from your republican perch, take off your
flimsy disguise, and proclaim a despotism, 'tis what you aim at, so let's have
it. The writer has no objections, but is opposed to the deception practiced
in the name of liberty, giving us the stalking shadow of a free government,
while the substance of a royal despotism is seen behind this skeleton of Radi-
camism.

dead in unhallowed ground, and wondering, that if the "Sandusky Register," and "New York Tribune," were cast into the "bottomless pit," thus nauseating it, could it throw up a fouler combination than the custodians of Johnson's island, and their sympathizers in Sandusky city.

"A FAREWELL TO JOHNSON'S ISLAND."

Penciled by an unknown hand upon a wall of one of the prison buildings at Johnson's island, it will, doubtless, prove interesting to those who have been inmates of that prison; nor will it, it is hoped, fail to strike the eyes and move the hearts of those who have friends that rest beneath the soil of the lake-girdled isle:

> "Hoarse sounding billows of the white-capped lake,
> That 'gainst the barriers of our hated prison break,
> Farewell! Farewell thou giant inland sea;
> Thou, too, subservest the modes of tyranny,—
> Girding this isle, washing its lonely shore
> With moaning echoes of thy melancholy roar,
> Farewell, thou lake! Farewell, thou inhospitable land!
> Thou hast the curses of this patriot band—
> All, save the spot, the holy sacred bed,
> Where rest in peace our Southern warriors dead!

We left Johnson's island on the 1st day of September, 1862. The morning was ominous of a gloomy trip; dark and portentous clouds hung loweringly o'er us, and boded storm. The little baggage we possessed, was sent to Sandusky, the day before, where was witnessed a scene of plunder on a scale that would have rivalled the exploits of an Alaric or Atilla. Mercury, the God of thieves, would have been an honest man in Sandusky. They broke open trunks; many things that were not stolen were damaged, and a perfect spirit of vandalism seemed to actuate the examiners of our baggage, who searched valises for mountain howitzers, and trunks for twenty-four pound parrots, while they would examine pockets for Springfield muskets.

We do not hold the United States government responsible for this outrage, but wish to show that a government must not always be held responsible for the malfeasance of its underlings. I hope the citizens of the North will understand and appreciate the application.

We reached Sandusky city, that hole of Abolitionism, and took our respective stations on the cars. Being well seated and comfortable, while waiting for the cars to start, a generous gentleman stepped to the window, (I have forgotten his name,) and handed a bottle of the ardent and a large pound-cake; said he was a good democrat, and true to his flag, but could not be insulting to prisoners, as most of the citizens of that place were. The next day we arrived at Indianapolis. At this point our traveling sorrows began; and here, again, was exhibited either the stupidity or rascally meanness of underlings. We were crowded into cattle cars with narrow plank benches, and like a drove of wild animals, were rushed off. We were on these cars, in this crowded, I may say packed, manner thirty-six hours, and the reader can imagine we would be necessarily ill, sore, bruised. We suffered so much in one or all of these discomforts, and were so covered with filth, that we were piteous objects to behold. Giving way to sleep, I would fall between the narrow apertures that separated the planks, and while one companion, who used the weed, would squirt the juice of a bad article of "Old Virginia," in one eye, he being half asleep, another chum would advise me of the fact that he wore boots, by closing my other eye with the heel of one of them. This was all bad enough, and it seemed as though our powers of endurance had been strained to their utmost tension, yet worse treatment was in store for us.

Cairo* is reached; a city that has no equal in the number of its bad smells, except, possibly, the city of Cologne as described by some traveler, and, I am sure, that the different qualities of mean whiskey far exceed the number of bad smells. We were immediately driven on board the Choteau, a crazy old tub, and in such a condition that the engineer kindly suggested to us not to shift rapidly in any numbers from one side of the boat to the other, as her boilers were very weak, and an explosion

---

* Cairo, *under the press influence*, controlled by that prince of *editors, John Oberly, Esq.*, has improved wonderfully since.

might be the result. However, they dove-tailed one thousand one hundred and thirty of us, excluding us from the cabin, it being reserved for the guard and the sick. I'll assure the reader it was quite lively, locating one thousand one hundred and thirty men on the outside of an old boat, stowing us on the coal heaps, 'midst the machinery, with one little stove for us all to cook on. It was an outrage of most glaring character, as they could have obtained other boats, furnishing us with comfortable transportation. Under the pretence, that we must wait for other prisoners to fill up the convoy, they detained us at Cairo four days and nights, exposed to the broiling sun, rain, and foul air, many of us sick and half-fed, during the sickly season of the year. Again we say, we don't hold the government responsible, but our treatment from subordinates was frightfully cruel. While here, we saw one of the many evidences of radical inconsistency. I had requested permission of Lieutenant Lennelle, to step to the wharf to speak to some one who had asked for me, when to my astonishment, I saw a brawny-looking specimen of the Puritan race, laying on unmercifully, with a large horse-whip, to several Negroes who were basking in the sunshine; he yelling, cursing, and slashing, alternately. I turned to Lieutenant Lennelle, whose face was a study for a painter, and asked him if he was not astonished. '

"Why, captain, that is the grossest outrage I ever saw committed, it is inhuman, I will report that man," said the astonished lieutenant, "and have him punished, if possible."

"Lieutenant Lennelle, I never saw a slave, in my years of experience in the South, so brutally beaten, even when convicted of crime, and it seems strange that such a spectacle attracts so little attention in the free State of Illinois. Lieutenant, the slave has merely changed masters."

At last we prepared to depart, and in anticipation of the terrible trip from Cairo to Vicksburg, were sad and dejected, yet there were some master-spirits with us whose energies never flag, and who are ever alive and equal to

all issues and occasions where the man is called upon, to do, to suffer, or to die, if needs be, for his kind. Among the most active and zealous, being that noble gentleman Captain C. F. Johnson,* of that *Old Roman* Buckner's† staff, who chartered a boat, the Diligent, assumed the responsibility of payment, which was two thousand dollars, for accommodations for one hundred passengers. Thanks to the kind offers of my friend Johnson, I was one of the favored. The owner of the boat had recommended her highly, and it was with pleasurable emotions that we changed from the Choteau, to the Diligent. Although it was painful to leave our comrades on the old Choteau, yet we could not do them any good by remaining, and increased their comfort by leaving. It seems to me that if Captain Johnson could have chartered a boat, the authorities could have done the same, showing there was no necessity for herding us like cattle in our own filth, as was the case on the Choteau. I had not a *soumarque*, but the word of a Confederate soldier in 1862, was good to a brother soldier. Out we steamed into the river, and our tortuous passage began. Gun-boats in front of us, gun-boats in the rear of us, and some six thousand emaciated creatures between them. They said, " many of us looked well !" True, those who had fine constitutions, stood it, but they were " few and far between." Many of the regiment to which I was attached, looked well, yet out of four hundred men led into prison, April the 8th, 1862, over one hundred were taken out feet foremost before September 1st, of the same year, (four months and twenty-one days,) a terrible ratio for men who were so *well* treated. On getting fairly started, we examined our floating elephant, and found sleeping accommodations for thirty persons, in state-rooms, that had been used a score of trips for the conveyance of wounded and dying soldiers, the effluvia from whose bodies had impregnated every pore in the room, defying a Hercules to cleanse them. I opened the door of one room, but my olfactories rebelled,

---

* Captain Johnson is (now 1868) of the firm Tyler, Johnson & Co., Louis-ville, Kentucky.

† Buckner, editing in Louisville, that sterling paper the " Louisville Journal."

and I concluded to sleep on the deck.   To regulate matters, straws were drawn ; those sleeping in the state-rooms, eating at the second and third tables ; those on deck, at the first table.   Plenty to eat, and fresh air, under exposure is preferable to a foul state-room and a deficiency of aliment

We moved on, and in a few days were off Memphis, having had nothing to disturb the monotony of the trip, only the sad spectacle of the burial, at different landings, of the sixty poor fellows who died on the trip ; a terrible bill of mortality, one per cent. in thirteen days.   We came to anchor off the Bluff city, on a lovely day in September, the bluff's fourth Chickasaw, (that form so beautiful a crown for the Egyptian Queen of our modern Nile,) were garnished with the beauty, and fashion of the city. Lovely women and brave men were there to give us welcome.   There were many of the latter, whose hearts were in the cause, who remained at home, for reasons unnecessary to mention in this connection ; and it had been better, if many of those who did go into the Confederacy, had followed their example, as too many, who from a sense of pride left their hearths and firesides, to follow in the wake of our armies, or to pitch their social tent in some one of the many distracted circles of the South, did no good, and set the pernicious example of wild speculation, one of the most demoralizing elements of the war ; whereas, had they remained, they could have rendered much service, in ameliorating the condition of prisoners, and assisting the families of those whose protectors were in the army.

I with others, who had loved ones in Memphis, was anxious to reach the shore.   Hour after hour passed, and no prospect of our desire being gratified.   At last a small skiff was seen to leave the shore, the occupant rowing for the steamer we were on.   He soon reached the boat, and we found 'twas a news-boy, with the daily papers.   While those who had eagerly purchased them, were reading them with avidity, I changed my military coat for one of linen, loaned me by that generous gentleman, Lieutenant George Martin, of the artillery, and walked quietly down to the boiler-deck, where I found Lieutenant " Si " Hayman in citizen's dress, conversing with the news-boy; in a few moments Hayman jumped into the boat, and I followed, the boy quietly remonstrating. I told him, to hand me the oars, take his seat in the stern, and with Hayman in the bow, I pulled for the shore, reaching it at the foot of Beale street, about twenty feet from one of the enemy's mortar-boats; gave the boy the only half-dollar I had, and walked up the street, meeting a host of friends, while *en route* for the Gayoso hotel, my objective point on landing. Under the influence of a famous caterer of the time, Frank Madden's combinations, I was enabled to withstand the flood of friendly greetings, that well-nigh o'erwhelmed me. Memphis was alive, and the blood of her generous heart was coursing through Colonel John Martin, Captain Ad. Storm, Colonel Samuel P. Walker, F. L. Warner, Colonel J. Knox Walker,* and many others, who were running to and fro, dealing out money and other necessaries, with the liberality that none but the generous can appreciate.

The Confederate prisoners who were in that fleet, will never forget those whole-hearted men, or their posterity. Even children were carried away by the promptings of generosity. One little girl in particular, poorly clad and bare-footed, with a basket of apples on her arm, when asked the price of them by a soldier, replied, "Nothing to Confederate soldiers;" and, suiting the action to the word, threw basket and contents into the crowd. For one, I can never forget the material courtesies extended me, by Samuel P. Walker, Ad. Storm, Frank Hyde, John Johnston, and John A. Henry.

While lying at the wharf, as some of the boats had come in for coaling and other purposes, one of those

---

* Colonel J. Knox Walker was one of the most courtly gentlemen I ever knew. His failing health compelled him to leave the service of the cause he loved so well, (but his heart was in it.) He was eminent, as a politician and financier, and one of the most genial gentlemen the South ever produced. I can almost hear his ringing laugh, as we parted, while he hummed:

"If you get there before I do,
Tell them I'm a coming to."

But the gallant Walker had too great a soul for a frail body, and he has gone to that land, where the curses of a vandal foe are not heard. Peace to his ashes!

seeming inconsistencies in the character and conduct of our custodians was exhibited. Captain Wash Gordon, of Tennessee, was on board of one of the boats, quite ill, from a disease contracted at Cairo, during our exposure at that place, and desired to be left at Memphis until convalescent, confident that the trip to Vicksburg would kill him; which it did, he dying a few days after our arrival at that port. His request was urged by some of the most influential citizens of the place, added to the importunity of his sister, Mrs. Sarah C. Law, of whom we have spoken previously, yet the authorities sternly refused, while at the same time indulgencies were granted in less deserving cases.

There were Federal officers stationed at Memphis, who were kind to our people, while in the faithful discharge of duty to their government, and the names of Chetlain and Hoge, should ever be kindly remembered.

We left Memphis in a storm of cheers and tears, 'midst the waving of handkerchiefs and the God-speed of thousands of sympathizing hearts. On arriving at Helena, General Steele, commanding that department, came on board to visit Colonel Wood, of Louisiana, a West Point classmate, who had the bearing that education and gentle association alone can furnish. We are off again for Vicksburg, nothing to enliven us except now and then the appearance of a contraband, who would emerge from the woods with all his worldly effects in a handkerchief, and with a woe-begone look, signal the gun-boat to stop for him, finding we would not, would retire sulkily to cover.

On the 17th day of September, 1862, ever memorable to the Confederate soldiers who formed that human cargo of that fleet, thirteen days on the river, making seventeen from Johnson's island, a trip that should have been made in five days, were means used for our destruction, whether the object was accomplished or not. At last, we stepped on shore in Dixie. How different from the few months before, not a drum beat, bugle blast, nor cheer heard, not a flag unfurled, or a handkerchief waved; it rained in torrents, I had handed my overcoat to my bed-fellow, at Johnson's island, Captain John Farabe,* of Shelby county, Tennessee, and hence, got a thorough soaking, yet trudged on from wharf to town, through the mud of Vicksburg.   It was a gloomy time, no enemy to stimulate us from without, and none to stimulate us within, and no shelter, but at intervals, a friendly shed.   Six thousand soldiers, with the blues, were adrift at Vicksburg, on a rainy day; the citizens had fed soldiers until they had nothing more to give, and self-preservation had become a law of nature, yet our troops did not force themselves on any one, they fought for their hearths and firesides, without bounty, pay, half-clad, hungry and suffering, yet they were subordinate to moral and social rights.   On wandering around the streets in search of shelter, I noticed the name of A. Gennella, on one of the many signs in the commercial part of the city.   This gentleman, one of Vickburg's most hospitable sons, had known my father in my school-boy days, and recognizing me, like a good Samaritan, cared for me and my two friends, Colonel Henderson and Captain Bibb, of the Fortieth Tennessee, who will join me in grateful remembrance of the generous hospitality of A. Gennella, and his estimable family.

Our orders were to report to General Tilghman,† at Jackson.   On arriving at the depot, we attempted to mount the platform of the car, when the guard halted us.

"Can't go to Jackson on this train, captain."

"Why not, sergeant?"

"Against orders, captain."

Remonstrances were of no avail, and I turned to leave, when an old sergeant in my first company, (the Gayoso Guards,) Charlie Lay, accosted me.   Fortunately for me, he commanded the guard, and obtained me a seat in the car.   Charlie Lay is a genial, generous fellow, earned his promotion honestly, and wears his honors most becomingly. After a few hour's ride, passed in pleasant conversation with the gallant Colonel Heiman, of the Tenth Tennessee, who occupied the seat with us, the sonorous tones of the conductor announced "Jackson."   We take quarters at the

* Captain Farabe died at his home, in Marshall county, Mississippi, in 1866.
† Tilghman killed at the battle of Baker's Creek.

Dixon house. Here we find Colonel Jim Jackson, General William H. Carrol,* Colonel Autry, Major John Dean, and "Uncle" Jimmy Hewitt, (as he was familiarly called.) Colonel Jim Jackson is as well known in the South, particularly in North Alabama, as "Old Hickory" himself. He was badly wounded at Manassas, but saved his life by giving a Federal soldier his watch to carry him out of reach of shot and shell. Jackson is one of the few men whose courage is never questioned under any circumstances. Colonel Autry commanded the Twentieth Mississippi, and was a meritorious officer. Colonel H. W. Walter, General Bragg's assistant adjutant general, was also at the Dixon house, possessing one of the finest legal minds in the South, which added to his military abilities, render him a worthy counsellor of the inflexible Bragg.

I reported to General Tilghman, one of the most distinguished officers furnished the South by the "dark and bloody ground," during the war, and to him and his aid-de-camp, Captain George Moorman, an officer every way worthy of the confidence of the courteous Tilghman, I was indebted for a twenty days' leave of absence, (an exception to the rule.)

On the strength of which I left for Richmond, seeking promotion not at the "cannon's mouth," but through lobby influence at the capitol. On reaching Charlotte, North Carolina, we found no trains left until the following evening, as they observe the Sabbath in that State. Four o'clock, the next afternoon, found us at the depot in company with Major Greene, of the Fifty-sixth Virginia, who, like myself, was anxious to reach Richmond. We attempted an entrance into the car, and were checked by the guard, who referred us to his commanding officer, Major Inge, who, with his battalion, was on his way to the front via. Richmond. I appealed to the major, but for the time uselessly.

" I would like to accommodate you, captain, but can't

---

* General Carroll died in exile, in Montreal, Canada, in 1868, a victim to Brownlow's tyranny, while he had when in power, this wretch treated with great kindness.

consistently, do it. I pressed these cars for my battalion, and there is barely standing room for them."

"But, major, I must go on to Richmond, I am acting under orders."

By this time Inge became excited, and closed his remarks with an expletive, in response to which, I said with a severity of expression—

"Let me tell you, Major Inge, in refusing me a seat you have done yourself and the service, a grievous wrong."

In passing through Augusta, Georgia, I purchased two bottles of the best "peach and honey" produced in that State, and as a "quid pro quo" for your contumacy, not one drop of the oleaginous fluid will "whet your whistle."

"By George, captain," says Inge, "you shall have my seat, sir. I think I have seen you somewhere before. You must excuse my abruptness, but I have been so annoyed to-day, that I have overlooked some of the cardinal points in military etiquette. Come in, let me introduce you to Colonels Peyton and Foreshay, the former from Virginia, and who was promoted from the ranks to a majority, for gallantry at the first Manassas; the latter, a Texan, and one of the most accomplished officers of the engineer corps."

I found Major Inge one of the most companionable gentleman I ever met, and am sure he makes a good officer.

Moral. In traveling, there is no stronger card of introduction than *good spirits*.

On arriving at the capital, we stopped at the American hotel, finding things sadly changed for the worst in the morale of the Confederacy. Carrington, the proprietor, advising us, when we dined, to take our hats to the table with us, as sixteen had been feloniously abstracted the day previous. Among the first notables met in our promenade, was General Jeff Thompson, of Missouri. After passing the compliments of the day, I remarked:

"General, I don't like to bring up unpleasant reminiscences, knowing you to be an advocate of 'temperance reform,' but on my first introduction to you, at the Gayoso hotel, Memphis, Tennessee, by the Honorable John Park, mayor at that time, (and one of the most sensible ones

she ever had,) we indulged in three consecutive cock-
tails?"

"So-so," says Jeff, "and to show you I've not forgotten
the taste, come to my room at Ballard's," to which place
we adjourned.

In spite of what may be said of his *idiosyn yoin crasies*,
he was a tower of strength to the Confederacy.

The next notable we met was Captain T. Harrison
Baker, of the ill-fated privateer "Savannah." Captain
Baker was in Fort Lafayette and elsewhere, fourteen
months. He is a regular "old salt," frank and fearless,
and a fine commander, and the city of Charleston may
well be proud of her distinguished son.

We again move on, steering for the war department,
inflated with anticipations of promotion. On reaching
the entrance to the capitol building, we enjoy the sight of
one of our warmest friends, Colonel B. D. Harman.
Harman made character in Mexico, as a splendid cavalry
officer, and was colonel of the First Confederate infantry,
now consolidated; one of the most popular officers in
Richmond, and is true to his friends.

We finish our business at the war department,) thanks
to the courtesy of Colonel Burton N. Harrison, private
secretary to the President,) to our satisfaction, and make
our exit. In the vestibule, we meet Captain John T.
Shirley, of gun-boat notoriety. Shirley was one of the
most indefatigable men in the service. He took the contract for building the famous ram "Arkansas," afterwards
commanded by Captain Isaac N. Brown, formerly a
lieutenant in the United States navy, and which ran the
gauntlet of the enemy's fleet at Vicksburg, a courageous
performance that redounds to his credit. Some of the
most pleasant moments of my life, have been spent in the
society of John T. Shirley, whose genial companionship
is still fresh in my memory. One of Shirley's aids in his
gunboat operations, was Captain D'Haven. This officer
is from that down-trodden State, Missouri; was the
first steamboatman that raised the Confederate flag on the
Mississippi river; has been a great sufferer for our cause,
is to the manor born, and as a friend and companion,

stands par-excellence in any social circle. As we reach our hotel, we find ourselves grasped by the hand with a grip as few men possess like Captain Marsh Miller. Miller was captain of the improvised gun-boat Grampus, He was a nervously energetic officer, and did the cause much good at Columbus, Island Ten, and New Madrid. After paying our board, we found that we hadn't sufficient to purchase emblems for our increasing rank, involving an expense of five dollars for two stars. I called at the paymaster's department, and saw a very discouraging sign pendant, "no funds to-day," which many brother officers will remember, whose daily attendance was greeted with the same ominous characters. Finding my friend, St. Clair, was a clerk in the department, and explaining my case to him, he introduced me to his chief, Major John M. Mason, son of the distinguished diplomat John M. Mason, of Louisina, who, appreciating the urgency of my case, furnished me with the desired funds. Charley St. Clair was Judge of the Supreme Court of Utah. Under the auspices of Albert Sidney Johnson, he was also a member of the Virginia legislature. Charley St. Clair had too much sentiment to combat the jagged points of life, and any dereliction of moral duty resulted more from impulse than confirmed principle of error. After being flushed with funds, and armed with a letter of introduction from the Honorable G. A. Henry, of Tennessee, to the Secretary of State, Judah P. Benjamin, I presented myself to that gentleman. My mission was unsuccessful, as my crime of having been a delegate to the Bell and Everett convention, at Baltimore, could not be palliated by my past services. Benjamin showed his fine teeth, gave me a politician's smile, and bowed me out. As my leave of absence had nearly expired, I left Richmond. On arriving at Knoxville, learning that the troops were falling back from Kentucky, I concluded to remain in Knoxville, hoping that I might meet some of my old companions in arms, in which desire I was very fortunate. General Preston Smith,* one of the bravest

* General Smith killed, during the celebrated Georgia campaign, from Dalton to Atlanta.

19

officers in the army; Colonel Milton A. Haynes, military commandant of the post, a West Pointer, of enlarged military views. Knoxville was surfeited with troops. Had it not been for Colonel Ed. Dyer, paymaster for McCowan's division, and his staff, it is possible I might have quartered in the streets. Captain Charlie Smith, his chief assistant; James Armour, and the *Good Friday* of the department, Major Jim Torrey,* the "old chief," as the boys called him.

Jim Torrey is called a desperate man; but I have seen his good feelings express themselves on one occasion, and owe him an everlasting debt of gratitude, for his kind attentions to a sick family on another, when it was troublesome to be attentive to the wants of others.

It would be impossible for me, to mention all the friends I met in Knoxville. General M. J. Wright,† formerly of the One Hundred and Fifty-fourth Senior Regiment, Tennessee Volunteers. Marcus J. Wright, is a self-made man, and most eminently deserves the position his energies have enabled him to attain. Colonel J. C. Cole, Fifth Confederate Regiment, Henry, Nelson, and Bob Bowles Rucker, of Island Ten notoriety, Major Ed. Austin, of New Orleans, and many other gallant soldiers, whose march of seven hundred miles on that unsuccessful campaign, had fatigued, but not dispirited, were coursing through the streets, trying to make the most of the rest that the halt at Knoxville, had permitted them to enjoy the streets of the little city, were a perfect jam, so much so, that pedestrianism for civilians was uncomfortable. To relieve the pressure, General Bragg issued an order, that no one under the rank of Brigadier-General, should appear on the street, without a written permit, and Lieutenant Waddell, with a squad of cavalry, was ordered to clear the streets.

I was conversing with Captain Charles Bradley, of the quarter-master's department, when I saw the cavalry coming. Bradley remarked:

---

* Jim Torrey, the "old chief," resides in Memphis.
† General M. J. Wright, farming near Memphis, Tennessee.

" Step in the door, and after they pass, we will go out again."

Every soldier in Knoxville seemed instinctively to do the same, crowding into every available opening in the city, reappearing as the guard disappeared in the distance. Several similar efforts were made with equal success. That army that contained eighteen hundred barefooted soldiers, prostrated with their late disastrous movement into Kentucky, and a majority of them without blankets, the ground being covered with snow, were not in a condition to submit to military orders that were cruel, as well as inexpedient. Major Dick Wintersmith, one of the best business men in the army in his department, of unquestioned courage, a full-blooded Kentuckian, connected with one of the oldest families in the State, and who, I think could have filled one cabinet office at Richmond, better than the incumbent, was the last friend whose hand I shook on leaving Knoxville, October 17, 1863. After passing the night with Lieutenant Hutchinson, of the Southern Guards of Memphis, in the attic of a building well ventilated, as one of the gable ends was knocked out, this added to our other discomforts, enabled us to leave Knoxville with but few regrets.

On arriving at Jackson, Mississippi, reported with my increased rank to General Pemberton, who ordered me to report, by letter, to Richmond. The post at Jackson was commanded by Lieutenant-colonel Gus. Fonte, who, although not an experienced military commander, adapted himself to the necessities of the position, and made a popular officer. At last, through the influence of Honorable S. R. Mallory, I was transferred to the bureau of conscription, and appointed Inspector-General for the department of Tennessee, Alabama, Mississippi, and East Louisiana, where I am for the present, Micawber-like, waiting for something to *turn up*.

APPENDIX.

TO THE YOUTH OF THE SOUTH.

WHEN the charge is made, that your fathers treated their prisoners badly, read this to their false accusers: That in a country filled with supplies, and with boundless resources, out of five thousand and twenty-five (5,025) Confederates, imprisoned in *Elmira*, in the spring of 1865, thirteen hundred and eleven (1,311) died in four months, a bill of mortality, not exceeded by the "Black Hole of Calcutta." The following is official:

"THE REBEL PRISONERS AT ELMIRA.

"A paragraph has been going the rounds of the Republican press, as follows:

" 'From the records of the Elmira prison, which were taken to Washington, for use in the Surratt trial, it is found that during the spring of 1865, 5,025 rebel prisoners were confined here during that time, and that only six deaths occurred in three months.'

" The Elmira 'Gazette' corrects this statement, and gives the figures to prove its falsity. That paper has taken pains to ascertain the facts, and finds that of that number confined at that place, during the spring of 1865, viz: 5,025, there were during the three months 884 deaths —a slight discrepancy of 878! In March, the number of deaths was 495; in April, 265; in May, 124; making a total of 884. And if February was included, which gives 426 more, the total for four months will be 1,311! Much has been said concerning the mortality of Union soldiers in Southern prisons, but such a record should awaken inquiry at home."—Buffalo "Courier."

Tell them that at camp Douglas, on lake Michigan, in the depth of winter, six (6) blankets were issued to one hundred and sixty (160) men, and that dogs and rats were daily eaten. Tell them, that at Point Lookout, that your fathers were guarded by Negroes, who shot at them as they would at game. That there was one stove to ten thousand (10,000) men ; and many froze to death, from lying on the bare ground, without a blanket. Tell them, that at camp Douglas prisoners were tied up by the thumbs, (in one instance, that of the gallant John D. Levett, afterwards Captain Levett,) for three hours, for slight infractions of the oppressive rules of the prison.

Tell them, that in all the prison pens of the North, many of the custodians of those sinks of oppression, allowed atrocities to be committed, at the recital of which the heart of civilization revolts. I append compilations, from official and other reliable data, which, I hope, every true child of the South—who love their ancestry and their heroic deeds—will read carefully, and when the lying historian, of a fanatical party, speaks of the so-called horrors of Andersonville, let the youth of the South know, that it is written, to hide the cruelties, practiced by our enemies upon Confederate prisoners.

In every large prison at the North, cruelty was systematically practiced for the purpose of forcing prisoners to take the oath of allegiance to the Federal government, or, in case of their refusal, of enfeebling their health to such an extent as to render them unfit for military service, on their return to the South. The treatment of some of the prisoners was so severe, that when they were taken from the cells, the blood gushed from their ears.

Sometimes prisoners, thinly clad, were removed long distances from one prison to another, in the coldest weather. No provisions were taken for them, and benevolent people along the route were forbidden to give them either food or clothing. On such occasions large numbers of the wretched sufferers died in the cars ; but they gained a happy release. No one can read the accounts of the treatment of Southern prisoners, in most

Hanging Prisoners by the Thumbs.

of the large prisons at the North, without feeling that those who died soonest were the most favored.

At camp Douglas, on lake Michigan, during an intensely cold spell in the winter of 1862, when icicles hung from the roof of the prison, within two inches of the stove pipe, and the breath froze on the beards of the prisoners, six blankets were issued to about 160 men—the only blankets issued during the winter. Few of those detailed to bring in fuel returned without being frost-bitten; many were brought back insensible, or in a helpless condition; some had their arms frozen stiff around the wood and could not open them. The food was very scanty, and rats and dogs were eaten whenever they could be procured. "Men," says one prisoner, "talk of the horrors of Andersonville. If those who now sleep on the shores of Lake Michigan could tell the story of their sufferings, Andersonville would appear as a paradise in comparison."

In one instance when a negro guard had shot into a crowd of over two hundred Southern prisoners, at Point Lookout, without provocation, killing and wounding five men, the officer of the day, in presence of the prisoners, told him when his ammunition gave out to let him know, and he would furnish more. Men were frozen to death by being forced to sleep on the ground with only one blanket and no fire. The rations were just enough to keep soul and body together. "The fiendish brutality practiced by the Fifth Massachusetts Cavalry, on the defenseless unfortunates at this post, can never be forgotten or forgiven." "I was a prisoner for eight long months," says one man, "and the sufferings I witnessed during that time, I never before had any conception of. I am told by those who experienced the tortures of Fort Delaware, that they were still worse."

Tying up by the thumbs was a punishment practiced daily at Fort Delaware, for the slightest infraction of prison rules; men were frequently tied up in this way for two and three hours at a time. At eight o'clock every morning, one small piece of mixed corn and wheat bread, and about an ounce of salt, were issued to each prisoner.

The same quantity was issued at two o'clock, with the addition of a pint of filthy soup. This was all they had. A poor boy from Charlottesville, Virginia, was shot dead for throwing some water from a cup out of a window of the barracks. One stove was all that was allowed about ten thousand men in the coldest winter months. A lieutenant, for a very slight offense, was ordered by General Schoepf, to have his hands manacled behind his back, and to be hung up by his elbows. He was kept hanging, until he fainted, from excruciating agony. A surgeon was detailed, to watch the operation, and to replace the shoulders of the unfortunate sufferer, when they became dislocated. This was repeated several times, after which the prisoner was placed in solitary confinement for ten days. The corpses of prisoners were sold, and bodies taken from the graves, for the use of medical colleges and surgeons.

"In reply to a resolution of the House of Representatives, says the Washington "Union," calling upon the Secretary of War, for the number of prisoners of either side held, and that died during the war, he makes the following report: Number of Union prisoners South, 261,000; number of Confederate prisoners North, 200,000; number of Union prisoners died, 22,576; number of Confederate prisoners died, 26,535. Out of 261,000 Union Prisoners, 22,500 died. The Union prisoners exceeded the Confederate prisoners 61,000, yet the deaths of the Union prisoners fell below those of the Confederate prisoners six thousand. Two Yankee prisoners died out of every twenty-three, in Southern pens. Two Confederate prisoners died out of every fifteen, in Northern pens.

It is due to the truth of history and to the cause of the Southern Confederacy, that these figures published by the authority of the United States Secretary of War, Mr. Stanton, should be widely circulated. From them we learn that, although the Southern Confederacy had more Northern prisoners in its hands, than the Northern Government had of Southern prisoners, the mortality in the Northern prisons was more than twice as great as in the

Southern. It is thus that facts and figures disprove the the violent calumnies which were set afloat in a time of passion, regarding the treatment of Union prisoners by the Southern government and its agents. The reader will not readily forget the shocking charges which were made during the war, not only against such men as Captain Wirz, but against high-minded, honorable, christian men, like Mr. Jefferson Davis, himself. Had these stories been true, they would necessarily show a largely disproportionately excess of mortality in Southern prisons. The official records—not of the Southern States, be it remembered, but of the Northern States, show that the death rate was much greater in the North, than in the South.

We do not pretend to say that there were not hardships, nay, grevious sufferings experienced in both the Northern and Southern pens. To say this, would be to say what was not the case. But it is evident that if the results are to be taken, as indicating the character of the treatment received, and we think they may be very fairly so taken, the Northern prisoners in the hands of the Confederacy were treated more leniently, than were the Southerners who had the misfortune to fall into the hands of their Northern oppressors. Assuming that the mode of treatment was the same in the North as in the South, the death rate in the Southern prisons ought to have been greater than in the Northern. For it is an indisputable fact that a Northern man will naturally suffer more in a Southern climate, than a Southern man will in a Northern climate. Besides, during the war, the Northern Government experienced no want of wholesome provisions wherewith to feed the prisoners who fell into their hands, if they had intended to treat them well, whilst the Confederacy was not so highly favored. Taking all these circumstances together, they go to show, that without the exercise of any extraneous influence, the mortality in the South, ought to have been much greater than in the North. That the opposite was the case—and to a very great extent too—must be taken as uttterly disproving the charges of wanton cruelty against the South, which were so common at the time, and which, grossly exaggerated by artistic imagination, helped to disfigure the pictorial columns of "Harper's Weekly."

We would have allowed this subject to slumber on, as it has been doing lately, were it not for the publication of the official figures, which come so opportunely, to relieve every resident of the Southern States, whether man or woman, whether abroad or at home, of the opprobrium which interested parties have sought to cast upon them, by the circulation of the most glaring falsehoods; and because even now, Radical sheets in the Northern States, do not hesitate to fling the accusation in the face of Mr. Jefferson Davis, with a view of influencing public opinion against him, whilst he is retained in custody, and, of course, debarred from replying to the falsehoods. Impartial history will record that the Southern people fought their cause with a nobleness of conduct, which did them honor. They fell, but falling could say in the memorable words of another people, who, like themselves, had striven, but in vain, for independence, "All is lost save honor." There was no fouler charge made against the Southern people, than that of having cruelly treated Northern prisoners. By the mouths of their enemies have they been fully vindicated.

TREATMENT OF JEFFERSON DAVIS.

THE following account of the treatment of the President of the late Confederate States, Jefferson Davis, by a so-called civilized government, is without a parallel in the history of civilization. Louis Napoleon, (after his two failures at invasion of his own country, from a foreign shore at Boulogne and Strasburg,) while confined at Ham, was treated in a manner, becoming his distinguished social position. Lafayette, during his five years' confinement at Olmutz, received deferential consideration at the hands of his jailors. Since time immemorial, State prisoners have received from all governments, no matter how barbarous, gentle treatment, until trial—but in the United States of America, a party of fanatics in power, have been led to the commission of unconstitutional and inhuman acts, that causes any conservator of peace and morals, to blush for his countrymen; their criminal abuses being so palpable—as in the case of Jefferson Davis, who has not been brought to trial, simply from the fact, that his acquittal, (a settled fact before an impartial jury,) would result in the establishment of the principle of State rights, and show to the world, that the late crusade against the South, was an Abolition raid, into which many honest men were led, imagining they were fighting for the integrity and oneness of the Union.

"MANACLED.

" Stop, soldier, stop! this cruel act
   Will ring through all the land,
Shame on the heart that planned the deed!
Shame on the coward hand

That drops the sword of justice bright
  To grasp these iron rings!
On them, not me, dishonor falls,
  To them this dark shame clings.

"Manacled? O, my God! my God!
  Is this a christian land?
And did our countries ever meet
  And grasp each other's hand?
O, Mexico! on thy red fields
  I battled 'midst the fray;
My riflemen, with steady aim,
  Won Buena Vista's day.

"Manacled! far down the South
  Let this one word speed fast,
My country, thou hast borne great wrongs,
  But this, the last, the last,
Will send a thrill through thy high heart,
  Despair will spurn control,
And these hard irons pressing *here*
  Will enter *thy* proud soul.

"Manacled! O, word of shame!
  Ring it through all the world!
My countrymen, on you, on you,
  This heavy wrong is hurled.
We flung our banners to the air;
  We fought as brave men fight;
Our battle-cry rang through the land;
  Home! liberty! and right!

"Manacled! For this I am here,
  Clanking the prisoner's chain.
We fought—and nobly did we fight—
  We fought, but fought in vain:
Down in that billowy sea of blood
  Went all our jewels rare,
And Hope rushed wailing from the scene
  And took herself to prayer!

"Manacled! manacled! Words of woe,
  But words of greater shame;
I've that within me which these wrongs,
  Can never, never tame;
And standing proud in conscious worth,
  I represent my land,
And that Lost Cause for which she bled,
  Lofty, heroic, grand!'"

HOW MR. DAVIS WAS IMPRISONED AT FORTRESS MONROE.

The Ironing Business—The True Relation of Facts.

STATEMENT OF EVENTS CONNECTED WITH THE FETTERING OF JEFFERSON DAVIS, WHEN A PRISONER AT FORTRESS MONROE, AS DERIVED FROM, AND VERIFIED BY THE PRISONER AND AN OFFICER OF THE DAY.

INCORRECTNESS OF CRAVEN'S BOOK.

WHEN Jefferson Davis was brought a captive to Fortress Monroe, he was confined in a gun-room of a casemate, the embrasure of which was closed with a heavy iron grating, and the doors which communicated with the gunner's room were closed with heavy double shutters, fastened with cross bars and padlocks. The side openings had been closed up with fresh masonry, the plastering of which was soft to the touch, the top being an arch to support the earth of the parapet. Two sentinels, with muskets loaded and bayonets fixed, paced to and fro across this small prison. Two other sentinels and a commissioned officer occupied the gunner's room, the doors and windows of which were strongly secured. The officer of the day had the key of the outer door, and sentinels were posted on the outer pavement in front of it. There were also sentinels on the parapet overhead. The embrasure looked out on the west ditch, say sixty feet wide, the water in which was probably from seven to ten feet deep, the scarp and counterscarp revetted with dressed masonry. Beyond the ditch, on the glacis, was a double chain of sentinels, and in the casemate rooms, on each side of the prison, were quartered that part of the guard which was not on post.

Borne down by privation, over exertion and exposure, he was in no condition, when thrown into prison, to resist exciting causes of disease. The damp walls, the food too coarse and bad to be eaten, the deprivation of sleep, caused by the tramping of sentries around the iron cot, the light of the lamp, which shone full upon it, the loud calling of the roll, when another relief was called out, the noise of unlocking the doors, the tramp of the sentinels, who came to relieve those on post, produced fever, and rapidly wasted his strength. Without mechanical aid, though his efforts were not interrupted, no one could have removed the grating from the embrasure. If that had been done, and any one could have swam across the ditch, and climbed up the revetment on the opposite side, which was doubtful, he then would have encountered the sentinels on the glacis. The circumstances, together with many manifestations, indicating feeling towards him, led him to the conclusion, that it was not the belief that these things were necessary to prevent his escape, but a purpose to offer an indignity, to inflict physical pain, and perhaps to deprive him of life.

On the 23d of May, 1865, the officer of the day, Captain J. Titlow, of the Third Pennsylvania artillery, came into his prison with two blacksmiths, bearing a pair of heavy leg irons coupled together by a ponderous chain. Captain Titlow, in a manner fully sustaining his words, informed him that with great personal reluctance, he came to execute an order to put irons upon him. Mr. Davis asked whether General Miles had given that order, and on being answered in the affirmative, said he wished to see General Miles. Captain Titlow replied that he had just left General Miles, who was leaving the fort. Mr. Davis then asked that the execution of the order should be postponed until General Miles returned. Captain Titlow said his orders would not permit that, and that to an old soldier it was needless to say that an officer was bound to execute an order as it was given to him. Mr. Davis told him that it was too obvious, that there could be no necessity for the use of such means to render his imprisonment secure; and on Captain Titlow's repeating that his duty was to execute his orders, Mr. Davis said it was not such an order as a soldier could give, or should receive, and he would not submit to it; that it was evidently the intention to torture him to death; that he would never tamely be subjected to indignities by which it was sought in his person to degrade the cause of which he was a representative. The officer of the day with evident kind feeling endeavored to dissuade him from resistance. The officer of the guard came in from the front room with the officer of the day, to induce him to yield. It was needless to show what was very apparent, that resistance could not be successful, and Mr. Davis' answer was that he was "a soldier and a gentleman, that he knew how to die," and pointing to the sentinel who stood ready, said, "let your men shoot me at once." He faced round with his back to the wall, and stood silently waiting. His quiet manner led the officer to suppose that no resistance would be made, and therefore the blacksmiths were directed to do their work. As one of them stooped down to put on the fetters, Mr. Davis slung him off so violently as to throw him on the floor; he recovered and raised his hammer to strike, but the officer of the day stopped him; simultaneously one of the sentinels cocked and lowered his musket, advancing on the prisoner, who had turned to encounter his assailant, and thus did not see the purpose of the blacksmith. Captain Titlow saw the new danger, and promptly interposed, telling the sentinels that they were not to fire. Ordered the officer of the guard to bring in four of the strongest men of the guard without firearms, for the purpose of overcoming by muscular strength the resistance which was threatened.

Mr. Davis had nothing with which to defend himself, even his pen-knife having been previously taken from him. The contest was brief, and ended in his being thrown down, four men being on his body and head. He could not see the blacksmiths when they approached to put on the irons, but feeling one of them, he kicked him off from him against the wall. The smith recovered, and with the aid which the other men could give him, succeeded in the second attempt to rivit one fetter, and secure the padlock which held the other. Mr. Davis scornfully asked his assailants if they "called"

20

themselves "soldiers," and said "the shame is yours, not mine." The object being effected, the officer of the day withdrew the men he had brought in. The prisoner lay down on the cot, covered his ironed limbs with the blanket, and felt only more intense contempt for the brutality with which he was treated than when a few minutes before he had announced his belief that he was to be tortured to death, and defied the power which attempted to degrade him. Of the dramatic account published in Dr. Craven's book, he said it could not have been written by one who either knew the facts, or had such personal knowledge of him as to form a just idea of what his conduct would be under such circumstances. The fact (he added) was that very little was said either by Captain Titlow or by himself, and that whatever was said, was uttered in a very quiet and practical manner. For himself he would say, he was too resolved, and too proudly conscious of his relation to a sacred, though unsuccessful cause, for such acclamations and manifestations as were imputed to him by Dr. Craven's informant, and given to the public in his books.

THE MURDERED WIRZ.

LETTER OF LOUIS SCHADE, ESQ.

THE youth of the South will consider the facts so truth-fully presented in the following letter of Louis Schade, esq., that eminent counsellor, which proves that our late beloved chief was innocent of any participation in the so-called atrocities of Andersonville, and that the murdered Wirz was more sinned against than sinning. The author knows that on one occasion, that when passing the depot while the sick Federal prisoner was being removed from the cars, that the persecuted and murdered Wirz, did assist in lifting a sick man in his own arms, and in this connec-tion permit the writer to say, that no people on the earth have ever treated prisoners as cruelly as the Abolition fanatics of the North, and no prisoners have been treated with more humanity (so far as compatible, with the capa-city of the government) than the Federal prisoners in Con-federate prisons:

Intending to leave the United States for some time, I feel it my duty, before I start, to fulfil in part a promise which, a few hours before his death, I gave to my unfor-tunate client, Captain Wirz, who was executed at Wash-ington, on the 10th day of November, 1865. Protesting up to the last moment his innocence of those monstrous crimes with which he was charged, he received my word, that, having failed to save him from a felon's doom, I would, as long as I lived, do everything in my power to clear his memory. I did that the more readily, as I was then perfectly convinced that he suffered wrongfully. Since that time, his unfortunate children, both here and in Europe, have constantly implored me to wipe out the terrible stains which now cover the name of their father. Though the times do not seem propitious for obtaining full justice, yet, considering that man is mortal, I will, before entering upon a perilous voyage, perform my duty to those innocent orphans, and also to myself.

I will now give a brief statement of the causes which led to the arrest and execution of Captain Wirz. In April, 1865, President Johnson issued a proclamation stating that from evidence in the possession of the "Bureau of Military Justice," it appeared that Jefferson Davis was implicated in the assassination of Abraham Lincoln, and for that reason the President offered a reward of 100,000 on the capture of the then fugitive ex-President of the Southern Confederacy. That testimony has since been found to be entirely false and a mere fabrication, and the suborner, Conover, is now under sentence in the jail of this city, the two perjurers, whom he suborned, having turned State evidence against him, whilst the individual, by whom Conover was suborned, has not yet been brought to justice.

Certain high and influential enemies of Jefferson Davis, either then already aware of the character of the testimony of those witnesses, or not thinking their testimony quite sufficient to hang Jefferson Davis, expected to find the wanting material in the terrible mortality of the Union prisoners at Andersonville. Orders were issued accordingly to arrest a subaltern officer, Captain Wirz, a poor, friendless and wounded prisoner of war, (he being included in the surrender of General Johnston,) and besides a foreigner by birth. On the 7th of May, he were placed in the old Capital Prison at Washington, and from that time the greater part of the Northern press was busily engaged in forming the unfortunate man in the eyes of the Northern people into such a monster that it became almost impossible for him to obtain counsel. Even his countryman, the Swiss Consul General, publicly refused to accept money to defray the expenses of the trial. He was doomed before he was heard, and even the permission to be heard according to law was denied him. To increase the excitement and give eclat to the proceeding, and to inflame still' more the public mind, the trial took place under the very dome of the capitol of the nation. A military commission, presided over by one of the most arbitrary and despotic generals in the country, was formed, and the paroled prisoner of war, his wounds still open, and so feeble that he had to recline during the trial on a sofa, carried before the same. How that trial was conducted, the whole world knows. The enemies of generosity and humanity believed it then a sure thing to get at Jefferson Davis.

Therefore, the first charge was that of conspiracy between Wirz, Jefferson Davis, Seddon, Howell Cobb, R. B. Winder, and a number of others, to kill the Union prisoners. The trial lasted for three months, but unfortunately for the blood-thirsty instigators, not a particle of evidence was produced, showing the existence of such a conspiracy; yet, Captain Wirz was found guilty of that charge! Having thus failed, another effort was made. On the night before the execution of the prisoner a telegram was sent to the Northern press from this city, stating that Wirz had made important disclosures to General L. C. Baker, the well-known detective, implicating Jefferson Davis, and that the confession would probably be given to the public. On the same evening some parties came to the confessor of Wirz, Rev. Father Boyle, and also to me, one of them informing me that a high Cabinet officer wished to assure Wirz, that if he would implicate Jefferson Davis with the atrocities committed at Andersonville, his sentence would be commuted. He, the messenger, or who ever he was, requested me to inform Wirz of this. In presence of Father Boyle I told Wirz next morning what had happened. The Captain simply and quietly replied: "Mr. Schade, you know that I have always told you that I do not know anything about Jefferson Davis. He had no connection with me as to what was done at Andersonville. If I knew anything about him I would not become a traitor against him or anybody else, even to save my life." He likewise denied that he had made any statement whatever to General Baker. Thus ended the attempt to suborn Captain Wirz against Jefferson Davis. That alone shows what a man he was. How many of his defamers would have done the same? With his wounded arm in a sling, the poor paroled prisoner mounted, two hours later, the scaffold. His last words were that he died innocent—and so he did. The 10th day of November, 1865, will indeed be a black stain upon the pages of American history.

To weaken the effect of his declaration of innocence, and of the noble manner in which Wirz died, a telegram was manufactured here and sent North, stating that on the 27th of October, Mrs. Wirz, (who actually was 900 miles on that day away from Washington,) had been prevented by that Stantonian *deus ex machina* General L. C. Baker, *from poisoning her husband!* Thus, on the same day when the unfortunate family lost their husband and father, a cowardly and atrocious attempt was made to blacken their character also. On the next day I branded the whole as an infamous lie, and since then I never have heard of it again, though it emanated from a Brigadier-General of the United States army.

All those who were charged with having conspired with Captain Wirz have since been released, except Jefferson Davis, the prisoner of the American Castle of Chillon, Captain Winder, was let off without trial, and if any of the others have been tried, which I do not know, certainly none of them have been hung. As Captain Wirz could not conspire alone, nobody will now, in view of that important fact, consider him guilty of that charge. So much, then, for charge No. 1.

As to charge No. 2, to wit: Murder, in violation of the laws and customs of war, I do not hesitate to declare that about 145 out of 160 witnesses on both sides, declared during the trial, that Captain Wirz never murdered or killed any Union prisoners, with his own hands or otherwise. All those witnesses (about twelve to fifteen,) who testified that they saw Captain Wirz kill a prisoner, have sworn falsely, abundant proofs of that assertion being in existence. The hands of Captain Wirz are clear of the blood of prisoners of war. He would certainly have at least intimated to me a knowledge of the alleged murders with which he was charged. In most all cases no names of the alleged murdered men could be given, and where it was done, no such persons could be identified. The terrible scene in court, when he was confronted with one of the witnesses, and the latter insisting that Wirz was the man who killed a certain Union prisoner, which irritated the prisoner so much that he almost fainted, will still be remembered. That man (Grey) swore falsely, and God alone knows what the poor innocent prisoner must have suffered at that moment. That scene was depicted and illustrated in the Northern newspapers as if Wirz had broken down on account of his guilt. Seldom has mortal suffered more than that friendless and forsaken man.

Fearing lest this communication will be too long, I will merely speak of the principal and most intelligent of these false witnesses, who testified to individual murder on the part of Captain Wirz. Upon his testimony the Judge Advocate in his final argument laid particular stress on account of his intelligence. This witness prepared also pictures of the alleged cruelties of Wirz, which were handed to the Commission, and are now on record, copies of which appeared at the time in Northern illustrated papers. He swore that his name was Felix de la Baume, and represented himself as a Frenchman, and grand-nephew of Marquis Lafayette. After having so well testified and shown so much zeal, he received a recommendation signed by the members of the Commission. On the 11th day of October, before the taking of the testimony was concluded, he was appointed to a clerkship in the Department of the Interior. This occurred whilst one of the witnesses for the defence (Duncan) was arrested in open court and placed in prison before he had testified. After the execution of Captain Wirz some of the Germans of Washington, recognized in de la Baume a deserter from the Seventh New York (Steuben) Regiment, whose name was not de la Baume, but Felix Oeser, a native of Saxony. They went to Secretary Harlan, and he dismissed the impostor and the important witness in the Wirz trial on the 21st of November, eleven days after the execution. Nobody who is acquainted with the Conover testimony, in consequence of which the President of the United States was falsely induced to place a reward of $100,000 upon the head of an innocent man, will be astonished at the above disclosures of the character of testimony before military commissions. So much for charge No. II.

If from twelve to fifteen witnesses could be found who were willing to testify to so many acts of murder on the part of Wirz, there must certainly have been no lack of such who were willing to swear to minor offences. Such was the unnatural state of the public mind against the prisoner at that time, that such men regarded themselves, and were regarded, as heroes, after having testified in the manner above described; whilst on the other hand, the witnesses for the defence were intimidated, particularly after one of them had been arrested.

But who is responsible for the many lives that were lost at Andersonville, and in the Southern prisons? That question has not fully been settled, but history will tell on whose heads the guilt for those sacrificed hecatombs of human beings is to be placed. It was certainly not the fault of poor Captain Wirz, when, in consequence of medicines having been declared contraband of war by the North, the Union prisoners died for the want of the same. How often have we read during the war that ladies, going South, had been arrested and placed in the old Capitol Prison by the Union authorities, because some quinine, or other medicines, had been found concealed in their petticoats! Our navy prevented the ingress of medical stores from the sea-side, and our troops repeatedly destroyed drug stores, and even the supplies of private physicians in the South. Thus, the scarcity of medicines became general all over the South. Surgeon J. C. Pilot writes, September 6th, 1864, from Andersonville, [this letter was produced by the Judge Advocate in the Wirz trial]: "We have little more than the indigenous barks and roots with which to treat the numerous forms of disease to which our attention is daily called. For the treatment of wounds, ulcers, &c., we have literally nothing, except water. Our wards, some of them, are wild with gangrene, and we are compelled to fold our arms and look quietly upon its ravages, not even having stimulants to support the system under its depressing influence; the article being so limited in supply that it can only be issued for cases under the knife."

That provisions in the South were scarce, will astonish nobody, when it is remembered how the war was carried on. General Sheridan boasted, in his official report that, in the Shenandoah valley alone, he burned two thousand barns filled with wheat and corn, and all the mills in the whole tract of country; that he destroyed all factories of cloth, and killed, or drove off, every animal, even to the poultry, that could contribute to human sustenance. And those desolations were repeated in different parts of the South, and that so thoroughly, that last month, two years after the end of the war, Congress had to appropriate a million of dollars, to save the people of those regions from actual starvation. The destruction of railroads, and other means of transportation, by which food should be supplied by abundant districts to those without it, increased the difficulties in giving sufficient food to our prisoners.

The Confederate authorities, aware of their inability to maintain their prisoners, informed the Northern agents of the great mortality, and urgently requested that the prisoners should be exchanged, even without regard to the surplus which the Confederates had on the exchange roll from former exchanges, that is, man for man, but our War Department did not consent to an exchange. They did not want to " exchange skeletons for healthy men." Finally, when all hopes of exchange were gone, Colonel Ould, the Confederate Commissioner, offered, early in August, 1864, to deliver up all the Federal sick and wounded, without requiring an equivalent in return, and

pledged that the number would amount to ten or fifteen
thousand, and, if it did not, he would make up that number with well men.   Although this offer was made in
August, the transportation was not sent for them (to
Savannah) until December, although he urged and implored, (to use his own words,) that haste should be made.
During that very period, the most of the deaths at
Andersonville occurred.   Congressman Covode, who lost
two sons in Southern prisons, will do well if he inquires
who these "skeletons" were which the Honorable Secretary of War did not want to exchange for healthy men!
If he does, he will hereafter be perhaps less bitter against
the people of the South.

But has the North treated her Southern prisoners so
well that she should lift up her hands and cry "anathe-
ma" over the South.   Mr. Stanton's reports to Congress,
July 19, 1866, that of Southern prisoners there died in
the North 26,436, and of Northern prisoners in the South
22,576.   What a fearful record!   Over 26,000 prisoners dying in the midst of plenty!   Mr. Stanton gives
the total number of prisoners in the North at 220,000,
and in the South at 126,940.   Suppose this to be correct, though this statement comes certainly from no impartial source, there died of prisoners in the South, without medicines and provisions, the fifth part, and in the
North, with medicines and provisions, the eighth part.
But in the number of Southern prisons in the North, are
probably included the paroled prisoners of Lee's, Johnston's and Smith's armies, who never entered a Northern
prison.   If that be so, the mortality of Southern prisoners in the North, will be even greater than that of the
Federal prisoners in the South.

We used justly to proclaim in former times, that ours
was "the land of the free and the home of the brave."
But when one half of the country is shrouded in a despotism which now only finds a parallel in Russian Poland,
and when our generals and soldiers quietly permit that
their former adversaries in arms shall be treated worse than
the Helots of old, brave soldiers though they may be, who,
when the forces and resources of both sections were more

equal, have not seldom seen the backs of our best generals, not to speak of such as Butler and consorts, then we may well question whether the "star-spangled banner still waves over the land of the free or the home of the brave." A noble and brave soldier never permits his antagonist to be calumniated and trampled upon after an honorable surrender. Besides, notwithstanding the decision of the highest legal tribunal in the land that military commissions are unconstitutional, the earnest and able protestations of President Johnson, and the sad results of military commissions, yet such military commissions are again established by recent legislation of Congress all over he suffering and starving South.

History is just, and, as Mr. Lincoln used to say, we cannot escape history. Puritanical hypocracy, self-adulation and self-glorification will not save those enemies of liberty from their just punishment.

Not even a christian burial of the remains of Captain Wirz was allowed by Secretary Stanton. They will lie side by side with those of another and acknowledged victim of military commissions, the unfortunate Mrs. Surratt, in the yard of the former jail in this city.

If anybody should desire to reply to this, I politely beg that it may be done before the first of May next, as then I shall leave the country to return in the fall. After that day letters will reach me in care of the American Legation, or Mr. Benedette Bolzani, Leipzig street, No. 38, Berlin, Prussia.

LOUIS SCHADE,
Attorney at Law.

WASHINGTON, April 4, 1867.

TREATMENT OF FEDERAL PRISONERS AND REBEL WITNESSES.

The following letter from one of the counsel of Captain Wirz effectually contradicts the false statements of the "Chronicle" with regard to the manner of the dismissal of Colonel Ould, and other distinguished Southern men, who were summoned as witnesses for the defense upon that trial, but were not allowed by the prosecution to testify :

WASHINGTON, D. C., September 5, 1868.

To THE EDITOR OF THE NATIONAL INTELLIGENCER:

My attention has been called to the following extract from an article contained in the " Chronicle," of the 27th of August last, to wit :

" The statements in Robert Ould's letter, that though announced as a witness for the defense in the Wirz case, he was dismissed by the prosecution, is authoritatively pronounced a malicious perversion of the facts. In military trials all witnesses are both summoned and dismissed by the Judge Advocate ; and had Wirz's counsel designed that Mr. Ould should be put upon the stand, it would have been done, though he would not have been allowed to make an entirely irrelevant statement in defense of the rebel system of exchange."

The words "authoritatively pronounced" induce me to believe that the said article emanates from one of the participants in the trial of the unfortunate Captain Wirz. They tremble for fear that retribution will soon follow, and are, consequently, trying to exculpate themselves by false statements. But there is no escaping for them !

Last spring a report of the Wirz trial was published by order of Congress. Though somewhat mutilated and curtailed, it will yet serve to expose the above falsehood of the " Chronicle." On page 615 of that report I find the following :

" The Judge Advocate (Colonel Chipman)—There is another point which I desire to submit to the court. During the progress of this trial, I have sought to exercise, as properly as I knew how, the discretion placed in my hands by the court, upon the subject of subpœnaing witnesses. Some witnesses, who may properly be termed rebel functionaries, have been subpœnaed by me inadvertently. I have signed such subpenas, made out by my clerk, with great haste, and without noticing the fact. Others were subpenaed by me deliberately, but upon further consideration, *I deemed it my duty to revoke the subpena.* This remark applies to a certain class of witnesses, which the court will understand: it embraces men, who have been leaders in the rebellion, such as General Lee, Mr. Seddon, Mr. Mallory, Surgeon-General Moore, *Commissioner Ould,* and others." * * * *

It will be observed, that the Judge Advocate, having in the eyes of his superiors committed the great blunder of permitting the defense to have such witnesses subpenaed, whose testimony could not be otherwise but damaging to the blood-thirsty plans of Stanton, Holt, and their tool, Grant, tries to excuse himself, by stating that he had corrected his error, and revoked the subpenas. On page 617 he again says :

* * "Certain political questions involved in subpenaing such persons as General Lee would suggest themselves to any mind. After it came to my knowledge, that those witnesses were to be brought here for purposes other than those indicated by counsel, I acted on what I thought a wise discretion, and revoked the subpenas to General Lee and others. In every case where I revoked subpenas, or declined to issue them, the evidence implicates the party as an accessory either before or after the fact, a principal in the first or second degree, or co-conspirator."

In page 618 he expressed the following kind feeling towards Colonel Ould :

* * "Colonel Ould is connected with those atrocities, or he will be connected with them before the conclusion of the trial, and the court cannot allow him to testify for his associate. Colonel Ould was in position where the facts regarding the prison at Andersonville must have come to his knowledge."

Colonel Ould had, therefore, a narrow escape from becoming an inmate of the Old Capitol, and sharing the fate of poor Wirz. Had the real Andersonville murderers only imagined that some years later he would expose to the world their terrible and cruel crimes toward their own soldiers, I doubt very much whether Colonel Ould would ever have been permitted to return to Richmond, for " dead men tell no tales."

It is almost superfluous, after citing the above extracts from the official record, to state in addition that the sub-peneas of General Lee, Colonel Ould, and other Southern witnesses, were stopped or revoked without the consent and even the knowledge of the counsel of Captain Wirz. As the whole trial was nothing but a most wretched farce, those gentlemen, even if they had succeeded in appearing as witnesses before the commission, would not have been permitted to say anything in favor of the prisoner and the cause of justice and humanity. Perhaps they may have shared the fate of one of the witnesses for the defence, (Duncan,) who was arrested in open court before he had time to testify. At any rate, they would have been sub-ject to the over-bearing insolence of the President of the commission, General Lew Wallace, whilst at the other end of the table the Judge Advocate, by sneering ques-tions and insulting insinuations, would have taxed to the utmost the forbearance of the rebels, as he politely used to denominate the Southern witnesses. In fact, after it had become apparent that the defense would not be allowed to produce any evidence in favor of the prisoner, particu-larly after the above mentioned subpenas had been coun-termanded or revoked without our knowledge, no further attempt was made on our part to bring these gentlemen before the commission. Captain Wirz told me several times that even to save his life he would not place his cherished, brave and noble chieftain, General Lee, in the position of being exposed to the insults of such a man as Lew Wallace.

The recent revelations by Colonel Ould must, indeed, be a terrible blow to the participants in the murder of Captain Wirz; for murder it was, and has so been decided by the highest tribunal of the country. Wirz, as he pro-mised before his death, is already haunting them by day and night. No Loyal Leagues and Grand Armies of the Republic can protect them against that terrible spectre.

The remains of the man who spurned life at the cost of becoming a traitor or suborned witness against his former compatriots lie still side by side with those of poor Mrs. Surratt, buried in one of the warehouses of the arsenal in this city, and still denied the right of christian burial. Nobody any longer doubts that they have been murdered. The Supreme Court has declared those commissions by which they were convicted to be unconstitutional. Yet their orphan children are not even permitted to weep at their graves ! . How savage this nation has become!

Can it be true that the star-spangled banner still waves " over the land of the free and the home of the brave."

   Respectfully,

      LOUIS SCHADE.

Formation of the Southern Confederacy and State Governments,

With dates of their admission to, and withdrawal from, the Confederation of the United States.

FORMATION OF THE SOUTHERN CONFEDERACY.

THE independence of the Southern Confederate States, commenced by the withdrawal of the State of South Carolina from the old Federal Union of the United States. The ordinance of secession was passed on December 20th, 1860, by a unanimous vote. The withdrawal of South Carolina from the old Union was followed successively by the States of Florida, Mississippi, Alabama, Georgia, and Louisiana. A convention of delegates from the six seceding States assembled in Congress at Montgomery, Alabama, to organize a Provisional Government, on the 4th day of February, 1861. The Hon. R. M. Barnwell, of South Carolina, was appointed temporary chairman.

A. R. Lamar, esq., of Georgia, was then appointed temporary secretary, and the deputies from the several States represented, presented their credentials in alphabetical order, and signed their names to the roll of the convention.

The following is the list:

Alabama.—R. W. Walker, R. H. Smith, J. L. M. Curry, W. P. Chilton, S. F. Hale Colon, J. McRae, John Gill Shorter, David P. Lewis, Thomas Fearn.

Georgia.—Robert Toombs, Howell Cobb, F. S. Bartow, M. J. Crawford, E. A. Nisbet, B. H. Hill, A. R. Wright, Thomas R. R. Cobb, A. H. Kenan, A. H. Stephens.

Mississippi.—W. P. Harris, Walter Brooke, N. S. Wilson, A. M. Clayton, W. S. Barry, J. T. Harrison.

South Carolina.—R. B. Rhett, R. W. Barnwell, L. M. Keitt, James Chesnut, Jr., C. G. Memminger, W. Porcher Miles, Thomas J. Withers, W. W. Boyce.

Florida.—James B. Owens, J. Patten Anderson, Jackson Morton, (not present.)

Louisiana.—John Perkins, Jr., A. Declonet, Charles M. Conrad, D. F. Kenner, G. E. Sparrow, Henry Marshall.

The constitution of the Confederate States, was adopted on Friday, February 8, 1861. On Saturday the 9th, Congress proceeded to the election of a President and Vice-President. Jefferson Davis, of Mississippi, and Alexander H. Stephens, of Georgia, were unanimously elected. On the 18th of the same month, President Davis was inaugurated.

The Presidential term of one year of the Provisional Government, under the constitution, began on the 18th day of February, 1861, and will expire on the 22d day of February, 1862. The first election, under the Confederate constitution, for President and Vice-President for the first regular Presidential term of six years, was held on the 6th day of November, 1861, in each State throughout the Confederacy.

GOVERNMENT OF THE CONFEDERATE STATES.

JEFFERSON DAVIS, of Mississippi, President.

ALEXANDER H. STEPHENS, of Georgia, Vice-President.

Colonel JOSEPH DAVIS, of Mississippi, Aid to the President.

Captain R. JOSSELYN, of Mississippi, Private Secretary of the President.

R. M. T. HUNTER, Virginia, Secretary of State; William M. Browne, Assistant Secretary of State; P. P. Dandridge, Chief Clerk.

C. G. MEMMINGER, South Carolina, Secretary of the Treasury; P. Clayton, Georgia, Assistant Secretary of

21

the Treasury; H. D. Capers, Chief Clerk of the Department; Lewis Cruger, South Carolina, Comptroller and Solicitor; Bolling Baker, Georgia, First Auditor; W. H. S. Taylor, Louisiana, Second Auditor; Robert Tyler, Virginia, Register; E. C. Elmore, Alabama, Treasurer.

J. P. BENJAMIN, Louisiana, Secretary of War; A. T. Bledsoe, Virginia, Chief Clerk of the Department; S. Cooper, Virginia, Adjutant and Inspector General of the Confederate States Army; Lieutenant-Colonel B. Chilton and Captain J. Withers, South Carolina, Assistants Adjutant and Inspector General; Colonel R. Taylor, Kentucky, Quartermaster General; Colonel A. C. Myers, South Carolina, Assistant Quartermaster General; Lieutenant-Colonel Northrop, South Carolina, Commissary General; Colonel J. Gorgas, Virginia, Chief of Ordnance; Colonel S. P. Moore, (M. D.,) South Carolina, Surgeon General; Captain C. H. Smith, (M. D.,) Virginia, Assistant Surgeon General; Captain Leg. G. Capers, (M. D.,) South Carolina, Chief Clerk of the Medical Department; Major D. Hubbard, Alabama, Commissioner of Indian Affairs.

S. R. MALLORY, Florida, Secretary of the Navy; Commodore E. M. Tidball, Virginia, Chief Clerk of the Department; Commodore D. N. Ingraham, South Carolina, Chief of Ordnance, Construction, and Repair; Captain George Minor, Virginia, Inspector of Ordnance; Commodore L. Rosseau, Louisiana, Chief of Equipment, Recruiting Orders, and Detail; Captain W. A. Spotswood, (M. D.,) Virginia, Chief of Medicine and Surgery; Captain John Debree, Chief of Clothing and Provisions.

Ex-Governor BRAGG, North Carolina, Attorney General; Wade Keys, Alabama, Assistant Attorney General; R. R. Rhodes, Mississippi, Commissioner of Patents; G. E. W. Nelson, Georgia, Superintendent of Public Printing; R. M. Smith, Virginia, Public Printer.

JOHN H. REAGAN, Texas, Postmaster General; H. S. Offut, Virginia, Chief Contract Bureau; B. N. Clements, Tennesse, Chief Appointment Bureau; J. L. Harrel, Alabama, Chief Finance Bureau; W. D. Miller, Texas, Chief Clerk of Department.

South Carolina—Settled by colonies of French, German and Irish, in 1670; adopted the Federal Constitution in 1780; passed the ordinance of secession, December 20th, 1860. Area of square miles, 29,385.

Florida—Settled by Spain, 1516; ceded to Great Britain, 1763; retaken by the Spaniards, 1781; ceded by them to the United States in 1819; admitted into the Union, 1845; passed the ordinance of secession, January 8th, 1861. Area, 59,268.

Mississippi—Settled by the French at Natchez, 1716; this State, together with parts of Georgia, Alabama and Florida, formed the Mississippi Territory in 1816; was admitted into the Union, 1817; passed ordinance of secession January 9th, 1861. Area, 47,156 square miles.

Alabama—Admitted into the Union, 1820; passed ordinance, January 11th, 1861. Area, 50,722 square miles.

Georgia was settled by General Oglethorpe in 1733; made a royal colony in 1752; adopted the Federal Constitution in 1798; passed ordinance of secession, January 19th, 1861. Area, 58,000 square miles.

Louisiana—Settled by the French in 1699; ceded to Spain in 1762; purchased by the Federal Union in 1803; admitted as a State in 1812; passed ordinance of secession January 26th, 1861. Area, 41,866 square miles.

Texas—Settled by the Spaniards, 1690; made part of the Mexican Republic, 1826; war with Mexico for independence commenced in 1833, ended in 1836, making her an independent State; admitted to the Union, 1845; passed ordinance of secession, February 1st, 1861. Area, 237,504 square miles.

Virginia—Settled by the English in 1607; adopted the Constitution, 1776; passed ordinance of secession, April 18th, 1861. Area, 61,352 square miles.

Tennessee—Settled, 1757; territory ceded to the United States, 1790; admitted as a State, 1796; passed ordinance of secession, May 2d, 1861. Area, 45,600 square miles.

Arkansas was part of the Louisiana purchase, made into a separate territory, 1819; admitted as a State, 1836;

passed ordinance of secession, May 6th, 1861.   Area,
52,198 square miles.

North Carolina.—Settled by emigrants from Virginia
in 1660; was divided into two territories, 1720, (North
and South Carolina;) adopted the Constitution, 1790;
passed ordinance of secession may 21st, 1861.   Area.
50,704 square miles.

Missouri—Settled by the French in 1764; territorial
government formed in 1804; admitted to the Union,
1821; passed ordinance of secession, October 28, 1861.
Area, 64,000 square miles.

The entire white population of the Confederate State
in 1860, was 6,867,239.   Colored, 3,644,676.   Total,
10,510,915.

STATE GOVERNMENTS OF THE CONFEDERATE STATES.

States.	Capitals.	Governors.	Term Expires.	Salary	Legislature Meets.	General Election.
Alabama.	Montgomery.	J. H. Shorter.	December, 1863.	$4000	2d Monday Nov.	1st Monday Aug.
Arkansas.	Little Rock.	Henry M. Rector.	November, 1861.	2500	1st Monday Nov.	1st Thursday Sept.
Georgia.	Milledgeville.	Joseph E. Brown.	November, 1863.	4000	1st Monday Nov.	1st Monday Oct.
Louisiana.	Baton Rouge.	Thos. O. Moore.	January, 1864.	4000	3d Monday Jan.	1st Monday Nov.
Mississippi.	Jackson.	John J. Pettus.	November, 1863.	4000	1st Monday Nov.	1st Monday Oct.
North Carolina.	Raleigh.	Henry T. Clark.	January, 1862.	3000	3d Monday Nov.	1st Thursday Aug.
South Carolina.	Columbia.	F. W. Pickens.	December, 1863.	3800	4th Monday Nov.	2d Monday Oct.
Tennessee.	Nashville.	Isham G. Harris.	October, 1863.	3000	1st Monday Oct.	1st Thursday Aug.
Texas.	Austin.	F. R. Lubbock.	December, 1864.	3000	1st Monday Nov.	1st Monday Aug.
Virginia.	Richmond.	John Letcher.	January, 1864.	5000	1st Monday Dec.	4th Thursday May.
Florida.	Tallahassee.	John Milton.	October, 1865.	2500	4th Monday Nov.	1st Monday Oct.
Missouri.	Jefferson City.	Claib. F. Jackson.	December, 1864.	3000	1st December.	1st Monday Aug.

ORGANIZATION OF THE CONFEDERATE STATES ARMY, NOVEMBER, 1861.

THE army of the Potomac is under the supreme command of General J. E. Johnston. It embraces three grand divisions : the largest and most important, at Manassas, being commanded by General P. T. G. Beauregard, and those at Aquia Creek and Shenandoah Valley, by Brigadiers-General T. H. Holmes, of North Carolina, and Thomas J. Jackson, of Stone Wall Bridge, respectively. General Beauregard's command is subdivided into four divisions, commanded respectively by General Gustavus W. Smith, Major-General Edmund Kirby Smith, Earl Van Dorn, and James Longstreet. Under these officers are the numerous brigades composing the army, each composed as nearly as possible of regiments belonging to the same State, and commanded by their own Brigadiers General. The Department of the Northwest remains under command of General Lee ; that of the Yorktown Peninsula, under Major-General Magruder ; that of Norfolk, under Major-General Huger ; that of Eastern Virginia, South of the James river, under Brigadier-General Pemberton ; and that of Richmond, under Brigadier-General Winder. The coast defences of North Carolina are under command of Brigadier-General Gatlin, assisted by Brigadiers-General J. R. Anderson and D. H. Hill. Those of South Carolina are in charge of Brigadier-General Ripley : those of Georgia, of Brigadier-General Lawton ; those of Alabama, of Brigadier-General Withers ; those of Louisiana, of Major-General Lovell ; and those of Texas, of Brigadier-General Hebert. Until his death, Brigadier-General Grayson commanded in East Florida. The supreme command in Kentucky, is vested in General A. S. Johnston ; and in Tennessee, in Major-General Polk.

ARMY WAGES.

The following is a statemen of the monthly pay of officers and privates in the service of the Confederate States :

RANK.	Infantry.	Cavalry.	Artillery.
Colonels..........................	$180 00	$210 00	$210 00
Lieutenant-Colonels	180 00	185 00	185 00
Majors	150 00	162 00	152 00
Captains.........................	130 00	140 00	130 00
First Lieutenants................	90 00	100 00	90 00
Second Lieutenants.............	80 00	90 00	80 00
Orderly Sergeants...............	20 00	20 00	20 00
Other Sergeants................	17 00	17 00	17 00
Corporals and Artificess.......	13 00	13 00	13 00
Musicians.......................	12 00	12 00	12 00
Privates...........	11 00	11 00	11 00

The monthly pay of Generals of divisions, or brigades, is $301. Privates and non-commissioned officers receive one ration a day, and a yearly allowance for clothing : commissioned officers are not allowed to draw rations.

INHUMAN TREATMENT

OF

CONFEDERATE PRISONERS.

———

Mr. Bicking, a prominent citizen of Bristol, Pa-, known to hundreds of citizens of Pennsylvania as a gentleman of integrity and reliability, says: "I was standing at the depot at Bethlehem, Pa., on the arrival of a train of cars, with four hundred rebel prisoners aboard, en route for one of our military prisons. They had eaten nothing since leaving Pittsburg, (forty-eight hours,) and were well nigh starved. The better class of citizens, irrespective of party, of Bethlehem, gave them food, which they ravenously devoured. The treatment of these prisoners was a disgrace to the country, as there was no excuse for the outrage, which it most certainly was, of starving human beings in a country filled with provisions."

This is but one of the thousand instances, that can be proven from individual and official sources, proving the outrageous manner in which prisoners were treated, while at the same time, a volume of evidence can be furnished that the Confederate authorities were kind and humane in their management of prisoners. I merely give one instance of thousands that could be cited, to prove this statement. By referring to chapter 8, page 107, of the history of the One Hundred and Fourth Pennsylvania Regiment, at that time commanded by Colonel W. W. H. Davis, the following paragraph appears: "That night the enemy occupied my head-quarter cabin, which was filled with their own, and our wounded. Among the oc-

cupants was General Roger A. Pryor, who treated our
wounded with great kindness, a box of nice wines and
brandy was found in the cabin, some of which, he gave
to each wounded soldier.   All the concurrent testimony
proves that the enemy were kind to our wounded, that
fell into their hands."   And ever were, in spite of the
brutalities to which their families were subjected, by the
many marauding bands of the enemy.   One instance
cited, of ten thousand such, is related by Colonel Davis,
chapter 16, page 210, of the same work: "On the first
of June, 1863, Colonel Montgomery, with his negro
regiment, made a raid up the Cumbahee river, to get
recruits.   He brought back eight hundred darkies, who appeared to be much better fitted to hoe cotton, than to
carry a musket.   There may be a difference between
stealing negroes from their homes, on the Congo, in
Africa, and stealing them from the Cumbahee, in South
Carolina, but, many people, are not able to see the difference.   Colonel Montgomery in this raid burned thirty-
four private dwellings, without a shadow of excuse, the
families, mostly women and children, were summari-
ly turned out of doors, and their homes destroyed before
their eyes.   Colonel Montgomery told the negroes ' that
the country would belong to them after the war, and as
they would have no use for the large houses, they might
burn them.'   The operation was a disgrace to our arms.
How often they were disgraced during the war by men
higher in rank than Colonel Montgomery, and *the acts
applauded, instead of being censured, and the guilty
officer dismissed the service.*"   No one will question the
statement of General W. W. H. Davis, that distinguished
soldier of Pennsylvania, whose honesty, integrity, and
military record, is a part of the history of the country,
and yet, Confederates treated their prisoners well, in spite
of the desolating fiends, who were murdering, robbing
and burning throughout the South.

J. P. Benjamin's and Robt. Ould's Letters.

UNANSWERABLE ARGUMENTS.

THE RESPONSIBILITY OF ANDERSONVILLE RESTS WITH THE ABOLITIONISTS.

————o————

J. P. BENJAMIN'S LETTER.

His Views of the Treatment of Federal Prisoners.

To THE TDITOR OF THE TIMES:

SIR: I find on arriving in England, that public attention is directed afresh to the accusation made by the Federal authorities that prisoners of war were cruelly treated by the Confederates—not merely in exceptional cases by subordinate officials—but systematically, and in conformity with a policy deliberately adopted by President Davis, General Lee and Mr. Seddon. As a member of the Cabinet of President Davis from the date of his first inauguration under the Provisional Constitution to the final overthrow of the Confederate Government by force of arms, as a personal friend, whose relations with Jefferson Davis have been of the most intimate and confidential nature, I feel it imperatively to be my duty to request your insertion of this letter in vindication of honorable men, who, less fortunate than myself, are now held in close confinement by their enemies, and are unable to utter an indignant word in self-defense.

A very material fact in relation to this charge of cruelty was omitted in the recent letter from your late "Richmond correspondent," who was probably not aware of it, but which I can attest from personal knowledge. During the difficulties which prevented the exchange of prisoners of war, cases arose which appealed so strongly to humanity that it was impossible for the most obdurate to remain insensible. The Federal authorities, therefore, empowered Colonel Mulford, their Commissioner of Exchange, to consent to mutual delivery of such sick and disabled prisoners as were incapable of of performing military service. To this class was the exchange of prisoners rigorously restricted. Colonel Ould, the Confederate Commissioner of Exchange, (who has recently been honorably acquitted, by the Federals themselves, of the same false charge of cruelty to prisoners,) made to the President, to the Secretary of War, and to myself, repeated complaints that prisoners on both sides were frequently delivered in a condition so prostrate, as to render death certain, from exposure during the transit between James river and Washington, or Annapolis. Efforts were made, in vain, to check this evil. In spite of surgeon's certificates, that they were too ill for removal without imminent danger; sick men on both sides, wearied by long confinement, fearful that the exchange would be again interrupted, longing for the sight of home and friends, would either insist on their ability to endure the journey, or, professing that recovery was hopeless, would piteously implore to be allowed to see their families before death. The lifeless bodies of numbers of Confederates, shipped from the North under these circumstances, were delivered to us at City Point, and the like result attended the delivery from our side. Rigid care was taken by the authorities of the United States to exclude from the exchange, all cases of slight illness, in accordance with their avowed policy of preventing our armies from being recruited by returned prisoners, this being our only resource for filling our thinned ranks, while they were able to procure unlimited recruits from this side of the Atlantic. From the class just mentioned the most emaciated specimens were chosen by our enemies, and exhibited as conclusive evidence that we exercised habitual cruelty towards prisoners of war. The most wretched and desperate cases were even made the originals for "photographs which cannot lie," and the revolting pictures of human infirmity, thus procured, were affixed as embellishments to sensational reports, manipulated by Congressional committees and sanitary commissions.

It is not my purpose to examine in detail the question whether on us or on the Federals rests the responsibility of interrupting the exchange of prisoners, and thus producing a mass of human misery and anguish of which few examples can be found in history. The published correspondence of the Commissioners of Exchange and certain revelations made by Federal officials in public speeches and in newspaper articles, will be sufficient to satisfy on this point the few who take the pains to ascertain the truth; but in response to the allegations imputed, in the latest news from America, to General Hitchcock, that "for the delays in exchanging and the consequent sufferings of the prisoners, the fault rested entirely with the Confederates," I would recall the following facts :

The first effort to establish a cartel of exchange was made by the Confederates, when I was temporarily in charge of the war office at Richmond, toward the close of the Provisional Government. General Howell Cobb, on our part, and General Wool, on the part of the United States, agreed on a cartel, which was submitted to their respective governments for approval. In my instructions to General Cobb, he was specially directed to propose that, after exhausting exchanges, the party having surplus prisoners in possession, should allow them to go home on parole, till the other belligerent should succeed in capturing an equivalent number for exchange. When this proposal was made by us, we held a large number of prisoners more than were in the hands of the enemy. It was accepted by General Wool as one of the terms of the cartel, but, unfortunately, some successes of our enemies intervened before ratification by their government. They obtained, in their turn, an excess of prisoners, and at once refused to ratify the cartel. In the ensuing year, while General Randolph was Secretary of War, the Confederates were a second time in possession of an excess of prisoners, and succeeded in negotiating a cartel, under which they liberated many thousands of prisoners on parole, without any present equivalent, thus securing in advance the liberation of a like number of their own soldiers that might afterward fall into the enemy's hands. This cartel remained many months in operation. No check or difficulty occurred, as long as we made a majority of captures.

In July, 1863, the fortune of war became very adverse to the Confederacy. The battle of Gettysburg checked the advance of General Lee on the Federal capital, while almost simultaneously the fall of Vicksburg and Port Hudson gave to our enemies a large preponderance in the number of prisoners. The authorities at Washington immediately issued general orders, refusing to receive from General Lee the prisoners held by him, until they should be reduced to possession in Virginia, thus subjecting their own men to the terrible sufferings glanced at by Colonel Fremantle, in order to embarrass General Lee's movements. They further refused to restore to us the excess of prisoners held by them, after having received, for nearly or quite a year, the benefit of the special provision of the cartel, when it operated in their favor ; and during the entire war, they never once consented to a delivery to us of any prisoners, in excess of the number for which we were prepared to return an immediate equivalent.

It requires no sagacity to perceive, that every motive of interest, as well as of humanity, operated to induce us to facilitate the exchange of prisoners, and to submit even to unjust and unequal terms, in order to recover soldiers, whom we could replace from no other source. On the other hand, interest and humanity were at war in their influence on the Federal officials. Others must judge of the humanity and justice of the policy, which consigned hundreds of thousands of wretched men to captivity, apparently hopeless, but I can testify unhesitatingly to its sagacity and efficiency, and to the pitiless sternness with which it was executed. Indeed, this refusal of exchange was one of the most fatal blows dealt us during the war, and contributed to our overthrow more, perhaps, than any other single measure. I write not to make complaint of it, but simply to protest against the attempt of the Federals to divide the consequences of their own conduct, as to throw on us the odium attached to a cruelty plainly injurious to us, obviously beneficial to themselves.

The sense of duty which prompts this letter, would be but imperfectly satisfied were I to withold at this juncture the testimony which none so well as myself can offer in relation to the charge of inhumanity made against Jefferson Davis. For the four years, during which I have been one of his most trusted advisers, the recipient of his confidence, the sharer, to the best of my abilities, in his labors and responsibilities, I have learned to know him better, perhaps, than he is known by any other living man. Neither in private conversation, nor in cabinet council, have I ever heard him utter one unworthy thought, one ungenerous sentiment. On repeated occasions, when the savage atrocities of such men as Butler, Turchin, McNeill and others, were the subject of anxious consideration, and when it was urged upon Jefferson Davis, not only by friends in private letters, but by members of his Cabinet in council, that it was his duty to the people, and to the army, to endeavor to repress such outrages by retaliation, he was immovable in his resistence to such counsels, insisting that it was repugnant to every sentiment of justice and humanity, that the innocent should be made victims for the crimes of such monsters. Without betraying the confidence of official intercourse, it may be permitted me to say, that when the notorious expedition of Dahlgren, against the city of Richmond had been defeated, and the leader killed in his flight, the papers found upon his body showed that he had been engaged in an attempt to assassinate the President and the heads of the Cabinet, to release the Federal prisoners confined in Richmond, to set fire to the city, and to loose his men and the released prisoners, with full license to gratify their passions on the helpless inhabitants.

The instructions to his men had been elaborately prepared, and his designs communicated to them in an address; the incendiary materials for firing the town formed part of his equipment. The proof was clear and undeniable. In the action, in which Dahlgren fell, some of his men were taken prisoners. They were brought to Richmond, and public opinion was unanimous, that they were not entitled to be considered as prisoners of war; that they ought to be put to trial as brigands and assassins, and executed as such if found guilty. In cabinet council the conviction was expressed, that these men had acquired no immunity from punishment for their crimes, if guilty, by the fact of their having been admitted to surrender by their captors, before knowledge of their offenses. A discussion ensued, which became so heated as almost to create unfriendly feeling, by reason of the unshaken firmness of Mr. Davis, in maintaining that although these men merited a refusal to grant them quarter in the heat of battle, they had been received to mercy by their captors as prisoners of war, and such were sacred; and that we should be dishonored if harm should overtake them after their surrender, the acceptance of which constituted, in his judgment, a pledge that they should receive the treatment of prisoners of war. To Jefferson Davis alone, and to his constancy of purpose, did these men owe their safety, in spite of hostile public opinion, and in opposition to two-thirds of the cabinet.

I forbear from further trespass on your space, although I am in possession of numerous other facts, bearing on the subject, that could not fail to interest all who are desirous of seeing justice done to the illustrious man, of whose present condition I will not trust myself to speak.

I remain, sir, your obedient servant,

J. P. BENJAMIN.

ANDERSONVILLE.

ROBERT OULD'S LETTERS.

" On the 16th of August, 1864, I addressed the following communication to Brigadier-General John E. Mulford, (then major,) Assistant Agent of Exchange:

"'RICHMOND, August 10, 1864.

"'MAJOR JOHN E. MULFORD, ASSISTANT AGENT OF EX- CHANGE:

"'SIR: You have several times proposed to me to ex- change the prisoners, respectively held by the two bel- ligerents—officer for officer, and man for man. The same offer has also been made by other officials having charge of matters connected with the exchange of pris- oners.

"'This proposal has heretofore been declined by the Confederate authorities, they insisting upon the terms of the cartel, which required the delivery of the excess on either side on parole. In view, however, of the very large number of prisoners now held by each party, and the suffering consequent upon their continued confine- ment, I now consent to the above proposal, and agree to deliver to you the prisoners held in captivity by the Con- federate authorities, provided you agree to deliver an equal number of Confederate officers and men. As equal numbers are delivered from time to time, they will be declared exchanged. This proposal is made with the understanding that the officers and men, on both sides, who have been longest in captivity will be first delivered where it is practicable.

"'I shall be happy to hear from you as speedy as pos- sible, whether this arrangement can be carried out.

"'Respectfully, your obedient servant,

"'RO. OULD,

"'AGENT OF EXCHANGE."

"The delivery of this letter was accompanied with a

statement of the mortality which was hurrying so many Federal prisoners, at Andersonville, to the grave.

"On the 22d day of August, 1864, not having heard anything in response, I addressed a communication to Major-General E. A. Hitchcock, United States Commissioner of Exchange, covering a copy of the foregoing letter to General Mulford, and requesting an acceptance of my propositions.

"No answer was ever received to either of these letters. General Mulford, on the 31st of August, 1864, informed me in writing, that he had no communication on the subject from the United States authorities, and that he was not, at that time, authorized to make an answer.

"This offer, which would have instantly restored to freedom thousands of suffering captives, which would have released every Federal soldier in confinement in Confederate prisons, was not even noticed. As the Federal authorities, at that time, had a large excess of prisoners, the effect of the proposal which I had made, if carried out, would have been to release all Union prisoners, while a large number of the Confederates would have remained in prison, awaiting the chances of the capture of their equivalents.

This is startling enough, but what will the christian world think of what follows? On the 24th of January, 1864, Mr. Ould wrote to General Hitchcock, the Federal Agent of Exchange:

"In view of the present difficulties attending the exchange and release of prisoners, I propose that all such on each side shall be attended by a proper number of their own surgeons, who, under rules to be established, shall be permitted to take charge of their health and comfort.

"I also propose that these surgeons shall act as commissaries, with power to receive and distribute such contributions of money, food, clothing and medicines, as may be forwarded, for the relief of prisoners. I further propose that these surgeons be selected by their own governments, and that they shall have full liberty at any

22

and all times, through the agents of exchange, to make reports, not only of their own acts, but of any matters relating to the welfare of prisoners."

The writer adds:

" To this communication no reply of any kind was ever made. I need not state how much suffering would have been prevented, if this offer had been met in the spirit in which it was dictated. In addition, the world have had truthful accounts of the treatment of prisoners on both sides, by officers of character, and thus much of that misrepresentation which has flooded the country, would never have been poured forth. It will be borne in mind that nearly all of the suffering endured by Federal prisoners, happened after January, 1864. The acceptance of the proposition made by me, on behalf of the Confederate government, would not only have furnished to the sick, medicines and physicians, but to the well an abundance of food and clothing, from the ample stores of the United States.

The statements go on increasing in interest. Witness the next:

" When it was ascertained that exchanges could not be made either on the basis of the cartel, or officer for officer and man for man, I was instructed by the Confederate authorities to offer to the United States government their sick and wounded, without requiring any equivalents. Accordingly, in the summer of 1864, I did offer to deliver from ten to fifteen thousand of the sick and wounded, at the mouth of the Savannah river, without requiring any equivalents, assuring at the same time the agent of the United States, General Mulford, that if the number for which he might send transports could not readily be made up from sick and wounded, I would supply the difference with well men. Although this offer was made in the summer of 1864, transportation was not sent to the Savannah river until about the middle or last of November, and then I delivered as many prisoners as could be transported—some thirteen thousand in number, amongst whom were more than five thousand well men.

More than once I urged the mortality at Andersonville

as a reason for haste on the part of the United States authorities. I know, personally, that it was the purpose of the Confederate government to send off from all its prisons, all the sick and wounded, and to continue to do the same, from time to time, without requiring any equivalents for them. It was because the sick and wounded, at points distant from Georgia, could not be brought to Savannah within a reasonable time, that the five thousand well men were substituted."

Again, Mr. Ould says, and appeals to General Mulford and other Federal officers, to support what he says:

"In the summer of 1864, in consequence of certain information communicated to me, by the Surgeon General of the Confederate States, as to the deficiency of medicines, I offered to make purchases of medicines from the United States authorities, to be used exclusively for the relief of Federal prisoners. I offered to pay gold, cotton or tobacco for them, and even two or three prices if required. At the same time I gave assurances that the medicines would be used exclusively in the treatment of Federal prisoners, and moreover agreed, on behalf of the Confederate States, if it was insisted on, that such medicines might be brought into the Confederate lines by the United States surgeons, and dispensed by them. To this offer I never received any reply. Incredible as this appears, it is strictly true.

"General John E. Mulford is personally cognizant of the truth of most, if not all the facts which I have narrated. He was connected with the cartel from its date until the close of the war. During a portion of the time he was Assistant Agent of Exchange on the part of the United States. I always found him to be an honorable and truthful gentleman. While he discharged his duties with great fidelity to his own government, he was kind, and I might almost say, tender to confederate prisoners. With that portion of the correspondence with which his name is connected, he is familiar. He is equally so with the delivery made at Savannah, and its attending circumstances, and with the offer I made as to the purchase of

medicines for the Federal sick and wounded.   I appeal
to him for the truth of what I have written."

We now come to a matter which not only has a touch-
ing but a local interest.   On the shelves of all the public
and many of the private libraries of Philadelphia, will be
found a volume got up during the fiercest excitement of
the war, and under the auspices, strange to say, of the
Sanitary Commission, whose business one would think
was to heal, not to stimulate, asperities, descriptive of
the cruelties inflicted on our prisoners.   It was issued
under the immediate approval of the Honorable J. Clark
Hare—now Radical candidate for the District Court—
Doctor Ellerslie Wallace, and other eminent lawyers, and
was adorned with a frightful photograph of emaciated
and dying Northern prisoners landed at Annapolis.
Judge Ould gives the secret history of this infamous
imposture:

"On two occasions, at least, we were asked to send
forward the very sick and most desperately wounded of
the prisoners in our hands.   Accordingly, the hospitals
were searched for the worst cases, and after they were
delivered they were taken to Annapolis, and there photo-
graphed as specimen prisoners."

· ROSTER

OF

PRISONERS,

CONFINED AT JOHNSON'S ISLAND, AND EXCHANGED SEP-
TEMBER, 1862.

PRISONERS CONFINED AT JOHNSON'S ISLAND.

Name.	Rank.	Regiment.	Co.	Where Captured.	When Capt'd.
Acre, J. G.	2d Lieut.	50th Tennessee.	D	Fort Donaldson.	Feb. 16, '62
Adams, W. H.	Chaplain.	42d Tennessee.		"	"
Adams, A. G.	2d Lieut.	7th Texas.	D	"	"
Adcock, P.	Captain.	1st Tennessee Batt.	C	"	"
Adams, W. S.	2d Lieut.	55th Tennessee.	E.	"	"
Aikin, J. H.	Captain.	9th Bat. Tenn. Cavalry.	C	"	"
Alexandria, D. G.	2d Lieut.	3d Tennessee.	D	"	"
Alexander, I. T.	1st Lieut.	4th Mississippi.	C	"	"
Allen, J. A.	Captain.	45th Tennessee.	B	Island 10.	April 8, '62
Allen, J. A.	2d Lieut.	2d Kentucky.	G	Fort Donaldson.	Feb. 16, '62
Allen, J W.	Private.	15th Mississippi.	A	Fishing Creek.	Jan. 19, '62
Allen, S. F.	1st Lieut.	50th Tennessee.	I	Fort Donaldson.	Feb. 16, '62
Allen, T. W.	2d Lieut.	15th Mississippi.	E	Fishing Creek.	Jan. 19, '62
Allen, W. C.	2d Lieut.	50th Tennessee.	A	Fort Donaldson.	Feb. 16, '62
Allison, James	Sergeant.	8th Kentucky.		"	"
Anderson, C. B.	2d Lieut.	49th Tennessee.	G	"	"
Anderson, G. H.	1st Lieut.	14th Mississippi.	I	"	"
Anderson, H. M.	Private.	Mouserrat Bat.		Nashville, Tenn.	April 17, '62
Anderson, Isaac	3d Lieut.	49th Tennessee.	I	Fort Donaldson.	"
Anderson, J.	2d Lieut.	53d Tennessee.	E		
Anderson, J. N.	2d Lieut.	33d North Carolina.		Newbern, N. C.	March 14, '62

Name	Rank	Regiment	Co.	Place	Date
Anderson, W. C.	2d Lieut.	32d Tennessee.	D	Fort Donaldson.	Feb. 16, '62
*Andrews, Robert	1st Lieut.	27th Alabama.		"	"
Andrews, William H.	2d Lieut.	1st Alabama.	E	Island 10.	April 8, '62
Anthony, Jake	Adjutant.	41st Tennessee.	G	Fort Donaldson.	Feb. 16, '62
Anthony, W. P.	1st Lieut.	30th Tennessee.		"	"
Anvil, D. M.	Colonel.	139th Virginia.	C	Beverly, Va.	April 10, '62
Arnett, R. F.	1st Lieut.	5th Kentucky.		Shiloh, Tennessee.	April 7, '62
Ash, J. R.	Lieut.	Morgan's Cavalry.	D	Lebanon, Tennessee.	May 6, '62
Ashby, W. F.	2d Lieut.	14th Mississippi.	A	Fort Donaldson.	Feb. 16, '62
*Atkins, T. M.	Captain.	49th Tennessee.	A	"	"
Austin, J. B.	1st Lieut.	49th Tennessee.	D	"	"
Averritt, S. W.	Lieut.	Confederate States Navy.		Island 10.	April 8, '62
*Avery, O. N.	Colonel.	33d North Carolina.		Newbern, N. C.	March 14, '62
*Avery, W. T.	Lt. Col.	1st Alabama, Tenn. and Miss.		Island 10.	April 8, '62
Aynett, H. H.	Captain.	53d Tennessee.		Fort Donaldson.	
Aymett, W. H.	3d Lieut.	"	K	"	"
Alexander, W. E	Captain.	3d Tennessee.		"	"
Ake, T	Captain.	Missouri.		Randolph County.	May 13, '62
*Baker, Alpheus	Colonel.	1st Alabama, Tenn and Miss.		Island 10.	April 8, '62
Bailey, L. L.	2d Lieut	Forrest Cavalry.	D	Fort Donaldson.	
Baker, G.	2d Lieut.	1st Bat. Tennessee Infantry.	B	"	"
Baker, J. M.	1st Lieut.	41st Tennessee.		"	"
Baker, L. B.	2d Lieut.	40th "	A	Island 10.	April 8, '62
Ballard, G. M.	3d Lieut.	55th "	-	"	"
Ballinger, E.	1st Lieut.	7th Texas.	K	Fort Donaldson.	
Bandy, W. T.	Captain.	18th Tennessee.		"	"

PRISONERS CONFINED AT JOHNSON'S ISLAND.—Continued.

Name.	Rank.	Regiment.	Co.	Where Captured.	When Capt'd.
*Banks, T. C.	2d Lieut.	32d Tennessee.	H	Fort Donaldson.	
Barber, F. C.	Captain.	3d "	K	"	
Barker, Peter	1st Lieut.	27th Alabama.	A	"	
Barbiere, Joe	Captain.	1st Alabama, Tenn. and Miss.	A	Island 10.	April 16, '62
Barksdale, H.		30th Tennessee.	G	Fort Donaldson.	
Barns, John	Private.	Cavalry.	F.	Clark county, Ky.	Oct. 24, '61
Barnett, W. H.	2d Lieut.	49th Tennessee.	K	Fort Donaldson.	
*Barnett, T. J.	1st Lieut.	3d Kentucky	K	Shiloh, Tennessee.	April 6, '62
Barringer, W. E.	"	41st Tennessee.	B	Fort Donaldson.	
Barthel, J. P.	Citizen.			"	
Barthel, F. N.	2d Lieut.	31st Virginia.	K	Lebanon, Virginia.	April 23, '62
Barton, I. C.	"	26th Mississippi.	B	Fort Donaldson.	
Bass, J. M.	1st Lieut.	32d Tennessee.	B	"	
*Bates, L.		42d "		"	
Battel, Joel A.	Colonel.	20th "		Shiloh.	April 7, '62
Beall, T. J.	Serg. Maj.	7th Texas	E	Fort Donaldson.	
Beal, D. T.	1st Lieut.	26th Mississippi.		"	
Bean, C. H.	Captain.	41st Tennessee.	E	"	
Bearden, W. S.	2d Lieut.	"	F	"	
Beasemen, W. T.	1st Lieut.	2d Kentucky.	A	"	
*Beaumont, Thomas	Captain	50th Tennessee.			

Name	Rank	Regiment	Co.	Where Captured	Date
Becker, O.	Surgeon.			Nashville.	Feb. 22, '62
Beckham, T. J.	Citizen.			Dover.	
*Bedford, H. L.	1st Lieut.	Artillery.		Fort Donaldson.	
Bell, O.	2d Lieut.	32d Tennessee.	F	"	
Bell, Thomas	2d Lieut.	30th "	H	"	
Bell, W. E.	2d Lieut.	2d Kentucky.	I	"	
Benoil, James W.	Captain.	14th Mississippi.	K	Island 10.	April 8, '62
*Benson, N. J.	Captain.	1st Alabama, Tenn. and Miss.	L		"
Benson, Joseph P.	2d Lieut.	1st Alabama.	B		"
Benson, N. J.	1st Lieut.	30th Tennessee.	A	Fort Donaldson.	"
Berrie, A. G.	"	10th "	H		
Bibb, Porter	Captain.	40th "	E	Island 10.	
Bifle, A. B.	1st Lieut.	9th Bat Tenessee Cavalry.	C	Fort Donaldson.	
Bibb, P. W.	Captain.	Tennessee Artillery.	H	Island 10.	
Bingham, Jabez	"	8th Kentucky.	B	Fort Donaldson.	
Black, A. D.	3d Lieut.	11th Arkansas.	H	Island 10.	
Blain, G. A.	Private.	7th Texas.	G	Fort Donaldson.	
Blair, F.	1st Lieut.	1st Georgia.		Fort Pulaski	April 11, '62
Blair, W. J.	Private.	29th Tennessee.	G	Fishing Creek.	Jan. 19, '62
Blair, R. L.	2d Lieut.	19th "		Shiloh	April 7, '62
Blake, C. H.	1st Lieut.	Kentucky Cavalry	G	Hickman, Ky.	March 23, '62
Bledsoe, I. D.	"	55th Tennessee.	C	Island 10.	
Blevin, Calvin	Private.	26th "	K	Fort Donaldson.	
Blon, J. H.	2d Lient.	25th Georgia.		Fort Pulaski.	April 11, '62
Boggers, A. F.	Captain.	26th Tennessee.	A	Fort Donaldson.	
Bohannon, N.	1st Lieut.	28th North Carolina.	I	Hanover C. H. Va.	May 27, '62

PRISONERS CONFINED AT JOHNSON'S ISLAND.—Continued.

Name.	Rank.	Regiment.	Co.	Where Captured.	When Capt'd.
*Bolen, J. N.	Captain.	Cavalry.		Fort Donaldson.	Feb. 16, '62
Bond, L. S.	1st Lieut.	Tennessee Cavalry.	A	Clarkesville, Tenn.	"
Bonds, J. B.	Private	26th Mississippi.	C	Fort Donaldson.	Feb. 18, '62
Bonner, I. G.	2d Lieut.	8th Kentucky.		Island 10.	
Book, L. F.	1st Lieut.	Tennessee Artillery.	E	Fort Donaldson.	
Boone, A. S.	Captain.	41st Tennessee.	K	"	
Boone, Ben	2d Lieut.	"			
Bost, J. L.	1st Lieut.	37th North Carolina.	E	Hanover C. H. Va.	May 27, '62
*Betts, Leonidas	"	1st Alabama, Tenn. and Miss.	B	Island 10	
Bottles, J. L.	Captain.	26th Tennessee	F	Fort Donaldson.	
*Bowdry, W. S.	2d Lieut.	3d Mississippi.	B	"	
Bowers, S. C.	"	18th Tennessee.	A	"	
Bowlings, T. B.	3d Lieut.	26th "	B	"	
Boyd, Thomas	2d Lieut.	1st Mississippi.	C	"	
Braddock, W. A.	"	2d Kentucky	1	"	
Bradley, A. T.	3d Lieut.	30th Tennessee.	G	"	
Bradley, G. T.	Private.	7th Texas.	F	"	
*Bradshaw, L. N.	2d Lieut.	10th Tennessee.	G	"	
Bridges, E. L. C.	1st Lieut.	3d "			
Brindley, G. I.	2d Lieut.	40th "	*?	Island 10.	April 8, '62
Brooks, A. J.	1st Lieut.	50th "	C	Fort Donaldson,	

Name	Rank	Regiment	Co.	Where Captured	Date
Broom, I. W.	1st Lieut.	49th Tennessee.	E	Fort Donaldson.	
Broughton, E. T.	Captain.	7th Texas.	C	"	
Broughton, I. S.	1st Lieut.	32d Tennessee.	K	"	March 14, '62
Brown, C. H.	2d Lieut	Unattached.			
Brown, H. D.	Major.	Forrest Cavalry.	G	Newbern, N. C.	
Brown, I. S.	Captain.	46th Tennessee.		Fort Donaldson.	
Brown, John W.	1st Lieut	7th Texas.	C	Island 10.	
Brown, I. W.	Adjutant.	8th Kentucky.	B	Fort Donaldson,	
*Brown, O. T.	1st Lieut.	1st Alabama, Tenn. and Miss.			
Brown, T. B.	2d Lieut	26th Tennessee.	I	Island 10	
Brown, N. C.	Captain.	27th Alabama.	I	Fort Donaldson.	
*Brown, P. W.	2d Lieut	18th North-Carolina.	A	Hanover C. H., Va.	May 27, '62
*Bryan, J. W.	Captain.	10th Tennessee.	K	Fort Donaldson.	
Bryant, A.	1st Lieut	55th "	H	Island 10	
Bryant, A. D.	Captain.	53d "	E	Fort Donaldson.	
Bryant, D. F.	1st Lieut.	3d Alabama Bat.	A	"	
Bryant, J. H.	Captain.	1st Bat., Tennessee.	B		
Buchanan, P. M.	2d Lieut.	1st Arkansas.	H	Pea Ridge, Ark.	March 8, '62
Budwell, I. B.	Private.	Virginia Artillery.	F	Fort Donaldson.	
Buford, S.	2d Lieut.	15th Mississippi.	G	Fishing Creek.	Jan. 19, '62
Burch, R. M.	1st Lieut.	32d Tennessee.	E	Fort Donaldson.	
Burchard, L. E.	3d Lieut.	8th Kentucky.	A	"	
Burgess, W. H.	2d Lieut.	49th Tennessee.	I	"	
Burke, T. H.	3d Lieut.	14th Mississippi.	A	"	
Burke, M.	3d Lieut.	10th Tennessee.	C	"	
Furlon, I. F.	2d Lieut.	30th "			

PRISONERS CONFINED AT JOHNSON'S ISLAND.—Continued.

Name.	Rank.	Regiment.	Co	Where Captured.	When Capt'd.
Burton, M. T.	Captain.	26th Mississippi.	I	Fort Donaldson.	
Bush, E. I.	Private.	30th Tennessee.		"	
Batler, I. F.	2d Lieut.	26th "	F	"	
*Batler, W. R.	Captain.	18th "	C	"	
Bryne, Alex.	"	15th Arkansas.	F	"	
Barnhart, H. M.	"	1st Texas Legion.	A	Corinth	June 12, '62
Branden, W.	Ch. Eng.	Confedcrate States Navy.		Off Memphis.	June 6, '62
Brickers, W. M.	2d Lieut.	3d Tennessee.	B	Fort Donaldson.	
Benson, N. O.	As. Eng.	Confederate States Navy.		Off Memphis.	June 6, '62
Barton, W. C.	Colonel.	Missouri Regiment.		Howard County, Mo.	March 27, '62
Cain, Peter	Private.	40th Tennessee.	B	Island 10.	
Caldwell, J. P.	Captain.	1st Division, Missouri S. G.	D	Silver Creek.	June 8, '62
Callaway. I E.	2d Lieut.	46th Tennessee.	D	Island 10.	
Campbell, A. J.	Captain.	48th "		"	
*Campbell, I. P.	Q. M. S.	32d "	B	Fort Donaldson.	
Camp, Thomas B.	1st Lieut.	7th Texas.	A	"	
Cantey, Henry	Captain.	20th Mississippi.	I	"	
Cantrell, Elijah	1st Lieut.	48th Tennessee.		"	
Cantrell, C. B.	Adjutant.	1st Tennessee Bat., Infantry.		"	
Cavey, S. Q.	Captain.			Howard County, Va.	March 15, '62
Carriger, Christian	2d Lieut.	41st Tennessee.	A	Fort Donaldson.	

Name	Rank	Regiment	Co.	Place	Date
Carruth E. B.	Com'ry.	7th Mississippi.	C	Shiloh, Tennessee	April 6, '62
Carter, H.	2d Lieut.	10th Tennessee.		Fort Donaldson.	
Caruthers, J. S.	1st Lieut.	51st "		"	
Caruthers, T. I.	"	Tennessee Artillery.		Island 10.	
Caruthers, W.	3d Lieut	42d Tennessee.	A		
Center, A. J.	2d Lieut.	1st B. A., Jeff Thompson's Brig.		Cape Girardau, Mo.	March 13, '62
Church, T. H.	"	9th Bat. Tennessee Cavalry.		Fort Donaldson.	
Chaffin, B.	1st Lieut	41st Tennessee.	C	"	
Champlin, W. S.	2d Lieut	20th Mississippi.	E	"	
Chatfield, William M.	Captain.	"	I	"	
Cheatham, L. R.	2d Lieut.	48th Tennessee.	G	"	
Childers W. G.	Private.	Recruit.		Clark County, Ky.	Oct. 24, '61.
*Childress, J. W. Jr.,	1st Lieut.	Comb's Tennessee Bat.		Fort Donaldson.	
Christian, J. H.	2d Lieut.	1st Alabama, Tenn. and Miss.	C	Island 10.	
Clark, C. J.	Captain.	3d Tennessee.	A	Fort Donaldson.	
Clark, F.	3d Lieut	40th "	H	Island 10.	
Clark, J. B.	Private.	9th Louisiana.		Huntsville Ala.	April 11, '62
Clark, J. D.	Drill M.	32d Tennessee.		Fort Donaldson.	
Clark, J M.	Colonel.	46th "	C	Island 10.	
Clark, L R.	Captain.	55th "			
Clark, R. M.	2d Lieut.	1st Bat. Mississippi Cavalry.		Hickman, Ky.	March 23, '62
Clark, Zack	Private.	Recruit.	B	Clark County, Ky.	Oct. 24, '61
*Clarkson, W. P.	Captain.	6th Missouri.		Missouri.	Dec. 21, '61
Clift, I. T.	1st Lieut.	11th Arkansas.	D	Island 10.	
Clopton, P. H.	2d Lieut	56th Virginia.	K	Fort Donaldson.	
Colb, H. B.	1st Lieut.	15th Arkansas.	D	"	

PRISONERS CONFINED AT JOHNSON'S ISLAND.—Continued.

Names.	Rank.	Regiment.	Co.	Where Captured.	When Capt'd.
Cole, J M.	Captain.	5th Georgia.	E	Huntsville, Ala.	April 11, '62
Cole, T. W.	1st Lieut.	20th Mississippi.		Fort Donaldson.	
Coleman, W. A.	"	50th Virginia.		"	
Coleman, A.	2d Lieut.	1st Alabama, Tenn. and Miss.	G	Island 10.	
Collett, J. H.	1st Lieut	7th Texas.	G	Fort Donaldson.	
Collins, S. S.	2d Lieut.	2d Kentucky.	E	"	
Collins, W. F.	1st Lieut	53d Tennessee.	B	"	
Collins, W. R.	2d Lieut	32d Tennessee.	A	"	
Connelly, N. F.	"	16th Arkansas.	C	Pea Ridge, Ark.	March 9, '62
Conner, G. W.	Captain.	9th Kentucky.	H	Prestonburg, Ky	Jan. 13, '62
Conner, J. A.	2d Lieut.	26th Mississippi.	B	Fort Donaldson.	
Cook, A. J.	Private.	"	D	Clarksville, Tenn.	Feb. 18, '62
Cook, I. C.	2d Lieut	50th Tennessee.	H	Fort Donaldson.	
Cook, T. B.	"	Tennessee Artillery.		Island 10	
Cooper, Charles	Private.	11th Tennessee.		Bowling, Ky.	Jan., 1862
Cooper, R. T.	Captain.	3d Tennessee.	D	Fort Donaldson.	
Cooper, S. C.	"	46th Tennessee.	H	Island 10.	
Cooper, W. M.	Private.	41st Tennessee.		Fort Donaldson.	
Coppage, W. D.	1st Lieut.	18th Tennessee.	K	"	
Cording, J. B.	Captain.	49th Tennessee.	D	"	
Corkran, J.	Private.	26th Missouri.	B	"	

Name	Rank	Regiment	Co.	Where captured	Date
Corn, J. B.	3d Lieut.	27th Alabama.	F	Fort Donaldson.	
Couch, John	Adjutant.	8th Kentucky.	A	"	
Couch, Quincy	1st Lieut.	15th Arkansas.	A	"	
Couch, William	3d Lieut.	"	K	"	
Covington, H. L.	1st Lieut.	30th Tennessee.	B	"	
Coven, J. H.	2d Lieut.	7th Texas.		"	
Cowan, J. H.	Captain.	42d Tennessee.	G	"	
Cowan, R. H.	1st Lieut.	Forrest Cavalry.	H	"	
Cowden, W. M.	Private.	41st Tennessee.		Shiloh.	April 8, '62
Cowlay, E. H.	Captain.	1st Arkansas.		Fort Donaldson.	
Cowlay, S. A.	1st Lieut.	48th Tennessee.		"	
Cox, J. H.	2d Lieut.	14th Mississippi.		"	
Cox, R. S.	1st Lieut.	26th Mississippi.	C	Island 10.	
Craig, J. M.	3d Lieut.	7th Texas.	C	"	
Crank, R. H.	1st Liaut.	46th Tennessee.	H	Fort Donaldson.	
Crawford, A. A.	Captain.	11th Arkansas.	D	Island 10.	
Criner, W. C.	2d Lieut.	27th Alabama.	D	Fort Donaldson.	
Crockett, R. J.	2d Lieut.	1st Alabama.	F	Island 10.	
Cronch, J. H.	2d Lieut.	51st Tennessee.	C	Fort Donaldson.	
Cron, R. N.	2d Lieut	11th Arkansas.	A		
*Crowder, J. G.	2d Lieut.	1st Tennessee Bat.	I		
Croxton, B. M. }	As. Surg.	3d Alabama Bat.	A		
Crozier, J.	Private.	3d Kentucky.			
Crum, D.	3d Lieut.	1st Kentucky Cavalry.	G	Huntsville, Ala.	April 11, '62
Crump, W. J.	2d Lieut.	14th Mississippi.	E	McDowell's City, Va.	April 3, '62
Crumpton, W. F.	Captain.	"	H	Fort Donaldson.	

PRISONERS CONFINED AT JOHNSON'S ISLAND.—Continued.

Name.	Rank.	Regiment.	Co.	When Captured.	When Capt'd.
Culbertson, J.	1st Lieut.	Artillery Corps.		Fort Donaldson.	
Culbertson, J. C.	1st Lieut.	1st Mississippi.	D	"	
Culbertson, N. R.	2d Lieut.	Tennessee Artillery.		"	
Cummings, J. W.	Private.	1st Kentucky Cavalry.	A	Nicholas county, Ky.	Oct. 11, '61
Cunningham, A.	Captain.	11th Arkansas.	I	Island 10.	
Cunningham, T.	Private.	19th Tennessee.		Gallitin, Ten.	April 3, '62
Curlee, T. G.	1st Lieut.	18th Tennessee.	H	Fort Donaldson.	
Curtis T. M.	2d Lieut.	50th Tennessee.	K	"	
Campbell, J. F.	2d Lieut.	32d Virginia.		Lewisburg, Ky.	May 23, '62
Carson, J. L.	Captain	30th Tennessee.	C	Fort Donaldson.	
Carter, R.	A. Q. M.			Booneville, Miss.	June 3, '62
Covert, John	Com'ry.	129th Virginia.			May 9, '62
Court, R. D.	1st Lieut.	C. S. Navy.		Off Memphis.	June 6, '62
Clayton, A.	As. Eng.	C. S. Navy.		"	"
Copher, D. T.				Boone co., Mo.	Jan. 15, '62
Daly, John	1st Lieut.	13th Louisiana.	A	Shiloh, Tenn.	April 7, '62
Daly, R. T.	2d Lieut.	53d Tennessee.	A	Fort Donaldson.	
Daniel, M. V.	Captain.	Williams' Kentucky Regiment.		Demassville, Ky.	Sept. 20, '61
Daniel, W. H.	Lieut.	Morgan Cavalry.		Fort Donaldson,	"
Dansby, R. C.	2d Lieut.	10th Tennessee.	I	"	"
Dardue, B. G.	"	3d Tennessee.	F		

Name	Rank	Regiment	Co.	Where captured	When captured
*Darnall, B. F.	2d Lieut.	3d Mississippi.	F	Fort Donaldson.	
D'Aubigne, Don	1st Lieut.	Pt. Cupee Artillery.	A	Island 10.	
Dougherty, A.	Private.	5th Kentucky.	A	Whipporwill, Tenn.	Dec. 5, '61
Davidson, J. M.	1st Lieut.	8th Kentucky.	K	Fort Donaldson.	
Davis, J. H.	2d Lieut.	18th Tennessee.	C	"	
Davis, J. N.	"	1st Mississippi.	D	"	
Davis, W. F.	3d Lieut.	15th Arkansas.	A	Island 10.	
Dawson, J. S.	Adjutant.	46th Tennssee.	C	Fort Donaldson.	
Day, J. W.	2d Lieut.	3d Mississippi.	D	"	
*Darzey, N. L.	1st Lieut.	"			
Deavenport, T. D.	Captain.	32d Tennessee.		Shiloh.	April 7, '62
Declowet, A.	4th Sergt.	Orleans G Battery.		"	"
Declowet, P. L.	1st Lieut.	"			
Dedneau, G.	Captain.	2d Kentucky.	I	Fort Donaldson.	
Degarnette, J. P.	Private.	Recruit.		Clark county.	Oct. 24, '61
Demeut, J. J.	Surgeon.	27th Alabama.		Fort Donaldson.	
Dennis, J. J.	2d Lieut	8th Kentucky.	H	"	
*Dickson, D. R.	"	3d Mississippi.	B	"	
Diggons, G. A.	1st Lieut.	10th Tennessee.	E	"	
Dickson, J. E.	Surgeon.	9th Bat. Tennessee Cavalry.	G	McDowell's City.	April 3, '62
Dickson, J. O.	2d Lieut.	1st Kentucky Cavalry.	E	Fishing Creek.	Jan. 19, '62
Donc, J. L.[!	Private.	25th Tennessee.			
Dockery, I. M.	1st Lieut.	Murray Artillery.			
Dodson, P. L.	2d. lieut.	20th Mississippi.	D	Fort Donaldson.	
Donahou, L. B.	1st Lieut.	10th Mississippi.	D	"	
Donally, L. P.	1st Lieut.	7th Texas.	E	"	

PRISONERS CONFINED AT JOHNSON'S ISLAND.—Continued.

Name.	Rank.	Regiment.	Co.	Where Captured.	When Capt'd.
Dorsey, B. J.	2d Lieut.	10th Tennessee.	G	Fort Donaldson.	
Doss, H. W.	"	14th Mississippi.	G	"	
Douglass, A. H.	1st Lieut.	14th Tennessee.	F	"	
Douglass, C. L.	Adjutant.	14th Tennessee.		"	
Douglass, W. D.	"	7th Texas.	H	"	
Douglass, J. W.	1st Lieut.	3d Mississippi.	G	"	
Douglass, J. M.	2d Lieut.	18th Tennessee.		"	
Douglass, R. E.	Adjutant.	49th Tennessee.	B	"	
Doyle, J. A.	2d Lieut.	3d Tennessee.		"	
Drake, R. B.	1st Lieut.	Floyd's Brigade.	C	"	
Draughon, M. J.	3d Lieut.	49th Tennessee.	A	Mills Spring.	Jan. 19, '62
Drewitt, James	Private.	19th Tennessee.		Cross Lanes, Va.	Aug. 12, '62
Drayfuss, L.	"	Casky's Virginia Cavalry.		Fort Pulaski.	April 11, '62
Drummond,	Lieut.	1st Georgia.		Hawk Nest, Va.	Aug. 25, '61
Daff, J. H.	Private.	8th Virginia Cavalry.	I	Fort Donaldson.	Feb. 16, '62
Dugan, P. B.	Captain.	14th Mississippi.	D	"	
Dunahoo, H.	2d Lieut.	26th Mississippi.	K	"	
Dunaway, F. E.	"	41st Tennessee.			
Duncan, A. M.	"	1st Alabama, Tenn. and Miss.	K	Island 10.	April 8, '62
Duncan, G. C.	"	40th Tennessee.	D	"	
Duncan, W. S.	"	Missouri Regiment.		Fullow.	Dec. 25, '61

Name	Rank	Regiment	Co.	Where Captured	Date
Dunn, John	1st Lieut.	34th Tennessee.	E	Fort Donaldson.	Feb. 14, '62
Denning, W. L.	3d Lieut.	8th Kentucky.	B	"	
Durham, J. Q.	2d Lieut.	50th Tennessee.	C	"	
Dural, C. H.	"	31st Virginia.	1	Blooming Gap, Va.	
Dwyer, Mill	3d Lieut.	10th Tennessee.	C	Fort Donaldson.	
Delesdenier, L. F.	Purser.	C. S. Navy.	G	Off Memphis.	June 6, '62
Early, A. E.	Captain.	26th Mississippi.	A	Fort Donaldson.	
Easby, D. J.	2d Lieut.	42d Tennessee.	A	"	
Eastham, G. A.	1st Lieut.	1st Bt. Tennessee Infantry.	E	Island 10.	
Evans, A. J.	1st Lieut.	1st Alabama, Tenn. and Miss.	A	Fort Donaldson.	
Eddins, O. F.	2d Lieut.	1st Mississippi.		Island 10.	
Edmonston, J. W.	Com'ry.	40th Tennessee.		Fort Donaldson.	
Edwards, C. H.	As. Surg.	32d Tennessee.		Fort Donaldson.	
Eggers, J. S.	1st Lieut.	37th North Carolina.		Hanover C. H.	May 27, '62
Edwards, G. M.	2d Lieut.	Tennessee Heavy Artillery.	H	Island 10.	
Elam, Thomas A.	"	4th Mississippi.	I	Fishing Creek.	Jan. 19, '62
Eldridge, L. D.	1st Sergt.	35th Tennessee.	E	Shiloh, Tenn.	April 7, '62
Elliott, S. N.	Private.	15th Mississippi.	B	Fort Donaldson.	
Ellis, R. D.	2d Lieut.	51st Tennessee.		Fort Donaldson.	
*Ellis, Leslie	Captain	10th Tennessee.	D	Huntsville, Ala.	April 7, '62
Ellis, Stephen	2d Lieut.	31st Alabama.	C	Fort Donaldson.	
Ellison, W. F.	"	32d Tennessee.	E	"	
English, R. H.	1st Lieut.	7th Texas.		Fort Donaldson.	
Enoch, E. R.	"	4th Mississippi.		"	
Erwin, Robert	Captain.	1st Georgia.	K	Fort Pulaski.	April 11, '62
Erwin, R. N.	Serg. Maj	10th Tennessee.		Fort Donaldson.	

PRISONERS CONFINED AT JOHNSON'S ISLAND—Continued.

Name.	Rank.	Regiment.	Co.	Where Captured.	When Capt'd.
Erwin, W. B.	1st Lieut.	9th Bat. Tennessee Cavalry.	D	Fort Donaldson.	
Estis, B. H.	3d Lieut.	3d Mississippi.	D	"	
Evans, H. C.	1st Lieut.	26th Tennessee.	K	"	
Evans, J. W.	"	42d Tennessee.		"	
Evans, R. L.	Act. Adj	53d Tennessee.		"	
Evans, W. B.	1st Lieut.	49th Tennessee.	K	"	
Ewing, L. M.	2d Lieut.	32d Tennessee.		"	
Ezell, F. L.	As. Com.			"	
Faikes, B. R.	2d Lieut.	18th Tennessee.	K	Island 10.	
Farned, James	3d Lieut.	1st Alabama, Tenn. and Miss.	E	"	
*Farrabee, J. R.	Captain.	1st Alabama, Tenn. and Miss.	H	"	May 27, '62
Farthing, N. Y.	"	37th North Carolina.	C	Hanover C. H.	
Finey, J. R.	2d Lieut.	41st Tennessee.	H	Fort Donaldson.	
Felton, W. R.	3d Lieut.	1st Alabama.	A	Island 10.	
Furguson, A. H.	3d Lieut.	40th Tennessee.	E	"	
Field, J. A.	2d Lieut.	56th Virginia.	C	Fort Donaldson.	
Field, Logan,	"	8th Kentucky.	H	"	
Finnancan, J. P.	3d Lieut.	10th Tennessee.	E	"	
Finney, J. J.	Captain.	32d Tennessee.		"	
Fisher, A. D.	Sergeant.	G Battery.		"	
*Fisher, James A.	Captain.	Tennessee Artillery		Island 10.	

Name	Rank	Regiment	Co.	Place	Date
Fisk, D.	2d Lieut.	1st Tennessee Bat.	D	Fort Donaldson.	
Fitzgerald, P. G.	"	Maury Artillery.		"	
Flemings, R. J.	Private.	20th Tennessee.	D	Fishing Creek.	
Fletcher, D. R.	3d Lieut.	42d Tennessee.	H	Fort Donaldson.	
Fletcher, Thomas	1st Lieut.	13th Arkansas.	K	Shiloh.	
*Flint, J. B. B.	Captain.	5d Mississippi.	F	Fort Donaldson.	
Flournoy, N. A.	1st Lieut.	56th Virginia.	E	"	
Floyd, H.	Private.	25th Tennessee.		Break Grove, Tenn.	Jan. 20, '62
Floyd, Joshua	2d Lieut.	1st Alabama, Tenn. and Miss.	H	Island 10.	
Fogg, J. F.		32d Tennessee.	K	Fort Donaldson.	
Foley, John	Major.	1st Georgia.		Fort Pulaski.	April 11, '62
Fanrille, W. B.	1st Lieut.	41st Tennessee.	E	Fort Donaldson.	
Ford, A.	3d Lieut.	7th Texas.	D	"	
Forester, Stephen	"	42d Tennessee.	B	"	
Forrest, O. P.	1st Lieut.	7th Tennessee.	H	"	
Forrester, A. H.	"	26th Tennessee.	C	"	
Foster, J. W.	Captain.	Kentucky Cavalry.		Clark county.	Oct. 24, '61
Fosh, F. F.	3d Lieut.	42d Tennessee.	C	Fort Donaldson.	
Foster, W. H.	2d Lieut.	3d Alabama Bat.		"	
Freas, L. H.	1st Lieut.	18th Tennessee.	L	"	
Freeman, William	Private.	19th Tennessee.		Madison Co., Ala.	
Freeman, E. F.	1st Lieut.	1st Georgia.		Island 10.	
Freeman, H. C.	"	15th Mississippi.	B	Fort Pulaski.	April 30, '62
Freeman, P. H.	Private.		E	Fishing Creek.	April 11, '61
Frisbee, R. H.	Captain.	8th Kentucky.	C	Fort Donaldson.	Jan. 19, '62
Fyke, M. V.	"	49th Tennessee.		"	

PRISONERS CONFINED AT JOHNSON'S ISLAND.—Continued.

Name.	Rank.	Regiment.	Co.	Where Captured.	When Capt'd.
Gaba, J. R.	2d Lieut.	26th Tennessee.	B	Fort Donaldson.	
Gailland, R.	1st Lieut.	1st Alabama.	B	Island 10.	
Gallaher, D. L.	Captain.	26th Mississippi.	B	Fort Donaldson.	April 7, '62
Gallaher, D. P.	1st Lieut.	2d Texas.		Shiloh, Tenn.	
Gallaway, J. B.	2d Lieut.	9th Bat. Cavalry.	B	Fort Donaldson,	
Gallaway, M. G.	Captain.	1st Arkansas.	F	Pea Ridge, Ark.	March 8, '62
Gauble, H. A.	1st Lieut.	1st Tennessee Bat.	D	Fort Donaldson,	
Gardner, Uriah	2d Lieut.	51st Tennessee.	E	"	
Gorman, John H.	"	1st Mississippi.	L	"	
Garner, J. T.	Private.	15th Mississippi.	H	Fishing Creek.	Jan. 19, '62
*Garrett, G. W. B.	Captain.	3d Mississippi.	C	Fort Donaldson.	
Garrett, Young	Private.	15th Mississippi.	I	Mills Spring.	"
Gassaway, S. A.	Serg. Maj	3d Mississippi.		Fort Donaldson.	
Gee, Joseph J.	Captain.	4th Mississippi.	H	"	
Gennette, J.	"	15th Tennessee.	B	Shiloh, Tenn.	April 7, '62
Gentry, J. F.	2d Lieut.	Forrest Cavalry.	G	Fort Donaldson.	
George, J. H.	Captain.	41st Tennessee.	D	"	
George, James Z.	"	20th Mississippi.	C	"	
George, S. J.	"	48th Tennessee.	L	"	
George, W. P. A.	1st Lieut.	32d Tennessee.	E	"	
*Gibson, A. C.	"	Isaqina Artillery.		"	

Name	Rank	Regiment	Co.	Place	Date
*Gibson, A. J.	Captain.	3d Mississippi.	A	Fort Donaldson.	
Gibson, Elijah	2d Lieut.	11th Arkansas.	H	Island 10.	
Gibson, Thomas	1st Lieut.	10th Tennessee.	C	Fort Donaldson.	
Giddings, James	2d Lieut.	3d Tennessee.		"	
Giles, J. R.	"	15th Arkansas.		"	
Gilmore, W. D.	1st Lieut.	Jackson Bat.			
Gilmore, J. N.	2d Lieut.	18th Tennessee.	F	Huntsville, Ala.	April 11, '62
Glass, J. D.	Private.	9th Louisiana.		At Home, Virginia.	April 29, '62
Good, Alexander	Lieut.	60th Virginia.		Fort Donaldson.	
Goodwin, A. S.	Captain.	48th Tennessee.	H	"	
Gold, J. C.	1st Lieut.	49th Tennessee.	H	"	
Gooch, Nat	2d Lieut.	18th Tennessee.	C	"	
Goodlett, D. Z.	1st Lieut	1st Alabama.	D	Island 10.	
Goodlow, J. H.	"	8th Kentucky.	H	{Fort Donaldson.	
Gordon, E. H. F.	Captain.	3d Tennessee.	B	"	
*Gordon, G. W.	"	48th Tennessee.	C	"	
Gordon, John	Com'ry.	41st Tennessee.	H	"	
Gordon, J. C.	Captain.	26th Tennessee.	H	"	
Gordon, N. S.	1st Lieut.	50th Tennessee.	G	"	
*Gould, A. W.	Captain.	50th Tennessee.		"	
Gould, P. F.	Surgeon.	"			
Grace, J. M.	Captain.	1st Alabama, Tenn. and Miss.	K	Island 10.	
Gracy, W. L.	Q. M.	1st Tennessee Bat.		Fort Donaldson.	
Graham, H. W.	2d Lieut.	26th Tennessee.	F	"	
Graham, Sam.	Captain.	50th Tennessee.	D	"	
Graham, T. B.	"	20th Mississippi.	F	"	

PRISONERS CONFINED AT JOHNSON'S ISLAND.—Continued.

Name.	Rank.	Regiment.	Co	Where Captured.	When Capt'd.
*Grant, J. F.	Surgeon.	32d Tennessee.		Fort Donaldson.	Feb. 14, '62
Gray, R. L.	2d Lieut.	31st Virginia.	C	Blooming Gap.	
Gray, H. L.	Captain.	20th Louisiana.		Fort Donaldson.	
Graves, Rice E.	"	Light Artillery.		"	
Green, B.	3d Lieut.	41st Tennessee.		"	
Green, E.	Sergeant.	"		"	
Green, Rufus	Private.	26th Tennessee.	K	"	
Green, T.	Q. M. S.	"	B	"	
Green, W. H.	2d Lieut.	2d Kentucky Cavalry.			
Gregory, H. A.	1st Lieut.	11th Arkansas.	F	Island 10.	Jan. 20, '62
Gregory, W. H. M.	Private.	16th Alabama.		Beech Grove.	
Griffin, H.	Surgeon.	50th Virginia.		Fort Danaldson.	
Griffin, J.	Captain.	1st Alabama, Tenn. and Miss.	B	Island 10.	
Griffin, T. D.	2d Lieut.	41st Tennessee.	D	Fort Donaldson.	
Grigsby, T. K.	Captain.	49th Tennessee.	B	"	
Grimes, G. L.	2d Lieut.	9th Bat. Tennessee Cavalry.		"	
Grimes, H. M.	"	49th Tennessee.	B	"	
Grison, J. D.	1st Lieut.	1st Tennessee Bat.	C	"	
*Griswold, D. B.	"	Sapper and Miner.		New Madrid, Mo.	May 1, '62
*Guervaut, J.	2d Lieut.	Floyd's Brigade.		Fort Donaldson.	
Gilmartin, L. J.	Captain.	1st Georgia.		Fort Pulaski.	April 11, '62

Name	Rank	Regiment	Co.	Where captured	Date
Gupton, A. J.	As. Surg.	42d Tennessee.		Fort Donaldson.	Feb. 7, '62
Gutherie, Ed. S.	Private.	8th Virginia Cavalry.		JumpingBranch.	
Gutherie, G. W.	3d Lieut.	30th Tennessee.	E	Fort Donaldson.	
Gutherie, J. J.	A. Mas.	C. S. Navy.		Island 10.	
*Guy, J. H.	Captain.	Floyd's Va. Artillery Grays.		Fort Donaldson.	
Gwin, W. H.	2d Lieut.	3d Mississippi.	D	"	April 25, '62
Hogan, R. H.	Private.	1st Kentucky Cavalry.		War Trail, Tenn.	
Hailey, S. D.	2d Lieut.	51st Tennessee.	D	Fort Donaldson.	
Hailey, W. B.	"	18th Tennessee.	D	"	
Haisled, E. G.	"	50th Virginia.	E	"	
Hakill, F. M.	Private.	40th Tennessee.	B	Island 10.	
Hale, J. C.	3d Lieut.	18th Tennessee.	F	Fort Donaldson.	
Hale, W. B.	Captain.	4th Mississippi.	A	"	
Hall, B. F.	2d Lieut.	55th Tennessee.	B	Island 10.	
Hall, D. S.	"	1st Alabama.	K	"	
Hall, John G.	Captain.	51st Tennessee.	L	Fort Donaldson.	
Hall, Z. M.	2d Lieut.	1st Alabama, Tenn. and Miss.	E	Island 10.	
Hallam, W. M.	"	4th Mississippi.	A	Fort Donaldson.	
Hallam, S. C.	1st Lieut.	"	A	"	
Hamilton, J. G.	2d Lieut.	"	G	"	
Hamlet, S. F.	3d Lieut.	"	D	"	
Hamm, Thomas D.	2d Lieut.	51st Tennessee.	H	"	
Hammock, A. G.	Captain.	40th Tennessee.	K	Island 10.	
Hammond, E. W.	2d Lieut.	3d Tennessee.	E	Fort Donaldson.	
Haoby, J. W.	Private.	16th Tennessee.		Nashville.	
Hancock, J. C.	1st Lieut.	3d Mississippi.	F	Fort Donaldson.	

PRISONERS CONFINED AT JOHNSON'S ISLAND.—Continued.

Names.	Rank.	Regiment.	Co.	Where Captured.	When Capt'd.
Handy, John II.	Captain.	10th Tennessee.	I	Fort Donaldson.	
Hanna, D. C.	Lieut.	53d Tennessee.		"	
Hannah, D. H.	1st Lieut.	3d Tennessee.	D	"	
Hannah, J. M.	Captain.	46th Tennessee.	H	Island 10.	
Hanson, Isaac S.	Citizen.			Fort Donaldson.	
*Harbin, M. P.	1st Lieut.	3d Mississippi.	B	"	
Harbison, S. B.	2d Lieut.	10th Tennessee.	I	"	
Hardu, William	1st Lieut.	3d Tennessee.	H	"	
*Harlow, E. W.	2d Lieut.	10th Tennessee.	G	"	
Harris, G. L.	Q. M.	55th Tennessee.		Island 10.	
Harris, L.	1st Lieut.	26th Mississippi.	B	Fort Donaldson.	
Harris, L. D.	"	14th Mississippi.	K	"	
Harris, L. D. R.	"	10th Arkansas.	H	Island 10.	
Harris, W. B.	2d Lieut.	18th Tennessee.	I	Fort Donaldson.	
*Harris, N. H.	Captain.	Adams' Cavalry.		Lebanon, Tenn.	May 6, '62
Harris, W. T.	Private.	7th Texas.	G	Fort Donaldson.	
*Harrison, H. V.	2d Lieut.	49th Tennessee.	C	"	
Harrison, T. H. Jr.,	"	20th Mississippi.	H	"	
Hart, G. W.	1st Lieut.	46th Tennessee.	B	Island 10.	
Harvey, G. W.	2d Lieut.	40th Tennessee.	C	Fort Donaldson.	
Hatcher, B. M.	Q. M.	9th Bat. Tennessee Cavalry.			

Name	Rank	Command	Co.	Where Captured	Date
Hansen, R. A.	Lieut.	33d North Carolina.		Newburn, N. C.	
Howkins, J. M.	2d Lieut.	53d Tennessee.		Fort Donaldson.	April 11, '62
Hawze, G. W.	Captain.	14th Virginia.	C	At Home, Virginia.	
Hawes, S. B.	2d Lieut.	2d Kentucky.	G	Fort Donaldson.	
Hay, G. W.	"	56th Virginia.	K	"	
Hay, P. T.	1st Lieut.	26th Mississippi.	F	"	
Haydon, John A.	Captain.	Engineers.		Fort Henry.	Feb. 6, '62
Haus, N. S.	3d Lieut.	1st Tennessee Bat.	A	Fort Donaldson.	
Hayman, S. R.	1st Lieut.	Tennessee Artillery.		Island 10.	
Haynes, H. H.	Sergeant.	20th Tennessee.	D	Fishing Creek.	Jan. 19, '62
Haynes, W. D.	1st Lieut.	46th "	I	Island 10.	
Head, J. D.	2d Lieut.	Forrest Cavalry.	F	Fort Donaldson.	
Headly, F. M.	Captain.	8th Kentucky.		"	
*Hedden, W. H.	1st Lieut.	Green's Bat.		"	
Hemphill J. R.	2d Lieut.	20th Mississippi.	K	Island 10.	
Henderson, C. C.		40th Tennessee.		"	
Henderson, Joseph	2d Lieut.	1st Alabama.	B	Fort Donaldson,	
Henderson, J. D.	2d Lieut.	7th Texas.	C	"	March 21, '62
Henderson, S. H.	Private.	1st Kentucky Cavalry.		Pike county, Ky.	
Henderson, W. F.	"	15th Mississippi.	G	Fishing Creek.	Jan. 19, '62
Hendrick, J.	2d Lieut.	49th Tennessee.	L	Fort Donaldson.	
Hendrickson, T. W.	Private.	9th Louisiana.		Huntsville, Ala.	April 11, '62
Hendrix, B.	2d Lieut.	26th Tennessee.	B	Fort Donaldson.	
Hendrix, R. B.	3d Lieut.	46th "	H	Island 10.	
Hester, J. F.	Private.	8th Virginia Cavalry.		Hawks Nest, Va.	Aug. 25, '61
Hickey, A. C.	1st Lieut.	26th Tennessee.	K	Fort Donaldson.	

PRISONERS CONFINED AT JOHNSON'S ISLAND.—Continued.

Name.	Rank.	Regiment.	Co.	Where Captured.	When Capt'd.
Hickey, D. H.	Private.	Kentucky Cavalry.		Clark county, Ky.	Oct. 24, '61.
Hicks, J. S.	Private.	"			"
Higgins, H. H.	Major.	40th Tennessee.		Island 10.	
Higgins, Joel	1st Lieut.	2d Kentucky.	B	Fort Donaldson.	
High, Robert A.	Private.	7th Texas.	G	"	
*Hill, R. J.	Captain.	3d Mississippi.	B		
Hilles, W. G.	1st Lieut.	McRai, Arkansas.	E	Pea Ridge, Ark.	March 8, '62.
Hillsman, B. T.	2d Lieut.	55th Tennessee.	G	Island 10.	
*Hodge, J. R.	Captain.	51st "	B	Fort Donaldson.	July 24, '62
Hogane, J. T.	Captain.	Engineers.		New Madrid, Mo.	March 1, '62
Hogan, J.-R.	Private.	9th Louisiana,		Huntsville, Ala.	April 11, '62
Rogan, E.	Chaplain.	11th Arkansas.		Island 10.	
Holden, W. B.	Captain.	53d Tennessee.	B		
Holland, W.	2d Lieut.	51st Virginia.	C	Bloomey Gap, Va.	Feb. 14, '62
Holliday, J. M.	2d Lieut.	55th Tennessee.	C	Island 10.	
Holloman, J. W.	3d Lieut.	8th Kentucky.	L	Fort Donaldson.	
Hollowell, J. L.	Captain.	McRai, Arkansas.	D	Pea Ridge, Ark.	March 7, '62
Holmes, M.	Private.	9th Louisiana,		Huntsville, Ala.	April 11, '62
Homan, G. W.	Private.	Crescent, New Orleans.		Shiloh, Tennessee.	April 7, '62
Hopkins, E.	A. Q. M.	1st Georgia.		Fort Pulaski.	April 11, '62
Hopkins, M. H.	1st Lieut.	"			"

Name	Rank	Regiment	Co.	Where Captured	Date
Hombeak, E. A.	1st Lieut.	9th Bat. Tennessee Cavalry.	H	Fort Donaldson.	
Horne, T. M.	1st Lieut.	2d Kentucky.	K	"	
Hostetler, J. W.	2d Lieut.	3d Mississippi.		"	
Hostetler, J. B.	Com'ry.	Green's Bat.	I	Island 10.	
Honlihau, P.	Private.	1st Alabama.	G	Fort Donaldson.	
Howard, J. B.	1st Lieut.	49th Tennessee	E	"	
Howard, J. D.	Captain.	48th "	E	Island 10.	
Howard, J. H.	Captain.	55th "	E	Fort Donaldson.	
Howell, J. A.	1st Lieut.	26th "	G	"	
Howlett, S. S.	2d Lieut.	48th "	F		
Howze, W. D.	"	1st Mississippi.			
Hoyle, L. C.	"	1st Tennessee Cavalry.	C	Big Creek Gap.	March 14, '62
Hottle, H. H.	"	51st Virginia.	G	Bloomey Gap, Va.	Feb. 14, '62
Hubbard, J. C.	Captain.	40th Tennessee.	F	Island 10.	
Hubbard, J. R.	2d Lieut.	42d "	A	Fort Donaldson.	
Huddleston, P. H.	1st Lieut	18th "	A	"	
Hudson, John	"	40th "	H	Island 10.	
*Hughes, A. J.		Tennessee Artillery.		"	
Hughes, G. E.	Corporal.	20th Tennessee.	D	Fishing Creek.	Jan. 19, '62
Hughes, G. M.	Private.	5th Bat. Tennessee Cavalry.	A	"	
Hughes, G. W.	2d Lieut.	8th Kentucky.	E	Fort Donaldson.	
Hughes, O. D.	Captain.	1st Mississippi.	K	"	
Hughes, M. T.	2d Lieut.	10th Tennessee.		"	
Hughlett, James		30th "			
Hull, J. H.	Captain.	5th Georgia.	I	Huntsville, Ala.	April 11, '62
Hulme, T. N.	"	42d Tennessee.	H	Fort Donaldson.	

PRISONERS CONFINED AT JOHNSON'S ISLAND.—Continued.

Name.	Rank.	Regiment.	Co.	Where Captured.	When Capt'd.
Humes, W. Y. C.	Captain.	Tennessee Artillery.	C	Island 10.	April 11, '62
Hurling, H. B.	Private.	9th Louisiana.		Huntsville, Ala.	
Hurt, D.	3d Lieut.	55th Tennessee.	G	Island 10.	
Hurt, John	2d Lieut.	30th Tennessee.	D	Fort Donaldson.	
Hussey, C.	"	1st Georgia.		Fort Pulaski.	April 11, '62
Hyde, R. R.	1st Lieut.	18th Tennessee.	G	Fort Donaldson.	
Hutton R. P.	3d Lieut.	26th Mississippi.	D	" "	
Harper, A. G.		Tennessee Cavalry.		Boonville, Miss.	June 3, '62
Henry, J. H.	1st Lieut.	4th Mississippi.	B	Fort Donaldson.	
Hogan, J. E.	2d Lieut	Tennessee Cavalry.		Corinth.	May 29, '62
Holt, G. W.	Captain.	5th Tennessee.	K	"	May 28, '62
Hopkins, J. W.	3d Lieut.	40th "	E	Island 10.	
Hunter, E. L. H.		26th "	E	Fort Donaldson.	
Henthorne, T. E.	1st Lieut.	Confederate States Navy.		Off Memphis.	June 6, '62
Hayden, W. W.	Pilot.	" "		"	"
Henthon, N. J.	1st Lieut.	" "		"	"
Hurt, J. H.	Captain	" "		"	"
Hall, William	Marine.	" "		"	"
Inge, W. H.	Captain.	1st Missouri.	D	Narsaw, Missouri.	Feb. 16, '62
Ingraham, J.	"	Light Artillery.		Fort Donaldson.	
Inks, L. P.	1st Lieut.	McRai's, Arkansas.		Pea Ridge.	March 7, '62

Name	Rank	Regiment	Co.	Where Captured	Date
Innis, R. H.	2d Lieut.	2d Kentucky.	F	Fort Donaldson.	April 11, '62
Irvine,, J. A.	"	9th Bat. Tennessee Cavalry.	A	"	
Irwin, H. B.	Captain.	27th Alabama.	D	"	
Isbill, W. A.	3d Lieut.	27th "			
Jackson, J. V.	Private.	9th Louisiana.	C	Huntsville, Ala.	
Jackson, F. M.	Surgeon.	42d Tennessee.		Fort Donaldson.	
Jackson, E. P.	Captain.	50th Tennessee.		"	
Jackson, T. E.	"	Floyd's Artillery.	A	"	
James, N. W.	"	41st Tennessee.	K	"	
Jameson, T. E.	"	48th Tennessee.		Milford, Missouri.	Dec. 19, '61
Jameson, W. E.	"	1st Div. Mo. State Guards.	K	Fort Donaldson.	
Jamicon, H.	"	4th Tennessee.	B	Shiloh.	April 7, '62
Jenkins, D. C.	Lieut.	4th Louisiana.	C	Huntsville.	April 11, '62
Jenkins, W. W.	Private.	9th Louisiana.	K	Fort Donaldson.	
Jennings, W. S.	2d Lieut	3d Tennessee.	F	"	
Jennigan, S. B.	3d Lieut	30th "		"	
Jett, E. P.	Private.	41st "	A	"	
Jerrell, S. W.	Com'ry.	8th Kentucky.	E	"	
Johnson, A. D.	3d Lieut.	41st Tennessee.		"	
Johnson, A. O.	"	49th Tennessee.	H	Island 10.	
*Johnson, C. F.	A. D. C.	To General Buckner.	F	Fort Donaldson.	
Johnson, H. F.	2d Lieut.	49th Tennessee.	F	"	
Johnson, J. W.	Lt. Col.	46th Tennessee.	D	Carnafax Ferry, Va.	Oct. 15, '61
Johnson, O. R.	3d Lieut.	1st Alabama.			
Johnson, R. Y.	"	49th Tennessee.			
Johnston, E. P.	Private	50th Virginia.			

PRISONERS CONFINED AT JOHNSON'S ISLAND.—Continued.

Name.	Rank.	Regiment.	Co.	Where Captured.	When Capt'd.
Johnston, G. B.	Captain.	28th North Carolina.		Hanover C. H., Va.	May 27, '62
*Jones, G. R. G.	1st Lieut.			Fort Henry.	Feb. 6, '62
Jones, G. W.	Captain.	3d Tennessee.	F	Fort Donaldson.	
Jones, H. L.	"	4th Tennessee Division.		Fort Henry.	Feb. 6, '62
Jones, J. H.	"	42d Tennessee.		Fort Donaldson.	
Jones, J. L.	"	30th Tennessee.	K	"	
Jones, J. P.	Private.	Cavalry Recruit.		Clark county, Ky.	Oct. 24, '61
Jones, L. L.	2d Lieut	1st Mississippi.	D	Fort Donaldson.	
Jones, R. W.	1st Lieut.	15th Wississippi.		Shiloh, Tennessee.	April 7, '62
Jones, Sol.	Captain.	55th Tennessee.	D	Island 10.	
Jones, L. B.	2d Lieut.	55th "	A	"	
Jones, F. B.	3d Lieut.	8th Kentucky.	A	Fort Donaldson.	
Jones, W. A.	Lt. Col.	55th Tennessee.		Island 10.	
Jones, W. H.	2d Lieut.	3d "	K	Fort Donaldson.	
*Joplin, Josiah	Adjutant.	Mississippi Regiment.		Milford, Missouri.	Dec. 19, '61
Joice, E.	Captain.	2d Kentucky.		Fort Donaldson.	
*Jorgner, W. H.	"			"	
Johns, Jas. C.	1st Lieut.	18th Tennessee.	B	Leesburg, Va.	May 23, '62
Kavanagh, J. R	Major.	12th Virginia.	B	Huntsville, Ala.	April 11, '62
Kavanagh, P.	Private.	9th Louisiana.		Fishing Creek.	
Keith, E. M.	Captain.	15th Mississippi.	E	Fort Donaldson.	
		41st Tennessee.			

Rank	Regiment	Co.	Where captured	Date
1st Lieut.	1st Alabama, Tenn. and Miss.	D	Island 10.	
2d Lieut.	40th Tennessee.	C	"	
3d Lieut.	1st Arkansas.	D	Shiloh, Tennessee.	April 6, '62
Private.	22d Virginia.		Nicholas co., Va.	Oct. 15, '61
3d Lieut.	11th Arkansas.	F	Island 10.	
2d Lieut.	9th Bat. Tenn. Cavalry.	C	Fort Donaldson.	
Captain.	3d Mississippi.	E	"	
Private.	4th Louisiana.		Shiloh.	
"	33d Tennessee.	B	Fort Donaldson.	
2d Lieut.	20th Mississippi.	C	"	
"	13th Arkansas.	F	"	
"	48th Tennessee.	A	"	
"	10th Tennessee.			
"	40th Tennessee.	B	Island 10.	
1st Lieut.	13th Mississippi.	C	Mill Springs.	
2d Lieut.	1st Alabama.	H	Island 10.	
Major.	"		"	
Private.	7th Virginia Cavalry.	F	Springfield, Va.	Jan. 14, '62
"	9th Louisiana.		Huntsville, Ala	April 11, '62
2d Lieut.	1st Georgia.		Fort Pulaski	"
"	8th Kentucky.	I	Fort Donaldson.	
1st Sergt.	Tennessee Artillery.		Island 10.	
2d Lieut.	2d Kentucky.	H	Fort Donaldson.	
3d Lieut.	1st Alabama, Tenn. and Miss.	A	Island 10.	
2d Lieut.	1st Alabama, Tenn and Miss.	D	"	
Private.	51st Virginia.		Carnafax Ferry.	Oct. 11, '61

PRISONERS CONFINED AT JOHNSON'S ISLAND—Continued.

Name.	Rank.	Regiment.	Co.	Where Captured.	When Capt'd.
Lane, R. G.	3d Lieut.	Forrest Cavalry.	D	Fort Donaldson.	
Lanie, J. H.	1st Lieut.	40th Tennessee.	K	Island 10.	April 7, '61
Lastraps, L.	Private.	Crescent, La.		Shiloh.	
Law, L. J.	Captain.	40th Tennessee.		Island 10.	
Lawrence, R. J.	"	14th Mississippi.		Fort Donaldson.	
Learson, E. S.					
Ledbetter, G. C.	2d Lieut.	42d Tennessee.	H	Fort Donaldson.	
Lee, Phil.	Captain.	2d Kentucky,	C	"	
Leech, E. C.	"	3d Alabama Bat.	C	Fort Henry	Feb. 6, '62
Leftrich, L.	1st Lieut.	41st Tennessee.	A	Fort Donaldson.	
Legendre, E. C.	2d Lieut.	Pt. Cupee Artillery.	B	Island 10.	
*Levy, A. S.	Q. M.	1st Alabama, Tenn. and Miss.		"	
Lewis, David	2d Lieut.	3d Mississippi.	G	Fort Donaldson.	
Lewis, John	Private.	15th Tennessee.		Brownsville, Ky.	Feb. 26, '62
Lewis, J. A.	2d Lieut.	1st Tennessee Batt.	E	Fort Donaldson.	
Lewis, W. P.	1st Lieut.	53d Tennessee.		"	
Lewter, H.	2d Lieut.	26th Mississippi.	B	"	
Liddell, C. J.	1st Lieut.	4th Mississippi.	C	"	
Liddell, J. M.	"	20th "	C	"	
Lillard, J. D.	Citizen.				
Lillard, C. C.	1st Lieut.	2d Kentucky.	I	Fort Donaldson.	

Rank	Regiment	Co.	Where captured	Date
2d Lieut.	Floyd's Artillery.		Fort Donaldson.	
As. Surg.	49th Tennessee.		" "	
2d Lieut.	3d Tennessee.			Sept. 12, '61
1st Sergt.	Tennessee Artillery.	E	Island 10.	
2d Lieut.	7th Texas.	D	Fort Donaldson.	
1st Lieut.	Tennessee Artillery.		Island 10	
Lieut.	41st Tennessee.		Fort Donaldson.	
Private.	1st "	A	Cheat Mountain.	
3d Lieut.	30th "	F	Fort Donaldson.	
"	30th "	D	" "	
Captain.	1st Alabama.	G	Island 10.	Feb. 14, '62
3d Lieut.	" "	A	"	
2d Lieut.	11th Arkansas.	G	"	
Captain.	31st Tennessee.	E	Bloomery Gap.	
"	11th Arkansas.	G	Island 10.	
"	Forrest Cavalry.	G	Fort Donaldson.	
"	12th Tennessee.	C	" "	April 10, '62
1st Lieut.	10th "	C	Nashville, Tenn.	
"	3d "	D	Fort Donaldson.	
Com.Serg.	26th Mississippi.	C	"	
2d Lieut.	48th Tennessee.	I	"	
1st Lieut.	30th "	I	"	
Captain.	30th "			Feb. 14, '62
Captain.	31st Virginia.	A	Bloomery Gap	
Q. M. S.	42d Tennessee.	A	Fort Donaldson.	
2d Lieut.	42d			

PRISONERS CONFINED AT JOHNSON'S ISLAND.—Continued.

Name.	Rank.	Regiment.	Co.	Where Captured.	When Capt'd.
Lowe, G. H.	Captain.	18th Tennessee.	E	Fort Donaldson.	April 8, '62
Lowe, J. C.	1st Lieut.	8th Texas.	A	Shiloh.	May 27, '62
Lowe, S. D.	Major.	28th North Carolina.		Hanover C. H., Va.	Jan. 19, '62
Lowny, W. M.	Private.	16th Alabama.	G	Fishing Creek.	April 11, '62
Lysle, J. W.	"	9th Louisiana.		Huntsville, Ala.	
*Lytle, F. H.	1st Lieut.	18th Tennessee.	C	Fort Donaldson.	
Maddox, R.	2d Lieut.	46th Tennessee.	G	Island 10.	
Magby, Chas.	Private.	3d Arkansas.	F	Cheat Mountain.	Sept. 12, '61
Magee, J T.	2d Lieut.	4th Mississippi.	G	Fort Donaldson.	
Mahau, R. W.	3d Lieut.	8th Kentucky.	F	"	
Margs, J. W.	Private.	50th Tennessee.	.	Clarksville, Tenn.	March 20, '62
Maitland, J. J.	1st Lieut.	Floyd's Artillery.		Fort Donaldson.	
Malory, F. E.	3d Lieut.	50th Tennessee.	E	"	
Maney, D. D.	4th Sergt	32d Tennessee.	H	"	
Mann, R.	Private.	15th Mississippi.	E	Fishing Creek.	
Manny, L. F.	Captain.	11th Arkansas.	F	Island 10.	
*Martin, D. B.	1st Lieut.	14th Tennessee.	B	Fort Donaldson.	
Martin, D. S.	2d Lieut.	3d Tennessee.	A	"	
Martin, G. S.	1st Lient.	Tennessee Artillery.		Island 10.	
*Mortin, J. W.	2d Lieut.	1st Bat. Tennessee Infantry.	B	Fort Donaldson.	
Martin, L.	Private.	15th Mississippi.	I	Fishing Creek.	

Name	Rank	Regiment	Co.	Where captured.	Date.
Martin, M. T.	Captain.	1st Tennessee Bat.	A	Fort Donaldson.	
Martin, W. P.	3d Lieut.	11th Arkansas.	E	Island 10.	
Martiniere, E T.	2d Lieut.	14th Mississippi.	A	Fort Donaldson.	
Marsey, C. K.	Captain.	20th Mississippi.	D	"	
Mathews, J. B.	2d Lieut.	18th Tennessee.	G	"	
Mathews, J. P.	Captain.	11th Arkansas		Island 10.	
Mathews, S. W.	2d Lieut.	15th "	L	Fort Donaldson.	
Mathews, B. F.	Captain.	3d Tennessee.		"	
Mauldin, B. R.	Private.	41st "	A	"	
Mauldin, J. H.	2d Lieut.	3d Mississippi.	A	"	
Mayberry, H.	1st Lieut.	48th Tennessee.	H	"	
Mayes, R. E.	Captain.	30th "		"	March 14, '62
Maheu, T. W.	Captain.	33d North Carolina.	G	Newbern, N. C.	
Mays, Samuel.	2d Lieut.	50th Tennessee.		Fort Donaldson.	
McAlpin, W.	Lieut.	1st Texas.		Island 10.	
McArcher, A. G.	2d Lieut.	1st Georgia.		Fort Pulaski.	April 11, '62
McCadoo, H. M.	3d Sergt.	Tennessee Artillery.		Fort Donaldson.	
McCaleb, A.	2d Lieut.	9th Bat. Tennessee Cavalry.	B	Island 10.	
McCall, C. C.	1st Lieut.	1st Alabama, Tenn. and Miss.	F	Fort Donaldson.	
McCallum, R. D.	1st Lieut.	51st Tennessee.	H	"	
*McCaul, R.	2d Lieut.	32d Tennessee.	K	"	Feb. 16, '62
McCauley, J. J.	"	50th Tennessee.		Buchanan co., Va.	
McClanahan, A.	Citizen.			Fort Donaldson.	April 11, '62
*McClellan, R. H.	2d Lieut.	9th Bat. Tennessee Cavalry.		"	
McClung, L. H.	1st Lieut.	49th Tennessee.	B	Clark county, Ky.	Oct. 24, '61
	Private.	Kentucky Cavalry.			

PRISONERS CONFINED AT JOHNSON'S ISLAND.—Continued.

Name.	Rank.	Regiment.	Co	Where Captured.	When Capt'd.
McClung, R. L.	1st Lieut.	15th Arkansas.	F	Fort Donaldson.	
McConnell, W. H.	2d Lieut.	14th Mississippi.	D	"	
McCoy, T. E.	"	3d Tennessee.	K	"	
McCoy, Wm.	1st Lieut.	10th Tennessee.	I	"	April 11, '62
*McCranie, G. W.	Captain.	9th Louisiana.	K	Huntsville, Ala.	
McCullum, G. B.	Sergeant.	3d Tennessee.	A	Fort Donaldson.	
McCullum, D. M.	2d Lieut.	33d Tennessee.	F	Island 10.	
*McDaniels, J. W.	1st Lieut.	Tennessee Artillery.		"	
McDavid, P. J.	2d Lieut.	7th Texas.	I	Fort Donaldson.	
McDonald, J. E.	Captain.	55th Tennessee.	G	Island 10.	
McDonald, Ed. H.	"	2d Alabama.	H	Fort Donaldson.	
McDougal, W. C.	Serg.-Maj.	26th Mississippi.	D	"	
McDougal, W. H.	Private.	20th Tennessee.		Fishing Creek.	
McDowell, E. C.	Lieut.	11th Arkansas.		Island 10	
McDowell, Harry	Captain.	2d Kentucky.	F	Fort Donaldson.	
McDuffie, R. N.	Private.	26th Tennessee.	I	"	
McEachern, J. E.	2d Lieut.	1st Alabama.	F	Island 10.	
McElwee, Wm E.	"	26th Tennessee.	I	Fort Donaldson.	
McFall, W. H.	"	9th Bat. Tennessee Cavalry.		"	
McFarland, C. D.	Captain.	26th Tennessee.	G	"	
McGehee, J. T.	Adjutant.	1st Alabama.		Island 10.	

Name	Rank	Regiment		Place	Date
McGehee, F. M.	1st Lieut.	27th Alabama.	K	Fort Donaldson.	Feb. 14, '62
McGowan, J. P.	Captain.	14th Mississippi.	D	"	Dec. 25, '61
McGuire, J. P.	2d Lieut.	32d Tennessee.	C	"	May 5, '62
McIntire, Thos.	Captain.	31st Virginia.	H	Bloomery Gap, Va.	
McIntyre, D. H.	Captain.	3d Missouri.	A	Fulton, Mo.	
McIntire, Jno.	Lieut.	Morgan's Cavalry.	B	Lebanon.	May 5, '62
*McKay, W. D.	1st Lieut.	40th Tennessee.	K	Island 10.	
*McKee, Nelson	"	48th Tennessee.	G	Fort Donaldson.	
*McKee, S. F.	Lieut.	Morgan's Cavalry.	F	Lebanon, Tenn.	
McKinny, H. U.	Captain	8th Kentucky	A	Fort Donaldson.	
McLanoleau, J.	1st Lieut.	48th Tennessee.	F	Fort Henry.	
*McLaughlin, J.	Q. M.	10th Tennessee.	D	Fort Donaldson.	
McLean, F. J.	2d Lieut.	9th Bat. Tenn. Cavalry.	K	Mills Spring.	
McLemore, A J.	Private	15th Mississippi.		Fort Donaldson.	
McClellan, R. C.	2d Lieut.	26th Mississippi.		Huntsville, Ala.	
McLeroy, W. S.	"	9th Louisiana.	C	Lexington, Mo.	Dec. 18, '61
McLure, W. P.	Captain.	1st Missouri Cavalry.	A	Clarksville.	Feb. 20, '62
*McMacon, J. O.	Sergeant.	20th Mississippi.		Fort Pulaski.	April 11, '62
McMahon, J.	Captain.	1st Georgia.		"	"
McMullen, M. J.	"	25th Georgia.	F	Fort Donaldson.	
McNabb, J. W.	2d Lieut.	26th Tennessee.	C	Henry co , Tenn.	
McNutt, G. W.	"	25th "	A	Fort Donaldson.	March 20, '62
McRody, J A.	Com'ry.	53d Tennessee.		Island 10.	
McRae, C. M.	1st Lieut.	1st Alabama.	F		
McReady, J. M.					
McRea, A.	Private.	15th Mississippi.	F	Mills Spring	

PRISONERS CONFINED AT JOHNSON'S ISLAND.—Continued.

Names.	Rank.	Regiment.	Co.	Where Captured.	When Capt'd.
McVay, L. D. F.	Com'ry.	1st Alabama, Tenn. and Miss.		Island 10.	
McWharter, H. J.	Captain.				
McWharter, F. P.	1st Lieut.	49th Tennessee	G	Fort Donaldson.	
McWharter, G. W.	Captain.	3d Mississippi.	H	Island 10.	
Medows, J. D.	"	1st Alabama.	C	Fort Donaldson.	
Meek, R. D.	2d Lieut.	4th Mississippi.	B	Island 10.	
Melton, P. M.	Captain.	55th Tennessee.	C	"	
Menefra, J. T.	1st Lieut.	1st Alabama, Tenn. and Miss.	E	"	
Milan, P. G.	"	55th Tennessee.			
Miller, M. S.	Lt. Col.	11th Arkansas.		Island 10.	
Mills, W. B.	As. Surg.	50th Tennessee.		Fort Donaldson.	
*Minter, J. H.	Lt. Col.	40th Tennessee.		Island 10.	
Mitchell, J. M.	Private.	8th Virginia Cavalry.	B	Jumping Branch.	Feb. 9, '62
Mitchell, R. A.	1st Lieut.	3d Tennessee.	D	Fort Donaldson.	
Mitchell, T. F.	2d Lieut.	50th Tennessee.		Carnafax Ferry.	Sept. 3, '61
Mitchell, W. C.	Colonel.	14th Arkansas.		Pea Ridge, Ark.	March 7, '62
Mitchell, W. T.	2d Lieut.	3d Tennessee.	B	Fort Donaldson.	
Mofley, Levi	"	25th Tennessee.	D	"	
Mofley, M. L.	"	1st Mississippi.	F	"	
Moffat, A.	"	51st Tennessee.	I	"	
Montfort, T. W.	1st Lieut.	25th Georgia.		Fort Pulaski.	April 11, '62

Name	Rank	Regiment	Co.	Where captured	Date
Moody, L. F.	Sergeant.	7th Texas.	C	Fort Donaldson.	April 29, '62
Moody, W. L.	Captain.	"	C	"	
Moore, A. W.	1st Lieut.	4th Mississippi.	I	"	
Moore, C. C.	2d Lieut.	1st Alabama, Tenn. and Miss.	B	Island 10.	
Moore, C. F.	1st Lieut.	7th Texas.	F	Fort Donaldson.	
*Moore, F. D.	2d Lieut.	15th Sr. Regt. Tenn. Vol.	I	Purdy, Tenn	
Moore, G. W.	Com.Serg	53d Tennessee.		Fort Donaldson.	
Moore, G. W.	Private.	"	E	"	
Moore, Isaac	"	15th Mississippi.	E	Mills Spring.	
Moore, J. B.	Captain.	4th Mississippi.	B	Fort Donaldson.	
Moore, J. T.	Private.	15th Mississippi.	G	Mills Spring.	
Moore, Jno. W.	"	14th Mississippi.	I	Fort Donaldson.	
*Moore, J. Y.	2d Lieut.	3d Mississippi.	C	"	
Moore, R. J.	"	26th Mississippi.	H	"	
Moore, R. N.	Captain.	9th Bat. Tennessee Cavalry.	B	Island 10.	
Moore, S. B.	3d Lieut.	1st Alabama.	D	Fort Donaldson.	
Moore, V. B.	2d Lieut.	50th Tennessee.	B	"	
Moore, W. A.	1st Lieut.	"	B		
Mooramu, G. T.	Lieut.	Artillery.	A	At Home, sick.	March 20, '62
Morgan, P. A.	2d Lieut.	46th Tennessee.	E	Fort Donaldson.	Feb. 16, '62
*Morgan, St. Clair	Captain	10th Tennessee.	K	Island 10.	
Morgan, W. J.	2d Lieut.	11th Arkansas.	G	"	
Morphis, J. L.	Captain.	1st Alabama, Tenn. and Miss.	K	Fort Donaldson.	
Morrill, J. R.	"	26th Tennessee.	C	"	
Morris, J. T.	1st Lieut.	49th Tennessee.	C	"	
Morris, N. S.	2d Lieut.	1st Alabama.	D	Island 10.	

PRISONERS CONFINED AT JOHNSON'S ISLAND.—Continued.

Name.	Rank.	Regiment.	Co.	Where Captured.	When Capt'd.
Morrison, J. P.	Captain.	48th Tennessee.	F	Fort Donaldson.	
Morton, J. W. jr.	1st Lieut.	1st Tennessee Artillery.		"	
Morton, J. H.	Captain.	52d Tennessee.	H	"	
Mosley, C. W.	2d Lieut.	56th Virginia.	B	"	
Mosley, G. M.	Captain.	1st Mississippi.	A	"	
Moss, J. C. C.	"	11th Arkansas.	F	Island 10.	
Moss, J. W.		2d Kentucky.	A	Fort Donaldson.	
Moss, J. W.	Private.	10th Mississippi.	L	Mills Spring.	
Moss, L. C.	2d Lieut.	2d Kentucky.	A	Fort Donaldson.	
Moss, T. B.	1st Serg't.	11th Arkansas.	E	Island 10.	
Moss, T. E.	Serg. Maj	2d Kentucky.		Fort Donaldson.	
Moss, W. A.		11th Arkansas.		Island 10.	
Muldoon, H. S.	2d Lieut.	14th Mississippi.	C	Fort Donaldson.	
Murff, R. S.	2d Lieut.	20th Mississippi.	B	"	
Murphy, C. N.	2d Lieut.	1st Georgia.		Fort Pulaski.	
Murphy, J. B.	1st Lieut.	3d Tennessee.	F	Fort Donaldson.	
Murphy, T.	Citizen.			Galletin co., Ky.	Dec. 27, '61
Murray, J. J.	2d Lieut.	53d Tennessee.	B	Fort Donaldson.	
Murrell, W. E.	Lieut.	41st Tennessee.		"	
Myers, J. J.	2d Lieut.	4th Arkansas.	D	Pea Ridge, Ark.	March 7, '62
Martin, J. T.	Major.	Arkansas.		Randolph co., Ark.	May 13, '62

Name	Rank	Regiment	Co.	Place	Date
Nabers, F. M.	1st Lieut.	14th Mississippi.	E	Fort Donaldson.	
Nanney, W. H.	3d Lieut.	1st Mississippi.	K	"	Sept. 12, '62
Napier, R. S.	As. Surg	49th Tennessee.	K	Cheat Mountain.	Jan. 19, '62
Nassauer, L.	Private.	1st Tennessee.	I	Fishing Creek.	
Nations, W. W.	Private.	15th Mississippi.	E	Huntsville, Ala.	April 11, '62
Neal, J. C.	Private.	15th Mississippi.		Fort Donaldson.	
Neal, S. J.	Private.	9th Louisiana.	A	"	
Neely, Moses S.	As. Surg.	51st Tennessee.	G	"	
Neal, Lea	2d Lieut.	26th Tennessee.	G	"	
Nelson, T. P.	Captain.	4th Mississippi.	F	"	
Nelson, W. R.	1st Lieut.	20th Mississippi.			
New, Luke W.	2d Lieut.	26th "			
Nichols, Alex.	1st Lieut				
Nichols, T. W.		50th Tennessee.	B	Island 10.	
Nooner, J. J. R.	3d Lieut.	11th Arkansas.	L	Fort Donaldson.	
Norman, J. T.	1st Lieut.	41st Tennessee.	K	"	
Norton, E. A.	Private.	41st "	H	"	
Norvell, J. S.	2d Lieut.	7th Texas.	A	"	
Nunney, H. M.	1st Lieut	49th Tennessee.	I	"	
Olive, J. J.	3d Lieut	27th Alabama.	C	"	
Oldham, S. T.	1st Lieut.	20th Mississippi.	K	"	
Olmstead, C. H.	Colonel.	1st Georgia.	A	Fort Pulaski.	April 11, '62
*O'Neal, John	Captain.	10th Tennessee.	I	Fort Donaldson.	
O'Neal, W. P.	"	32d "	H	"	
Osborne, J. C.	"	41st "	G	"	
Outlaw, W. D.	2d Lieut.	14th Mississippi.			

PRISONERS CONFINED AT JOHNSON'S ISLAND.—Continued.

Name.	Rank.	Regiment.	Co.	Where Captured.	When Capt'd.
Overtown, G. B.	Chaplain.	2d Kentucky.		Fort Donaldson.	
Overton, J. F.	Captain.	Forrest Cavalry.	A	"	
Overton, R. B.	Private.	"	A	"	
*Overton, F. D.	Lieut.	41st Tennessee.		"	
Owen, G. W.	"	Morgan's Cavalry.		Lebanon, Tenn.	May 5, '62
Owen, W. G.	Surgeon.	Grave Bat.		Fort Donaldson.	
Owens, R. A.	Chaplain.	46th Tennessee.	I	Island 10.	
*Owing, G. W.	3d Lieut.	26th "	H	Fort Donaldson.	
Ong, J. W.	Pilot.	8th Virginia Cavalry.		Off Memphis.	May 15, '62
Oldham, J. P.		Confederate States Navy.		"	June 6, '62
Orn, Wm.	As. Eng.	" "			
Palmer, P. H.	1st Sergt.	15th Mississippi.	B	Mills Spring.	
Palmer, R. D.	Chaplain.	4th "	E	Fort Donaldson.	
Pardue, G. M.	1st Lieut.	42d Tennessee.	C	"	
Pardue, W. J.	4th Sergt.	" "	C	"	
Pardue, W. P.	1st Lieut.	26th Mississippi.	H	"	
Parmele, W. J.	3d Lieut.	4th "	E	"	
Parker, G. W.	1st Lieut.	21st Alabama.	E	Shiloh, Tenn.	April 7, '62
Parker, J. T.	Private.	15th Mississippi.	E	Mills Spring.	
Parker, J. W.	1st Lieut.	50th Tennessee.	H	Fort Donaldson,	
Paschal, E.	2d Lieut.	46th "	K	Island 10.	

Rank	Regiment	Co.	Where Captured	Date
Lieut.	Adam's Cavalry.		Lebanon, Tenn.	May 5, '62
3d Lieut.	26th Tennessee.	E	Fort Donaldson.	
Captain.	49th "	E	Mills Spring.	
Private.	15th Mississippi.	F	Fort Donaldson.	
2d Lieut.	30th Tennessee.	B	"	
1st Lieut	50th "		"	
2d Lieut.	4th Mississippi.	K	"	
"	" "	B	"	
Captain.	1st "	L	"	
2d Lieut.	51st Tennessee.	A	"	
"	14th Mississippi.	L	"	
Captain	15th Arkansas.	E	Shiloh, Tenn.	April 7, '62
1st Lieut.	Crescent, New Orleans.	H	Fort Donaldson,	
2d Lieut.	42d Tennessee.	B	Island 10.	
3d Lieut.	42d "	K	Huntsville, Ala.	April 11, '62
2d Lieut.	1st " Art.		Fort Donaldson.	
Private.	9th Louisiana.	G	"	
1st Lieut.	4th Mississippi.	D	Fort Donaldson.	
Private.	26th "	C	Island 10.	
2d Lieut	32d Tennessee.		Fort Donaldson.	
Sergeant.	Tennessee Artillery.	H	Island 10.	
2d Lieut.	3d Tennessee.	A	Fort Donaldson.	
3d Lieut.	11th Arkansas.		Island 10.	
Major.	" "		Nicholas co., Va.	Sept 10, '61
Private.	8th Virginia Cavalry.		Fort Donaldson.	
A. Q. M.	49th Tennessee.			

PRISONERS CONFINED AT JOHNSON'S ISLAND.—Continued.

Name.	Rank.	Regiment.	Co.	Where Captured.	When Capt'd.
*Pointer, H. P.	Captain.	3d Tennessee.	E	Fort Donaldson.	
Polk, R. J.	2d Lieut.	Tennessee Artillery.		Island 10	April 11, '62
Pollard, L.	Private.	15th Mississippi.	L	Mills Spring.	
Pond, W. G.	1st Lieut.	30th Tennessee.	E	Fort Donaldson.	
Porter, T. L.	"	9th Batt. Tennessee Cavalry.	B	"	
Powell, J.	Captain.	1st Kentucky.	I	"	
Powell, J. A.	Private.	9th Lousiana.		Huntsville, Ala.	
Powell, W. H.	3d Lieut.	49th Tennessee.	E	Fort Donaldson.	
Poiner, J. C.	Captain.	46th Tennessee.	F	Island 10.	
Pratt, T. F.	As. Surg.	Morgan Cavalry.		Lebanon.	May 5, '61
Presson, J. N.	2d Lieut.	55th Tennessee.	E	Island 10.	Dec. 5, '61
Provines, J. G.	Captain.			Fulton. Mo.	
Pruett, J. E.	1st Lieut	1st Alabama.	L	Island 10.	
Pryor, J. H.	Private.	15th Mississippi.	G	Mills Spring.	
Pugh, A. J.	2d Lieut.	9th Batt. Tennessee Cavalry.		Fort Donaldson.	
Purifoy, H. M.	Captain.	15th Arkansas.		"	
*Purrell, J. B.	3d Lieut.	3d Mississippi.	B	"	
Putnam, W. L.	Captain	18th Tennessee.	I	"	
Palmer, B.	"	6th Tennessee.		Bolivar, Tenn.	
Pastal, O.	Pilot.	C. S. Navy.		Off Memphis.	
Pell, J. N.	Pilot.	"		"	June 6, '62

Phelps, J. M.	Colonel.	Q. M. of Gunboat Arkansas.		Arkansas.	
*Quarrels, W. A.		42d Tennessee.		Fort Donaldson.	
Radosky, Jus.	Private.	31st Virginia.	I	Green Brier River.	Oct. 16, '61
*Ragan, W. S.	3d Lieut.	3d Mississippi.	F	Fort Donaldson.	
25 Ragsdale, F. A.	Captain.	40th Tennessee.	B	Island 10.	
Rainey, J. K.	Lieut.	50th Tennessee.		Fort Donaldson.	
Raisler, C. W.	Captain.	40th Tennessee.		Island 10.	
Ramsey, D. W.	"	1st Alabama.	B	"	
Rand, Oscar R.	"	26th North Carolina.		Newbern, N. C.	March 14, '62
Randall, P. H.	1st Lieut.	46th Tennessee.	G	Island 10.	
Randolph, J. G.	2d Lieut.	18th Tennessee.	C	Fort Donaldson.	
Rankin, J. E.	"	Grave's Battery.		"	
Ray, Asa	"	1st Alabama, Tenn. and Miss.	D	Island 10.	
Ray, C. A.	1st Lieut.	26th Mississippi.	G	Fort Donaldson.	
Ray, R. M.	"	18th Tennessee.	E	"	
Reagan, M.	2d Lieut.	53d Tennessee.	A	"	
Reed, A. M. L.	3d Lieut.	15th Arkansas.		"	
Reed, C. S.	2d Lieut.	26th Tennessee.	G	"	
Reed, J. M.	"	42d Tennessee.		"	
Reed, W. G.	1st Lieut.	41st Tennessee.		"	
Reiley, John	Lieut.	5th Louisiana.	F	Chickahominy.	
Richards, A. C.	Captain.	50th Virginia.	E	Fort Donaldson.	
Richardson, J. C.	2d Lieut.	27th Alabama.	K	Fort Henry.	Feb. 6, '62
Richardson, S. L.	Private.	1st Tennessee.		Cheat Mountain.	Sept. 12, '61
Richardson, W. C.	Captain.	53d Tennessee.	G	Fort Donaldson.	
*Riddlesperger, J. H.	1st Lieut	3d Mississippi.		"	

PRISONERS CONFINED AT JOHNSON'S ISLAND.—Continued.

Names.	Rank.	Regiment.	Co.	Where Captured.	When Capt'd.
Riley, N. B.	2d Lieut.	8th Kentucky.	G	Fort Donaldson.	
Riley, R. H.	1st Lieut.	1st Alabama.	G	Island 10.	
*Roberts, E.	2d Lieut.	3d Mississippi.	E	Fort Donaldson.	
Roberts, Jas. A.	"	20th Mississippi.	B	"	
Roberts, Rich'd.	Captain.	49th Tennessee.	F	"	
Robertson, H. L.	2d Lieut	"	I	"	
*Robinson, H. H.	Chaplain	3d Mississippi			
Rodger, Jas.	Private.	1st Alabama, Tenn. and Miss.	K	Island 10.	
Rodgers, J. W.	2d Lieut	2d Kentucky.	C	Fort Donaldson.	
Rodgers, H. B.	1st Lieut.	"	D	"	
Rogers, F. A.	Captain.	2d Regt. Missouri S. G.	C	Milford, Mo.	Dec. 19, '61
Roe, T. B.	2d Lieut.	Tennessee Artilery.		Island 10.	
Roffu, W. D.	Private.	23d Virginia.	I	Fayette County, Va	Sept. 13, '61
Roffe, T. J.	"	"	I	"	"
Rodger, J. B.	1st Lieut.	40th Tennessee.	D	Island 10.	
Rodger, W. J.	As. Surg.	26th Mississippi.		Fort Donaldson.	
Rorer, W. A.	Captain.	20th "	B	"	
Rose, W. H.	3d Lieut.	32d Tennessee.	F	"	
Russore, L.	Captain.	40th "	C	Island 10.	
Rowland, J. C.	2d Lieut	1st Georgia.		Fort Pulaski.	
Rowland, H T.	Sergeant.	8th Kentucky.	C	Fort Donaldson.	

Name	Rank	Regiment	Co.	Place	Date
Rude, E.	3d Lieut.	15th Arkansas.			
Rudolph, W. H.	1st Lieut.	49th Tennessee.	F	Fort Donaldson.	
Ruffin, J. E.	"	50th "	F	"	
Rupert, W. H.	2d Lieut.	Tennessee Artillery.	E	Island 10.	
Rush, J. W.	Captain.	1st Alabama, Tenn. and Miss.			
Rushing, W. R.	"	18th Tennessee.	C	Fort Donaldson.	Nov. '61
Russell, G. W.	Private.	8th Virginia Cavalry.	A	Guyandotte, Va.	
Russell, J. C.	2d Lieut.	41st Tennessee.		Fort Donaldson.	
Rand, N.	Adjutant.	22d Virginia.	B	Lewisburg, Va.	
Ransom, W. B.	1st Lieut.	10th Texas Cavalry.		Booneville, Miss.	June 3, '62
atliff, O.	"	27th Alabama.	H	Fort Donaldson.	
Richardson, G. L.	2d Lieut	Confederate States Navy.		Off Memphis.	June 6, '62
Rawson, J. E.	"	" "			"
*Saddler, A. D.	"	" "			
Saffle, R. M.	1st Lieut.	3d Mississippi.	E	Fort Donaldson.	
Sale, T. S.	2d Lieut	26th Tennessee.	F	"	
*Salmon, H. W.	Captain.	1st " Artillery.		"	Dec. 3, '61
Sample, W. T.	"	1st Missouri Cavalry.	F	Versailles, Mo.	
Sams, J.	Private.	30th Tennessee.	K	Fort Donaldson.	
Sanders, J. M.	Captain.	29th "	C	Mills Spring.	
Sanford, J. H.	2d Lieut.	11th Arkansas.	A	Island 10.	
Sanford, M. A.	Private.	1st Alabama.	A	"	
Sanders, F. F.	Captain.	"	K	"	
Sayer, A.	Citizen.	3d Mississippi.		Fort Donaldson.	Dec. 26, '61
Sayer, J. M.	"			Warsaw.	"
Schneeider, T.	Lieut.	20th Louisiana.		Shiloh, Tennessee	April 7, '62

PRISONERS CONFINED AT JOHNSON'S ISLAND.—Continued.

Name.	Rank.	Regiment.	Co.	Where Captured.	When Capt'd.
Scott, C.	2d Lieut.	28th North Carolina.	C	Hanover C. H.	May 27, '62
Scott, J. D.	Captain.	41st Tennessee.	G	Fort Donaldson.	
Scott, F. T.	1st Lieut.	11th Arkansas.	G	Island 10.	
Scott, T. J.	2d Lieut.	8th Kentucky.	H	Fort Donaldson.	
Subert, J. L.	1st Lieut.	31st Virginia.		Bloomery Gap, Va.	Feb. 14, '62
Sellers, V. J.	Lieut.	Morgan's Cavalry.		Lebanon, Tenn.	May 5, '62
Sellers, W. F.	Private.	50th Virginia.	D	Carnifax Ferry.	Sept. 13, '61
Selvage, W.-R.	1st Lieut.	11th Arkansas.	E	Island 10.	
Sewell, W. M.	Private.	15th Mississippi.		Fishing Creek.	
Sexton, E. G.	Captain.	50th Tennessee.	H	Fort Donaldson.	
*Seymoore, R.	1st Lieut.	10th Tennessee.	K	"	
Shackleford, W. A. H.	Captain.	26th Mississippi.	H	"	
Shackleford, T. H.	"	1st Alabama, Tenn. and Miss.	E	Island 10.	
Shacklet, A. R.	"	8th Kentucky.	H	Fort Donaldson.	
Shankley, J. H.	3d Lieut.	55th Tennessee.	H	Island 10.	
Sharp, M. D. M.	2d Lieut.	26th Mississippi.	E	Fort Donaldson.	
Sharp, H. K. W.	1st Lieut.	55th Tennessee.	A	Island 10.	
Sharp, J. G.	Captain.	26th Mississippi.	E	Fort Donaldson.	
Shaw, B. F.	2d Lieut.	49th Tennessee.	K	"	
Shawhau, T. S.	Private.	1st Kentucky Cavalry	A	Paintsville, Ky.	Jan. 10, '62
Shearin, J. T.	2d Lieut.	1st Alabama, Tenn. and Miss.	K	Island 10.	

Name	Rank	Regiment	Co.	Where captured.	Date.
Shepherd, D. T.	Act. H. S.	Crescent, New Orleans.		Shiloh.	
Shepherd, J. A.	1st Lieut.	11th Arkansas.	A	Island 10.	
Shepherd, M. N.	2d Lieut.	"	A	"	
Sherter, W. B.	Private.	28th Tennessee.	F	Fishing Creek.	Dec. 7, '61
*Simmons, Jas.	Captain.	Unattached.		Saline county. Mo.	
Simonton, G. F.	Adjutant.	1st Mississippi.		Fort Donaldson.	
Simonton, J. M.	Colonel.	"		"	
Simpson, C. N.	1st Lieut.	3d Mississippi.	I	"	
Simpson, S. R.	Q. M. S.	30th Tennessee.		"	
Simpson, W. M.	Captain.	1st Tennessee Bat.		"	
Sims, M. L.	1st Lieut	Forrest Cavalry.	D	Fort Pulaski.	
Sims, T. W.	Captain.	1st Georgia.		Island 10.	
Sistunk, A. J.	2d Lieut.	1st Alabama, Tenn. and Miss.	C	Lebanon.	May 5, '62
Skillman, W. H.	"	2d Kentucky Cavalry.		Fort Donaldson.	
Skinner, T. E.	Act. Ord.	8th Kentucky.	A	"	
Slaughter, R. C.	Captain.	8th "	A	"	
*Smith, A. F.	2d Lieut.	49th Tennessee.	A	"	
Smith, F. M.	1st Lieut.	3d Mississippi.	F	Island 10.	
Smith, G. W.	2d Lieut.	55th Tennessee.		Fort Donaldson.	
Smith, G. W.	Q. M. S.	26th Mississippi.	G	Island 10.	
Smith, H. C.	Private.	11th Arkansas.		"	
Smith, J. M.	Colonel.	"		Fort Donaldson.	
Smith, T.	2d Lieut.	French Virginia Artillery.	G	Island 10.	
Smith, W. J. S.	Private.	11th Arkansas.	H	"	
Smith, W. L.	2d Lieut.	46th Tennessee.		Fort Donaldson.	
Smith, W. M.	"	27th Alabama.	A	"	

PRISONERS CONFINED AT JOHNSON'S ISLAND.—Continued.

Name.	Rank.	Regiment.	Co.	Where Captured.	When Capt'd.
Smith, W. R.	Sergeant.	41st Tennessee.		Fort Donaldson.	
Smith, W. S.	2d Lieut.	1st Alabama, Tenn. and Miss.	F	Island 10.	
Smith, W. W.	Ac. Mast.	Confederate States Navy.		"	
Snider, C.	2d Lieut.	40th Tennessee.	K	"	
Snodgrass, D.	Captain	1st Bat. Tennessee Infantry.	D	Fort Donaldson.	
Soule, George		Crescent City Guards.	A	Shiloh, Tenn.	
Southall, R. M. G.	2d Lieut.	10th Tennessee.	K	Fort Donaldson.	
Spain, T. J.		1st Alabama, Tenn. and Miss.	A	Island 10.	
Sparkman, J. M.	1st Lieut.	Maney's Bat.		Fort Donaldson.	
Spear, F. J.	2d Lieut.	18th Tennessee.	H	"	
Spearz, E. F.	1st Lieut.	2d Kentucky.	G	"	
Speer, W. H. A.	Captain.	28th North Carolina.		Hanover C. H.	
Spencer, G. M.	2d Lieut.	Artillery.		Fort Danaldson.	
Spencer, J. D.	Citizen.			Gallitin county, Ky.	Dec. 27, '61
Spencer, S.	1st Lieut.	Issaquera Artillery.		Fort Donaldson.	
Spinks, W. L.	"	14th Mississippi.	H	"	
Spradhir, W. H.	2d Lieut.	30th Tennessee.	E	"	
Stafford, F. M.	Cadet.	4th Mississippi.		"	
Stankrewitz, P. K.	Captain.	Thetman's Bat.		"	
Stark, G. M. R.	2d Lieut.	30th Tennessee.	B	"	
Steel, T. H.	"	51st Virginia.		Gloomery Gap, Va.	Feb. 14, '62

Name	Rank	Regiment	Co.	Where Captured	Date
Steele, J B.	2d Lieut.	1st Bat. Arkansas Cavalry.	E	Fayetteville, Ark.	Feb. 23, '62
Steele, R. L.	1st Lieut.	32d North Carolina.		Hanover C. H.	
Steel, T.	Surgeon.	2d Kentucky.	A	Lexington, Ky.	Jan. 21, '62
Steel, W. T.	Private.	Forrest Cavalry.		Fort Donaldson.	
Stegin, J. H.	Captain.	1st Georgia.	F	Fort Pulaski.	April 11, '62
Sterling, E. R.	2d Lieut.	20th Mississippi.	L	Fort Donaldson.	
Stevens, J. R.	"	4th Mississippi.	C	"	
Stewart, E. H.	"	11th Arkansas.		Island 10.	
Stewart, G.	Serg. Maj	26th Tennessee.		Fort Donaldson.	
Stewart John	Captain.	89th Virginia.	H	Gloomery Gap.	
Stewart, J. B.	2d Lieut.	46th Tennessee.		Island 10.	
Stewart, W. A.	1st Lieut.	37th North Carolina.	I	Hanover C. H.	
Stewart, W. E.	Captain.	40th Tennessee.		Island 10.	
Stinson, H. C.	2d lieut	Grave's Bat.		Fort Donaldson.	
St. John, H. J.	Captain.	18th Tennessee.	D	"	
St. John, M. E.	2d Lieut.	"	D	"	
*Stockell, C. H.	1st Lieut.	53d Tennessee.		"	
Stodard, A. A.	2d Lieut.	20th Mississippi.	C	Hanover C. H.	Feb. 16, '62
Stowe, S. N.	Captain.	28th North Carolina.	B	Shiloh.	
Strebe, F.	As. Surg.	20th Louisiana.	H	Fort Donaldson.	
Stuart, J. B.	Captain.	27th Alabama.		Johnson's co., Ky.	
Stuart, J. E.			C	Island 10.	
Stubbs, J. P.	Captain.	1st Alabama.	K	Fort Donaldson.	Feb. 24, '62
Sudduth, A. D.	2d Lieut.	3d Mississippi.		Island 10.	
Sullins, S. B.	A. C. S.	1st Alabama.		Island 10.	
Sullivan, W. M.	1st Lieut.	48th Tennessee.	G	Fort Donaldson.	

PRISONERS CONFINED AT JOHNSON'S ISLAND.—Continued.

Name.	Rank.	Regiment.	Co.	Where Captured.	When Capt'd.
Sutton, J. D. N.	2d Lieut.	25th Georgia.	F	Fort Pulaski.	
Swaffin, S.	"	4th Mississippi.		"	
Swanson, J. M.	Employe.			Island 10.	
Sweeney, William	1st Lieut.	10th Tennessee.	G	Fort Donaldson.	
Sweeney, W. J.	2d Lieut.	40th "	G	Island 10.	
Smindoll, W. C.	"	3d Mississippi.	I	Fort Donaldson.	
Sykes, T. D.	1st Lieut	20th "	B		
Symons, J. J.	"	1st Georgia.		Fort Pulaski.	
Saffin, W.	Lieut.			Decatur, Ala.	
Shadburn, R. A.	1st Lieut.	Morgan's Cavalry.		Lebanon, Tenn.	May 5, '62
Sprigg, J. T.	Captain.	Virginia.	B	Allegheny co., Va.	May 16, '62
Steele, Thos.	1st Lieut.	4th Kentucky.	E	Shiloh.	
Swift, Joseph	Ch. Eng.	Confederate States Navy.		Off Memphis.	June 6, '62
Sareleting, Peter	As. Eng.	" "		"	"
Sryne, R. G.	Captain.	Virginia.	G	Allegheny co., Va.	May 16, '62
Tabb, W. H.	1st Lieut.	14th Mississippi.	C	Fort Donaldson.	
Talbott, L. W.	3d Lieut.	Forrest Cavalry.		"	
Talliaferro, E. T.	Surgeon.	26th Tennessee.		"	
*Tally, J.	1st Lieut.	Floyd's Va. Artillery.		Fort Henry.	Feb. 6, '62
*Taylor J.	Captain.	1st Tennessee Artillery.		Fort Donaldson.	
Taylor, J. M.	Surgeon.	26th Mississippi.			

Name	Rank	Regiment	Co.	Where Captured	Date
Taylor, N. J.	Chaplian	14th Mississippi.	K	Fort Donaldson.	
Taylor, S. T.	Captain.	Virginia Militia.		Green Brier co., Va.	
Teasly, L. W.	2d Lieut	49th Tennessee	K	Fort Donaldson.	
Tennett, G. W.	"	Confederate States Navy.		Fort Pulaski.	
Terry B. D.	1st Lieut.	Green's Battery.		Fort Donaldson.	
Tharp, W. A.	Captain.	46th Tennessee.	C	Island 10.	
Thomas, Arch	3d Lieut.	30th "	A	Fort Donaldson.	
Thomas, C.	Private.	53d		"	
Thomas, C. H.	1st Lieut.	2d Kentucky.	C	Island 10.	
Thomas, J. S.	Private.	4th Arkansas Bat.	B	Fort Donaldson.	
Thomas, R. F.	2d Lieut.	50th Tennessee.	B	Island 10.	
Tidmarsh, T. U.	1st Lieut.	Artillery.			
Tidwell, F. L.	2d Lieut.	7th Texas.	G	Fort Donaldson.	
Tillman, J. D.	"	Tennessee Infantry.		Island 10.	
Titsworth, J. P.	1st Lieut.	1st Tennessee Battalion.	C	Fort Donaldson.	
Thompson, E. B.	Captain.	27th Alabama.	C	"	
Thompson, E. B.	2d Lieut.	Manny's Artillery.		"	
Thompson, J. J.	"	Pt. Cupee Artillery.	B	Island 10.	
Thompson, J. W.	"	26th Mississippi.	A	Fort Donaldson.	
*Thompson, J. S.	A. Q. M.	3d "		"	
Thompson, M V.	1st Lieut.	9th Bat. Tennessee Cavalry.	K	"	
Thompson S. M.	Captain.	10th Tennessee.	G	"	
Towns, W. S.	2d Lieut.	30th "	E	"	
Towsend, L. R.	"	4th Mississippi.		"	
Tracey, E. G.	"	Floyd's Va. Artillery.		"	
Trepagnier, F. O.	3d Lieut.	Orleans Guards Bat.	A	Shiloh, Tenn.	April 7, '62

PRISONERS CONFINED AT JOHNSON'S ISLAND.—Continued.

Name.	Rank.	Regiment.	Co.	Where Captured.	When Capt'd.
Trice, J. L.	Captain.	4th Kentucky	B	Shiloh, Tenn.	
Trotter, A.	2d Lieut	14th Mississippi.	D	Fort Donaldson.	
*Tryon, F.	"	2d Kentucky.	E	"	
Tucker C. G.	Captain.	32d Tennessee.	C	"	
Tucker, H. H.	2d Lieut.	32d Tennessee.	C	"	
Tucker, M. A.	"	55th Tennessee.	C	Island 10.	
Tungett, W. H.	2d Lieut.	53d Tennessee.		Fort Donaldson.	
Turner, C.	"	1st Tennessee Bat. Infantry.		"	
*Turner, J. C.	1st Lieut.	3d Mississippi.	D	"	
Turner J. H.	Captain.	30th Tennessee.	E	"	
Turner, L. W.	2d Lieut.	56th Virginia.	B	"	
Turner, W. V.	As. Surg.	50th Tennessee.		"	
Turntine, J. J.	1st Lieut.	40th "	A	Island 10.	
Tuttle C. E.	2d Lieut.	1st Alabama.	K	. "	
Trothy, S. C.	1st Lieut	40th Tennessee.	E	"	
Tyler, J. M.	Private.	15th Mississippi.	E	Fishing Creek.	
Tripplet, M.	Captain.	Virginia Rangers.	C	Allegheny co., Va.	May 16, '62
Umback, C. H.	2d Lieut.	1st Georgia.		Fort Pulaski.	
Ursey, R. L.	"	2d Kentucky.	D	Fort Donaldson.	
Vance, M. D.	Captain.	11th Arkansas.	A	Island 10.	
VanMater, D. S.	Lieut.	50th Tennessee.		Fort Donaldson.	

Name	Rank	Regiment	Co.	Where captured	When captured
VanZandt, K. W.	Captain.	7th Texas.	D	Fort Donaldson.	
Vasser, W. H.	Com'ry.	14th Mississippi.		"	
Vison, J. W.	2d Lieut.	26th North Carolina.	B	Newbern, N. C.	March 14, '62
Vorhies, A. H.	Surgeon.			Fort Henry.	
Wade, F. T.	2d Lieut.	32d Tennessee.	G	Fort Donaldson.	
Waldrop, H. W.	1st Lieut.	1st Mississippi.		"	
Walker, C. H.	Captain.	3d Tennessee.		"	
Walker, J. F.	"			"	
Walker, J. W.	"	9th Batt. Tennessee Cavalry.	A	Island 10.	
Walker, J. W.	"	42d Tennessee.	B	Fort Pulaski.	
*Walker, J. W.	1st Lieut.	40th "	C	Island 10.	
Walker, R. D.	Captain.	1st Georgia.	G	Fort Donaldson.	
Walker, R. M.	"	40th Tennessee.	I	Island 10.	
Walker, R. S.	2d Lieut.	53d "	K	Fort Donaldson.	
Walker, S. P.	1st Lieut.	40th "	D	"	
Walker, W. D.	2d Lieut.	48th "	E	"	
Walters, J. C.	1st Lieut.	26th Mississippi.	B	Island 10.	
Wall, J. W.	2d Lieut	49th Tennessee.	D	Mills Spring.	
Wall, J. Q.	"	Pt. Coupee Bat.	G	Shiloh.	April 7, '62
Walton, J. L.	Private.	20th Tennessee.	G	Fort Donaldson.	
Womack, W. J.	3d Lieut	38th Tennessee.		Lebanon.	
*Ward, J. S.	1st Lieut.	50th Tennessee.	G	Island 10.	
Warfield, C.	2d Lieut.	Morgan's Cavalry.	K	Fort Donaldson.	
Warlick, J. N.	Serg. Maj	55th Tennessee.	G	"	
Warren, J. A.	1st Lieut.	3d Mississippi.			
Waters, R. B.	2d Lieut.	8th Kentucky.			

PRISONERS CONFINED AT JOHNSON'S ISLAND—Continued.

Name.	Rank.	Regiment.	Co.	Where Captured.	When Capt'd.
Watkins, C.	1st Lieut.	11th Arkansas.	B	Island 10.	Feb. 6, '62
Watts, W. O.	"	1st Tennessee Artillery.		Fort Henry.	
Weaver, H.	2d Lieut.	41st Tennessee.		Fort Donaldson.	
Webb, B. F.	Captain.	18th Tennessee.	F		Dec. 7, '61
Weed, F. F.	"	Missouri State Guards.		Saline co., Mo.	
Weir, D. L.	2d Lieut.	14th Mississippi.	B	Fort Donaldson.	"
Wiesinger, A. J.	Com'ry.	4th Mississippi.		"	
Wiesinger, G. J.	Private.	15th Mississippi.	I	Mills Spring.	
Welcker, B. F.	Captain.	26th Tennessee.	A	Fort Donaldson.	
Weldon, James W.	"	46th Tennessee.	H	Island 10.	
Wells, E. M.	"	3d Mississippi.		Fort Donaldson.	
Werner, C.	2d Lieut.	1st Georgia.		Fort Pulaski.	
Westbrook, J. W.	"	4th Mississippi.		Fort Donaldson.	
Weston, J. A.	1st Lieut.	40th North Carolina.		Newbern.	March 14, '62
Wheatly, H. D.	As. II. S.	50th Tennessee.		Fort Donaldson.	
Wheeler, W.	1st Lieut.	40th North Carolina.		Newbern.	March 14, '62
Whealing, C. E.	Private.	1st Tennessee.	I	Cheat Mountain.	Sept. 12, '61
White, A. H.	2d Lieut.	7th Texas.	I	Fort Donaldson.	
White, A. L.	1st Lieut.	51st Virginia.		Bloomery Gap.	Feb. 16, '62
White, J. A.	3d Lieut.	1st Bat. Tennessee Infantry.	E	Fort Donaldson.	
White, J. M.	1st Lieut.	32d Tennessee.	D	"	

Name	Rank	Regiment	Co.	Where Captured	Date
White, J. R.	Captain.	53d Tennessee.	I	Fort Donaldson.	April 11, '62
White, W. E.	"	17th Alabama.	B	Huntsville, Ala.	
Whiteside, S. A.	"	48th Tennessee.	K	Fort Donaldson.	
Whitfield, J. F.	"	1st Alabama.		Island 10.	
Whitfield, J. H.	Serg. Maj.	42d Tennessee.	G	Fort Donaldson.	
Whitfield, J. R.	2d Lieut.	11th Arkansas.	B	Island 10.	
Whitfield, T. J.	Captain.	42d Tennessee.	B	Fort Donaldson.	
Whittey, J. R.	1st Lieut.	55th Tennessee.	E	Island 10.	
Whitty, J. T.	1st Lieut.	Tennessee Bat. Infantry.	E	Fort Donaldson.	
Whitson, S. M.	Captain.	9th Bat. Tennessee Cavalry.		"	
Wilbourne, J. G.	1st Lieut.	1st Mississippi.	H	"	
Wilkerson, T.	1st Lieut.	15th Arkansas.		"	
Willard, P. F.	2d Lieut.	2d Div. Mo. State Guards.	D	Kirksville, Mo.	Nov. 28, '61
Wilford, G. H.	2d Lieut.	8th Kentucky.		Fort Donaldson.	
*Willhite, J. F.	1st Lieut.	Missouri Rcts.	C	Milford, Mo.	Dec. 19, '61
Williams, B. F.	2d Lieut.	26th Mississippi.	H	Fort Donaldson.	
Williams, G. G.	2d Lieut.	50th Tennessee.	G	"	
Williams, J. B.	2d Lieut	50th "	D	"	
Williams, J. C.	1st Lieut.	20th Mississippi.	K	"	
Williams, J. F.	2d Lieut.	4th Mississippi.	I	"	
Williams, J. V.	2d Lieut.	20th Mississippi.	I	"	
Williams, T.	2d Lieut.	26th Mississippi.	I	"	
Williams, T. L.	4th Sergt.	26th Mississippi.		"	
Williams, J. H.	1st Lieut.	46th Tennessee.	E	Island 10.	
Williams, J. T.	1st Lieut.	46th "		"	
Williamson, A. J.	2d Lieut.	40th "	A	"	

PRISONERS CONFINED AT JOHNSON'S ISLAND.—Continued.

Name.	Rank.	Regiment.	Co	Where Captured.	When Capt'd.
Williamson, W. T.	2d Lieut.	1st Alabama.	C	Island 10.	
Wills, M. C.	2d Lieut.	11th Arkansas.	B	"	
Willis, G. T.	3d Lieut.	26th Tennessee.	G	Fort Donaldson.	
Wilson, A. A.	Chaplain.	50th "		"	
Wilson, J. P.	2d Lieut.	42d "	A	"	
Wilson, D.	Captain	42d "		"	
Wilson, E. C.	Q. M.	15th Arkansas.		"	
Wilson, E. S.	Com'ry.	32d Tennessee.		"	
Wilson, J. D.	Serg. Maj	46th "	A	Island 10.	
*Wilson, R. A.	1st Lieut	49th "	A	Fort Donaldson.	
Wilson, R. M.	2d Lieut.	20th Mississippi.	H	Bloomery Gap, Va.	Jan 14, '62
Wilson, W.	1st Lieut.	89th Virginia.	F	Island 10.	
Wilson, W. W.	1st Lieut.	40th Tennessee.	A	Fort Donaldson.	
Wimberly, L. M.	1st Lieut.	3d Alabama Bat.		Island 10.	
Winger, H. C.	Adjutant.	11th Arkansas.	G	Fort Donaldson.	
*Winstead, J. M.	Captain.	32d Tennessee.	B	"	
Wimo, J. C.	Captain.	14th Mississippi.		Jacksboro'.	March 14, '62
Winston, E.		Gen. Zollicoffer's Brigade.		"	
Winston, W. C.	2d Lieut.	Tennessee Artillery.	K	Island 10.	
Withers, T. H.	2d Lieut.	40th Tennessee.		"	
*Witherspoon, A. J.	Chaplain	21st Alabama.		Shiloh, Tennessee.	April 8, '62

Name	Rank	Regiment	Co.	Place	Date
Wood, B. J.	Captain.	18th Tennessee.	I	Fort Donaldson.	
Wood, John H.	Captain.	1st Alabama.	E	Island 10.	April 7, '62
Wood, R. T.	2d Lieut.	1st Alabama, Tenn. and Miss.	I	"	
Wood, R. K.	1st Lieut.	1st Alabama Bat.	C	Fort Donaldson.	
Wood, W. C.	1st Lieut.	22d Alabama.		Shiloh.	April 7, '62
Wood, W. J.	Com'ry.	18th Tennessee.	I	Fort Donaldson.	Jan. 18, '62
Woods, A. F.	Private.	15th Mississippi.	E	Fishing Creek.	April 11, '62
Wooten, C. B.	Captain.	5th Georgia.	C	Huntsville, Ala.	
Wooten, R H.	2d Lieut.	51st Tennessee.	A	Fort Donaldson.	
Worley, W.	Captain.	31st Tennessee.		"	March 23, '62
Wren, W. T.	1st Lieut.	1st Bat Mississippi Cavalry.	E	Hickman, Ky.	
Wright, J. M.	2d Lieut.	32d Tennessee.		Fort Donaldson.	
*Wright, John R.	1st Lieut.	1st Alabama, Tenn. and Miss.	I	Island 10.	June 1, '62
Wen, Robert D.	2d Lieut.	Mississippi Cavalry.	B	Rienzi, Miss.	
Welcher, H. J.	Com'ry.	26th Tennessee.		Fort Donaldson.	
Willis, C. W.	1st Licut.	21st Louisiana.	8	Corinth.	May 28, '62
Wilson, N. J.	Captain.	Response Bat.		Shiloh.	April 7, '62
Wood, P. K.	Lieut.	4th Mississippi.	E	Fort Donaldson.	
Whelley, D.		Marine C. S. N.		Off Memphis.	June 6, '62
Williams, Geo.					"
Webb, F. S.	1st Lieut.	Tennessee.			
Young, J.	2d Lieut.	32d Tennessee.		Fort Donaldson.	
*Young, W. G.	3d Lieut.	3d Mississippi.	I	"	
*Young, W. F.	Captain.	49th Tennessee.	G	"	
Younghlood, R. A.	2d Lieut.	18th Tennessee.	A	"	

PAROLED PRISONERS ARRIVED IN PRISON.

Name.	Rank.	Regiment.	Co.	Where Captured.	When Capt'd.
Weller, F. J.	2d Lieut.	1st Tennessee Artillery.		Fort Henry	Feb. 6, '62
Morton, J. H.	Captain.	32d Tennessee.		Fort Donaldson.	Feb. 16, '62
King, John	Private.	1st Tennessee Regt.		Cheat Mountain.	
Steadman.	Colonel.	1st Alabama.		Island 10.	April 8, '62
Blanchard.				Shiloh.	
Wood.					
Carson.					

LIST OF COMMANDS IN PRISON.

The following commands, representing the eleven Confederate States, have their unfortunate representatives in prison—121 commands:

State	Command	No.
Kentucky	2d Inf.	23
	8th "	4
	5th "	15
	Morgan's Cav.	11
	3d Ky. Inf.	26
	9th "	1
	Williams' Regt.	7
	4th Regt.	20
	1st Cav.	10
Miss.	1 Bt. Cav.	
	Issaquena Art.	
Texas	1st Legn.	7
	8th	8
	10th Cy.	55
Tennessee	Forrest's Cavalry	50
	1 Batt. Infantry	42
	Tennessee Artillery	9
	Comb's Tenn. Batt.	3
	Murray's Artillery	45
	Maney's Artillery	49
	Jackson Batt.	53
	Grave's Battery	32
	Porter's "	41
	16th Tenn. Infantry	30
	154th Sr. Tenn.	40
	Adams' Cavalry	18
	Green's Batt. Art.	20
	Thetman's "	10
	Zollicoffer's Brigade	29
	1 Ala. Tenn. & Miss.	19
		46
		48
		11
		25
		54
		7
Arkansas	1 Batt. In.	11
	McRay's B	15
		16
		13
		10
		4
Ga.	Ga. Bat.	1
		25
		5
Louisiana	Pt. Coupee A.	9
	Orleans Gd. B	13
	Crescent Gds.	20
		4
		5
		21
Missouri	6th Mo. St. Gd.	130
	1st Mo. Cav.	31
	Eng'r Corps.	56
	Jeff Thompson's Brig.	32
Virginia	Virginia Artillery.	129
	Floyd's Brigade.	60
	French's Va. Art.	1?
	Caskey's Va. Cav.	51
	Va. Rangers.	22
		89
Ala.	27 Inf.	33
	1 "	28
	3 Batt.	37
	16 Inf.	32
	2 "	26
	21 "	40
	17 "	
	22 "	
N. C.	Con. States Navy.	
	Gunboat Flotilla.	

26

CASUALTIES AND CHANGES

AMONG

Commissoned Officers after Exchange;

AND RESIDENCE AND OCCUPATION OF THOSE LIVING, SO FAR
AS KNOWN.

————

Alpheus Baker, Brigadier-General, Eufaula, Ala., Lawyer.
Robert Andrews, Captain, Alabama, Farmer.
T. M. Atkins, Colonel, Allenville, Ky., Farmer.
W. T. Avery, transferred to P. O. Dept., Memphis, Tenn.,
Lawyer.
O. N. Avery, killed at the battle of the "Wilderness."
T. C. Banks, Williamson co , Tenn , Farmer.
T. J. Barrett, killed at the battle of Franklin, Tenn.
Thos. Beaumont, Colonel, killed in action in Georgia.
Joel A. Battel, Farmer, Tennessee.
H. L. Bedford, Memphis, Tennessee, Lawyer.
N. J. Benson, Captain, Mississippi, Farmer.
A. G. Berry, Tennessee, Teacher.
J. N. Bolan, Murray, Kentucky, Dentist.
Leonidas Betts, Mississippi, Merchant.
J. W. Bradshaw, Captain and Adjutant, Forrest's Cavalry,
Nashville, Merchant.
O. W. Brown, Alabama, Lawyer.
T. W. Brown, U. S. Publishing Company, 411 Broome st.,
New York.
J. P. Campbell, Adjutant, died in hospital during the war.
W. R. Butler, Colonel, Commission Merchant, Murfreesboro',
Tennessee.
J. W. Childress, Jr., Capt., Merchant, Murfreesboro', Tenn.

J. B. Budwell, Warrington, Va.
W. P. Clarkson, died in Texas, in spring of 1863.
B F. Darnell, Way's Bluff, Miss , Farmer.
J. B. B. Flint, Fulton, Miss., Druggist.
G. W. B. Garrett, Major, Pocahontas, Tenn., Merchant.
A. J. Gibson, Salem, Miss., Farmer.
D. R. Dickson, Crump's Mill, Miss., Merchant.
N. L. Daisy, Captain, Rickersville, Miss., Farmer.
W. S. Bowdry, Baldwin, Miss., Merchant.
J. Guerrant, Goochland C. H., Va.
W. H Hedden, Captain, Memphis, Tenn., Merchant.
T. T. Kirtland, Memphis, Tenn., Merchant.
R. J. Hill, Orizaba, Miss., Merchant.
M. P. Harbin, Orizaba, Miss , Farmer.
J. H. Kennedy, Baldwin, Miss., Farmer.
G. W. McCranie, Colonel, Monroe, Louisiana, Editor.
J. F. Wilhight, Rockport, Boone co., Mo., Farmer.
H. W. Salmon, Colonel, Clinton, Henry co., Mo.
A. J. Witherspoon, Alabama, Minister.
J. S. Thompson, Baldwin, Mississippi, Teacher.
J. C. Turner Captain, killed in action, 1865.
J. B. Purnell, Crump's Mill, Mississippi, Physician.
J. Y. Moore, deceased.
A. D. Saddler, Captain, Baldwin, Mississippi, Miller.
W. S. Rogan, Blackland, Mississippi, Farmer.
J. H. Riddlesperger, Captain, Ruckersville, Miss., Farmer.
W. C. Young, Captain, New Albany, Miss., Farmer.
J. A. Warren, Friar's Point, Mississippi, Physician.
A. D. Suddeth, Captain, Friar's Point, Mississippi.
H. H. Robinson, Cottonplant, Mississippi, Farmer.
E. Roberts, left the service.
E. M. Smith, dropped from the rolls.
John Shirley Ward, Nashville, Tennessee, Editor.
T. E. Mallory, Captain, Adam's Sta., Tenn., Merchant.
W. H. Harris, Major, New York city, Commission Merchant.
H. V. Harrison, Captain, Springfield, Tennessee, Merchant.
John O'Neil, Tennessee, Farmer
F. D. Overton, Nashville, Tennessee.
G. M. Parker, Colonel, Mobile, Alabama, (Woodruff & Parker,) Merchants.
W. G. Pease, Agent Fielding, Guinness & Co., New York.
W. R. Poindexter, Tobacco Inspector, Brooklyn, N. Y.
J. H. Gray, Richmond, Virginia, Lawyer.
D. B. Griswold, Captain, Friar's Point, Miss., Merchant.

R. H. McClellan, Captain, Charlotte, Tenn., Merchant.
J. M. Winstead, Colonel, Nashville, Tenn., Merchant.
John R. Wright, killed in action.
A. F. Smith, Clarksville, Tennessee, Merchant.
J. Tally, Captain, died since the war.
W. F. Young, Clarksville, Tennessee, Teacher.
T. U. Titmarsh, died in Memphis, Tennessee, 1867.
W. A. Quarles, Brig.-Gen., Clarksville, Tenn., Lawyer.
R. A. Wilson, Captain, New Providence, Tenn., Merchant.
St. Clair Morgan, killed at Chickamauga.
S. M Thompson, Colonel, Alabama, Farmer.
J. W. Bryan, Captain, Nashville, Tennessee, Farmer.
Thomas Gibson, Captain, Nashville, Tennessee, Merchant.
R. Seymour, Texas.
J. A. Minter, Colonel, Memphis, Tennessee, Merchant.
R. A. Mitchell, Captain, Lynnville, Tennessee, Merchant.
W. O. Watts, Major, New Orleans, Louisiana.
James A. Fisher, Tennessee, Farmer.
F. Tryon, killed in action.
J. W. Walker, Captain, Memphis, Tennessee, Merchant.
S. P. Walker, Jr., Captain, Memphis, Tenn., Lawyer.
J. Taylor, Mississippi, Farmer.
H. P. Pointer, Spring Hill, Tennessee, Farmer.
C. H. Stockdell. Nashville, Tennessee, Merchant.
B. F. Saunders, assassinated in North Carolina, in 1868.
T. S. Sale, Memphis, Tennsssee.
P. K. Stankewitz, Nashville, Tennessee, Janitor Med. Col.
James Simmons, died in Arkansas.
W. H. Joiner, Lieutenant-Colonel, Tennessee, Farmer.
U. S. Lipscomb, Captain, Cincinnati, Ohio, Cotton Broker.
E. W. Harlow, Nashville, Tennessee, Merchant.
J. R. Hodges, died at Johnson's Island, 1862.
A. J. Hughes, Nashville, Tennessee, Merchant.
F. H. Lytle, Memphis, Tennessee, Merchant.
A. J. Laird, Eufaula, Alabama.
L. J. Laird, Eufaula, Alabama.
A. S. Levey, Major, Memphis, Tennessee, Merchant.
J. W. Lindsey, Nashville, Tennessee, Merchant.
A. Lindsey, Nashville, Tennessee, Merchant.
Josiah Joplin, Myrtle Springs, Bowie county, Texas, Farmer.
C. F. Johnson, Colonel, Tyler, Johnson & Co., Louisville, Kentucky, Merchants.
G. R. G Jones, Memphis, Tennessee, Lawyer.
G. W. Gordon, died at Vicksburg, Miss., September, 1862.

A. W. Gould, killed in Tennessee.
J. F. Grant, Pulaski, Tennessee, Physician.
E. F. Freeman, Memphis, Tennessee, Physician.
Leslie Ellis, Nashville, Tennessee, Merchant.
John R. Farrabe, died in Mississippi, 1867.
A. C. Gibson, Major, Clinton, Mississippi, Farmer.
T. R. Kelsey, killed in action.
J P. Kirkman, frozen to death, near Columbia, Tennessee, 1867.
J. McDaniels, Nashville, Tennessee, Printer.
R. McCall, Captain, Bethesda, Tennessee, Merchant.
W. D. McKay, Captain, Louisville, Kentucky.
R. D Palmer, Nashville, Tennessee, Merchant.
A. J. McWhorter, Nashville, Tennessee, Merchant.
F. P. McWhorter, Nashville, Tennessee, Merchant
J. W. Martin, Captain, Nashville, Tennessee, Physician.
D. B. Martin, Union City, Tennessee.
F. D. Moore. Humboldt, Tennessee, M. & O. R. R. Officer.
J. W. Morton, Jr , Captain, Nashville, Tennessee, Physician.
M. Burke, Nashville, Tennessee, Steamboat Man.
J- G. Crowder, killed at Franklin, Tennessee

Six years have elapsed since these "scraps" were written. Constant travel since the war and want of opportunity has prevented their publication, yet the writer deems them as appropriate to-day as then, and has no alterations to make in them—regretting naught.

Ho! for a Trip 'Round the World.

The following card of the agencies of Dr. H. L. LEAF, is published as a complimentary gratuity, to a friend of the author's childhood.

The Pacific railroad, upon its completion, will open to the South an immense trade, uniting her with the world in commercial links. Much of this will find its way through New York and Philadelphia: and, as *'tis more than probable*, Dr. LEAF will be the *Philadelphia* agent of that railroad line—as he has been for so many years the competent representative of the steamship interests—it is well that the Southern people should know him. There are but few men of our day whose lives have been so full of adventure, as that of Dr. HARLAN L. LEAF—twenty-eight trips across the Isthmus, ventures to the Sandwich Islands, New Zealand and other parts of the world. Testamonials from communities for his humane efforts (in one instance risking health and life to assist in ameliorating the condition of his fellow man, which effort was recognized by the grateful recipients, and the gallant LEAF wears a magnificent watch, as a testimonial of their estimate of his worth); an Indian fighter during the Texas struggle; a traveler over the length and breadth of his own country, with a well stored mind, the result of a thorough classical education, stamps Dr. LEAF as one of the most remarkable men of our times; and it is to such a character that our Southern, traveling community should look for facilities, when their objective point is either of the four quarters of the globe. Dr. LEAF is a true man, with extraordinary business qualifications; is honest to the letter and spirit of his calling, and as a faithful agent he has no superior; and, while a staunch defender of the Union cause during our late struggle, he was ever humane and generous in his dealings with Southern citizens; and the traveling public South can rest assured, that all those desirous of going to any part of the world, will be furnished extra facilities by consulting, either by letter or in person, Dr. H. L. LEAF, (at Adams Express Co., 320 Chestnut street,) or that old hero of the Pacific and Neptune of the Atlantic, the courtly Captain F. R. BABY, the New York agent of the *Pacific Mail Steamship Company*, whose knowledge of his duties is alone excelled by his generosity. The author has crossed the Atlantic on the *Cunard, Inman, Collins and French Trans-Atlantic* lines, and deems the latter the best that ever crossed the ocean. GEORGE MACKENZIE, the agent at New York, is one of the most accomplished gentlemen and best business managers on the continent of America. But, if the traveler prefers an English line, advise with Messrs. HOWLAND and ASPINWALL, (or their agent, Dr. LEAF,) of New York, who are courteous in their business dealings, and represent one of the best English lines—the *London Steamship Company*. For a superior route to reach the North, take the Memphis and Louisville Road and the Atlantic and Great Western—they are the best, because Col. SAMUEL JONES, of the former, and Colonel SHATTUCK, of the latter, are the most competent railroad managers in the United States. If you move by water, take any boat that JOHN C. DAVIS or FRANK STEIN commands.

H. L. LEAF'S
STEAMSHIP PASSAGE AND FOREIGN FREIGHT OFFICE,

AT THE ADAMS EXPRESS COMPANY,

NO. 320 CHESTNUT ST., PHILADELPHIA.

Prices of Passage the same in Philadelphia as in New York.

Refer to
ADAMS EXPRESS CO.
HOWARD EXPRESS CO.
AMERICAN EUROPEAN EXPRESS CO.
WELLS, FARGO & CO.
HARNDEN EXPRESS CO.

Refer to
KINSLEY EXPRESS CO.
W. B. DINSMORE, President Adams Express Co.
DREXEL & CO.
JAY COOK & CO.
E. S. SANFORD, &c.

To California, Japan, China, Australia, New Zealand, South and Central America, &c., by the "Pacific Mail Steamship Co." via Panama. ☞On the 1st, 9th, 16th and 24th of each Month, except when these days fall on Sunday, then on the Saturday preceding.

To Havre and Brest, France, by the General Trans-Atlantic Mail Steamship Company.

To London, by "Howland & Aspinwall's" London and New York Steamship Line, to and from London.

To Liverpool, England, Ireland, Germany, and other Ports of Europe, by the Inman and other Steamship Lines, every Saturday and Wednesday.

To Rio de Janeiro, Brazil, &c.

To Havana, Cuba, and the West Indies.

To New Orleans, Savannah, Charleston, &c.

AGENCY FOR THE "AMERICAN EUROPEAN EXPRESS CO."

Anstiu Baldwin & Co., Proprietors, New York. The only recognized connection of the Express Companies of the United States with Europe, Asia, West Indies, and South America.

GOODS, FREIGHT AND PARCELS to all parts of Europe, Asia, &c., forwarded promptly twice each week.

Bills for £1 Sterling and to any amount, supplied at any time.

—o—

PRINCIPAL AGENCIES:

NEW YORK. Austin Baldwin & Co., 72 Broadway.
LONDON. H. Starr & Co., 22 Moorgate St., E. C.
LIVERPOOL. Stavely & Starr, 32 Dale Street.
DUBLIN. Royal Bank of Ireland.
PARIS. L. herbette Kane & Co., No. 8 Place de la Bourse.
ROME, Vienna, Hamburg, Stockholm, Copenhagen, &c.

—o—

☞ Any change in the above rates or sailing days, can be ascertained at the office.

100 pounds of baggage allowed each adult passenger, and 10 cents per pound will be charged on the excess.

Passengers by purchasing at *this office,* will avoid all imposition, have their *Passage* secured, and can remain with their families until the night previous to the sailing day, *and thus avoid hotel bills and other expenses in New York.* You will promote your interest and comfort, by purchasing of

H. L. LEAF, Agent.

At the Adams Express Co., No. 320 Chestnut St., Philadelphia.